History Alive!®
The United States Through Industrialism

TCi™

Chief Executive Officer: Bert Bower

Chief Operating Officer: Amy Larson

Director of Curriculum: Liz Russell

Managing Editor: Laura Alavosus

Editorial Project Manager: Nancy Rogier

Project Editor: Mali Apple

Copyeditor: Jennifer Seidel

Editorial Associates: Anna Embree, Sarah Sudano

Production Manager: Lynn Sanchez

Art Director: John F. Kelly

Senior Graphic Designers: Paul Rebello, Christy Uyeno

Graphic Designers: Don Taka, Victoria Philp

Photo Edit Manager: Margee Robinson

Photo Editor: Picture Research Consultants, Inc.

Production Project Manager: Eric Houts

Art Editor: Mary Swab

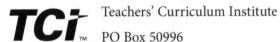

Teachers' Curriculum Institute

PO Box 50996

Palo Alto, CA 94303

Customer Service: 800-497-6138

www.teachtci.com

ISBN 978-1-58371-934-3

2 3 4 5 6 7 8 9 10 -MLI- 14 13 12 11

Acknowledgments

Program Director

Bert Bower

Program Author

Diane Hart

Creative Development Manager

Kelly Shafsky

Contributing Writers

Laura Alavosus

John Bergez

Susan Buckley

Jill Fox

Christine Freeman

Amy George

Brent Goff

Andrew Goldblatt

David M. Holford

Elspeth Leacock

Tedd Levy

Julie Weiss

Curriculum Developers

Joyce Bartky

April Bennett

Nicole Boylan

Vern Cleary

Terry Coburn

Julie Cremin

Erin Fry

Amy George

Steve Seely

Nathan Wellborne

Reading Specialist

Kate Kinsella, Ed.D.
Reading and TESOL Specialist
San Francisco State University

Teacher Consultants

Melissa Aubuchon
City of Ladue School District
St. Louis, Missouri

Terry Coburn
Brookside School
Stockton, California

Connie Davidson
San Leandro Unified School District
San Leandro, California

Amy George
Weston Middle School
Weston, Massachusetts

Nicolle Hutchinson
Broward County Public Schools
Miramar, Florida

Dawn Lavond
Moreland Middle School
San Jose, California

Julie Peters
Woodstock Community Union
School District #200
Woodstock, Illinois

Debra Schneider
Tracy Unified School District
Tracy, California

Acknowledgments

Scholars

Dr. Eric Avila
*University of California,
Los Angeles*

Maureen Booth
Maynard, Massachusetts

Dr. Eun Mi Cho
*California State University
Sacramento*

Dr. William Deverell
University of Southern California

Dr. Dan Dupre
*University of North Carolina,
Charlotte*

Dr. Ben Keppel
University of Oklahoma

Dr. Stanley J. Underdal
San Jose State University

Dr. Dan Wickburg
University of Texas, Dallas

**Readability
Consultant**

Jeanne Barry
*Jeanne Barry and Associates, Inc.
Incline Village, Nevada*

Cartographer

Mapping Specialists
Madison, Wisconsin

**Internet
Consultant**

Chuck Taft
*University School of Milwaukee
Milwaukee, Wisconsin*

**Diverse Needs
Consultants**

Erin Fry
Glendora, California

Colleen Guccione
Naperville, Illinois

Cathy Hix
*Swanson Middle School
Arlington, Virginia*

**Unit 9
A Modern
Nation
Emerges**

How to Use This Program:
History Alive! The United States Through Industrialism

Teaching with the TCI Approach means shifting to a student-centered, activity-based classroom. To meet this exciting challenge, this introduction to the Lesson Guide for *History Alive! The United States Through Industrialism* will give you the basics you need to start teaching this program with confidence right away.

The TCI Approach

Why is the TCI Approach so effective at igniting students' passion for learning? The TCI Approach consists of a series of instructional practices that allow students of all abilities to experience key social studies concepts. It has eight features.

Theory- and Research-Based Active Instruction

Lessons and activities are based on five well-established theories.

Understanding by Design   Grant Wiggins and Jay McTighe maintain that teaching for deep understanding must begin with planning the big ideas students should learn. That's why you will see an Essential Question at the start of every chapter in *History Alive! The United States Through Industrialism*.

Nonlinguistic Representation   Research by Robert Marzano and colleagues demonstrates that teaching with nonlinguistic activities helps improve comprehension and retention. Use of graphic organizers and movement are both key to TCI lessons.

Multiple Intelligences   Howard Gardner believes that all students are intelligent —just not in the same ways. TCI activities address Gardner's seven intelligences: verbal-linguistic, logical-mathematical, visual-spatial, body-kinesthetic, musical-rhythmic, interpersonal, and intrapersonal.

Cooperative Interaction   Elizabeth Cohen's research shows that cooperative groupwork leads to learning gains and higher student achievement. Working in small groups is a cornerstone of TCI activities.

Spiral Curriculum   Jerome Bruner championed the idea of the spiral curriculum, in which students learn progressively—understanding more difficult concepts through a process of step-by-step discovery. TCI questioning strategies spiral from simple recall to higher-order thinking skills such as analysis and evaluation.

Standards-Based Content

Dynamic lessons that integrate hands-on learning and content reading build mastery of state and national social studies standards.

Preview Activities

Short, engaging activities at the start of the lessons help you preview key concepts and tap students' prior knowledge and personal experience.

Multiple Intelligences Teaching Strategies

TCI activities incorporate six multiple intelligences teaching strategies:

- Visual Discovery
- Social Studies Skill Builder
- Experiential Exercise
- Writing for Understanding
- Response Group
- Problem Solving Groupwork

These six strategies are explained in detail on the following pages.

Considerate Text

Carefully structured reading materials enable students at all levels to understand what they read. Uncluttered pages present content in digestible "chunks." Engaging images reinforce content, while consistent vocabulary development improves student comprehension.

Graphically Organized Reading Notes

Easy-to-understand graphic organizers help students record key ideas and make meaning out of what they read. By using graphic organizers that display the underlying logic of and interconnections among concepts, students improve their comprehension and retention of content.

Processing Activities

End-of-lesson activities, involving multiple intelligences and higher-order thinking skills, challenge students to apply what they have learned in a variety of creative ways.

Assessments to Inform Instruction

Carefully designed chapter tests move students through a progression of thinking skills, from comprehension to skills application to critical thinking. Test results in these three areas show you where students are succeeding and where they need more instruction.

Multiple Intelligences Teaching Strategies

The TCI Approach uses the six teaching strategies described here to bring learning alive. All six appear in the *History Alive! The United States Through Industrialism* Lesson Guide with detailed, step-by-step instructions. Support materials for the chapter activities appear in the Lesson Masters, visuals, and placards; on *Sounds of History;* and online at TeachTCI (see page xxvi).

Visual Discovery

In Visual Discovery activities, students view, touch, interpret, and bring to life compelling images as they discover key social studies concepts. Seeing and interacting with an image in combination with reading and recording notes on the content help students remember salient ideas.

Here are some tips for Visual Discovery activities:

- Arrange your classroom so that projected images will be large and clear.
- Ask carefully sequenced questions that lead to discovery.
- Challenge students to read about each image and apply what they learn.
- Have students interact with each image to demonstrate learning.

Social Studies Skill Builder

In Social Studies Skill Builders, students work in pairs or small groups on fast-paced, skill-oriented tasks, such as mapping, graphing, analyzing artifacts, and forming hypotheses, to enhance their understanding of chapter content.

Here are some tips for Social Studies Skill Builders:

- Teach each skill through modeling and guided practice.
- Prepare students to work in pairs or small groups.
- Set clear expectations, allow students to practice each skill repeatedly, and give immediate feedback.
- Debrief the activity to help students make connections to key social studies concepts.

Experiential Exercise

In Experiential Exercises, participating in short, memorable experiences helps students grasp social studies concepts. Through the use of movement and introspection, students capture a moment or feeling that is central to understanding a particular concept, situation, or event.

Here are some tips for Experiential Exercises:

- Prepare students for a safe, successful experience by arranging the classroom appropriately, communicating clear behavioral and learning expectations, anticipating student reactions, and recognizing teachable moments.

- Bring authenticity to the experience by assuming an appropriate persona, hamming it up, and using simple props, costumes, music, and sound effects.
- Allow students to express their feelings immediately after the experience.
- Ask carefully sequenced questions to help students make connections between their experience and key concepts or events.

Writing for Understanding

Writing for Understanding activities give students a rich experience—such as viewing powerful images, role-playing, discussing complex issues, or acting out key events—to write about. Students develop ideas and form opinions during the experience, before beginning to write. The experience becomes a springboard for writing, challenging students to clarify ideas, organize information, and express what they have learned.

Here are some tips for Writing for Understanding activities:

- Have students record their ideas, thoughts, and feelings in prewriting activities.
- Guide students through the writing process.

Response Group

In Response Group activities, students work in small groups with thought-provoking resources to discuss critical thinking questions among themselves. A presenter then shares each group's findings with the class.

Here are some tips for Response Group activities:

- Create mixed-ability groups and a suitable classroom arrangement.
- Prepare students to answer provocative critical thinking questions.
- Allow groups time to prepare their responses.
- Facilitate a lively class discussion.

Problem Solving Groupwork

In Problem Solving Groupwork activities, students work in heterogeneous groups to create projects that require multiple abilities so that every student can contribute. Within a group, each student takes a defined role. After completing their task, groups present their projects to the class.

Here are some tips for Problem Solving Groupwork activities:

- Review ground rules for working cooperatively in groups.
- Give group members clearly defined roles and requirements.
- Give groups autonomy and time to prepare high-quality projects.
- After groups present their work, debrief each presentation for deeper meaning and accuracy.

Program Components

The components of *History Alive! The United States Through Industrialism* work together to maximize your time and creativity. Everything you need to provide insightful and stimulating classroom experiences is included in the program. There are also plenty of opportunities to add your own resources.

Lesson Guide

"Command central" for the program includes detailed, step-by-step procedures for implementing the classroom activities, as well as the following resources:

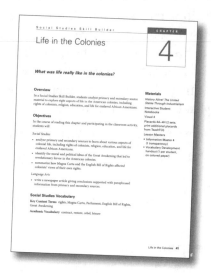

- Planning Guides detailing materials and timing for each part of the lesson

- social studies and language arts objectives

- Key Content Terms and academic vocabulary

- mini lesson guides for writing assignments tied to each Reading Further case study

- literature recommendations and information for accessing online resources

- recommendations for differentiating instruction for English language learners, students reading and writing below grade level, special education students, and advanced learners

- Guides to Reading Notes

- answers and rubrics for assessments

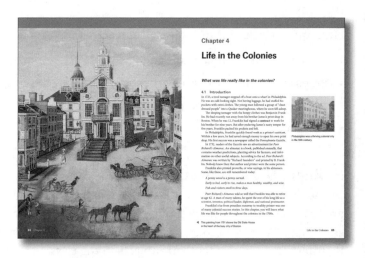

Student Edition

To help students focus their learning, each chapter of the text is organized around an Essential Question. In the Student Edition, you will find

- considerate text that is uncluttered and easy to navigate.

- powerful graphic elements that support visual learning, spark student interest, and foster comprehension.

- key concepts and vocabulary terms highlighted in the text and defined in the Glossary.

- Setting the Stage unit introductions that provide background on how the geography of the region affected its history. Each feature includes detailed maps that students use to complete Geography Challenge activities.

- unit timelines that appear at the end of every unit and capture the most important events of the region's history at a glance. The timelines include information that students use to complete Timeline Challenge activities.

- High-interest Reading Further case studies that explore the chapter concepts in depth.

Interactive Student Notebook

The Interactive Student Notebook is each student's personal repository of learning, all in one place. The Interactive Student Notebook includes

- Preview activities
- graphically organized Reading Notes
- Processing activities
- Reading Further writing activities

For more information, see "Using the Interactive Student Notebook" on pages xx–xxi.

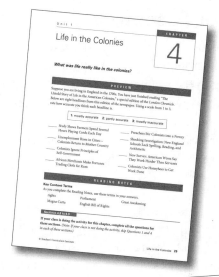

Lesson Masters

Reproducible pages support classroom activities. Follow the materials list in the Lesson Guide to know how many copies of each master to prepare before class.

- Student Handouts
- Information Masters
- chapter assessments
- sets of Timeline Challenge Cards

Visuals and Placards

Visual support for chapter activities, including

- maps, graphs, diagrams, and tables
- photographs

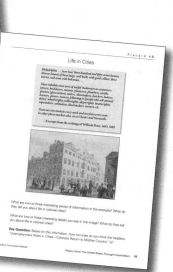

Sounds of History

Audio tracks, including dramatic readings, musical recordings, and sound effects, enhance the drama and realism of many of the activities.

Chapter Essentials

While students look forward to the wide variety of activities they will experience in a TCI classroom, they also reap the benefits of TCI's consistent organization of learning in the chapters. Following sound pedagogical practices, each lesson begins with a Preview activity to spark interest and connect to prior learning, progresses to visually engaging Reading Notes, then moves to a scaffolded writing task for Reading Further, and concludes with a Processing activity that asks students to apply what they have learned.

Preview

The Preview activity is a short, engaging task that foreshadows upcoming content. The goal is to ignite interest, activate prior knowledge, tap a wide range of intelligences, and prepare students to tackle new concepts. Students complete most of the Preview activities in their Interactive Student Notebooks.

Types of Preview activities include

- connecting personal experiences with key concepts
- predicting
- analyzing artifacts, maps, photographs, paintings, drawings, political cartoons, song lyrics, and music
- responding to hypothetical scenarios
- depicting and explaining historical information
- examining the contributions of historical figures

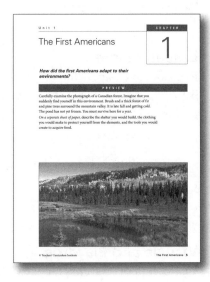

Reading Notes

One of the most powerful ways to improve students' comprehension and retention is to have them complete graphically organized Reading Notes for each chapter. Using this format helps students see the underlying logic of and interconnections among events, facts, and concepts. When students record information in engaging, visual ways, they are better able to recall content months and even years later. Students complete the Reading Notes in their Interactive Student Notebooks.

Types of graphically organized Reading Notes include

- T-charts
- labeled and annotated maps, charts, diagrams, and illustrations
- flowcharts
- spoke diagrams
- timelines
- Venn diagrams
- speech bubbles

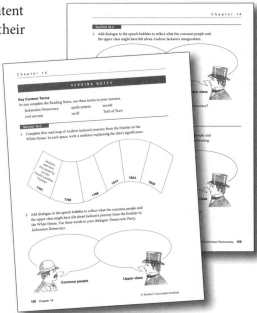

Reading Further

For each Reading Further, students complete a two-part writing activity about what they have read. The first part prepares them to write while the second part provides them with a guiding rubric for their work. Types of writing activities include

- letters
- newspaper articles
- debate arguments
- diary entries

Processing

Processing activities challenge students to synthesize the information in a chapter to demonstrate their understanding of it. The intent is to allow students to actively apply what they have learned so that you—and they—can assess their comprehension. Students complete the Processing activities in their Interactive Student Notebooks or on separate sheets of paper.

Products of Processing activities include

- song and poem verses
- newspaper articles
- posters
- illustrations
- pamphlets
- interviews
- collages

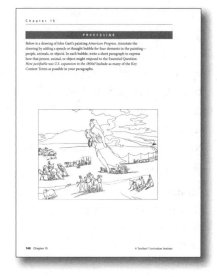

Using the Interactive Student Notebook

In the Interactive Student Notebook, all parts of the integrated lesson come together as students create a dynamic repository for their learning. Students should store their notebooks in a three-ring binder. Because the pages are perforated, it will be easy for you to collect only selected chapters to grade at one time, rather than whole binders.

Interactive Student Notebook Guidelines for Students

One of the most important steps for helping students to create successful notebooks is establishing clear guidelines. Decide ahead of time what you expect your students to produce in their notebooks. Clearly communicate your expectations on a single sheet of paper that students can glue into the inside front cover of their notebooks. Here are example guidelines that you might adapt for your own students.

Purpose Your Interactive Student Notebook will help you to become a creative, independent thinker and writer. You will use your notebook in class for completing all chapter Preview, Reading Notes, Reading Further, and Processing activities. It will also help you study for tests.

Materials You will need colored pencils, a glue stick, highlighters, scissors, tape, and a zipper pouch.

Grading To earn an A– or higher grade, you must keep a complete, neat notebook, produce quality work, and consistently take the time to extend your learning beyond classroom assignments. Notebooks will be checked for completeness periodically—usually every three to four weeks, except during the first few weeks of class, when they will be checked more regularly. You must keep an updated assignment sheet listing all class assignments, due dates, and point values. Also include columns for recording self-assessment points and teacher-assessment points.

Absence If you are absent, check the class assignment sheet the teacher has placed in the large envelope in the front of the class. It will list all assignments that are due.

Managing Assessment of Interactive Student Notebooks

If you teach four or five classes a day, you could have 150 or more student notebooks to monitor. Because so much of students' work appears in these notebooks, you will need an efficient and accurate system for assessing them.

Informal Assessment   Monitor student notebooks aggressively in the first few weeks of the course. Look at notebooks as you walk around, making positive comments and helpful suggestions. Here are some additional ideas:

* While students work on another assignment, conduct a quick review of the previous night's homework, giving students checks or special stamps to denote completed assignments.
* Provide a model of outstanding work for an assignment or set of class notes.
* Allow students to use their notebooks on a quiz or test. This will come as a pleasant surprise and reward for students with well-organized notebooks.

Formal Assessment   At the beginning of the course, clearly explain the criteria on which notebooks will be assessed, such as quality and completeness of assignments, visual appearance, neatness, higher-order thinking, and organization. Here are some additional ideas for assessing student work:

* Create a simple rubric that identifies the criteria you feel are most important.
* Stagger notebook collection so that you correct only one class set at a time.
* Grade selectively. Don't feel compelled to grade every notebook entry.
* Create an evaluation sheet like the one below to support your expectations of student work.

Notebook Assignment	Due Date	Possible Points	Student Assessment	Teacher Assessment
Chapter 6 Preview	11/8	5	3	4
Chapter 6 Reading Notes	11/9	20	19	17
Chapter 6 Processing	11/10	10	8	10
Chapter 9 Reading Notes	11/15	20	18	19
Chapter 9 Processing	11/16	10	9	8
Totals		65	57	58

Student Comments: I'm not used to these kinds of assignments, but I'm trying my best.

Teacher Comments: Your work is solid. Think about creating some of your excellent visuals for extra credit.

Organizing a TCI Classroom

Most of the activities in *History Alive! The United States Through Industrialism* require students to move into small groups of two, three, or four. With a brief training exercise, you can teach them how to do so quickly without wasting valuable time.

Moving Your Classroom Furniture

Tell students that they will be working in small groups of different sizes throughout the course. They must know how to move into each grouping quickly and efficiently with all their materials. When working in pairs, they should place their desks either side by side or face to face, with the edges touching. For groups of three or more, the front corners of the desks must touch.

With these expectations clear, allow students to practice moving into groups. Randomly assign students to groups and indicate where they should meet. Then say "Go!" and time them. If necessary, allow the class to discuss what went wrong and brainstorm ideas for getting into groups more efficiently. Have students repeat the process until they can do it in "record time."

Be prepared for students to think this exercise is silly. However, if you spend 20 minutes at the beginning of the course teaching this skill, you will save hours of instructional time. Your goal should be for students to be able to form various group configurations in less than one minute, without your needing to touch any student furniture.

Organizing Your Teacher Resources

History Alive! The United States Through Industrialism comes with all of the materials you need to excite your students about the history and legacy of the United States during this period. It will be up to you, however, to gather the materials for each chapter and organize them in a way that makes it fast and easy to conduct activities year after year. Here are some tips to save you time and make running your classroom much easier:

1. Begin preparation for each activity by gathering everything on the materials list, such as placards, visuals, and the audio tracks.

2. Make all the copies you will need of classroom masters, such as Student Handouts and Information Masters. Consider creating these copies from the online resources at TeachTCI.

3. When you finish each activity, place all the printed materials in a clear, resealable plastic bag (an ideal size is 10 by 12 in. and 4 mm thick) with the Lesson Guide on top as a "label." This will keep the many individual activity pieces together and will ensure that next year's preparation takes virtually no time.

4. Prepare the equipment you will use, including projectors and computers.

Creating a Cooperative, Tolerant Classroom

The interactive, experiential, and stimulating learning at the heart of the TCI Approach can happen only when students feel comfortable sharing ideas, taking risks, working cooperatively, tolerating differences, and disagreeing honestly and respectfully with you and their classmates. Thus you need to take purposeful steps to develop a "safe" community in your classroom.

Here are some tips for creating a cooperative, tolerant classroom:

- Greet your students at the door every day to make a personal connection with them as they enter your classroom.

- Explain your expectations for classroom behavior, using specific examples. You may also involve students in shaping class rules.

- Stage an icebreaker at the beginning of the course to help students feel more comfortable with their new classmates. For example, make a list of descriptions (likes to dance, speaks another language, and the like), give each student a copy, and ask the class to get the autograph of one person who fits each profile.

- Convince students that learning to work effectively with others will benefit them throughout their lives.

- Teach students how to move efficiently into groups of various sizes.

- Use role-playing activities to teach students cooperative skills.

- Form mixed-ability groups.

- Allow newly formed groups to engage in team-building activities to promote group cohesion.

- Allow students to engage in groupwork activities without unnecessary interventions by you.

Assessing Learning

Effective assessment requires many approaches—individual and group, informal and formal—to create a well-rounded understanding of student performance. Here are some tips for evaluating student work.

Informal Assessment

Assessment of day-to-day activities benefits both you and your students. You send the message that every activity is important. And by identifying what works and what doesn't, you are able to adjust your instructional plans. Try these methods:

- Make your expectations known in advance so students will know how they will be rated.
- Note students' answers to questions, both oral and written.
- Evaluate participation in act-it-outs and class discussions.
- Look for students' level of cooperation in pairs and small groups.
- Ask students to assess their own work.
- Skim Interactive Student Notebooks as students work in class.

Groupwork Assessment

Evaluating groupwork presents a lot of questions: Should you rate the product or the process? The individual or the group? The amount of effort or the quality of the result? Here are five steps that will help you assess groupwork equitably:

1. Set clear criteria for evaluation.
2. Make both individuals and groups accountable.
3. Record notes as groups work and while they present their final products.
4. Have students complete self-assessments to evaluate their individual contributions as well as the group's performance.
5. Determine group and individual grades.

Formal Assessment

In addition to classroom observations and evaluation of student notebooks, you will need formal measurements of how much your students have learned. Research has shown that the TCI Approach improves student comprehension and retention. (For research results, visit www.teachtci.com.)

History Alive! The United States Through Industrialism provides an assessment for each chapter. You will find reproducible test pages in the Lesson Masters and answers in the Lesson Guide. Each chapter assessment has three parts.

Mastering the Content   The first part contains multiple-choice questions that check students' understanding of the main concepts and content introduced in the chapter. These questions range from simple comprehension to application, analysis, and evaluation. They use the wording and formats most commonly found on standardized tests.

Applying Social Studies Skills   The second part has short-answer tasks and multiple-choice questions designed to assess how well students have mastered a wide range of history skills. Students are asked to read, compare, and analyze selected passages as well as a great variety of graphic elements, including maps, diagrams, illustrations, graphs, and tables of data. These skill assessments are scaffolded to guide students from simple tasks, such as identifying data, to more complex critical thinking tasks.

Exploring the Essential Question   The third part returns to the Essential Question, asking students to apply what they have learned to a constructed-response task. Each writing task is accompanied by a prompt that provides information for students to draw upon and is carefully scaffolded to help students gather and organize the information they will need to complete the task. The final work product may be a written piece or a visual representation of information, similar to those called for in state assessments that include constructed-response tasks.

You will find digital versions of the assessments online at TeachTCI (see page xxvi). You can use the tests as they are, randomize the order of questions, edit questions, or add your own questions.

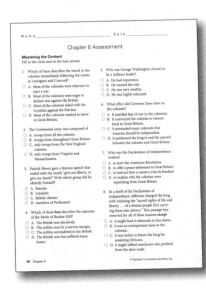

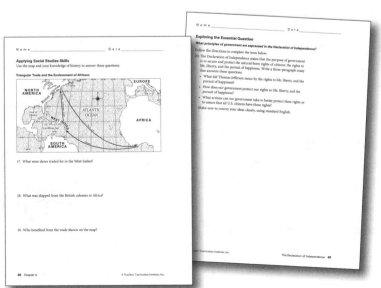

Enhancing Instruction with TeachTCI

Support for *History Alive! The United States Through Industrialism* extends beyond the box of print and audiovisual materials to a wealth of technology components. With a subscription to TeachTCI providing access to exclusive online resources, you will have the following tools to help you plan and extend lessons and customize assessments.

Teacher Resources Materials Online

Access digital versions of components—such as the Lesson Guide, Lesson Masters, and Interactive Student Notebook—all organized by chapter. Preview, print, and project items as needed.

Classroom Presenter

Project a digital Lesson Guide for each classroom activity from your Internet-connected computer. Hidden teaching notes pop up for your eyes only, while animated visuals show students what to do.

Student Edition

You and your students can view the Student Edition text and images online. You'll see what your students are reading as you assign them chapters and Reading Challenges.

Reading Challenges Scoring Manager

Assign Reading Challenges to your class and track results of both individual students and entire classes. You'll know how much your students understand and which topics need reinforcement.

Assessment Creator

Build customized assessments for your class. This tool lets you add, delete, edit, and sort questions and answers.

Lesson Tips from the TCI Community

Get ideas, engage in professional exchanges with teachers around the country, and share your own best practices. Our discussion groups are organized by program and chapter.

Enrichment Resources

Enhance student learning with chapter-related Web links and in-depth essays on selected topics.

Customized State Correlations

See how the content you are teaching aligns to your state standards in easy-to-read chart form.

Enhancing Engagement with LearnTCI

LearnTCI allows students to interact with *History Alive! The United States Through Industrialism* on any computer with Internet access. With a LearnTCI subscription, students have access to the following online tools and resources.

Student Edition Text and Images

Students can read their Student Edition anywhere they have access to a computer with an Internet connection. They can zoom in on any image and sharpen their reading skills with a wealth of features.

Text-to-Audio Tool for Accessibility

Students can highlight the text and have it read to them. You decide which students have access to this feature, which is geared primarily toward English language learners and students reading below grade level.

Text Highlighting Tool

Students can highlight what they think are the main ideas of each section.

Main Idea Viewer

After using the Text Highlighting Tool, students can compare their answers to the main ideas identified by the program. Again, you decide which students have access to this feature. It is especially helpful for English language learners and students reading below grade level.

Reading Challenges

In Reading Challenges, students analyze videos, visuals, or primary sources related to the text and then respond to questions. To answer correctly, they need to read and understand the text as well as the multimedia element. Students receive immediate feedback, so if they didn't answer a question correctly, they can reread the passage to discover the correct answer.

Enrichment Resources

Students can gain deeper understanding by exploring links to other chapter-related Web sites and reading in-depth essays on selected topics.

Learn more about TeachTCI and LearnTCI at **www.teachtci.com/tech-demo**.

Growing Professionally

There is much, much more to learn about igniting students' interest in history and creating insightful and memorable classroom experiences. For a complete explanation of the TCI Approach, the Interactive Student Notebook, and how to create a cooperative, tolerant classroom, we encourage you to read *Bring Learning Alive!* This book covers every aspect of TCI's methodology for the middle and high school social studies classroom. Please visit **www.teachtci.com** or call Customer Service at **800-497-6138** for more information or to order.

TCI Academy Training

After you have taught a few TCI lessons and seen your students' active interest in learning about history, you may find that they have reignited your passion for teaching. Help your colleagues remember why they went into teaching by bringing TCI Academy training to your school or district.

Trainings are built around immersion lessons, in which teachers become students to experience the power of active, student-centered instruction. TCI Academy trainers are classroom teachers themselves and debrief activities to provide immediate feedback. You can mix and match TCI Academy sessions to build a course that best meets your needs. Please visit **www.tciacademy.com** or call us at **800-840-2698** to get started.

Our Colonial Heritage

Our Colonial Heritage

Overview

This activity introduces geographic information essential to Unit 1. Students read and interpret maps to learn about the locations, physical features, and human geography of areas in North America claimed and colonized by Great Britain, France, Spain, and Russia. They annotate a map and answer questions in their Interactive Student Notebooks, and then discuss critical thinking questions. Their comprehension of content and proficiency in map-reading and higher-order thinking skills will help you gauge their readiness for the unit. The pages that follow include a completed map, answers to questions, a scoring guide to inform your teaching, and suggestions for modifications to meet specific student needs.

Essential Geographic Understandings

1. Location and physical geography of British, French, Spanish, and Russian land claims in North America

2. Key physical features: Appalachian Mountains, Rocky Mountains, Mississippi River, Ohio River, Missouri River, Lake Michigan, Lake Ontario, Lake Superior, Lake Huron, Lake Erie

3. Location of the 13 colonies that formed the original United States

4. Impact of physical geography on American Indian ways of life

5. Impact of physical geography on the development of the English colonies

Procedures

1 **Introduce the unit.** Tell students they will learn about the exploration, colonization, and peoples of what is now the continental United States.

2 **Create a KWL chart.** Ask students to identify what they know about the exploration and settlement of North America and what they want to learn. Use their responses to gauge how much additional background information they will need as you progress through the unit. Students will return to the KWL chart at the end of the unit and add the key information they have learned.

3 **Have students read Unit 1 "Setting the Stage" in the Student Edition.**

4 **Have students complete the Geography Challenge.** Monitor students as they answer the questions and complete the map. You may want to have them work in pairs. Use the guide on the next two pages to check their answers. You may wish to project the map from the Interactive Student Notebook and have students annotate it as the class works through the map-reading questions. Make sure students have grasped Essential Geographic Understandings 1 to 3.

5 **Discuss the "Critical Thinking" questions.** Help students understand the geographic relationships in Essential Geographic Understandings 4 and 5.

North America

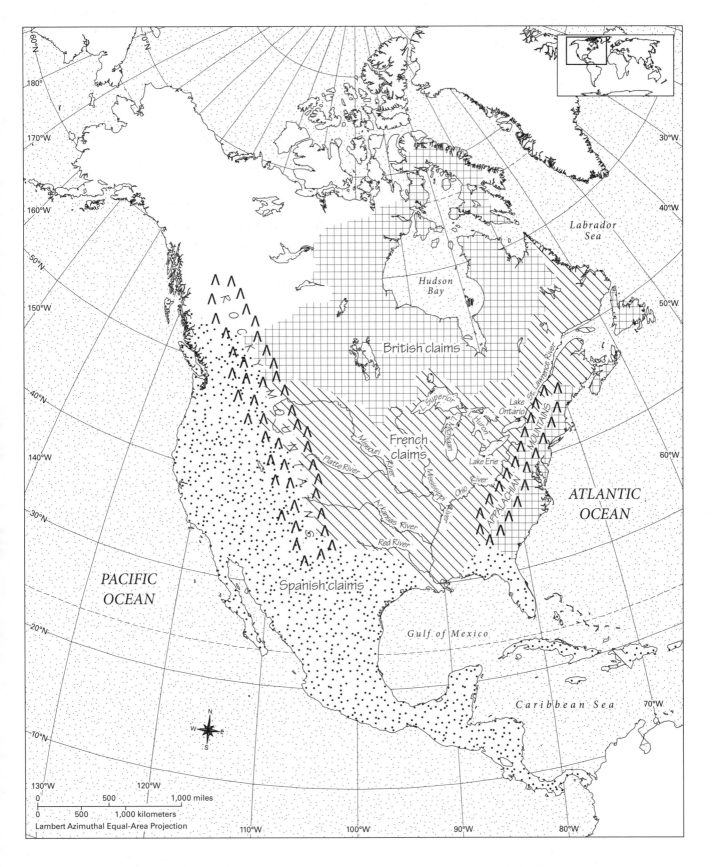

PACIFIC
OCEAN

ATLANTIC
OCEAN

Labrador
Sea

Hudson
Bay

British claims

French
claims

Spanish claims

Gulf of Mexico

Caribbean Sea

L. Superior

L. Michigan

Lake Huron

Lake Ontario

Lake Erie

St. Lawrence River

Missouri River

Platte River

Arkansas River

Red River

Mississippi River

Ohio River

ROCKY MOUNTAINS

APPALACHIAN MOUNTAINS

0   500   1,000 miles

0   500   1,000 kilometers

Lambert Azimuthal Equal-Area Projection

Geography Skills

Score 1 point for each correct answer. Use the map on the previous page to check shading and labeling.

1. Students should shade and label Spanish land claims.

2. Students should shade and label French land claims.

3. Students should shade and label British land claims.

4. The Appalachian Mountains fell mainly within Great Britain's land claims and bordered French land claims.

5. The Rocky Mountains fell mainly within Spain's land claims and bordered French and British land claims.

6. Accept any three of the following rivers: Missouri, Mississippi, Ohio, Platte, Arkansas, Red, St. Lawrence.

7. The colonies that became the original United States were part of Britain's land claims. The colonists who settled in this region sought American Indians' land.

8. American Indians hunted more in order to satisfy the French demand for furs.

Critical Thinking

Questions may have more than one correct answer. Score 1 to 3 points for each reasonable answer, depending on the strength of students' geographic reasoning. Possible answers are given here.

9. Other ways of making a living in these areas might have been hunting, fishing, or manufacturing goods.

10. The Appalachian Mountains. Possible answer: Traveling over land, a good way to cross the Appalachian Mountains might be to look for lower mountains or a low opening between mountains.

11. The land rises in elevation from the Mississippi River to the Rocky Mountains. West of the Rocky Mountains, elevation varies from mountains to lower-elevation land between the mountains and along the coast. (Some students may recognize these areas as valleys or coastal plains.) Farming might be easier on flatter land.

Using Scores to Inform Instruction

Geography Skills A score of 6 out of 8 or better indicates that students have acquired sufficient geographic information to proceed with the unit.

Critical Thinking A score of 6 out of 9 or better indicates that students are beginning to understand the relationships between physical geography and the different ways in which people live.

Modifying Instruction

ELL or Learners with Special Education Needs Consider focusing on map-reading questions or limiting the number of "Critical Thinking" questions.

Students with Weak Map or Critical Thinking Skills Assign appropriate pages from the Social Studies Skills Toolkit in the back of the Lesson Masters.

The First Americans

How did the first Americans adapt to their environments?

Overview

In a Social Studies Skill Builder, students hypothesize the geographic origins of American Indian artifacts to explore how the first Americans in eight cultural regions adapted to their environments.

Objectives

In the course of reading this chapter and participating in the classroom activity, students will

Social Studies

- trace the migration routes of the first Americans to the Americas.
- describe how American Indians viewed their environment.
- formulate hypotheses about the origins of American Indian artifacts.
- analyze ways in which American Indians of eight cultural regions adapted to their environments.

Language Arts

- clarify word meanings through the use of definitions and examples.

Social Studies Vocabulary

Key Content Terms migrate, environment, natural resource, culture, cultural region

Academic Vocabulary resourceful, revise, adapt, temporary, dominate

Materials

History Alive! The United States Through Industrialism

Interactive Student Notebooks

Visuals 1A and 1B

Placards 1A–1H (2 sets; create additional placards as needed)

Lesson Masters
- Information Master 1
- Vocabulary Development handout (1 per student, on colored paper)

Activity	Suggested Time	Materials
Preview	10 minutes	• Interactive Student Notebooks • VIsuals 1A and 1B
Vocabulary Development	30–40 minutes	• *History Alive! The United States Through Industrialism* • Interactive Student Notebooks • Vocabulary Development handout
Social Studies Skill Builder	100 minutes (2 regular periods) (1 block period)	• *History Alive! The United States Through Industrialism* • Placards 1A–1H (2 sets) • Information Master 1
Processing	20 minutes	• Interactive Student Notebooks
Assessment	40 minutes	• Chapter 1 Assessment

Preview

1   **Introduce the concept of an environment.** Project *Visual 1A: The Canadian Forest,* and tell students that this photograph shows the environment of a Canadian forest in the fall. Explain that an environment refers to the land, water, animals, and plants in a specific area. Ask students to point out some environmental features in the image.

2   **Have students complete the Preview activity.** Students will describe the shelter, clothing, and tools they would make to survive in this Canadian forest.

3   **Have students share their responses in pairs or with the class.**

4   **Introduce the concept of adapting to an environment.** Project *Visual 1B: An Ojibwa Camp,* and explain that this painting depicts an Ojibwa Indian camp in the same Canadian region students just wrote about. Ask,

   • What do you see here?

   • What were the Ojibwa houses made of? What type of clothing did the Ojibwa people wear?

   • What are some ways the Ojibwa people may have adapted to their environment?

5   **Explain the connection between the Preview and Chapter 1.** Explain to students that, just as the Ojibwa used natural resources for shelter, food, and clothing, so too did the many American Indian groups in the Americas. In this chapter, students will explore ways in which different groups of American Indians adapted to their environments.

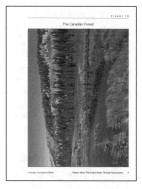

VIsual 1A

VIsual 1B

Vocabulary Development

1   **Introduce the Key Content Terms.** Have students locate the Key Content Terms for the chapter in their Interactive Student Notebooks. These are important terms that will help them understand the main ideas of the chapter. Ask volunteers to identify any familiar terms and how they might be used in a sentence.

2   **Have students complete a Vocabulary Development handout.** Give each student a copy of the Vocabulary Development handout of your choice from the Reading Toolkit at the back of the Lesson Masters. These handouts provide extra practice and support, depending on your students' needs. Review the completed handout by asking volunteers to share one answer for each term.

> **Writing: Written Language Conventions**
> Call attention to the spelling of *environment,* noting the second *n.* Explain that some words are often misspelled because of a silent letter or a sound that is left out when the word is pronounced—for example, *government, boundary, Arctic, parliamentary,* and *business.* Explain that students must simply learn these spellings or look them up.

Reading

1 **Introduce the Essential Question and have students read Section 1.1.** Then have students use information from the section and the chapter opener image to propose possible answers to the Essential Question: *How did American Indians adapt to their environments?*

2 **Have students complete the Reading Notes for Sections 1.2 to 1.4.** Have several volunteers share their responses. Use Guide to Reading Notes 1 to check their answers.

3 **Have students complete the remaining Reading Notes for Chapter 1.** Assign Sections 1.5 to 1.12 during the activity as indicated in the procedures for the Social Studies Skill Builder. Remind students to use the Key Content Terms where appropriate as they complete their Reading Notes.

Social Studies Skill Builder

1 **Prepare the classroom.** Post two sets of *Placards 1A–1H: American Indian Artifacts* on the walls. (**Note:** Create additional placards as needed.)

2 **Introduce the activity.** Explain that students will examine artifacts, or human-made objects, from eight American Indian cultural regions. They will hypothesize the geographic origins of the artifacts and then read to learn more about a specific cultural region.

3 **Place students in pairs and review the steps on *Information Master 1: Directions for Analyzing American Indian Artifacts.*** Emphasize that after examining each placard, pairs should raise their hands to indicate that they are ready for you to check their answers.

4 **Conduct the activity.** Have each pair go to an open placard to begin. When pairs indicate that they are ready for you to check their work, verify their answers using Guide to Reading Notes 1. If they have identified the correct cultural region, remind them to complete their Reading Notes for that region and then proceed to an open placard.

5 **Debrief the activity.** Once most pairs have completed most of the Reading Notes, review the answers. Then ask,

- Which cultural regions do you think would have been least challenging to adapt to? Most challenging? Why?

- In what ways did American Indians adapt to their environments?

Processing

Have students complete the Processing activity. Students will create an annotated diagram showing how American Indians in one cultural region adapted to their environment.

Placards 1A–1H

Information Master 1

Quicker Coverage

Use Fewer Placards Choose just four to six placards for students to review, and assign the remaining cultural regions for homework. Consider making three or four sets of the selected placards to help the activity proceed quickly.

Conduct a Jigsaw Have each pair join three other pairs to form groups of eight students. Then have each pair choose two placards to analyze and complete the corresponding Reading Notes. Finally, convene the original groups of eight, and have students share their answers to the Reading Notes.

Deeper Coverage

Play a Review Game When students complete the Processing assignment, tell them not to include the name of the cultural region. Post the completed annotated diagrams on the wall and have students hypothesize which cultural region each diagram depicts. Consider awarding points for each correct answer.

Expand the Processing Have students create annotated diagrams for all eight cultural regions on a poster, and display the posters around the room.

Assessment

Mastering the Content

1. C	5. C	9. C	13. A
2. A	6. C	10. D	14. B
3. C	7. B	11. D	15. C
4. D	8. D	12. B	16. B

Applying Social Studies Skills

17. Great Plains

18. Possible answers: forests or trees, lakes or rivers

19. Answers will vary. Students should show understanding of adaptability and provide at least one specific example to indicate that understanding. Possible answer: Unlike American Indians in most other cultural regions, the Southwest people had to adjust to harsh weather conditions. They found ways to use the little rainwater by digging irrigation ditches to carry water from streams to fields.

Exploring the Essential Question

20. Answers should include all of the elements requested in the prompt.

Scoring Rubric

Score	Description
3	Student completes all six parts of the task. Ideas are clearly stated, supported by details, and demonstrate command of standard English conventions.
2	Student responds to most or all parts of the task. Ideas may lack details or not be clearly stated.
1	Student responds to at least one part of the task. Ideas may contain factual or grammatical errors and may lack details.
0	Response does not match the task or is incorrect.

Digging Up the Past

1   **Introduce the idea that photographs and written materials provide information about past events.** Show students a photograph of a well-known event that occurred 40 to 50 years ago, such as the 1969 moon landing. Point out that this event happened before students were born, and ask them how they know about the event. Be sure they name written sources, such as newspapers and books, as well as television and the Internet.

2   **Discuss how people gather information about pre-literate cultures.** Ask,

   - How do we know about American Indian cultures and their lives in ancient times, before written history?

   - Suppose you find an artifact from an ancient American Indian group. If you knew nothing about the artifact or who made it—and there was no written information to tell you—what kinds of questions would you ask about it?

3   **Have students read the Chapter 1 Reading Further.** Tell students that Cahokia Mounds is an Illinois State Historic Site as well as a UNESCO (United Nations Educational, Scientific and Cultural Organization) World Heritage site. Archaeologists like Tim Pauketat still work there to solve the site's mysteries.

4   **Have students complete the Chapter 1 Reading Further in their Interactive Student Notebooks.** Discuss how asking good questions helps archaeologists, and then invite students to share and compare the research questions they have recorded.

5   **Point out that asking good questions is an important part of studying American history.** Discuss how historians, like archaeologists, begin their research with good questions, such as, *Why did this happen? How would history have been different if this event had not happened?*

English Language Learners

Create an Illustrated Dictionary Have students identify at least six words in the reading that they are unfamiliar with. Then have them complete the following steps for each of those words and for each Key Content Term:

- Define it in their own words.
- Use it in a sentence.
- Draw a symbol or simple picture to represent it.

Learners Reading and Writing Below Grade Level

Support the Activity During the Social Studies Skill Builder, provide students with a partially completed copy of the matrix from Guide to Reading Notes 1. Have students use this matrix to help them match the artifacts on each placard to a cultural region. Then have them read the corresponding sections and complete the Reading Notes.

Learners with Special Education Needs

Model How to Analyze a Placard Before conducting the activity, project one of the placards and ask, *What do you see here? What do these artifacts suggest about the environment of this American Indian cultural region? Look at the four maps in Section 1.3 of your book. Which cultural region do you think these artifacts are from?* Reveal the answer and have students add two pieces of information to the matrix in their Reading Notes. Then have students work in pairs to complete the Reading Notes for the corresponding section.

Advanced Learners

Create an Annotated Map As an alternative to the Processing activity, have students create a three-dimensional annotated map, on butcher paper or poster board, of the eight cultural regions described in the text. Have them use the first map in Section 1.3 as a starting point. The annotated map should

- clearly show the eight American Indian cultural regions.
- include physical representations of the land in each cultural region.
- reflect the variety of climates in the cultural regions.
- display through two-dimensional or three-dimensional objects how American Indians adapted to the environments within each cultural region.
- have a key that explains any symbols used on the map.

Enrichment Resources

Find out more about American Indians by exploring the following Enrichment Resources for *History Alive! The United States Through Industrialism* at www.teachtci.com.

Enrichment Readings These in-depth readings encourage students to explore selected topics related to the chapter. You may also find readings that relate the chapter's content directly to your state's curriculum.

Internet Connections The recommended Web sites provide useful and engaging content that reinforces skills development and mastery of subjects within the chapter.

Literature Recommendations

The following books offer opportunities to extend the content in this chapter.

The First Americans: Prehistory–1600, 3d ed., by Joy Hakim (New York: Oxford University Press, 2003)

In a Sacred Manner I Live: Native American Wisdom by Neil Philip, Ed. (New York: Clarion Books, 2005)

Native American Migration by Tracee Sioux (New York: The Rosen Publishing Group, 2004)

Section 1.2

1. Illustrations will vary. Exposed about 30,000 years ago, Beringia was a wide bridge of land between Asia and North America. It disappeared when the glaciers melted and the oceans rose.

2. The first Americans came from Siberia across what was land area during the last Ice Age. They migrated south down into North and South America.

Section 1.3

1. Possible answer: American Indians in the far north regions used natural resources to adapt to their environment by making warm, hooded clothing from animal skins. To avoid being blinded by the glare of the sun, they made goggles out of bone with slits to see through.

2. A culture is a way of life and includes a people's beliefs, customs, food, dwellings, and clothing.

3. Cultural regions will vary. American Indians living on the Plains would primarily wear clothing made from animal hide, fur, and plant materials. American Indians living in the Southeast would build rectangular houses with pointed leaf roofs. American Indians living in the Great Basin would eat animals and wild plants.

Section 1.4

American Indians viewed themselves as a part of the community of plants, animals, and other natural objects.

Sections 1.5 to 1.12

Symbols of cultural regions will vary.

	Section 1.5: Northwest Coast	Section 1.6: California	Section 1.7: Great Basin	Section 1.8: Plateau
Placard	E	H	G	A
Main geographic features	thick forests of fir, spruce, and cedar; rugged mountains	coast and coastal foothills, inland valley, deserts, mountains	desert, grasses, sagebrush, piñon trees	mountains, forests, grasses, sagebrush
Main food sources	shellfish, seaweed, seals, sea lions, whales, fish, deer, moose, bear	salmon, shellfish, deer, roots, berries, pine nuts, acorns	ducks, eggs, cattails, snakes, grasshoppers, plants, berries, jackrabbits	salmon, onions, carrots, camas, antelope, deer
Types of homes	large houses from logs or living trees, shingles from cedar bark	cone-shaped homes made of bark or reeds	temporary shelters of willow poles shaped into a cone and covered with brush or reeds	partly under-ground homes lined with logs and covered with saplings, reeds, and mud
Types of, and materials for, crafts and clothing	cedar-bark capes; baskets, mats, and blankets from inner bark	skirts and aprons from grasses or plants, animal hides, baskets and sifters from plant materials	robes from rabbit skins, baskets coated with pine sap	clothing from animal hides and decorated with seeds and shells; woven baskets and hats
Tools	seal harpoons, wooden wedges, sledgehammers, rope, needles, bone drills, stone knives	antler tools, baskets, fish traps	seed beaters (baskets to collect seeds), nets, decoys to attract ducks, sharp sticks	nets for catching salmon, spears, digging sticks

	Section 1.9: Southwest	Section 1.10: Great Plains	Section 1.11: Eastern Woodlands	Section 1.12: Southeast
Placard	C	B	D	F
Main geographic features	canyons, mountains, deserts, flat-topped mesas, rivers	treeless grasslands	forests, lakes, streams	coastal plains, river valleys, mountains, swamps
Main food sources	corn, beans, squash, rabbits, chili peppers	farming, buffalo	deer, bears, beavers, birds, fish, greens, nuts, berries, corn, squash	corn, beans, squash, squirrels, rabbits, turkeys, deer, wild plants
Types of homes	apartment-like houses made from adobe bricks	tipis made from buffalo hides	log-frame homes covered with elm bark (longhouses)	tree strips woven in a rectangular frame and plastered with clay, roofs of leaves
Types of, and materials for, crafts and clothing	cotton clothes dyed with bright colors from plants and minerals	clothing and bags made from buffalo	deerskin skirts, capes, and moccasins	deerskin skirts
Tools	corn grinders, dams, clay pots, clay ovens	hardwood bows, arrows, bone knives and scrapers, spears, shields, rope	canoes, corn scrapers and grinders	hoes made of stone, shell, or bone; blowguns; bows and arrows

European Exploration and Settlement

How did Europeans explore and establish settlements in the Americas?

Overview

In a Visual Discovery activity, students analyze and bring to life images depicting European exploration and settlement to discover how European nations explored and established settlements in the Americas.

Objectives

In the course of reading this chapter and participating in the classroom activity, students will

Social Studies

- identify the motives behind European exploration of the Americas.
- explain how Europeans established territorial claims in the Americas.
- compare the Spanish, French, English, and Dutch settlements in the Americas.
- describe the impact of European exploration and settlement of the Americas on indigenous peoples and West Africans.

Language Arts

- communicate the perspective of a historical character by using well-chosen details to relate a clear and coherent event.
- write a narrative that reveals the significance of the event.

Social Studies Vocabulary

Key Content Terms Columbian Exchange, slavery, conquistadors, colony, missionaries, coureurs de bois

Academic Vocabulary domesticate, convert, revolt, impact, technique

Materials

History Alive! The United States Through Industrialism

Interactive Student Notebooks

Visuals 2A–2E

Lesson Masters

- Student Handouts 2A and 2B (1 of each for every 4 students)
- Vocabulary Development handout (1 per student, on colored paper)

Activity	Suggested Time	Materials
Preview	10 minutes	• Interactive Student Notebooks
Vocabulary Development	30–40 minutes	• *History Alive! The United States Through Industrialism* • Interactive Student Notebooks • Vocabulary Development handout
Visual Discovery	100–150 minutes (2–3 regular periods) (1–1.5 block periods)	• *History Alive! The United States Through Industrialism* • Visuals 2A–2E • Student Handouts 2A and 2B
Processing	20 minutes	• *History Alive! The United States Through Industrialism* • Interactive Student Notebooks
Assessment	40 minutes	• Chapter 2 Assessment

Preview

1   **Have students complete the Preview activity.** Students will consider where to start a new community and rank relevant factors from most to least important.

2   **Have students share their responses in pairs or with the class.**

3   **Explain the connection between the Preview and Chapter 2.** Tell students that the factors they just considered about where to start a new community are similar to those that early Europeans considered when determining where to settle in the American continents. In this chapter, students will discover how European nations explored and established settlements in the Americas.

Vocabulary Development

1   **Introduce the Key Content Terms.** Have students locate the Key Content Terms for the chapter in their Interactive Student Notebooks. These are important terms that will help them understand the main ideas of the chapter. Ask volunteers to identify any familiar terms and how they might be used in a sentence.

2   **Have students complete a Vocabulary Development handout.** Give each student a copy of the Vocabulary Development handout of your choice from the Reading Toolkit at the back of the Lesson Masters. These handouts provide extra practice and support, depending on your students' needs. Review the completed handout by asking volunteers to share one answer for each term.

Reading

1   **Introduce the Essential Question and have students read Section 2.1.** Then have students use information from the section and the chapter opener image to respond to these questions:

   • Judging from the illustration that opens the chapter, what do you think some explorers feared? What other fears do you think explorers had?

   • Why might explorers have ventured into unknown lands?

   • What might explorers have done once they found new lands?

2   **Have students complete the remaining Reading Notes for Chapter 2.** Assign Sections 2.2 to 2.6 during the activity as indicated in the procedures for the Visual Discovery activity. Remind students to use the Key Content Terms where appropriate as they complete their Reading Notes.

Visual Discovery

1 **Place students in groups of four and introduce the activity.** Explain that students will examine images to hypothesize how European nations explored and established settlements in the Americas. They will "step into" two of the images to bring the related content to life.

2 **Introduce Section 2.2 by projecting *Visual 2A: Columbus Claims San Salvador for Spain*.** Ask,

- What do you see here?

- What are some of the things the men are carrying? Why might they be carrying these items?

- Who do you think the men in the foreground are?

- Who do you think the people on the far left are? What might they be thinking?

3 **Have students read and complete the Reading Notes for Section 2.2.** Use Guide to Reading Notes 2 to review the answers with the class.

4 **Have students prepare to bring the image to life.** Assign each group one of these four characters: Christopher Columbus, Priest, Soldier, Taino Indian. Distribute *Student Handout 2A: Creating an Act-It-Out About Columbus Claiming San Salvador* to each group and review the directions. Make sure groups understand that they are responsible only for portraying their assigned character. Give groups about five minutes to prepare for the act-it-out.

5 **Conduct the act-it-out.** Call up one actor for each character to stand in the appropriate location in front of the projected image, taking on that character's posture and facial expression. Acting as the on-scene reporter, ask the characters some of the questions from Student Handout 2A. (**Note:** Consider conducting the act-it-out a second time with new actors.).

6 **Introduce Section 2.3 by projecting *Visual 2B: Spanish Mission at San Carlos Borroméo de Carmelo*.** Tell groups to pretend they are detectives gathering clues to answer this question: *What was life like in this settlement?* Have groups find details, or "evidence," in the image that will help answer the question. For example, the crucifix is evidence that Christianity was practiced in this settlement. Then ask volunteers to come forward and place a sticky note on each piece of evidence and explain what it suggests about life in the settlement.

7 **Have students read and complete the Reading Notes for Section 2.3.** Review the answers with the class.

Visual 2A

Student Handout 2A

Visual 2B

8 **Introduce Section 2.4 by projecting *Visual 2C: Coureurs de Bois Working in New France*.** Ask,

- What do you see here?

- What are the men wearing? Why might they be dressed this way?

- What are the men holding? What might they do with these things?

- Who are these men? Where might they be from?

9 **Have students read and complete the Reading Notes for Section 2.4.** Review the answers with the class.

10 **Have students prepare to bring the image to life.** Assign each group one of these characters: Coureur de Bois Holding Fish, Coureur de Bois Holding a Fox, Huron Indian (not pictured), Iroquois Indian (not pictured). Distribute *Student Handout 2B: Creating an Act-It-Out About New France* to each group and review the directions. Make sure groups understand that they are responsible only for portraying their assigned character. Give groups about five minutes to prepare.

11 **Conduct the act-it-out.** Call up one actor for each coureur de bois to stand in the appropriate location in front of the projected image, taking on that character's posture and facial expression. Place the Huron and Iroquois Indian characters on opposite sides. Acting as the on-scene reporter, ask the characters some of the questions from Student Handout 2B. (**Note:** Consider conducting the act-it-out a second time with new actors.)

12 **Introduce Section 2.5 by projecting *Visual 2D: Settlers at Jamestown*.** Assign each group one of these four inanimate objects shown in the image: ax, barrel, small boat, tree. Tell groups to discuss how their object may have helped settlers adapt to the new environment. After a few minutes, tell groups to think of a simple way to position their bodies to represent the object. For example, a student representing a barrel might lie curled up on the floor. Have one member of each group assume the object's position. Then walk around and ask, *What are you? How will you help settlers adapt to their new environment?*

13 **Have students read and complete the Reading Notes for Section 2.5.** Review the answers with the class.

Visual 2C

Student Handout 2B

Visual 2D

Visual 2E

14 Introduce Section 2.6 by projecting *Visual 2E: Peter Stuyvesant and the Surrender of New Amsterdam.* **Ask,**

- What do you see here?

- Where might these people be from?

- What emotions do you think the man in the center is feeling? What emotions are the others feeling?

- What do you think the paper that the man is holding says?

15 Have students read and complete the Reading Notes for Section 2.6. Review the answers with the class.

Processing

Have students complete the Processing activity. Students will create a historical marker commemorating an early European settlement.

Quicker Coverage

Eliminate One or Both Act-It-Outs Instead, have students analyze the images and complete the Reading Notes for those sections.

Deeper Coverage

Conduct an Additional Act-It-Out After students complete the Reading Notes for Section 2.6, have them bring to life the image of Peter Stuyvesant on Visual 2E. Assign each group one of these characters: Peter Stuyvesant, Woman in Red on Left, Clergyman on Right, Man in Background Looking Out to Sea. Have groups prepare to answer the following questions:

- Groups representing Peter Stuyvesant: *Who are you? Why don't some people like you? What have you accomplished as governor? How do you plan to deal with the British demands? Do you think your resistance will be successful?*

- Remaining groups: *Who are you? What do you think of Governor Stuyvesant? How do you think Governor Stuyvesant is handling the English threat? What do you think should be done next?*

Call up one actor for each character to stand in the appropriate location in front of the projected image, taking on that character's posture and facial expression. Acting as the on-scene reporter, ask the characters some of the questions above.

Listening and Speaking: Comprehension

Before the presentation, remind students that listening actively requires framing questions about what is said, as well as thinking critically about how well each speaker played the role and delivered his or her message. After each speaker finishes, ask listeners to paraphrase the speaker's point of view, as well as to ask at least one question about the content and to make one evaluative comment about what the speaker did well.

Assessment

Mastering the Content

1. B	5. B	9. D	13. C
2. A	6. B	10. A	14. B
3. B	7. C	11. A	15. C
4. B	8. B	12. D	16. A

Applying Social Studies Skills

17. Answers may vary slightly. Samuel Champlain saw the Iroquois warriors make a move to fire at them.

18. B

19. C

Exploring the Essential Question

20. Answers should include all of the elements requested in the prompt.

Scoring Rubric

Score	Description
3	Student completes all three parts of the task. Ideas are clearly stated, supported by details, and demonstrate command of standard English conventions.
2	Student responds to most or all parts of the task. Ideas may lack details or not be clearly stated.
1	Student responds to at least one part of the task. Ideas may contain factual or grammatical errors and may lack details.
0	Response does not match the task or is incorrect.

Who Was the Real Columbus?

1 **Elicit students' ideas about Christopher Columbus.** Write "Christopher Columbus" on the board. Ask students for words or phrases that describe him, and record their responses.

2 **Discuss students' points of view about Columbus as reflected in their descriptions.** Ask, *What do these words and phrases say about your points of view about Columbus?*

3 **Have students read the first two pages of the Chapter 2 Reading Further.**

4 **Ask students to compare the motivations of Columbus and Las Casas.** Ask,

  • What was Columbus's motivation for traveling to North America?

  • What was Las Casas's motivation for traveling to North America?

  • How do you think Las Casas's point of view changed after he became a priest?

5 **Have students finish the reading.**

6 **Have students complete the Chapter 2 Reading Further in their Interactive Student Notebooks.** Ask them to share and discuss their summaries of the points of view of the encounter and among historians.

7 **Have students share their point-of-view paragraphs about a recent event in pairs or with the class.** Explore what factors can lead people to have differing points of view about the same topic. Ask, *Why do you think you and the other person had different points of view?*

English Language Learners

Provide Visuals and Questions Give copies of the visuals and corresponding questions to students the night before you conduct the activity so that they can be prepared to take part in the discussions the following day.

Learners Reading and Writing Below Grade Level

Support the Processing Give students a template like the one below to assist them with the Processing activity.

This historical marker commemorates the settlement of _____ .

This settlement was established in _____ .

It was established after . . . (describe how it was settled)

American Indians living near the settlement were treated _____ .
For instance, . . .

Ultimately the settlement _____
(write either did well or failed). The reasons for this include . . .

Learners with Special Education Needs

Support the Act-It-Outs Consider these tips:

- Place students in nonspeaking roles. For instance, for Visual 2A, assign students a nonspeaking character behind Columbus. For Visual 2C, have students take on the shape of inanimate objects, such as the mountain and house.

- Have students prepare a script by answering the questions on the corresponding handout. Allow them to read from that script during the act-it-out.

- Tell students which role they will be playing a few days in advance so that they can practice their part.

Advanced Learners

Create Illustrations from the Perspective of an American Indian Artist As an alternative to the Processing activity, challenge students to draw four pictures that show some feature of European exploration and settlement from the perspective of an American Indian artist living in the 17th century. Each picture should focus on one European group: the Spanish, French, English, or Dutch. Instruct students to write a dialogue to accompany one of the pictures that clearly demonstrates how American Indians felt about European exploration and settlement. The dialogue can be between two or more American Indians or between an Indian and a settler.

Enrichment Resources

Find out more about European exploration and settlement by exploring the following Enrichment Resources for *History Alive! The United States Through Industrialism* at www.teachtci.com.

Enrichment Readings These in-depth readings encourage students to explore selected topics related to the chapter. You may also find readings that relate the chapter's content directly to your state's curriculum.

Internet Connections The recommended Web sites provide useful and engaging content that reinforces skills development and mastery of subjects within the chapter.

Literature Recommendations

The following books offer opportunities to extend the content in this chapter.

Roanoke: Solving the Mystery of the Lost Colony by Lee Miller (New York: Penguin Books, 2002)

Exploring North America by Jacqueline Morley (New York: Peter Bedrick Books, 2002)

Wigwam and the Longhouse by David Yue and Charlotte Yue (New York: Houghton Mifflin, 2000)

Section 2.2

1. Spain sponsored the voyages of Christopher Columbus, an explorer who claimed territories in the Caribbean and South America for Spain. Spain later sent conquistadors like Hernán Cortés and Francisco Pizarro to discover and claim lands for Spain in the Americas.

2. Illustrations should include the labels *people, foods, domesticated animals,* and *diseases.* Descriptions should include the term *Columbian Exchange.*

Section 2.3

1. Spain sponsored several expeditions to North America. As conquistadors explored new territories, they claimed the areas for Spain. Ponce de León explored and established a colony in Florida. Francisco Coronado traveled as far north as the Great Plains in search of seven cities of gold, but all he found were seven little pueblos.

2. Illustrations should include the labels *presidio* and *mission.* Descriptions will vary.

3. The American Indians and the Spanish learned many things from each other. Pueblo people learned how to use new tools, grow new foods, and raise sheep for wool. Many converted to Catholicism through the work of missionaries. From the Indians, the Spanish learned new techniques for growing crops. Some Spanish settlers treated the American Indians harshly by enslaving them and whipping those who continued to practice their traditional rituals.

4. Students' maps should reflect the labeling on the map in Section 2.6.

Section 2.4

1. France sent explorers to the Atlantic coastline of North America. Jacques Cartier claimed Canada for France. Samuel de Champlain established the first settlement in Quebec. Robert de La Salle claimed the territory of Louisiana, which included everything west of the Mississippi River.

2. Illustrations should include the label *coureurs de bois.* Descriptions will vary.

3. The French made American Indians their business partners. An especially friendly relationship existed between the French and the Huron, who were enemies of the Iroquois. Fur trappers lived in Huron villages, learned the Huron language, and married Huron women.

4. Students' maps should reflect the labeling on the map in Section 2.6.

Section 2.5

1. John Cabot sailed across the Atlantic and claimed the island of Newfoundland for England. Sir Walter Raleigh tried to start a colony on Roanoke Island, but the colonists mysteriously disappeared. The London Company sent settlers to Virginia to start a moneymaking colony that became known as Jamestown.

2. Illustrations and descriptions will vary.

3. At first, the Indians were hesitant to trade with the settlers and many settlers died from hunger and disease. Pocahontas, the daughter of a powerful Indian chief, made friends with Jamestown leader John Smith and helped the settlers by bringing them food and keeping peace with her people. The American Indians refused to trade with the settlers during the "Starving Time." Relations improved when John Rolfe married Pocahontas.

4. Students' maps should reflect the labeling on the map in Section 2.6.

Section 2.6

1. Dutch merchants sponsored the trip of Henry Hudson, who claimed land along the Hudson River. The Dutch West India Company established a colony near present-day Albany, New York. The colony of New Amsterdam on Manhattan Island was governed by the unpopular Peter Stuyvesant, who peacefully surrendered it to the British in 1664.

2. Illustrations should include the labels *fur, Iroquois,* and *weapons.* Descriptions will vary.

3. The Dutch settlers were instructed to not use violence but to persuade or barter with the American Indians. The Dutch also established friendly relations with the Iroquois Confederacy and supplied them with weapons to fight the Huron.

4. Students' maps should reflect the labeling on the map in Section 2.6.

The English Colonies in North America

What were the similarities and differences among the colonies in North America?

Overview

In a Problem Solving Groupwork activity, students analyze the similarities and differences among the English colonies in North America by creating and visiting sales booths in a "colonial fair."

Objectives

In the course of reading this chapter and participating in the classroom activity, students will

Social Studies

- identify the various reasons for the settlement of the British colonies.
- compare religious practices and the different government systems—including the system set up in the Mayflower Compact—among the colonies.
- collaborate with others to showcase the economic, political, and religious features of a colony.
- synthesize key information about a colony by writing a postcard from the perspective of an American colonist.

Language Arts

- write a short narrative employing descriptive strategies.
- present detailed evidence, examples, and reasoning to support arguments.

Social Studies Vocabulary

Key Content Terms mercantilism, cash crops, charter, democratic, Mayflower Compact, slave trade

Academic Vocabulary economy, isolated, authorize, proprietor, prosperous

Materials

History Alive! The United States Through Industrialism

Interactive Student Notebooks

Visual 3

Lesson Masters

- Student Handout 3 (8 copies)
- Vocabulary Development handout (1 per student, on colored paper)

poster board or trifold posters

markers

Activity	Suggested Time	Materials
Preview	15 minutes	• Interactive Student Notebooks • Visual 3
Vocabulary Development	30–40 minutes	• *History Alive! The United States Through Industrialism* • Interactive Student Notebooks • Vocabulary Development handout
Problem Solving Groupwork	150–200 minutes (3–4 regular periods) (1.5–2 block periods)	• *History Alive! The United States Through Industrialism* • Student Handout 3 • poster board and markers
Processing	20 minutes	• Interactive Student Notebooks
Assessment	40 minutes	• Chapter 3 Assessment

Preview

1 **Project *Visual 3: Early English Colonies in North America*.** Explain that the early English colonies are often divided into New England, Middle, and Southern Colonies. Have students identify these three regions on the map. Then discuss these questions, having students record their answers:

- What are some interesting details you notice in the map?

- What similarities existed among the colonial regions?

- What differences existed among the colonial regions?

2 **Explain the connection between the Preview and Chapter 2.** Tell students that while the early English colonies shared some characteristics, they differed greatly in terms of geography, economic activities, religious practices, and types of government. In this chapter, students will analyze the similarities and differences among the English colonies in North America.

Visual 3

Vocabulary Development

1 **Introduce the Key Content Terms.** Have students locate the Key Content Terms for the chapter in their Interactive Student Notebooks. These are important terms that will help them understand the main ideas of the chapter. Ask volunteers to identify any familiar terms and how they might be used in a sentence.

2 **Have students complete a Vocabulary Development handout.** Give each student a copy of the Vocabulary Development handout of your choice from the Reading Toolkit at the back of the Lesson Masters. These handouts provide extra practice and support, depending on your students' needs. Review the completed handout by asking volunteers to share one answer for each term.

Reading

1 **Introduce the Essential Question and have students read Section 3.1.** Then have students use information from the section and the chapter opener image to propose possible answers to the Essential Question: *What were the similarities and differences among the colonies in North America?*

2 **Have students read and complete the Reading Notes for Section 3.2.** Have several volunteers share their responses. Use Guide to Reading Notes 3 to check their answers.

3 **Have students complete the remaining Reading Notes for Chapter 3.** Assign Sections 3.3 to 3.10 during the activity as indicated in the procedures for the Problem Solving Groupwork activity. Remind students to use the Key Content Terms where appropriate as they complete their Reading Notes.

Problem Solving Groupwork

1 **Introduce the activity.** Explain that groups will represent one of eight early English colonies in North America to create a colonial sales booth encouraging others to settle in their colony. They will then participate in a "colonial fair," where they will visit the booths and choose their ideal colony.

2 **Divide students into groups and assign colonies.** Place students into eight groups and assign each group one of eight colonies: Massachusetts, Rhode Island, Connecticut, New York, Pennsylvania, Maryland, Virginia, or Georgia. (**Note:** Ideally there will be four students per group. For fewer than 32 students, consider eliminating one or more of the colonies. For more than 32 students, create larger groups or add a fifth role of Historian to Student Handout 3 to lead the group in Step 2.)

3 **Review the steps for creating a colonial sales booth.** Distribute *Student Handout 3: Creating a Colonial Sales Booth* to each group and assign each group member a role. Review the steps on the handout, emphasizing that each group will have two teams. During the Colonial Fair, Team A (Advertising Director and Copywriter) will conduct the sales presentation while Team B (Graphic Artist and Salesperson) visits the other booths. Teams will then trade places.

4 **Monitor progress as groups prepare their booths.** Tell groups that when they complete a step, they should raise their hands to have you initial that step before they move on. When groups are ready, provide them with materials for creating their posters.

5 **Have groups set up their booths.** Have each group place two desks together at the periphery of the room and display their posters on the wall or on the desks.

6 **Conduct the Colonial Fair.** In a dramatic voice, announce that the Colonial Fair is open. Tell members of Team B to begin visiting booths. Tell students that as they visit each booth, they should complete part of their Reading Notes for that section. When most Team B members have visited all of the booths, have them switch places with Team A. (**Note:** Depending on the time available, you may want Team B members to visit the booths on one day and Team A members to visit them the next day.)

7 **Have students complete the remaining Reading Notes for Sections 3.3 to 3.10.** Use the Guide to Reading Notes to check their answers.

8 **Hold a follow-up discussion.** Ask,

- In which colony would you most like to have settled? In which colony would you least like to have settled? Why?

- What were the main similarities among the colonies?

- What were the main differences among the colonies? How do you think these differences might have affected the way the colonies interacted?

Student Handout 3

Listening and Speaking: Evaluation of Oral Communications

As students listen to each sales presentation, encourage them not only to listen for content, but also to identify any slant or bias. Is the speaker partial to his or her own colony? In what way is the sales presentation biased? How might the speaker eliminate that bias?

Processing

Have students complete the Processing activity on a separate sheet of paper. Students write a postcard from the perspective of a colonist persuading a friend to settle in an American colony.

Quicker Coverage

Eliminate the Sales Presentations Instead, have groups complete Steps 1 to 4 on Student Handout 3 to create posters promoting a colony and then display their posters. Then welcome students to the Colonial Fair and have them walk around to view the posters. Remind students to complete at least three spokes on each diagram in their Reading Notes.

Deeper Coverage

Create Advertising Brochures In lieu of posters, have groups create brochures encouraging others to move to their colony. Brochures should include the slogan, at least four visuals depicting the colony, and four paragraphs describing the key features of the colony including reasons for settlement, geography and climate, religion, and government. Before the fair, make copies of each brochure for groups to hand out during their sales presentations.

Assessment

Mastering the Content

1. B	5. D	9. A	13. B
2. D	6. A	10. D	14. D
3. C	7. D	11. B	15. A
4. C	8. A	12. D	16. B

Applying Social Studies Skills

17. New England

18. Southern

19. Possible answers: The mountains restricted the growth of the colonies. The mountains protected the colonies from American Indian tribes in the west. The mountains prevented the colonists from easily moving westward.

Exploring the Essential Question

20. Answers should include all of the elements requested in the prompt.

Scoring Rubric

Score	Description
3	Student completes all four parts of the task. Ideas are clearly stated, supported by details, and demonstrate command of standard English conventions.
2	Student responds to most or all parts of the task. Ideas may lack details or not be clearly stated.
1	Student responds to at least one part of the task. Ideas may contain factual or grammatical errors and may lack details.
0	Response does not match the task or is incorrect.

A Colonial Cast of Characters

1   **Survey students' ideas about the English colonists.** Create a T-chart on the board with two columns: "Characteristics of the Colonists" and "Reasons Why the Colonists Came." Ask students what words they would use to describe the colonists who settled the 13 English colonies. Then ask them for reasons that the colonists came to the Americas.

2   **Have students read the Chapter 3 Reading Further.** (**Note:** You might suggest that students research the recent debate over whether Equaino may have been born in South Carolina rather than Africa.)

3   **Add additional descriptions to the T-chart.** Discuss what new information and perceptions about colonial Americans students learned in the reading. Did they know, for example, that historians believe that around half of all European colonists came as indentured servants? Did they remember that African Americans were part of the story from the earliest days? You may wish to use a different color for adding the new entries to the T-chart.

4   **Have students complete the Chapter 3 Reading Further in their Interactive Student Notebooks.** Introduce the activity by talking about the importance of the Mayflower Compact as one of the founding documents of U.S. history. Although the Compact did not spell out the particulars of the government for the new colony, it made it clear that the colonists themselves were creating this "civil body politick" for "the generall good of the Colonie." This was a pattern of self-rule that would come to fruition more than 150 years later in the American Revolution and the new United States. (**Note:** Before students write their letters, you may want to review proper letter formatting using the Writing Toolkit. You may also want to ask some students to write contrasting letters from the position of the "Strangers," the *Mayflower* passengers who were not Separatists.)

5   **Invite students to share their letters about the Mayflower Compact.**

English Language Learners

Prepare a Cue Card For the sales presentations, have students prepare cue cards, like the one below, outlining their main points. Cards should include the colony's slogan as well as the lyrics to the jingle. Encourage students to practice their presentations using their cue cards.

Welcome to _____ (insert slogan)!

We believe this is the best colony for you to settle in. Here's why:

1.

2.

The pictures on our poster show our colony's best features. For example, this picture shows . . .

Our colony is really great. Here is a song that tells you about our colony:

Learners Reading and Writing Below Grade Level

Support the Reading Give students photocopies of the chapter. For Sections 3.3 to 3.10, have them underline or highlight information in four colors relating to these topics: reasons for settlement, geography and climate, religion, and government. This will help students complete their spoke diagrams.

Learners with Special Education Needs

Support the Activity Consider these tips:

- Give students a copy of Student Handout 3 the day before the activity. Make sure they understand the directions and let them choose a role.

- Add a fifth role of Sales Manager. This person will lead the groups in Step 7 by making sure the group follows the correct order of the sales presentation and by offering tips. During the Colonial Fair, this student will join Team B. When Team B gives its sales presentation, instruct this student to stand next to the poster and point to the corresponding information and visuals.

Advanced Learners

Conduct Additional Research Have students research more information about their colonies to add to their posters. In addition to having students meet the requirements on Student Handout 3, require that their posters include descriptions of the colony's founders, a primary source quotation from a founder or colonist, and information about the colony's economic livelihood.

Enrichment Resources

Find out more about the events that led to American independence by exploring the following resources for *History Alive! The United States Through Industrialism* at www.teachtci.com.

Enrichment Readings These in-depth readings encourage students to explore selected topics related to the chapter. You may also find readings that relate the chapter's content directly to your state's curriculum.

Internet Connections The recommended Web sites provide useful and engaging content that reinforces skills development and mastery of subjects within the chapter.

Literature Recommendations

The following books offer opportunities to extend the content in this chapter.

We the People: The Mayflower Compact by Phillip Brooks (Minneapolis: Compass Point Books, 2004)

The Landing of the Pilgrims by James Daugherty (New York: Random House, 2001)

Our Strange New Land: Elizabeth's Diary, Jamestown, Virginia, 1609 by Patricia Hermes (New York: Scholastic, 2000)

Section 3.2

Students' maps should show the regions outlined and the names of the colonies underlined and include at least two details for each region.

Section 3.3

Possible notes for Massachusetts (symbols will vary):

- *Settlers:* first by Pilgrims led by William Bradford; later by Puritans led by John Winthrop
- *Reasons for settlement:* to escape religious persecution
- *Climate and geography:* harsh winters and warm summers; rich pastures and forests
- *Economy:* crop and livestock farming, lumbering
- *Religion:* Puritan
- *Government:* self-governing, as described in the Mayflower Compact

Section 3.4

Possible notes for Rhode Island (symbols will vary):

- *Settlers:* former Puritans from Massachusetts led by Roger Williams and Anne Hutchinson
- *Reasons for settlement:* religious freedom from the Puritans
- *Climate and geography:* humid summers and cold winters; coastal lowlands and rocky woodlands
- *Economy:* farming, lumbering, shipbuilding, fishing, whaling
- *Religion:* various faiths
- *Government:* self-governing

Section 3.5

Possible notes for Connecticut (symbols will vary):

- *Settlers:* Former Massachusetts Puritans led by Thomas Hooker
- *Reasons for settlement:* to establish a new settlement apart from Massachusetts Puritans
- *Climate and geography:* cold winters and mild summers; forested hills and seacoast
- *Economy:* farming, shipbuilding, fishing, whaling
- *Religion:* Puritan
- *Government:* self-governing, with written constitution

Section 3.6

Possible notes for New York (symbols will vary):

- *Settlers:* Dutch and English
- *Reasons for settlement:* to make money
- *Climate and geography:* cold winters and hot summers; wetlands and forested mountains
- *Religion:* various faiths
- *Government:* British-appointed governor and council; eventually an elected assembly

Section 3.7

Possible notes for Pennsylvania (symbols will vary):

- *Settlers:* English Quakers led by William Penn
- *Reasons for settlement:* to safely practice their religion
- *Climate and geography:* cold winters and hot summers; rolling hills and fertile soil
- *Economy:* farming, trade, lumbering, and shipbuilding
- *Religion:* various faiths
- *Government:* elected assembly

Section 3.8

Possible notes for Maryland (symbols will vary):

- *Settlers:* English Catholics and Protestants
- *Reasons for settlement:* to find religious and political freedom
- *Climate and geography:* cold winters, hot summers; low, fertile land surrounding Chesapeake Bay
- *Economy:* farming, lumbering, shipping, fishing, iron mining
- *Religion:* various faiths, particularly Catholic
- *Government:* elected assembly

Section 3.9

Possible notes for Virginia (symbols will vary):

- *Settlers:* English landowners and skilled laborers
- *Reasons for settlement:* to make a profit
- *Climate and geography:* mild winters and hot summers; coastal lowlands and wooded mountains
- *Economy:* farming
- *Religion:* Church of England
- *Government:* elected assembly (House of Burgesses)

Section 3.10

Possible notes for Georgia (symbols will vary):

- *Settlers:* debtors from English prisons, and other Europeans
- *Reasons for settlement:* to find religious freedom and cheap land
- *Climate and geography:* mild winters and hot summers; wetlands and forested mountains
- *Religion:* various faiths
- *Government:* ruled by James Oglethorpe for 12 years, then an elected assembly

Life in the Colonies

What was life really like in the colonies?

Overview

In a Social Studies Skill Builder, students analyze primary and secondary source material to explore eight aspects of life in the American colonies, including rights of colonists, religion, education, and life for enslaved African Americans.

Objectives

In the course of reading this chapter and participating in the classroom activity, students will

Social Studies

- analyze primary and secondary sources to learn about various aspects of colonial life, including rights of colonists, religion, education, and life for enslaved African Americans.

- identify the moral and political ideas of the Great Awakening that led to revolutionary fervor in the American colonies.

- summarize how Magna Carta and the English Bill of Rights affected colonists' views of their own rights.

Language Arts

- write a newspaper article giving conclusions supported with paraphrased information from primary and secondary sources.

Social Studies Vocabulary

Key Content Terms rights, Magna Carta, Parliament, English Bill of Rights, Great Awakening

Academic Vocabulary contract, restore, rebel, leisure

Materials

History Alive! The United States Through Industrialism

Interactive Student Notebooks

Visual 4

Placards 4A–4H (2 sets; create additional placards as needed)

Lesson Masters

- Information Master 4 (1 transparency)
- Vocabulary Development handout (1 per student, on colored paper)

Activity	Time	Materials
Preview	10–15 minutes	• *History Alive! The United States Through Industrialism* • Interactive Student Notebooks
Vocabulary Development	30–40 minutes	• *History Alive! The United States Through Industrialism* • Interactive Student Notebooks • Vocabulary Development handout
Social Studies Skill Builder	100 minutes (2 regular periods) (1 block period)	• *History Alive! The United States Through Industrialism* • Interactive Student Notebooks • Visual 4 • Placards 4A–4H (2 sets) • Information Master 4 (1 transparency)
Processing	30 minutes	• Interactive Student Notebooks
Assessment	40 minutes	• Chapter 4 Assessment

Preview

1   **Have students complete the Preview activity.** Students will consider the accuracy of several fictitious headlines from an English newspaper during the mid-1700s.

2   **Have students share their responses in pairs or with the class.** Do not reveal the correct answers, as students will be working further with the headlines in the Social Studies Skill Builder.

3   **Explain the connection between the Preview and Chapter 4.** Explain to students that, as reflected in several of the fictitious headlines, British citizens in the mother country often had inaccurate and disparaging ideas about the American colonies. In this chapter, students will take on the role of investigative journalists in the mid-1700s and travel to eight places to uncover the truth of what life was really like in the colonies.

Vocabulary Development

1   **Introduce the Key Content Terms.** Have students locate the Key Content Terms for the chapter in their Interactive Student Notebooks. These are important terms that will help them understand the main ideas of the chapter. Ask volunteers to identify any familiar terms and how they might be used in a sentence.

2   **Have students complete a Vocabulary Development handout.** Give each student a copy of the Vocabulary Development handout of your choice from the Reading Toolkit at the back of the Lesson Masters. These handouts provide extra practice and support, depending on your students' needs. Review the completed handout by asking volunteers to share one answer for each term.

Reading

1   **Introduce the Essential Question and have students read Section 4.1.** Then have students use information from the section and the chapter opener images to propose possible answers to the Essential Question: *What was life really like in the colonies?*

2   **Have students complete the Reading Notes for Chapter 4.** Assign Sections 4.2 to 4.9 during the activity as indicated in the procedures for the Social Studies Skill Builder. Remind students to use the Key Content Terms where appropriate as they complete their Reading Notes.

> **Writing: Written English Language Conventions**
>
> Use the chapter vocabulary and other key terms to teach or review some rules of capitalization.
>
> 1. Capitalize key words in the names of important documents (Magna Carta, English Bill of Rights).
>
> 2. Capitalize the names of government bodies (Parliament).
>
> 3. Capitalize the names of major historical events (Great Awakening).

Social Studies Skill Builder

1 **Prepare the classroom for the activity.** Post two sets of Placards 4A–4H on the walls, spacing the placards a few feet apart. (**Note:** Create additional placards as needed.)

2 **Introduce the activity.** Tell students that they will now step into the role of investigative journalists in the mid-1700s and travel through the colonies to scrutinize the claims made by the *London Chronicle*. Explain that to uncover the truth, an investigative journalist inspects actual documents and makes thorough observations, sometimes while undercover. Students will "investigate" eight aspects of colonial life, discuss them with their partners, record notes, and draw their own conclusions about life in the colonies.

3 **Project *Visual 4: Life on a Farm* and conduct part of an investigation as a class.** Tell students to pretend they are standing on a country road observing the scene shown. Discuss the questions on the visual with the class.

4 **Place students in pairs and project *Information Master 4: Analyzing Information About Life in the Colonies*.** Review the steps to explain how pairs will investigate and gather information on eight aspects of colonial life. (**Note:** When you check responses to the Key Question, focus on the appropriateness of the evidence that students cite rather than their evaluation of the headline's accuracy.)

5 **Conduct the activity.** Have each pair of students go to an open placard to begin the investigation. Continue the activity until most pairs have analyzed most of the placards and completed the corresponding Reading Notes. (**Note:** You can have students finish any Reading Notes not completed in class as homework.)

6 **Review Placards 4B to 4H as a class.** Have students complete any unfinished responses to the Key Questions in their Reading Notes during the review. (**Note:** To make reviewing the placards easier, you may want to make and project copies of them.)

- Display the first placard.

- Have one pair come to the front of the class and share their response to the questions on the placard.

- Ask the class whether they agree with the response. Have volunteers explain why they agree or disagree, citing evidence from the placard.

- Repeat the procedure with the remaining placards.

Placards 4A–4H

Visual 4

Information Master 4

7 **Debrief the activity.** Ask,

- How many of the original headlines turned out to be mostly inaccurate? Did any of the answers surprise you?

- Do you think you would have liked to live in the American colonies at this time? Why or why not? Support your opinion with information from your Reading Notes.

- How did your ideas about life in the colonies change over the course of your investigation? What did you discover about what life was *really* like in the colonies?

Processing

Have students complete the Processing activity. As investigative journalists, they will write a newspaper article entitled "What Life Is *Really* Like in the Colonies" to be published in a more reputable British newspaper.

Quicker Coverage

Decrease the Number of Placards Choose four placards for students to review in class and assign the Reading Notes for the remaining aspects of colonial life as homework. You might choose Placards 4C (rights of colonists), 4D (life for African Americans), 4E (religion), and 4F (education).

Shorten the Placard Review Abbreviate the class review of the placards by projecting a transparency of one of the placards, stating the corresponding headline, and having volunteers explain whether they believe the headline is mostly accurate or inaccurate and why.

Deeper Coverage

Create a Newspaper from the Time Period Place students in groups of four. Assign each student in the group one of the six topics of colonial life that had an inaccurate headline. Have them write an article about their assigned topic using their rewritten headline and their Reading Notes. Then have groups lay out their articles to create a newspaper. Encourage them to add features they would find in a typical newspaper of the day, such as a header, illustrations, political cartoons, and advertisements.

Create an Investigative Journalist's Sketchbook After they complete each section of Reading Notes, have students create an original sketch—with captions and annotations for that aspect of colonial life—to add to an investigative journalist's sketchbook of their travels through the colonies.

Assessment

Mastering the Content

1. D	5. D	9. B	13. D
2. D	6. A	10. A	14. A
3. A	7. B	11. C	15. A
4. A	8. A	12. D	16. B

Applying Social Studies Skills

17. D

18. Possible answers: Massachusetts is a New England Colony, while the others are Southern Colonies, which were almost completely dependent upon agriculture. Shops line the streets. The city looks relatively large for those times, and Massachusetts had a large city, Boston.

19. Answers will vary. Students might mention the importance of religion, class differences, tradespeople, or merchants and shops.

Exploring the Essential Question

20. Answers should include all of the elements requested in the prompt.

Scoring Rubric

Score	Description
3	Student completes all three parts of the task. Ideas are clearly stated, supported by details, and demonstrate command of standard English conventions.
2	Student responds to most or all parts of the task. Ideas may lack details or not be clearly stated.
1	Student responds to at least one part of the task. Ideas may contain factual or grammatical errors and may lack details.
0	Response does not match the task or is incorrect.

A Great Awakening

1 **Discuss the idea of an awakening.** Write "A Great Awakening" on the board, and ask students what they think the phrase means. Elicit the notion that an awakening can imply "waking up to a new day," as in having a new outlook on life.

2 **Have students read the first two pages of the Chapter 4 Reading Further.** When they have finished, point out that Nathan Cole was a New England resident, and ask,

- What do you know about the importance of religion in the New England colonies?

- How do you think the Puritans would have responded to George Whitefield?

3 **Have students finish the reading.** Then read aloud this sentence, which was spoken by a New Light preacher: "The common people claim as good a right to judge and act for themselves as civil rulers or the learned clergy." Ask students,

- What did the preacher mean when he spoke these words?

- How does this differ from what a Puritan might have said?

4 **Have students complete the Chapter 4 Reading Further in their Interactive Student Notebooks.** Discuss the answers to the questions, and then have students write their diary entries.

5 **Invite students to share their diary entries in pairs or with the class.**

English Language Learners

Annotate the Placards Annotate Placards 4A–4H with points of clarification, vocabulary definitions, and hints for students as they investigate the historical evidence on each placard. For example, on Placards 4B and 4C, you might write the main idea of each paragraph in the margin to help focus students' reading.

Learners Reading and Writing Below Grade Level

Adjust the Processing Instead of having students write a newspaper article detailing two or three conclusions about colonial life, have them explain just one conclusion.

Learners with Special Education Needs

Support the Processing Consider these tips:

- Provide computer access so students can type their ideas.
- Allow students to report their answers on a voice recorder.
- Instead of having students write a newspaper article, have them write one or two sentences explaining their conclusion about each placard's topic.

Create Cloze Reading Notes Omit several answers on a copy of Guide to Reading Notes 4 and give students copies of this altered version. For example, eliminate the answers to the Key Questions and the headline prompts and leave the majority of the answers that come directly from the reading.

Advanced Learners

Assign a More In-Depth Processing Challenge students to integrate the information from their Reading Notes into a dramatic story about an 18th-century character. Have them make up a fictitious name for a colonial hero or heroine, determine a colonial setting, and find ways to make reference to at least six of the topics covered in their notes.

Enrichment Resources

Find out more about life in the American colonies by exploring the following Enrichment Resources for *History Alive! The United States Through Industrialism* at www.teachtci.com.

Enrichment Readings These in-depth readings encourage students to explore selected topics related to the chapter. You may also find readings that relate the chapter's content directly to your state's curriculum.

Internet Connections These recommended Web sites provide useful and engaging content that reinforces skills development and mastery of subjects within the chapter.

Literature Recommendations

The following books offer opportunities to extend the content in this chapter.

The Bill of Rights by Michael Burgan (Minneapolis, MN: Compass Point Books, 2002)

Religion in Colonial America by Jon Butler (New York: Oxford University Press, 2000)

Jonathan Edwards by Samuel Willard Crompton (New York: Chelsea House, 2004)

Section 4.2

1. Check for evidence from the placard that supports the student's opinion about this headline's accuracy.

2. nine-tenths

3. Possible answers: Trees had to be cleared from the land before building roads and homes. When families became too large, everyone would help build rooms onto the house. Chores included making everything from furniture and tools to cloth and soap.

4. Possible headlines: "Colonial Farms Produce Everything Needed," "Colonists' Chores Start Before Sunrise"

Section 4.3

1. Check for evidence from the placard that supports the student's opinion about this headline's accuracy.

2. one-twentieth

3. Possible answer: I see iron tools in a blacksmith's shop. I hear gossip and stories being told in a tavern and bells ringing in a church. I smell rotting garbage all over the city, burning grease in "betty lamps," and bayberry candles in a home. I taste food and drink in a tavern. I feel flies and mosquitoes biting me; I touch a new coat in a tailor shop.

4. Possible headlines: "Economy Thrives in Colonial Cities," "Colonial Cities: Dangerous Firetraps"

Section 4.4

1. Check for evidence from the placard that supports the student's opinion about this headline's accuracy.

2. American colonists saw themselves as English citizens. This was important because they expected to have the same rights as English citizens had in England.

3. Possible answers:

    - 1215: Magna Carta limits the power of the king and says he must follow the law.

    - 1265: A group of lawmakers called Parliament is created to approve laws.

    - 1689: The English Bill of Rights guarantees such rights as trial by jury, petitioning the king, and choosing representatives to create taxes.

4. Possible headlines: "Colonists View Themselves Equal to All English Citizens," "Colonists Cherish Lawmaking Rights"

Section 4.5

1. Check for evidence from the placard that supports the student's opinion about this headline's accuracy.

2. Slavery was found in all three colonial regions. It expanded most rapidly in the Southern Colonies, because slaves were used to help raise the many crops grown there.

3. Slaves had little hope of making a better life in the colonies because their position was fixed at the bottom of colonial society.

4. Possible headlines: "Colonial Merchants Build Fortunes in Slave Trade," "The Middle Passage: A Nightmare for Slaves"

Section 4.6

1. Check for evidence from the placard that supports the student's opinion about this headline's accuracy.

2. Possible answers:

    - *organized:* Horns and drums were used to call people to worship. A "seating committee" carefully assigned seats.

    - *strict:* Houses were searched to make sure everyone went to church.

    - *long:* Services could last five hours. After lunch people returned to church.

3. The sentences should be numbered in this order: 4, 1, 3, 5, 2. Possible answer:

Causes and Effects of the Great Awakening

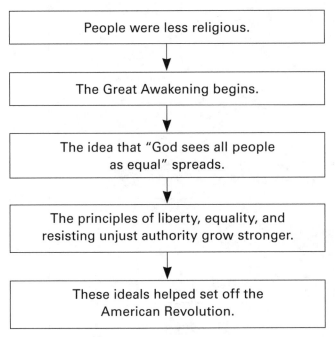

People were less religious.

↓

The Great Awakening begins.

↓

The idea that "God sees all people as equal" spreads.

↓

The principles of liberty, equality, and resisting unjust authority grow stronger.

↓

These ideals helped set off the American Revolution.

4. The original headline is mostly accurate.

Section 4.7

1. Check for evidence from the placard that supports the student's opinion about this headline's accuracy.

2. *New England Colonies* ★: Every town with 50 families or more had to hire a teacher. Towns with 100 families or more had to build a school.

   Middle Colonies: Every religious group or family had to decide whether to build a school or educate children at home.

   Southern Colonies: A few neighbors might hire a teacher together. Tutors were also hired, or students were sent to other cities for school.

3. Possible answer: Schools had a single room. Pencils and paper were scarce. Students wrote on bark. Some used one book, the *New England Primer.* Many people believed that boys needed more schooling than girls.

4. Possible headlines: "New England Towns Provide Education for Children," "Colonial Schools Lack Basic Supplies"

Section 4.8

1. Check for evidence from the placard that supports the student's opinion about this headline's accuracy.

2. Possible answer:

Colonial Marriage	Marriage Today
Colonists could not marry if they were indentured servants.	People can marry regardless of social status.
People generally married in their early to mid-20s.	People marry at many different ages.

3. Possible answers: Farm families needed help with all the chores. Some families included many stepchildren and orphans. Family members were expected to take care of grandparents or other relatives that needed help.

4. The original headline is mostly accurate.

Section 4.9

1. Check for evidence from the placard that supports the student's opinion about this headline's accuracy.

2. A bee was an event in which colonists combined work and play to get a task completed quickly.

3. Possible activities: coasting downhill on sleds, billiards, playing cards, horse racing, wrestling matches, dance contests

4. Possible headlines: "Colonists Share Work and Fun at Barn Raisings," "Study Shows Card Playing a Favorite Pastime"

Our Colonial Heritage

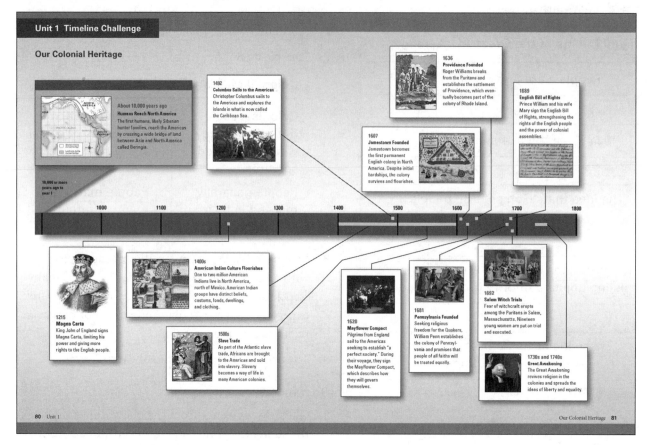

Our Colonial Heritage

1636
Providence Founded
Roger Williams breaks from the Puritans and establishes the settlement of Providence, which eventually becomes part of the colony of Rhode Island.

1689
English Bill of Rights
Prince William and his wife Mary sign the English Bill of Rights, strengthening the rights of the English people and the power of colonial assemblies.

1492
Columbus Sails to the Americas
Christopher Columbus sails to the Americas and explores the islands in what is now called the Caribbean Sea.

1607
Jamestown Founded
Jamestown becomes the first permanent English colony in North America. Despite initial hardships, the colony survives and flourishes.

About 10,000 years ago
Humans Reach North America
The first humans, likely Siberian hunter families, reach the Americas by crossing a wide bridge of land between Asia and North America called Beringia.

10,000 or more years ago to year 1

1000 1100 1200 1300 1400 1500 1600 1700 1800

1215
Magna Carta
King John of England signs Magna Carta, limiting his power and giving more rights to the English people.

1400s
American Indian Culture Flourishes
One to two million American Indians live in North America, north of Mexico. American Indian groups have distinct beliefs, customs, foods, dwellings, and clothing.

1500s
Slave Trade
As part of the Atlantic slave trade, Africans are brought to the Americas and sold into slavery. Slavery becomes a way of life in many American colonies.

1620
Mayflower Compact
Pilgrims from England sail to the Americas seeking to establish "a perfect society." During their voyage, they sign the Mayflower Compact, which describes how they will govern themselves.

1681
Pennsylvania Founded
Seeking religious freedom for the Quakers, William Penn establishes the colony of Pennsylvania and promises that people of all faiths will be treated equally.

1692
Salem Witch Trials
Fear of witchcraft erupts among the Puritans in Salem, Massachusetts. Nineteen young women are put on trial and executed.

1730s and 1740s
Great Awakening
The Great Awakening revives religion in the colonies and spreads the ideas of liberty and equality.

Overview

This Timeline Challenge provides students with a review of the main events and ideas of this unit, as well as practice in reading and interpreting timelines. You can vary and expand the activity according to students' needs and the amount of time available.

Basic Procedure

1 **Introduce the timeline in the Student Edition.** Direct students to the Our Colonial Heritage timeline at the end of Unit 1 in the Student Edition. You may wish to have students read aloud and discuss the timeline entries.

2 **Introduce the Timeline Challenge in the Interactive Student Notebook.** Direct students to the Unit 1 Timeline Challenge in their notebooks. Point out the two types of questions, "Timeline Skills" and "Critical Thinking," and model how to answer each type.

3 **Have students complete the Timeline Challenge.** Monitor students as they work. Use the Guide to Unit 1 Timeline Challenge to check their answers. You may wish to project a transparency of this page as you work through the questions with the class and conduct a discussion of the "Critical Thinking" questions.

4 **Complete the KWL chart.** Return to the KWL chart created at the beginning of the unit, and ask students to list the key information they have learned.

Classroom Timeline

1 **Prepare the Timeline Challenge Cards.** Copy and cut the cards from *Student Handout TC1: Unit 1 Timeline Challenge Cards.* You may wish to laminate the cards for future use.

2 **Create a timeline on a classroom wall.** On an empty wall or a large bulletin board, make a timeline with masking tape or colored paper. Mark off the time intervals in advance, or ask students to do so in class.

3 **Have students place the Timeline Challenge Cards.** Distribute cards to individual students or pairs and have them tape the cards to the timeline in the correct locations. Call on students to provide more information on the timeline topics to review main events and issues.

Student Handout TC1

Internet Research

1 **Review students' suggestions for additional timeline entries.** Have students share their answers to the last question of the Timeline Challenge.

2 **Have students conduct Internet research.** Ask students to choose and research one of their suggested events.

3 **Have students create additional Timeline Challenge Cards.** Direct students to research an appropriate image for their cards and then use the computer to create an illustrated card, complete with timeline entry.

Timeline Skills

Score 1 point for each correct answer.

1. The first humans reached the Americas about 10,000 or more years ago by crossing a land bridge between Asia and North America.

2. Magna Carta limited the king's power and gave more rights to the English people.

3. One to two million American Indians lived north of Mexico. Groups differed in their beliefs, customs, foods, dwellings, and clothing.

4. Slavery in the Americas began in the 1500s.

5. Jamestown was the first permanent English colony in the Americas. It was founded in 1607.

6. The Mayflower Compact described how the Pilgrims would govern themselves.

7. Providence was founded 29 years after Jamestown. Pennsylvania was founded 45 years after Providence.

8. The English Bill of Rights strengthened the rights of the English people and the power of colonial assemblies.

9. They were accused of witchcraft.

10. The Great Awakening revived religion in the colonies and spread the ideas of liberty and equality.

Critical Thinking

Score 1 to 3 points for each answer, depending on the thoroughness of the response.

11. Possible answer: American Indians of the Great Basin spent most of the year traveling in small groups in search of food. They made temporary shelters using willow poles and ate mostly plants. American Indians in the Southwest made adobe homes and lived in large villages. Their diet consisted of corn, beans, and squash.

12. Answers will vary. Students must provide at least two reasons for their choice.

13. Both Magna Carta and the English Bill of Rights strengthened the colonists' belief that citizens had a voice in their government. Magna Carta limited the power of the king in England, and the English Bill of Rights gave lawmaking power to the people's elected representatives. American colonists saw themselves as English citizens and expected these same rights to be extended to the colonies.

14. Answers will vary. Students must explain why the events they chose merit inclusion.

Using Scores to Inform Instruction

Timeline Skills A score of 7 out of 10 indicates that students understand most of the key events of this unit.

Critical Thinking A score of 8 out of 12 indicates that students are able to think critically about most of the key issues of this unit.

If students score below these levels, consider reviewing timeline and critical thinking skills.

Revolution in the Colonies

Revolution in the Colonies

Overview

This activity introduces geographic information essential to Unit 2. Students read and interpret maps to learn about the locations, physical features, and human geography of the regions in North America where important fighting occurred during the American Revolution. They annotate a map of the 13 colonies and answer questions in their Interactive Student Notebooks, and then discuss critical thinking questions. Students' comprehension of content and proficiency in map-reading and higher-order thinking skills will help you gauge their readiness for the unit. The pages that follow include a completed map, answers to questions, a scoring guide to inform your teaching, and suggestions for modifications to meet specific student needs.

Essential Geographic Understandings

1. Location and physical geography of the 13 colonies that became the original United States

2. Key physical feature: Appalachian Mountains

3. Key cities: Boston, New York, Albany, Philadelphia, Charleston

4. Impact of physical geography on the American Revolution

5. Impact of human geography on the American Revolution

Procedures

1 **Introduce the unit.** Tell students they will learn about tension that arose in the colonies over British rule, how these tensions led to the American Revolution and the Declaration of Independence, and how independence was won.

2 **Create a KWL chart.** Ask students to identify what they know about the American Revolution and Declaration of Independence and what they want to learn. Use their responses to gauge how much additional background information they will need as you progress through the unit. Students will return to the KWL chart at the end of the unit and add key information they have learned.

3 **Have students read Unit 2 "Setting the Stage" in the Student Edition.**

4 **Have students complete the Geography Challenge.** Monitor students as they answer the questions and complete the map. You may want to have them work in pairs. Use the guide on the next two pages to check their answers. You may wish to project the map from the Interactive Student Notebook and have students annotate it as the class works through the map-reading questions. Make sure students have grasped Essential Geographic Understandings 1 to 3.

5 **Discuss the "Critical Thinking" questions.** Help students understand the geographic relationships in Essential Geographic Understandings 4 and 5.

The Thirteen Colonies

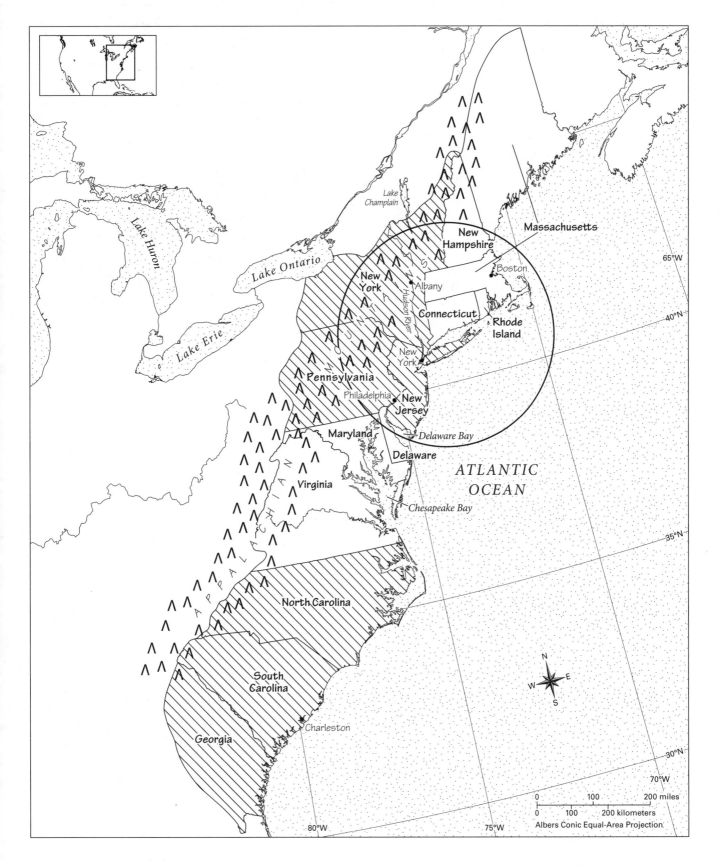

Geography Skills

Score 1 point for each correct answer. Use the map on the previous page to check shading and labeling.

1. Each of the four cities is a port and is located on or close to the Atlantic Ocean.

2. The population density in most of this region was between 2 and 15 people per square mile.

3. The most heavily populated colonial region included Boston, Philadelphia, and New York.

4. The New England Colonies had the fewest Loyalists.

5. The goal of independence would have been strongest in New England because that is where the fewest Loyalists lived.

6. Possible answer: The first British army could have come south from Canada along the Hudson River, while the second British army in New York City could have come north up the Hudson River, meeting up somewhere in between.

Critical Thinking

Questions may have more than one correct answer. Score 1 to 3 points for each reasonable answer, depending on the strength of students' geographic reasoning. Possible answers are given here.

7. Areas near the coast were generally more densely settled than areas farther inland. One possible reason is that coastal areas were settled first and the colonies gradually spread inland.

8. This was the most heavily populated area of the colonies, containing three of the colonies' four largest cities. Controlling this region would have given either side control of a large part of the colonies' total population.

9. Loyalists were strong in these colonies. The British might have expected that these Loyalists would help them in the war. Also, these colonies were not heavily settled, so there would be fewer people to conquer.

Using Scores to Inform Instruction

Geography Skills A score of 4 out of 6 or better indicates that students have acquired sufficient geographic information to proceed with the unit.

Critical Thinking A score of 6 out of 9 or better indicates that students are beginning to understand the relationships between physical geography and the different ways in which people live.

Modifying Instruction

ELL or Learners with Special Education Needs Consider focusing on map-reading questions or limiting the number of "Critical Thinking" questions.

Students with Weak Map or Critical Thinking Skills Assign appropriate pages from the Social Studies Skills Toolkit in the back of the Lesson Masters.

Toward Independence

When is it necessary for citizens to rebel against their government?

Overview

In a Response Group activity, students participate in a series of colonial town meetings to debate whether to rebel against British rule. In the process, they evaluate the events that deeply divided the American colonists and eventually caused them to rebel against the British government.

Objectives

In the course of reading this chapter and participating in the classroom activity, students will

Social Studies

- identify the roots of the nation's blend of civic republicanism, classical liberal principles, and English parliamentary traditions.

- assess the impact of such key events as the French and Indian War, the Boston Massacre, and the battles of Lexington and Concord on colonists' loyalty to the British government.

- analyze several actions of the British government between 1763 and 1775 that built resentment and divided the colonists in their feelings about British rule.

Language Arts

- write a persuasive composition that includes a well-defined thesis supported by evidence, examples, and reasoning.

Social Studies Vocabulary

Key Content Terms militia, tyranny, repeal, boycott

Academic Vocabulary violation, retain, restricted, authority

Materials

History Alive! The United States Through Industrialism

Interactive Student Notebooks

short quiz on any topic (1 copy per student; see the Preview)

Lesson Masters

- Student Handout 5 (1 copy, cut apart)
- Information Masters 5A and 5B (1 transparency of each)
- Vocabulary Development handout (1 per student, on colored paper)

Activity	Suggested Time	Materials
Preview	30 minutes	• short quiz on any topic • Interactive Student Notebooks
Vocabulary Development	30–40 minutes	• *History Alive! The United States Through Industrialism* • Interactive Student Notebooks • Vocabulary Development handout
Response Group	150 minutes (3 regular periods) (1.5 block periods)	• *History Alive! The United States Through Industrialism* • Interactive Student Notebooks • Student Handout 5 • Information Masters 5A and 5B
Processing	30 minutes	• Interactive Student Notebooks
Assessment	40 minutes	• Chapter 5 Assessment

Preview

1 **Introduce the school's "new policy."** Tell students you just received an important memo from the principal. Read the following fictitious memo to the class, which you may want to put on school letterhead for authenticity.

Funding for education has been drastically reduced due to shortfalls in state revenue. As a result, monies that ordinarily would be granted to _____ [your school] will not be forthcoming. The school faces severe financial problems, and the administration has been forced to consider alternative funding sources.

Therefore, a new policy is in immediate effect. Each student in social studies classes will be required to pay for all photocopied materials. The fee will be 10 cents per page. There will be no exceptions. Any student who does not pay the 10-cent fee will receive a zero for the assignment. While this may seem a burden, it is absolutely necessary. We must all work together to solve this temporary financial problem.

2 **Invite questions about the new policy.** This activity is designed to allow students to experience the sense of injustice about "taxation without representation" that colonists felt, so allow students to express their feelings in an appropriate manner. Expect them to show concern and anger. Adopt a neutral stance by validating their concerns and feelings, but make it clear that you must carry out the policy.

3 **Tell students they will now take a quiz.** Explain that they must pay 10 cents for the photocopied quiz. Those students that have no money can borrow money from a classmate or fill out an IOU. Ask a volunteer to collect the money. Mention that the volunteer's fee for the quiz will be waived.

4 **Pass out quizzes to students who paid the fee.** Remind students who did not pay the fee that they will receive a zero for the quiz, and have them sit quietly. After a minute or so, tell the class that the memo was fictitious and return students' money.

5 **Have students answer the Preview questions on a separate sheet of paper.**

6 **Have students share their responses in pairs or with the class.**

7 **Explain the connection between the Preview and Chapter 5.** Tell students that the feelings they experienced during this activity are similar to those felt by many colonists between 1763 and 1775, when a series of British laws were imposed on them without their input or consent. In this chapter, students will learn about the issues that led the colonists to mistrust and eventually rebel against British rule.

Vocabulary Development

1 **Introduce the Key Content Terms.** Have students locate the Key Content Terms for the chapter in their Interactive Student Notebooks. These are important terms that will help them understand the main ideas of the chapter. Ask volunteers to identify any familiar terms and how they might be used in a sentence.

2 **Have students complete a Vocabulary Development handout.** Give each student a copy of the Vocabulary Development handout of your choice from the Reading Toolkit at the back of the Lesson Masters. These handouts provide extra practice and support, depending on your students' needs. Review the completed handout by asking volunteers to share one answer for each term.

Reading

1 **Introduce the Essential Question and have students read Section 5.1.** Have students propose possible answers to the Essential Question: *When is it necessary for citizens to rebel against their government?* Then have them read Section 5.1. Afterward, have students respond to these questions:

- Who were the Patriots? Who were the Loyalists?

- What is happening in the illustration that opens this chapter? Who is the man on horseback?

- How might a Patriot view this scene? How might a Loyalist view it?

- What could have happened to cause the colonists to become so divided in their feelings about British rule?

2 **Have students read and complete the Reading Notes for Section 5.2.** Tell students that this section summarizes the French and Indian War, which set off a chain of events that greatly affected the colonists. Use Guide to Reading Notes 5 to check students' understanding.

3 **Have students complete the remaining Reading Notes for Chapter 5.** Assign Sections 5.3 to 5.8 during the activity as indicated in the procedures for the Response Group activity. Remind students to use the Key Content Terms where appropriate as they complete their Reading Notes.

Response Group

1 **Introduce the activity.** Tell students that they will now step into the roles of historical figures from the Revolutionary era to participate in a series of colonial town meetings where they will decide whether to rebel against the British government.

2 **Divide students into groups of three and assign roles.** Assign each group one historical figure from *Student Handout 5: Role Cards of Historical Figures.* Explain that each group will represent the viewpoint—Patriot, Loyalist, or Neutralist—of one historical figure during the upcoming colonial town meetings. Remind students of the difference between a Patriot and a Loyalist. Also discuss Neutralists, those colonists who have yet to support either side. If you do not need all the role cards, distribute them to create roughly equal numbers of Patriot, Loyalist, and Neutralist groups. You may want to mention that, in reality, Loyalists made up only 15 to 20 percent of the colonial population.

3 **Have groups prepare to represent their historical figures.** Project *Information Master 5A: Representing Your Historical Figure* and review the instructions. Clarify that many of the role cards give historical information about how the figures reacted to some of the events that will be discussed later. Give groups adequate time to complete Steps 1 and 2, and then have each group choose one member to be a spokesperson. Call on each group to introduce their historical figure in Step 3.

4 **Have students read and complete the Reading Notes for Section 5.3.**

5 **Project *Information Master 5B: Preparing for the Colonial Town Meetings* and have groups prepare for Colonial Town Meeting 1.** Reveal only the information for Colonial Town Meeting 1. Tell groups that the year is 1767. Remind students that since the end of the French and Indian War, the British government has taken many controversial actions in the colonies. For that reason, colonists have come together to decide whether to rebel against the British government. Direct students to use their books, Reading Notes, and role cards to complete the steps on Information Master 5B. Explain that during the town meeting, they will try to persuade everyone to join their side, but should focus especially on Neutralists. Circulate as students work, checking that their responses accurately reflect the historical figures. (**Note:** The historical figures are authentic, but the meetings are fictional.)

6 **Conduct Colonial Town Meeting 1.** One by one, have the spokespersons present their positions. They should begin by standing and reminding the other colonists of their name and allegiance (Patriot, Loyalist, or Neutralist). Encourage discussion by allowing other students to comment on the spokesperson's presentation and then allowing the spokesperson to defend the position. Have the current spokesperson choose the next spokesperson, until all have presented.

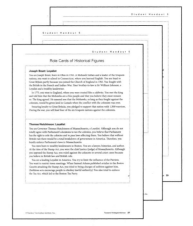

Student Handout 5

Information Master 5A

Information Master 5B

7 **Take a vote to decide whether the colonists should rebel against the government at this time.** Remind students to reflect their historical figure's perspective as they vote. Ask, *Who has decided to comply? To oppose? To rebel?* You may want to record the vote tally for each of the four meetings.

8 **Repeat Steps 5 to 7 to conduct the remaining town meetings.** Make these adjustments:

Colonial Town Meeting 2: Have students complete the Reading Notes for Sections 5.4 and 5.5. Then reveal "Colonial Town Meeting 2" on Information Master 5B. Inform students that the year is now 1770. The British government has continued to enact controversial laws, and a tragic event has taken place in Boston. Skip Step 6, and take a vote on whether the colonists should rebel.

Colonial Town Meeting 3: Have students complete the Reading Notes for Sections 5.6 and 5.7. Then reveal "Colonial Town Meeting 3" on Information Master 5B. Tell students that the year is now 1774 and that tensions between the colonists and the British government have increased dramatically. Conduct the town meeting, and then take a vote on whether the colonists should rebel.

Colonial Town Meeting 4: Have students complete the Reading Notes for Section 5.8. Then reveal "Colonial Town Meeting 4" on Information Master 5B. Tell students that it is late April 1775 and that the conflicts between the colonists and the British government have reached a crisis point. Skip Step 6, and take a vote on whether the colonists should rebel.

9 **Debrief the activity.** Ask,

- Did your historical figure's opinion change over the course of the town meetings? Explain.

- Did you agree with your historical figure's opinion throughout this activity? Why or why not?

- Think back to the fictitious memo about paying for photocopies. How were some of the events that took place between 1763 and 1775 in the American colonies similar to your experience in class?

- In general, when is it necessary for citizens to rebel against their government?

Processing

Have students complete the Processing activity. Students will create a pamphlet persuading colonists to rebel against or remain loyal to the British government.

Quicker Coverage

Use an Alternative Preview Use this alternative Preview activity to connect the chapter content to students' personal experience. Ask students to write a brief response to this prompt: *Suppose the following situation happened to you. During your second class, your friend tells you how much trouble he is having with a poster he needs to complete for a class project. On the way to your next class, you decide you want to help him by loaning him your art set, an expensive set that you use only for special occasions. But at lunch, before you have had a chance to give it to him, you find him sitting at a table working on his poster with your art set. You realize he took it out of your backpack sometime after your second class. How do you feel about this situation? Explain why you feel this way.*

Eliminate the Historical Figures Conduct the Response Group activity without having students step into the roles of historical figures. Simply place students into groups of three and have them debate the topics from their own points of view, using the Student Edition and their Reading Notes as resources.

Deeper Coverage

Expand the Discussions Conduct a full-class discussion for Colonial Town Meetings 2 and 4, following the same process used for the first town meeting.

Research Historical Figures Have students research their historical figures to find more information about their figures' beliefs, arguments, and opinions. Specifically, tell students to look for interesting quotations that will not only give them more information, but may also be used during the town meetings.

Assessment

Mastering the Content

1. A	5. A	9. B	13. A
2. C	6. A	10. B	14. C
3. C	7. C	11. B	15. B
4. A	8. B	12. C	16. D

Applying Social Studies Skills

17. B

18. A

19. Answers will vary. Students should cite evidence from the engravings to support their answer.

Exploring the Essential Question

20. Answers should include all of the elements requested in the prompt.

Scoring Rubric

Score	Description
3	Student completes all four parts of the task. Ideas are clearly stated, supported by details, and demonstrate command of standard English conventions.
2	Student responds to most or all parts of the task. Ideas may lack details or not be clearly stated.
1	Student responds to at least one part of the task. Ideas may contain factual or grammatical errors and may lack details.
0	Response does not match the task or is incorrect.

"I Love the Story of Paul Revere, Whether He Rode or Not"

1 **Introduce the poem "Paul Revere's Ride."** Read aloud the first two lines of the poem in the Chapter 5 Reading Further, and ask students if they have ever heard them before. Explain that these are the opening lines to one of the most famous poems in American literature—and that, in fact, it was this poem that made Paul Revere famous.

2 **Have students read the Chapter 5 Reading Further.** Encourage them to look up unfamiliar words, such as *belfry, steed,* and *spectral.*

3 **Have students respond to the purpose and characteristics of the excerpt.** Read the excerpt aloud, or have students read portions of it aloud (either individually or in groups), so students can experience the rhythms that Longfellow used in the poem. (If you prefer to read the entire poem, you will easily find it online.) Then ask,

   • How did Longfellow create a sense of action in this piece of writing?

   • Why might a poet create this kind of rhythm in a poem?

4 **Encourage interested students to conduct further research about Paul Revere and his ride.** You might have them explore the Internet Connections for Chapter 5 available through the Enrichment Resources for *History Alive! The United States Through Industrialism.*

5 **Discuss why Longfellow might have portrayed Paul Revere as a lone hero.** Ask,

   • At a time when many Americans feared the United States would be divided by civil war, why would Longfellow choose to write about an incident in the American Revolution?

   • Why do you think Longfellow decided to focus his poem on one person's actions?

6 **Have students complete the Chapter 5 Reading Further in their Interactive Student Notebooks.** You may want to have them share their definitions and descriptions of a hero. You may also want to create a class definition, combining and synthesizing the qualities students have identified.

7 **Have students share their descriptive paragraphs on local heroes.** Using the qualities students have described, discuss the various kinds of people who are considered heroes in a community and the kinds of civic participation that are valued.

English Language Learners

Ensure Students Are Prepared for the First Meeting
To make sure students are adequately prepared for the first colonial town meeting, have them complete the Reading Notes for Sections 5.2 and 5.3 in small groups or as a whole class. Then, when reviewing the steps for the first meeting on Information Master 5B, make sure everyone thoroughly understands what to do.

Create Cue Cards Have students use the prompt below to create a cue card of their comments. When they act as spokespersons for the colonial town meetings, they can read their comments directly from the cue cards.

I believe that the colonies should (comply/oppose/rebel).

I believe this because _____

_____.

Learners Reading and Writing Below Grade Level

Support the Processing Give students examples of actual pamphlets. Point out techniques used in the pamphlets to persuade readers, such as colorful pictures, attention-getting titles, and a limited amount of text. Also give students a prototype showing the pamphlet's basic content and structure to use as a guide as they create their own.

Learners with Special Education Needs

Support the Reading Notes Supply students with a copy of Guide to Reading Notes 5, omitting key words and phrases from the answers. As students read, have them fill in the missing words and add additional notes in their own words.

Advanced Learners

Assign Each Student a Historical Figure Instead of having each group represent one historical figure, distribute role cards so that each group has three different historical figures—all Patriots, all Loyalists, or all Neutralists. When groups prepare for the town meetings, have them present their historical figures to their group members only, rather than to the entire class. (**Note:** Distributing cards in this way will require repeating some roles.)

Enrichment Resources

Find out more about the events that led to American independence by exploring the following Enrichment Resources for *History Alive! The United States Through Industrialism* at www.teachtci.com.

Enrichment Readings These in-depth readings encourage students to explore selected topics related to the chapter. You may also find readings that relate the chapter's content directly to your state's curriculum.

Internet Connections The recommended Web sites provide useful and engaging content that reinforces skills development and mastery of subjects within the chapter.

Literature Recommendations

The following books offer opportunities to extend the content in this chapter.

Causes of the American Revolution by Dale Anderson (Pleasantville, NY: Gareth Stevens Publishing, 2006)

Countdown to Independence: A Revolution of Ideas in England and Her American Colonies, 1760–1776 by Natalie S. Bober (New York: Simon and Schuster, 2001)

Primary Source History of the Colony of Massachusetts by Jeri Freedman (New York: Rosen Publishing Group, 2006)

Section 5.2

1. Colonial governments elected their own assemblies, passed laws, and created taxes and decided how to use them.

2. Possible answers:

   In 1754, Washington and his men opened fire on a French scouting party in the Ohio Valley. This event began the French and Indian War.

   In 1759, British troops captured Canada. This was an important turning point for the Americans, who had suffered many losses to the French.

3. The territory in North America controlled by Great Britain expanded greatly. Colonists felt proud to be British and hopeful for the future.

Section 5.3

1.

2. Possible answers:

   Proclamation of 1763

   For: If the colonists move past the Appalachians, Indians will attack them.

   Against: The only new land available for settlement is on the other side of the Appalachians.

   Stamp Act

   For: The colonists pay few taxes compared to other British citizens. It is time for them to pay their fair share for the French and Indian War.

   Against: No taxation without representation! You have no right to tax us without our consent.

   Quartering Act

   Against: The soldiers take up space and do nothing. Why should we pay for them?

Law	What did this law require colonists to do?	How did some colonists protest this law?	How did the British government react to those protests?
Proclamation of 1763	Colonists could only settle land east of the Appalachian Mountains.	Colonists argued in letters and articles that it was tyranny, an unjust use of government power.	The British government ignored colonists' complaints and sent more troops to the colonies.
Stamp Act (1765)	Colonists had to buy a stamp for any paper they used, including newspapers and playing cards.	Colonists sent messages to Parliament, refused to buy stamps, and attacked tax collectors.	The British government repealed the Stamp Act.
Quartering Act (1765)	Colonial assemblies had to provide housing and supplies for British troops.	New York's assembly refused to give funds for some supplies.	The British government refused to allow the New York assembly to meet until it complied with the law.

Section 5.4

1. The Townshend Acts placed a duty, or tax, on certain goods the colonists imported from Great Britain. The acts were passed to raise money for Great Britain's army in the colonies.

2. Drawings should show a boycott of English goods. Women refusing to buy these goods should be included in the illustration.

3. Lord North repealed the Townshend Acts because the taxes were not raising enough money to cover the losses due to the boycott. Sketches should show that tea was left out of the repeal.

Section 5.5

1. Drawings from the Patriot point of view might show peaceful, unarmed colonists and British soldiers opening fire on them. Drawings from the Loyalist point of view might show colonists yelling insults at British soldiers and throwing ice balls and rocks at them.

2. John Adams defended the British soldiers who were accused of killing colonists at the Boston Massacre. He believed in upholding the law and that every person had the right to a fair trial.

Section 5.6

1. Possible answer: The Boston Massacre did not cause new protests against the British government, and the repeal of the Townshend Acts led to a period of calm in the colonies.

2. Possible answer:

   Argument for the Tea Act: It will lower the cost of tea in the colonies. It will keep the British East India Company from going bankrupt.

   Argument against the Tea Act: It will create a monopoly of the tea trade. It will cause colonists to worry that the British government will try to control other trades.

3. Possible answer:

   Loyalist: "Patriot Temper Tantrum at Boston Harbor": Loyalists saw the Patriots as rowdy, unreasonable, and difficult to control.

   Patriot: "Magnificent Moment of Defending Our Rights": Patriots believed this destructive action was necessary to defend their rights of representation in government.

Section 5.7

1. After the Boston Tea Party, King George no longer simply wanted to collect taxes from the colonists. He now wanted to take control of the colonies.

2. Possible answers:

Actions of the Intolerable Acts	How might this hurt you?
Closed Boston Harbor to shipping.	My business may lose money.
The British government now controlled the government in Massachusetts.	I have less say in my government than before. I can't even gather with other colonists at town meetings without the governor's permission.
A British soldier accused of murder would have his trial in England, not in the colonies.	People in England will not understand all the circumstances of the trial and will probably take the soldier's side. This might make it easier for soldiers to get away with murder.
More soldiers were sent to Boston to make sure colonists followed the laws.	More freedoms will be taken from us as the British government uses more force.

3. Possible actions (opinions will vary): Merchants in other colonies closed their shops to oppose the treatment of colonists in Massachusetts. Virginians called for a meeting of delegates from all the colonies to find a peaceful solution. Some towns and cities began to organize militias.

4. Patrick Henry urged colonists to unite by thinking of themselves as one group of people: Americans.

5. The First Continental Congress decided to send a message to King George asking him to recognize their rights. The Congress also called for a new boycott of British goods until the Intolerable Acts were repealed.

Section 5.8

Possible flowchart:

British troops leave Boston and march to Concord to seize gunpowder and weapons.

↓

Paul Revere and others warn colonists of the British approach.

↓

Minutemen and British troops fight in Lexington.

↓

British troops continue to Concord.

↓

British soldiers search for weapons and gunpowder in Concord.

↓

Colonists fight British soldiers at Concord's North Bridge.

↓

Colonists attack British soldiers on the retreat to Boston.

The Declaration of Independence

What principles of government are expressed in the Declaration of Independence?

Overview

Students learn about key events leading up to the writing of the Declaration of Independence and, in a Writing for Understanding activity, analyze key excerpts of the Declaration and the principles of government they express.

Objectives

In the course of reading this chapter and participating in the classroom activity, students will

Social Studies

- identify the final causes, such as the Battle of Breed's Hill and *Common Sense,* that brought about independence.

- analyze the principles of government expressed in the Declaration of Independence.

- recognize how delegates to the Second Continental Congress were able to preserve the slave trade by suppressing Jefferson's attempt to condemn it in the Declaration of Independence.

Language Arts

- write an essay with a coherent thesis and a clear, well-supported conclusion.

- support a thesis or conclusions with paraphrases, quotations, and comparisons.

- revise writing for word choice and appropriate organization.

Social Studies Vocabulary

Key Content Terms independence, petition, *Common Sense,* Declaration of Independence, natural rights

Academic Vocabulary debate, impose, policy, fundamental

Materials

History Alive! The United States Through Industrialism

Interactive Student Notebooks

Visual 6

Lesson Masters

- Student Handout 6A (1 per student)

- Student Handout 6B (10 copies, cut apart)

- Information Masters 6A and 6B (1 transparency of each)

- Vocabulary Development handout (1 per student, on colored paper)

Activity	Suggested Time	Materials
Preview	15 minutes	• Interactive Student Notebooks • Visual 6
Vocabulary Development	30–40 minutes	• *History Alive! The United States Through Industrialism* • Interactive Student Notebooks • Vocabulary Development handout
Writing for Understanding	Phase 1 100 minutes (2 regular periods) (1 block period) Phase 2 100 minutes (2 regular periods) (1 block period)	• *History Alive! The United States Through Industrialism* • Interactive Student Notebooks • Student Handouts 6A and 6B • Information Masters 6A and 6B
Processing (optional)	20 minutes	• Interactive Student Notebooks
Assessment	40 minutes	• Chapter 6 Assessment

Preview

1 **Introduce the Declaration of Independence.** Project *Visual 6: Signing the Declaration of Independence* and have students analyze the painting. Ask,

- What do you see in this painting?

- What famous document do you think is being signed? Cite evidence from the painting to support your idea.

Visual 6

Tell students that this famous painting depicts the signing of the Declaration of Independence. Featured in the center is the committee—including John Adams, Thomas Jefferson, and Benjamin Franklin—responsible for drafting the Declaration. Here they present the draft to the president of the Second Continental Congress, John Hancock. You may also want to share this information with students:

- Fifty-six delegates to the Second Continental Congress (mostly well-educated, white men) signed the Declaration of Independence.

- Among the groups not represented in the Congress were African Americans, women, working classes, Loyalists, and American Indians. In fact, voting rights at the time were generally extended only to white male property owners, who made up one of every four colonists.

- An assortment of colonial flags are displayed on the wall. Each flag bears the red cross of St. George, a symbol of the colonies' allegiance to Great Britain.

- In the center of the flags is a drum, used in this era to keep a beat for marching soldiers. The drum symbolizes the state of war between Great Britain and the colonies.

2 **Have students complete the Preview activity.**

3 **Have students share their responses in pairs or with the class.** It is possible that while many students may know of the Declaration of Independence and be familiar with its words, they may not be able to recall any quotations or their meanings. This Preview will establish a baseline of knowledge and give students a hint of what they will be doing in the activity.

4 **Explain the connection between the Preview and Chapter 6.** Tell students that the Declaration of Independence is one of the most important documents in our nation's history and still has great meaning for us today. In this chapter, students will build upon their existing knowledge to understand the principles of government expressed in the document and to evaluate how well the United States upholds those principles today.

Vocabulary Development

1 **Introduce the Key Content Terms.** Have students locate the Key Content Terms for the chapter in their Interactive Student Notebooks. These are important terms that will help them understand the main ideas of the chapter. Ask volunteers to identify any familiar terms and how they might be used in a sentence.

2 **Have students complete a Vocabulary Development handout.** Give each student a copy of the Vocabulary Development handout of your choice from the Reading Toolkit at the back of the Lesson Masters. These handouts provide extra practice and support, depending on your students' needs. Review the completed handout by asking volunteers to share one answer for each term.

Reading

1 **Introduce the Essential Question and have students read Section 6.1.** Have students identify the Essential Question: *What principles of government are expressed in the Declaration of Independence?* Then have them read Section 6.1. Afterward, have students respond to these questions:

- Who was Patrick Henry?

- What was the main idea of his speech to the Virginia House of Burgesses?

- How might his speech have pushed the colonies closer to declaring independence?

2 **Have students read and complete the Reading Notes for Sections 6.2 and 6.3.** Remind students to use the Key Content Terms where appropriate as they complete their Reading Notes. Use Guide to Reading Notes 6 to review answers with the class.

3 **Have students complete the remaining Reading Notes for Chapter 6.** Assign Sections 6.4 and 6.5 as indicated in the procedures for the Writing for Understanding activity.

Writing for Understanding

Phase 1: Analyzing the Declaration of Independence

1 **Examine the text of the Declaration of Independence.** Have students open to the Declaration of Independence at the back of their books, and ask them the questions below. Students can quickly skim the text to find answers. Have a few volunteers respond before revealing the answer.

- What does the Preamble say? *It says that the Declaration of Independence will tell the world why the colonies believe they should be independent.*

- What are some key ideas expressed in the second paragraph of the Declaration? *All men are created equal and have such basic rights as life, liberty, and the pursuit of happiness.*

> **Reading: Structural Features of Informational Materials**
>
> Have students identify the proposition, or opinion statement, that Jefferson offers about the "present King of Great Britain" and the "Facts" he uses to support his proposition. Ask them to explain how that support is structured. Then lead the class in a discussion of the probable effects of that structure on the audience. Students might also enjoy discussing whether all the "Facts" are, in actuality, facts.

- Look at the long list that begins with the words "He has refused his Assent." What is this a list of, and why do you think it was included? *It is a list of charges that explain how the king has violated the colonists' rights. It was included to prove that the king should not have the power to rule over the colonies.*

- Can you connect any of the charges on this list to events you have learned about before? *Students might mention "For Quartering large bodies of armed troops among us" or "For imposing Taxes on us without our Consent."*

- What do the representatives solemnly declare in the last paragraph? *Among other things, they declare "that these United Colonies are . . . Free and Independent States."*

2 **Place students in pairs and introduce the activity.** Tell students they will now work with their partners to examine and analyze key excerpts of the Declaration of Independence. Explain that it was written in the formal language of the late 1700s and can be challenging to understand.

3 **Analyze key excerpts of the Declaration.**
Give each student a copy of *Student Handout 6A: Analyzing Excerpts from the Declaration of Independence*, and review the step for Part 1 with the class. Instruct pairs to ignore Part 2 at this point. Pass out one card cut from *Student Handout 6B: Excerpts in Modern Language* to each pair and have students begin work. Have them continue until most pairs have completed Part 1. Use the key at right to check their answers.

Key
Excerpt 1: G
Excerpt 2: C
Excerpt 3: E
Excerpt 4: B
Excerpt 5: D
Excerpt 6: F
Excerpt 7: A

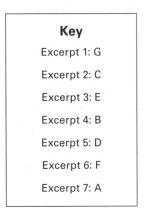
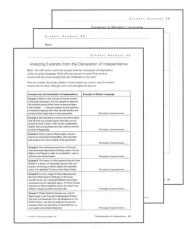

Student Handouts 6A and 6B

4 **Have students read and complete the Reading Notes for Section 6.4.**

5 **Examine four principles of government expressed in the Declaration.**
Project *Information Master 6A: Four Principles of Government in the Declaration of Independence.* Tell students that these are the principles of government Jefferson used in the Declaration to make his argument for independence from Great Britain. Have students find the principles on Part 2 of Student Handout 6A. Quickly clarify the meaning of each principle as students fill in the missing words. Explain that these ideas had been discussed for years throughout Europe during a period of time called the Enlightenment. In particular, the ideas of John Locke, a prominent philosopher of the Enlightenment, can be found in the Declaration of Independence.

Information Master 6A

6 **Match the principles with the excerpts from the Declaration.** Review the remaining steps for Part 2 with the class. Then have partners match the principles of government with the excerpts from the Declaration on Student Handout 6A. Answers will vary, but those shown in the key will be the most common.

7 **Debrief the activity.** For each of Principles 1 to 4, ask, *In which excerpt(s) did you find this principle? What did you underline to support your opinion?*

8 **Have students read and complete the Reading Notes for Section 6.5.**

Key
Excerpt 1: Principle 4
Excerpt 2: Principles 1 and 2
Excerpt 3: Principle 3
Excerpt 4: Principle 4
Excerpt 5: Principles 2 and 4
Excerpt 6: Principle 4
Excerpt 7: Principles 3 and 4

Phase 2: Writing an Essay

1 **Introduce the essay.** Tell students they will now write an essay evaluating how well the United States is upholding the principles of the Declaration of Independence.

2 **Have students write their first drafts.** Project *Information Master 6B: Writing an Essay About the Principles in the Declaration of Independence,* and review the directions. Have students write their first drafts neatly, in pencil. To facilitate the peer-checking activity to follow, ask them to write on every other line.

3 **Have students peer-check the first drafts.** Project Information Master 6B again, and have each student create a checklist by writing down the bulleted items for the writing assignment. Alternatively, make a copy of Information Master 6B for each student. Review the directions for the peer-checking activity below, and then have pairs complete it. (**Note:** You may want to make a transparency of a sample draft you have written and practice the steps as a class.)

Information Master 6B

- Exchange essays with your partner. Carefully read your partner's draft. Try to find each required item from the checklist in the essay.

- Put a check on the checklist next to each item you find. If you cannot find an item in the draft, leave that item blank.

- For the last two items on the checklist, place a star in the essay next to the idea that is expressed most clearly. Place another star next to the best piece of evidence that supports the thesis.

- When you are both done, review your checklist with your partner. Point out the items you found and any that seem to be missing. Then return the checklist and draft to the author.

4 **Give students time to write their final drafts.** Remind students to use the results of the peer-checking activity to improve their essays by including revisions of any required items that were missing or unclear. (**Note:** Consider collecting the first drafts, checklists, and final drafts to verify that students incorporated the feedback.)

Processing (optional)

1 **Understand the intent of the Processing activity.** The essay writing assignment serves as this chapter's Processing activity. Should you choose not to have students do the writing assignment, you might use the optional Processing activity in the Interactive Student Notebook.

2 **Have students complete the Processing activity.**

3 **Have students share their answers with partners or with the class.**

Quicker Coverage

Decrease the Number of Excerpts Eliminate Excerpts 1 and 6 on Student Handout 6A and the corresponding modern excerpts F and G on Student Handout 6B.

Eliminate the Peer-Checking Omit the peer-checking activity in Phase 2 of the Writing for Understanding activity.

Deeper Coverage

Analyze Other Documents Have students use the four principles of government given on Information Master 6A to examine other important documents. Take key excerpts from documents and create modern translation cards as in the activity and have students match them. For example, use excerpts from *Common Sense*, such as those below.

Excerpts from *Common Sense*	Excerpts in Modern Language
Excerpt 1: As a long and violent abuse of power, is generally the Means of calling the right of it in question.	When there is a history of misuse of power, the people can question a ruler's actions.
Excerpt 2: But the injuries and disadvantages we sustain by that connection, are without number; and our duty to mankind at large, as well as to ourselves, instruct us to renounce the alliance.	We have been wounded over and over again because of our bond to Great Britain. It is our responsibility to reject our ties with Great Britain.

Provide a Current Example Ask students to locate a report of a current event from a magazine, newspaper, or the Internet that is an example of a principle of government found in the Declaration of Independence. It can be an example of the government upholding or not upholding the principle. Have them report the information to the class or insert it in their Interactive Student Notebooks.

Assessment

Mastering the Content

1. A	5. A	9. D	13. D
2. A	6. C	10. B	14. A
3. A	7. D	11. A	15. A
4. D	8. B	12. D	16. B

Applying Social Studies Skills

17. molasses and sugar

18. rum and iron

19. Possible answer: merchants and businessmen

Exploring the Essential Question

20. Answers should include all of the elements requested in the prompt.

Scoring Rubric

Score	Description
3	Student completes all three parts of the task. Ideas are clearly stated, supported by details, and demonstrate command of standard English conventions.
2	Student responds to most or all parts of the task. Ideas may lack details or not be clearly stated.
1	Student responds to at least one part of the task. Ideas may contain factual or grammatical errors and may lack details.
0	Response does not match the task or is incorrect.

The Power of Common Sense

1 **Discuss the meaning of the phrase "common sense."** Elicit from students the idea that common sense means good judgment that most people would agree on, an understanding that does not require specialized knowledge. Encourage them to offer examples of what they consider to be common sense.

2 **Have students read the Chapter 6 Reading Further.** When they have finished, ask them to whom Paine addressed his pamphlet. Discuss the facts that he wrote for the general public, not for the government or another special audience, and that he wanted to convince all Americans that separation from England was just "common sense."

3 **Have students identify Paine's key ideas.** Based on what they have read, students should be able to summarize Paine's two key ideas:

   • Colonists do not automatically owe loyalty to any monarch.

   • Colonists should create an independent nation based on individual liberty.

4 **Have students complete the Chapter 6 Reading Further in their Interactive Student Notebooks.**

5 **Invite students to share their *Common Sense* covers and back cover copy.** Discuss the images students have created to reflect the theme on the front cover, and have them share their explanations of why revolutionary behavior seemed to be "common sense."

English Language Learners

Modify the Preview If students are newcomers from another country, they may have knowledge of the Declaration of Independence, but not be able to provide a phrase from it. Modify the Preview by providing a well-known excerpt from the Declaration of Independence, such as "all men are created equal," as a response to the first question.

Offer Vocabulary Support Ensure that students fully understand the terms *principle* and *delegate*. Consider adding these terms to the list of Key Content Terms so that students will practice their meanings on the Vocabulary Development handout.

Learners Reading and Writing Below Grade Level

Create a Glossary of Terms Supply the following terms with their definitions on a handout or the board for students to use as they match the modern excerpts with the actual excerpts during Phase 1 of the Writing for Understanding activity.

- *absolved*: released
- *allegiance*: loyalty
- *alter*: change
- *consent*: agreement
- *derive*: receive
- *dissolve*: end
- *endowed*: given
- *impel*: force
- *in direct object*: the goal of
- *institute*: establish
- *just*: fair
- *oppression*: unfair action
- *redress*: relief
- *secure*: defend
- *self-evident*: obvious
- *unalienable*: not to be taken away
- *usurpation*: illegal taking of power

Provide a Sample Essay Give students a sample essay to refer to as they write their own essays.

Learners with Special Education Needs

Modify Phase 1 Reduce the number of excerpts students need to match in the activity by giving them a copy of Student Handout 6A with some of the modern excerpts entered. Also provide some of the principle numbers.

Modify Phase 2 Modify the writing assignment by having students write just one paragraph. Students should still create a thesis. Their paragraph should contain a topic sentence, an explanation of one example in support of their thesis, and a concluding sentence.

Advanced Learners

Paraphrase the Declaration Instead of giving students cards from Student Handout 6B, have them rewrite each excerpt in their own words.

Expand the Writing Assignment Have students write three paragraphs in support of their thesis rather than two.

Enrichment Resources

Find out more about the Declaration of Independence by exploring the following Enrichment Resources for *History Alive! The United States Through Industrialism* at www.teachtci.com.

Enrichment Readings These in-depth readings encourage students to explore selected topics related to the chapter. You may also find readings that relate the chapter's content directly to your state's curriculum.

Internet Connections The recommended Web sites provide useful and engaging content that reinforces skills development and mastery of subjects within the chapter.

Literature Recommendations

The following books offer opportunities to extend the content in this chapter.

The Declaration of Independence by Kelly Barth, Ed. (San Diego, CA: Greenhaven Press, 2003)

George Washington by Cheryl Harness (Des Moines, IA: National Geographic, 2000)

The American Revolution by Stuart Murray (New York: Harper Collins, 2006)

Section 6.2

1. John Adams proposed George Washington be commander-in-chief. He believed that Washington, with his talent and character, would unite the colonies better than anyone else.

2. Possible flowchart:

Events in the Battle of Bunker Hill

Militiamen built a fort on Breed's Hill all through the night of June 16.

↓

When British general Howe saw the American fort, he ordered an attack.

↓

The Americans waited until the British were as close as possible before they fired on them.

↓

It took the British three tries to take the hill.

3. Possible answers:

Ticonderoga (Winter 1775–1776): Sketch could show Americans loading up supplies of cannons and ammunition. *Caption:* The Continental army was able to increase their supplies enough to attack Boston.

Boston (March 4, 1776): Sketch could show British troops and Loyalists leaving Boston on ships. *Caption:* The Continental army was able to regain Boston with very little bloodshed, and the British fled to Canada.

Section 6.3

1. Possible answer: There was no fighting for a year after the battles at Lexington and Concord and the British retreat from Boston, and many colonists still felt loyal to the king.

2. Possible answer:

Olive Branch Petition — *Common Sense*

Written to King George.

Colonists ask for an end to the quarrels and hope for peace.

King George rejects it and calls colonists traitors.

Give solutions to the problems between Great Britain and the colonies.

Written to colonists.

Claims Great Britain has hurt the colonists.

Thousands of colonists are persuaded to declare independence.

Section 6.4

1. Thomas Jefferson drafted the Declaration of Independence to officially state that the colonies were separating from Great Britain and becoming independent.

2. Possible ideas and explanations:

- *All people are born equal.* If everyone is treated the same, the world will be a more just place.

- *A government's power to rule comes from the people.* People don't have to feel powerless. The government does not have power over them.

- *The people can create a new government to protect their safety and happiness.* People don't have to wait around for someone to make their government better. They can create a new government that will keep them safe and happy.

Section 6.5

1. Possible answer: *Northern delegate:* This passage may offend New England merchants who benefit from the slave trade. *Southern delegate:* This passage may lead to a demand to end slavery. We need slaves to work on our farms.

2. Cartoons should show that delegates were endangering their lives by signing the Declaration of Independence. The caption should reflect this idea.

The American Revolution

How was the Continental army able to win the war for independence from Great Britain?

Overview

In an Experiential Exercise, students participate in a game of Capture the Flag. They compare their experience to the determining factors of the war for independence from Great Britain—examining the strengths and weaknesses of each side, important battles, and other key factors in the conflict—to determine how the British were defeated.

Objectives

In the course of reading this chapter and participating in the classroom activity, students will

Social Studies

- identify the impact of the American Revolution on other parts of the world.
- examine the course of the war for independence and the subsequent defeat of the British.

Language Arts

- analyze similes to understand the course and outcome of the war for independence.

Social Studies Vocabulary

Key Content Terms American Revolution, Continental army, strategy, ally

Academic Vocabulary democracy, rebellion, issue, crucial

Materials

History Alive! The United States Through Industrialism

Interactive Student Notebooks

Lesson Masters

- Information Master 7A (1 copy)
- Information Master 7B (1 transparency)
- Vocabulary Development handout (1 per student, on colored paper)

four small towels or cloths (1 red, 3 blue) to use as flags

four orange cones or other items to mark off the playing field

masking tape

whistle

small prizes (optional)

Activity	Suggested Time	Materials
Preview	15 minutes	• Interactive Student Notebooks
Vocabulary Development	30–40 minutes	• *History Alive! The United States Through Industrialism* • Interactive Student Notebooks • Vocabulary Development handout
Experiential Exercise	50 minutes (1 regular period) (0.5 block period)	• *History Alive! The United States Through Industrialism* • Interactive Student Notebooks • Information Master 7A • four small towels or cloths (1 red, 3 blue) • four orange cones or similar items • masking tape • whistle • prizes (optional)
Processing	25 minutes	• Interactive Student Notebooks • Student Handout 7B
Assessment	40 minutes	• Chapter 7 Assessment

Preview

1 **Introduce the game Capture the Flag.** Have students raise their hands if they have ever played the game. Ask for volunteers to describe the objective and rules of the game. (**Note:** See Step 3 of the Experiential Exercise for the objective and rules.)

2 **Have students complete the Preview activity in their Interactive Student Notebooks.**

3 **Have students share their responses in pairs or with the class.**

4 **Explain the connection between the Preview and Chapter 7.** Tell students that skills and experience are two of the important factors involved in winning a game. In this chapter, students will learn about the two "teams" that participated in the American Revolution. One side had more skills and experience in fighting wars, but it was not necessarily the side that won.

Vocabulary Development

1 **Introduce the Key Content Terms.** Have students locate the Key Content Terms for the chapter in their Interactive Student Notebooks. These are important terms that will help them understand the main ideas of the chapter. Ask volunteers to identify any familiar terms and how they might be used in a sentence.

2 **Have students complete a Vocabulary Development handout.** Give each student a copy of the Vocabulary Development handout of your choice from the Reading Toolkit at the back of the Lesson Masters. These handouts provide extra practice and support, depending on your students' needs. Review the completed handout by asking volunteers to share one answer for each term.

Reading

Have students complete the Reading Notes for Chapter 7. Assign Sections 7.1 to 7.8 during the activity as indicated in the procedures for the Experiential Exercise. Remind students to use the Key Content Terms where appropriate as they complete the Reading Notes.

Experiential Exercise

1 **Understand the intent of the activity.** In this activity, students will participate in six rounds of Capture the Flag. These rounds are analogous to the course of the war for independence from Great Britain. In each round, the teacher will change the rules just enough to tilt the outcome of the game in the Blue Team's favor. This illustrates how the Continental army was able to defeat the British. (**Note:** Historical analogies are noted in Step 4 below and on Information Master 7A. Do not share these connections with students until after the activity is completed.)

2   **Prepare the playing area.** Before class, mark off an area roughly 50 feet by 100 feet (or smaller, for fewer than 30 students) on a field, playground, or gym. Use cones (or trash cans or backpacks) to mark the four corners and tape to divide the field in half. (**Note:** If moving the activity out of your classroom is not possible, see the option under "Quicker Coverage" for an alternative way to conduct this activity.)

3   **Review the objective and rules of the game.** Take students to the playing area and explain the rules for Capture the Flag.

- The object of the game is to capture the other team's flag and bring it back to your team's side of the field without being tagged by a member of the other team.

- When you are on your side of the field, your job is to play defense and tag members of the other team if they come onto your side. If you go onto the other team's side of the field, your job is to play offense and try to capture their flag and bring it back to your side without getting tagged. You may not throw or hand the flag to another teammate.

- If you are tagged on the other team's side, you must leave the field immediately and sit next to the teacher. If you are tagged while the flag is in your hand, you must return the flag first. The teacher will tell you when you can reenter the game. If the teacher sees you tagged and you do not come out immediately, you will not be allowed to play for the remainder of the game.

- Only one student on each team can guard the team's flag, and he or she cannot touch or move the flag. All other team members must play offense or defense.

- When you hear the whistle, stop playing and return to your side of the field.

4   **Divide students into teams.** Follow these guidelines to create three teams.

- Have students form a single line, ordering themselves from those with the most experience playing Capture the Flag to those with no experience.

- Assign the quarter of the class with the least experience to the Blue team.

- Assign the half of the class with the most experience to the Red team, with one exception. Have the player with the most experience stand aside.

- Assign the student you removed from the experienced group to be the captain of the Blue team.

- Assign the remaining quarter of the class to the White team.

Historical analogy: The Continental army was much smaller and less experienced than the British military. However, George Washington, an experienced soldier, was commander in chief of the Continental army.

5 **Follow the steps on *Information Master 7A: Procedures for Rounds 1 to 6 of Capture the Flag* to have the class play six rounds of the game.** In Rounds 1 to 5, make sure to blow the whistle to end the round before the Red team can capture the Blue team's flag.

6 **Debrief the activity.** Return to the classroom and have students sit with their teams. Then ask these questions:

   • *To the Red and then the Blue team:* How did you feel at the very beginning of the game? Why?

   • *To the White team:* At the very beginning of the game, which team did you think would win? Why?

   • *To the Red and then the Blue team:* How did you feel as the game went on? Why?

   • *To all:* What rule changes or other factors helped the Blue team win?

7 **Connect the activity to the chapter.** Explain that students' experience in Capture the Flag was modeled after the major factors that allowed the Continental army to win the war. Ask a few volunteers to answer this question: *Is there anything that you experienced in this game that might help you understand how the Continental army was able to win the war for independence from Great Britain?* Tell students that in this chapter they will read about each phase of the war and compare it to their game of Capture the Flag.

8 **Introduce the Essential Question and have students read Section 7.1.** Have students identify the Essential Question: *How was the Continental army able to win the war for independence from Great Britain?* Then have them read Section 7.1 Afterward, have students respond to these questions:

   • Carefully look at the paintings on these two pages. Which army looks better prepared for battle? Explain.

   • In what ways was Joseph Martin an ideal soldier?

   • How did the army in New York compare to the British army when Joseph Martin entered the war?

   • What might have enabled the Continental army to win the war?

9 **Have students read and complete the Reading Notes for Sections 7.2 to 7.8.** As students complete each section, use Guide to Reading Notes 7 to review their answers and check that they have made the proper historical connections.

Processing

Have students complete the Processing activity on a separate sheet of paper. They will create a simile that shows how the Americans were able to defeat the British and win the war. Project *Information Master 7B: Simile for the Continental Army's Victory* to show students an example of how to create their similes.

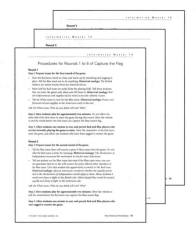

Information Master 7A

Information Master 7B

Quicker Coverage

Modify the Experiential Exercise Rather than actually playing the game, conduct a simulated game of Capture the Flag in the classroom. Move the desks aside and prepare a small playing field according to the procedures in the Lesson Guide. Review the objective and rules of the game, and then divide students into three teams as described in the Lesson Guide. For each of the six rounds of the game, have students prepare to play the round as described on Information Master 7A and then, rather than actually playing the round, simply discuss these questions in their teams: *How do you think the playing of this round would be different with these changes than without them? Given these changes, who do you think would win and why?* Have volunteers from each team—Red, Blue, and White—share their answers, and then move to the next round of the game.

Deeper Coverage

Hold a Class Discussion Facilitate a discussion about the most important contributing factors to the American victory in the war. Have the class brainstorm a list of seven to ten factors. Then divide students into groups of three. Have groups rank the factors in order from most important to least important and then prepare a spokesperson to present and defend their rankings to the class. Finally, have each group present. Allow time for comments from the class.

Assessment

Mastering the Content

1. A	5. D	9. A	13. D
2. A	6. C	10. C	14. C
3. D	7. C	11. B	15. C
4. B	8. D	12. A	16. C

Applying Social Studies Skills

17. Southern Colonies

18. the blockage of French warships

19. Possible answers: The British troops were outnumbered. The combined forces of the French and American troops prevented a British retreat. The French and American troops surrounded the British.

Exploring the Essential Question

20. Answers should include all of the elements requested in the prompt.

Scoring Rubric

Score	Description
3	Student completes all three parts of the task. Ideas are clearly stated, supported by details, and demonstrate command of standard English conventions.
2	Student responds to most or all parts of the task. Ideas may lack details or not be clearly stated.
1	Student responds to at least one part of the task. Ideas may contain factual or grammatical errors and may lack details.
0	Response does not match the task or is incorrect.

George Washington: A Warrior Spirit and a Caring Heart

1 **Elicit descriptions of George Washington.** Ask students for words and phrases that describe George Washington. You might begin the discussion by writing *The Father of Our Country* and *the face on a dollar bill* on the board.

2 **Have students read the Chapter 7 Reading Further.** Encourage them to look up such unfamiliar words as *momentous, plunder, diabolical, whit,* and *fortitude.*

3 **Using Washington as the example, discuss how people form impressions of historical figures.** Ask,

- What had you read or heard about Washington before today? What did you know about his actions? What did you know about his personality?

- What images of Washington have you seen? How do those rather formal images make you feel about him?

- How did the information in this reading change your impressions of Washington?

4 **Have students complete the Chapter 7 Reading Further in their Interactive Student Notebooks.** Before students write their letters, ask,

- What does the quotation from Joseph Plumb Martin reveal?

- What does the soldiers' concern for Washington's safety say about their attitude toward the general?

5 **Ask students to share the sentences they wrote using the words in the Word Bank.** Have them compare these words and sentences with the descriptions of Washington they gave earlier.

6 **Have students share their letters.**

English Language Learners

Partner Up for the Reading Notes Have students pair up to complete the Reading Notes. English language learners may require more assistance with the first questions in each section than with the last question, in which they relate their experience to history.

Support Vocabulary Development Assist students with difficult vocabulary in this chapter, such as the terms suggested below, by giving them a glossary of terms to use as they complete the reading.

- *defensive:* protecting yourself from danger or harm
- *mercenaries:* soldiers who fight for anyone who will pay them
- *pardon:* to forgive or excuse
- *surrender:* to give up

You may also want to remind students that sometimes a word's meaning may be found in the sentence in which it is used. For example, the third paragraph of Section 7.7 states, "Guerrillas—soldiers who are not part of a regular army—kept the American cause alive." Tell students that parentheses and commas are also sometimes used to signal the inclusion of a definition within a sentence.

Learners Reading and Writing Below Grade Level

Model How to Complete the Reading Notes Project and complete the Reading Notes for Section 7.2 as a class, and have students copy the class responses into their notebooks. Encourage students to use their now-completed first page of Reading Notes as a model for the remaining sections.

Learners with Special Education Needs

Assign Student Reporters Have students who are physically unable to participate in the Capture the Flag game serve as on-the-scene reporters. Give each reporter a spiral notebook and a pencil and ask them to record "reporter's notes" during each round of the game. These notes can be as simple as which side seems to be winning after each round, or they could be detailed summaries of what is occurring on the "battlefront." When debriefing the activity, have student reporters summarize the events of each round before analyzing the actions as a group.

Modify the Reading Notes Have students complete only the last question of each section of Reading Notes. Give them a copy of the Reading Notes pages with the answers to all but the last question, in which they annotate each round of the game, completed.

Advanced Learners

Research the Revolution Challenge students to complete in-depth library or Internet research on a single battle of the American Revolution. Students should display the results of their research on a poster that includes

- the name and the dates of the battle.
- the location of the battle on a map of North America.
- at least one specific battle map.
- one paragraph that summarizes the battle and its significance.
- directions for completing a round of Capture the Flag that would reflect what happened in that battle.

Enrichment Resources

Find out more about the American Revolution by exploring the following Enrichment Resources for *History Alive! The United States Through Industrialism* at www.teachtci.com.

Enrichment Readings These in-depth readings encourage students to explore selected topics related to the chapter. You may also find readings that relate the chapter's content directly to your state's curriculum.

Internet Connections The recommended Web sites provide useful and engaging content that reinforces skills development and mastery of subjects within the chapter.

Literature Recommendations

The following books offer opportunities to extend the content in this chapter.

George Washington, Spymaster: How America Outspied the British and Won the Revolutionary War by Thomas B. Allen (Des Moines, IA: National Geographic Society, 2004)

Why Not Lafayette? by Jean Fritz (New York: Puffin, 2001)

Prince Estabrook—Slave and Soldier by Alice Hinkle (Lexington, MA: Pleasant Mountain Press, 2001)

Sections 7.2 and 7.3

1. Possible answers:

American Strengths	British Strengths
• The Americans had patriotism on their side; people were willing to give their lives for their country. • The Americans received secret aid from the French. • George Washington was an experienced military leader who inspired courage and confidence.	• The British army had 50,000 soldiers, reinforced by 30,000 Hessian mercenaries, as well as Loyalists, Native Americans, and African Americans. • British soldiers were well trained and experienced. • British forces were well supplied with food, uniforms, ammunition, and weapons.
American Weaknesses	**British Weaknesses**
• The Continental army was small and always short of soldiers. • Few Americans were trained for battle. • The army was plagued by shortages of guns, gunpowder, food, and uniforms.	• Sending troops and supplies from Great Britain to North America was slow and costly. • The British people were not passionate about defeating the rebels. • The British had poor military leadership.

2. Completed annotations:

   • The Blue team is smaller. It has not warmed up. It hasn't played Capture the Flag as much as the Red team, just like . . . American forces were smaller and had less training and experience than the British.

   • The Red team is larger. It has warmed up. It has played the game more than the Blue team, just like . . . the British army was larger, better trained, and more experienced than the American forces.

   • The Blue captain has experience playing Capture the Flag, just like . . . George Washington was an experienced general.

   • The White team cheers for the Blue team, just like . . . the French secretly aided the Americans at the beginning of the war.

   • Half the Red team starts the game far from the field, just like . . . Great Britain was far from America and had to ship troops and supplies across the Atlantic.

Section 7.4

1. Many Americans believed that freedom and independence were goals worth fighting for.

2. The Declaration raised hopes and questions for African Americans. They wondered if the words "all men are created equal" applied to them and if independence would bring an end to slavery.

3. The British, with their greater numbers and superior training, overwhelmed the inexperienced Americans at New York and in other battles in 1776.

4. Completed annotations:

   • The teacher tells the Blue team they will get a prize if they win. This increases their motivation, just like . . . the Declaration of Independence increased the motivation of many Americans to fight and win the war.

   • Because they have more experienced players, the Red team is almost able to steal the Blue flag, just like . . . the British, with more numerous and experienced soldiers, almost defeated the Americans in 1776.

   • One Blue player is told he or she might not get a prize, even if the Blue team wins. That player must decide whether to stay on the Blue team or switch to the Red team, just like . . . African Americans were not sure whether fighting for independence would assure them either equal rights or the end of slavery. They had to decide whether to fight on the American or the British side.

Section 7.5

1. The message of Paine's *The Crisis* was to remind Americans that real patriots hold onto their beliefs, even in hard times.

2. Washington had his troops cross the Delaware River at night and take the enemy by surprise early the next morning.

3. Victories at Trenton and Princeton showed that the Americans could beat the British and their allies, which greatly boosted American morale.

4. Completed annotations:

   - The teacher gives the Blue team a pep talk and encourages them to keep fighting, just like . . . Thomas Paine's pamphlet *The Crisis* encouraged Americans to hold onto their beliefs, even during hard times.

   - The teacher adds a second Blue flag. This makes it harder for the Red team to win and boosts the Blue team's morale, just like . . . American victories at Trenton and Princeton showed the British it would be harder than they expected to win the war and boosted the Americans' morale.

Section 7.6

1. Washington avoided large battles that might put his army at risk. Instead, he fought a defensive war designed to tire out the British.

2. After the Battle of Saratoga, the French become allies of the Americans, and Spain also entered the war against Britain.

3. Baron Friedrich von Steuben of Prussia drilled the American soldiers and turned them into an organized fighting force. The Marquis de Lafayette of France used his own money to buy clothing for the soldiers.

4. Completed annotations:

   - The teacher tells the Blue team they do not have to capture the Red flag to win. Instead, they must keep the Red team from capturing all the Blue flags, just like . . . Washington told Congress that he would fight a defensive war to try to tire out the British.

   - The teacher tells the Blue team that if they can hold on for one more round, they may receive help, just like . . . after the American victory at the Battle of Saratoga, the French became allies of the Americans.

   - The teacher has one volunteer from the White team join the Blue team, just like . . . some Europeans, like von Steuben and Lafayette, aided the American cause.

Section 7.7

1. Americans in the South used guerrilla tactics, like hit-and-run raids, against the British.

2. The Continental army tired out the British in the South and eventually forced them to retreat to Yorktown, where they were defeated.

3. French troops and warships helped the Americans to trap the British army at Yorktown.

4. Completed annotations:

   - The teacher adds a third Blue flag. This makes it harder for the Red team to win, just like . . . successful American hit-and-run tactics in the South made it more difficult for the British to win the war.

   - The White team enters the game to help the Blue team, just like . . . the French sent troops and warships to help the Americans defeat the British at Yorktown.

Section 7.8

1. Most British people accepted the defeat at Yorktown, but King George did not want to accept defeat.

2. Three key provisions of the Treaty of Paris were (1) Great Britain recognized the United States as an independent country; (2) Great Britain handed over territory from the Atlantic Coast to the Mississippi River; and (3) the United States agreed to return all rights and property taken from Loyalists during the war.

3. The American Revolution helped inspire revolts against European rule throughout South America. The Americans also influenced the French Revolution.

4. Completed annotations:

- By the end of Round 6, many members of the Red team don't want to play anymore, but some do, just like . . . after Yorktown, many British were ready to accept defeat, though King George did not want to accept defeat.

- At the end of the game, the Blue, White, and Red captains shake hands. The Blue and White teams receive their prizes. The Red captain hands over the Red flag. The Blue team promises to be nice to the Red team, just like . . . at the end of the war, the Americans, French, and British signed a treaty in Paris. In the treaty, the United States received its independence. The British handed over territory to the Americans. The Americans promised to respect the rights and property of Loyalists.

Revolution in the Colonies

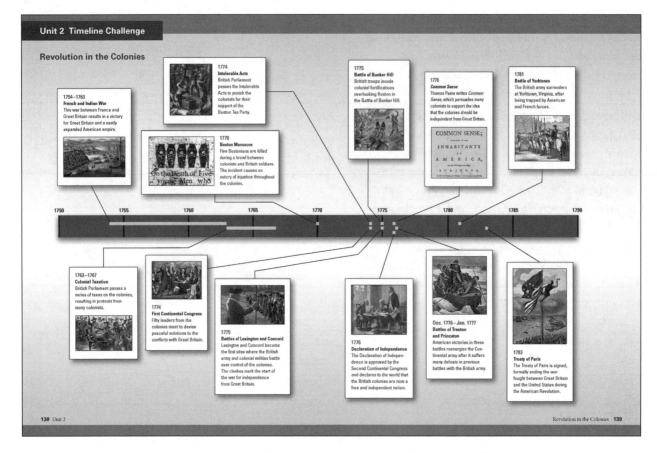

Overview

This Timeline Challenge provides students with a review of the main events and ideas of this unit, as well as practice in reading and interpreting timelines. You can vary and expand the activity according to students' needs and the amount of time available.

Basic Procedure

1   **Introduce the timeline in the Student Edition.** Direct students to the Revolution in the Colonies timeline at the end of Unit 2 in the Student Edition. You may wish to have students read aloud and discuss the timeline entries.

2   **Introduce the Timeline Challenge in the Interactive Student Notebook**. Direct students to the Unit 2 Timeline Challenge in their notebooks. Point out the two types of questions, "Timeline Skills" and "Critical Thinking," and model how to answer each type.

3   **Have students complete the Timeline Challenge.** Monitor students as they work. Use the Guide to Unit 2 Timeline Challenge to check their answers. You may wish to project a transparency of this page as you work through the questions with the class and conduct a discussion of the "Critical Thinking" questions.

4   **Complete the KWL chart.** Return to the KWL chart created at the beginning of the unit, and ask students to list the key information they have learned.

Classroom Timeline

1 **Prepare the Timeline Challenge Cards.** Copy and cut the cards from *Student Handout TC2: Unit 2 Timeline Challenge Cards.* You may wish to laminate the cards for future use.

2 **Create a timeline on a classroom wall.** On an empty wall or a large bulletin board, make a timeline with masking tape or colored paper. Mark off the time intervals in advance, or ask students to do so in class.

3 **Have students place the Timeline Challenge Cards.** Distribute cards to individual students or pairs and have them tape the cards to the timeline in the correct locations. Call on students to provide more information on the timeline topics to review main events and issues.

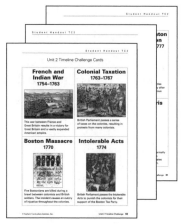

Student Handout TC2

Internet Research

1 **Review students' suggestions for additional timeline entries.** Have students share their answers to the last question of the Timeline Challenge.

2 **Have students conduct Internet research.** Ask students to choose and research one of their suggested events.

3 **Have students create additional Timeline Challenge Cards.** Direct students to research an appropriate image for their cards and then use the computer to create an illustrated card, complete with timeline entry.

Timeline Skills

Score 1 point for each correct answer.

1. France and Great Britain

2. British Parliament met with protests from the colonists because it taxed them without their consent.

3. the Boston Massacre and the Boston Tea Party

4. The First Continental Congress met in 1774 to find peaceful solutions to the conflicts with Great Britain.

5. *Common Sense* and the Declaration of Independence were both published in 1776. After reading *Common Sense,* many colonists supported independence for the American colonies, so *Common Sense* could be considered a "cause" and the Declaration of Independence could be considered an "effect."

6. The first battles between British troops and the colonists were at Lexington and Concord in 1775.

7. The war for independence began in Lexington and Concord in 1775, before the Declaration of Independence was issued.

8. The Battles of Trenton and Princeton were significant because they helped reenergize the Continental army. About six years elapsed between these battles and the end of the revolution.

9. The Continental army had the help of the French.

Critical Thinking

Score 1 to 3 points for each answer, depending on the thoroughness of the response.

10. Students should choose one event and give reasons for their choice.

11. Answers will likely focus on principles in the Declaration of Independence, including the following: everyone has certain rights that cannot be taken away; the government gets its power to make decisions and protect rights from the people; when the government does not protect the people's rights, the people have the right to change or remove the government.

12. Possible answers: Foreign aid from the French; the British were far from their supplies and reinforcements; colonists were motivated by the principles found in the Declaration of Independence; *The Crisis,* written by Thomas Paine, encouraged colonists to keep fighting; victories at Trenton and Princeton; colonists did not have to actually defeat the British but just keep them from winning.

13. Answers will vary. Students must explain why the events they chose merit inclusion.

Using Scores to Inform Instruction

Timeline Skills A score of 6 out of 9 indicates that students understand most of the key events of this unit.

Critical Thinking A score of 8 out of 12 indicates that students are able to think critically about most of the key issues of this unit.

If students score below these levels, consider reviewing timeline and critical thinking skills.

Forming a New Nation

Forming a New Nation

Overview

This activity introduces geographic information essential to Unit 3. Students read and interpret maps to learn about the human geographies of the 13 original states. They annotate a map of those states and answer questions in their Interactive Student Notebooks, and then discuss critical thinking questions. Students' comprehension of content and proficiency in map-reading and higher-order thinking skills will help you gauge their readiness for the unit. The pages that follow include a completed map, answers to questions, a scoring guide to inform your teaching, and suggestions for modifications to meet specific student needs.

Essential Geographic Understandings

1. Location, physical size, and comparative populations of the 13 original states

2. Location and size of the largest urban areas in the United States in 1790

3. Distribution and extent of slavery in the United States in 1790

4. Impact of population distribution and characteristics on the form of government the framers created in the Constitution

Procedures

1 **Introduce the unit.** Tell students they will learn how and why the Constitution was written. They will also learn about the Constitution's structure and content and the form of government the Constitution created—the government we live under today.

2 **Create a KWL chart.** Ask students to identify what they know about the Constitution and what they want to learn. Use their responses to gauge how much additional background information they will need as you progress through the unit. Students will return to the KWL chart at the end of the unit and add the key information they have learned.

3 **Have students read Unit 3 "Setting the Stage" in the Student Edition.**

4 **Have students complete the Geography Challenge.** Monitor students as they answer the questions and complete the map. You may want to have them work in pairs. Use the guide on the next two pages to check their answers. You may wish to project the map from the Interactive Student Notebook and have students annotate it as the class works through the map-reading questions. Make sure students have grasped Essential Geographic Understandings 1 to 3.

5 **Discuss the "Critical Thinking" questions.** Help students understand the geographic relationships described in Essential Geographic Understanding 4.

The United States, 1790

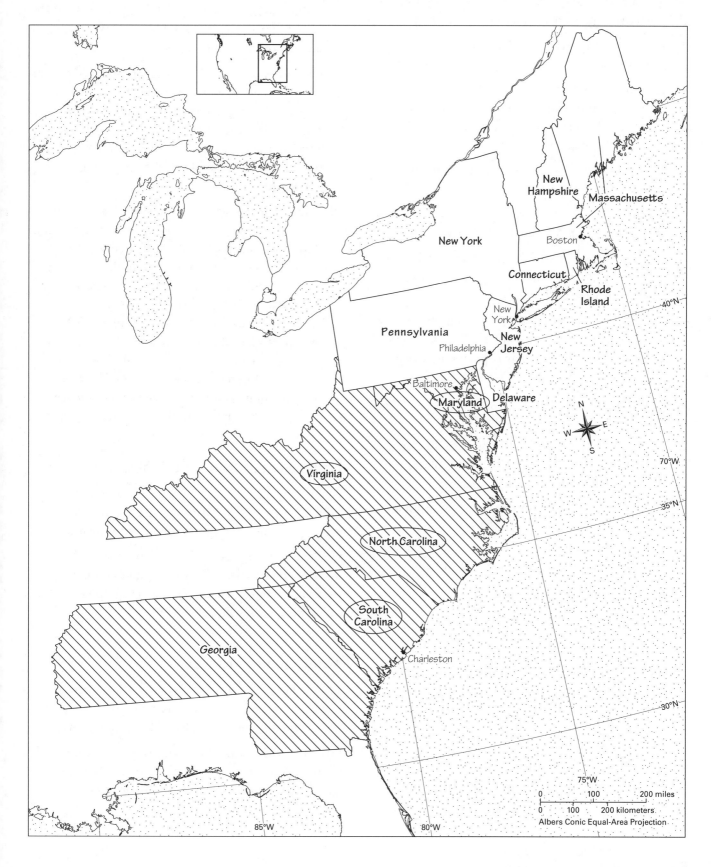

Geography Skills

Score 1 point for each correct answer. Use the map on the previous page to check shading and labeling.

1. Virginia and Pennsylvania had the largest populations.

2. The nation's five largest cities in 1790 were Baltimore, Maryland; Boston, Massachusetts; Charleston, South Carolina; New York, New York; and Philadelphia, Pennsylvania.

3. Only 6 of the nation's 24 largest cities and towns were located in the South.

4. The South's next four largest cities had populations of 2,500 to 5,000. All were located in Virginia.

5. Students should shade Georgia, Maryland, North Carolina, South Carolina, and Virginia. Most of these states were in the South.

6. Connecticut, Massachusetts, New Hampshire, New Jersey, New York, Pennsylvania, and Rhode Island had few or no slaves in their populations. These states were in the North.

7. Eighteen of the nation's 24 largest cities and towns were in states with few or no slaves.

8. Slaves were about one-third or more of the population in Georgia, Maryland, South Carolina, and Virginia.

9. Students should circle Virginia, North Carolina, Maryland, and South Carolina. Virginia would fall from the top rank to the same range as Pennsylvania. North Carolina and Maryland would fall below Massachusetts and New York. South Carolina also would fall a tier in the population rankings.

Critical Thinking

Questions may have more than one correct answer. Score 1 to 3 points for each reasonable answer, depending on the strength of students' geographic reasoning. Possible answers are given here.

10. Populous states like Virginia, Pennsylvania, Massachusetts, New York, North Carolina, and Maryland would likely support such a system because it would give them great power in the national government. Less-populous states like Rhode Island, Delaware, and Georgia would likely oppose it because they would have little power in a population-based legislature.

11. Less-populous states like New Jersey would benefit from a system of equal representation and would suffer in a population-based system. Proposed compromises will vary, but students might suggest a two-house legislature in which states are equally represented in one house and by population in the other.

12. Virginia, North Carolina, Maryland, and South Carolina had large slave populations. Not counting slaves for seats in a population-based legislature would reduce their power. This would indirectly benefit populous states with few or no slaves, like Pennsylvania, Massachusetts, and New York, which would likely favor such a plan for that reason. Suggested compromises might include a two-house, population-based legislature where slaves count in one house but not in the other, or counting only a portion of a state's slaves when determining its population.

Using Scores to Inform Instruction

Geography Skills A score of 6 out of 9 or better indicates that students have acquired sufficient geographic information to proceed with the unit.

Critical Thinking A score of 6 out of 9 or better indicates that students are beginning to understand the relationships between physical geography and the different ways in which people live.

Modifying Instruction

ELL or Learners with Special Education Needs Consider focusing on map-reading questions or limiting the number of "Critical Thinking" questions.

Students with Weak Map or Critical Thinking Skills Assign appropriate pages from the Social Studies Skills Toolkit in the back of the Lesson Masters.

Creating the Constitution

What compromises emerged from the Constitutional Convention?

Overview

In an Experiential Exercise, students examine the factors that led to the creation of a stronger central government under the U.S. Constitution by re-creating a key debate from the Constitutional Convention.

Objectives

In the course of reading this chapter and participating in the classroom activity, students will

Social Studies

- analyze the effectiveness of the Articles of Confederation.
- explain how the Northwest Ordinance helped establish new territory for the United States.
- determine the causes of Shays's Rebellion and its effects on the new nation.
- identify the main points of contention during the development of the Constitution, the arguments surrounding them, and their resolutions.
- describe the role of such leaders as George Washington and Roger Sherman in the writing and ratification of the Constitution.
- describe the underlying political philosophy of the Constitution championed by such men as James Madison and Alexander Hamilton.

Language Arts

- deliver a persuasive presentation that makes a clear and knowledgeable judgment and supports arguments with evidence, examples, and reasoning.

Social Studies Vocabulary

Key Content Terms Articles of Confederation, Northwest Territory, Northwest Ordinance, Constitutional Convention, Enlightenment, republic, constitution, Great Compromise, Three-Fifths Compromise, Electoral College, ratify, *The Federalist Papers*

Academic Vocabulary committed, liberal, framework, contradiction

Materials

History Alive! The United States Through Industrialism

Interactive Student Notebooks

Visual 8

radio

Lesson Masters

- Information Masters 8A and 8B (1 transparency of each)
- Student Handout 8A (1 copy, cut into cards)
- Student Handout 8B (1 copy; optional)
- Student Handout 8C (1 copy)
- Vocabulary Development handout (1 per student, on colored paper)

Activity	Suggested Time	Materials
Preview	30 minutes	• Interactive Student Notebooks • radio • Information Master 8A
Vocabulary Development	30–40 minutes	• *History Alive! The United States Through Industrialism* • Interactive Student Notebooks • Vocabulary Development handout
Experiential Exercise	100–150 minutes (2–3 regular periods) (1–1.5 block periods)	• *History Alive! The United States Through Industrialism* • Interactive Student Notebooks • Visual 8 • Student Handouts 8A and 8C • Student Handout 8B (optional) • Information Master 8B
Processing	25 minutes	• Interactive Student Notebooks
Assessment	40 minutes	• Chapter 8 Assessment

Preview

1   **Understand the intent of the Preview.** This Preview allows students to experience how difficult it was to pass laws under the Articles of Confederation. In the activity, groups will propose and vote on which radio station to listen to. Based on directions from you, some groups will undermine the process by not agreeing to any of the proposals. Expect students to feel some frustration as they participate in this activity.

2   **Introduce the activity.** Tell students that today they will get to listen to a radio in class and will vote on which station to listen to. Explain that you will divide the class into 13 groups. One group will make a proposal for a radio station, and all the groups will vote on the proposal. Each group will have one vote. To be chosen, a station must receive 9 votes.

3   **Form 13 groups and "rig" the activity.** Divide students into 13 groups, and tell the groups they have two minutes to come up with a radio station to propose. While the groups are discussing which station to propose, secretly tell 5 groups they will earn extra credit if they vote only for their own proposal. Emphasize that they will only earn the points if they do not let the other groups know about the extra credit.

4   **Guide the class through the process of choosing a radio station.** Have one group offer their proposal, and allow the class to discuss it. After a few minutes, conduct a vote, reminding students that 9 groups must vote for the station for it to be chosen. Continue allowing students to vote on proposals until you think they have experienced the difficulties and frustration of the process.

5   **Debrief the activity.** Ask,

  • How did you feel as you tried to reach an agreement?

  • What are the weaknesses of this type of decision-making system? What are the benefits?

  • What might be a better way to have the class make a decision?

6   **Have students complete the Preview.** Project *Information Master 8A: Experiencing the Weaknesses of the Articles of Confederation*, covering the entries below the headings on the T-chart. Reveal the first entry under "Articles of Confederation" and ask students to identify the part of today's activity that models this historical fact. Reveal the corresponding entry under "Classroom Experience" and have students record both entries on their own T-charts. Repeat this process for the remaining entries.

Information Master 8A

7 **Explain the connection between the Preview and Chapter 8.** Tell students that the ineffectiveness of the federal government under the Articles of Confederation concerned many Americans. In summer 1787, fifty-five delegates from 12 states met in Philadelphia to revise the Articles. The delegates at this Constitutional Convention quickly concluded that there was no hope for the old system of government and began working on a plan for a new one. The delegates confronted several challenging issues at the convention. In this chapter, students will learn about these issues and how the delegates compromised to resolve them, resulting in the creation of the Constitution.

Vocabulary Development

1 **Introduce the Key Content Terms.** Have students locate the Key Content Terms for the chapter in their Interactive Student Notebooks. These are important terms that will help them understand the main ideas of the chapter. Ask volunteers to identify any familiar terms and how they might be used in a sentence.

2 **Have students complete a Vocabulary Development handout.** Give each student a copy of the Vocabulary Development handout of your choice from the Reading Toolkit at the back of the Lesson Masters. These handouts provide extra practice and support, depending on your students' needs. Review the completed handout by asking volunteers to share one answer for each term.

Reading

1 **Introduce the Essential Question and have students read Section 8.1.** Have students identify the Essential Question: *What compromises emerged from the Constitutional Convention?* Then have them read Section 8.1. Afterward, have them respond to these questions:

   • What worried James Madison about the future of the United States?

   • Why did many members of Congress fear a strong central government?

   • What were some of the government's powers under the Articles of Confederation? What were some of its limitations?

2 **Have students read and complete the Reading Notes for Sections 8.2 and 8.3.** Use Guide to Reading Notes 8 to review answers with the class and check for understanding.

3 **Have students complete the remaining Reading Notes for Chapter 8.** Assign Sections 8.4 to 8.12 during the activity as indicated in the procedures for the Experiential Exercise. Remind students to use the Key Content Terms where appropriate as they complete their Reading Notes.

Experiential Exercise

Phase 1: Opening the Convention

1 **Before class, prepare the room.** Set up the classroom to re-create the Assembly Room in Independence Hall.

- Follow the diagram to arrange and label 12 groups of desks to represent the delegations at the convention. The circles indicate how many students to assign to each state for a class of 32 students. If you have fewer or more than 32 students, see Step 4 below for how to assign students to states. You will not assign any students to Rhode Island, as it did not send a delegation to the convention. Place an empty desk at the back of the room to represent its absence.

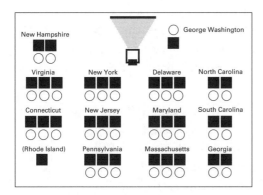

- Consider placing a candle and quill pen at each desk and explaining to students that the delegates used candles when they met at night. You might also place a gavel at George Washington's desk.
- Project *Visual 8: Assembly Room of Independence Hall.*

2 **Introduce the activity.** When students enter the room, tell them that it is summer 1787 and they are delegates to the Constitutional Convention. Explain that they originally came to Philadelphia to resolve the problems created by the Articles of Confederation, but now have decided to throw out the Articles and create a new government. Emphasize that some delegates are optimistic about this change and others are angered by it.

3 **Place students in groups.**

4 **Distribute and review role cards.** Pass out the appropriate role card cut from *Student Handout 8A: Role Cards for Constitutional Convention Delegates* to each student. For fewer than 32 students, pass out role cards in the order they appear in the Lesson Masters. For more than 32 students, give the extra students additional copies of the role cards of delegates from larger states, beginning with Pennsylvania and Virginia. Tell students to read their role cards carefully, explaining that they are each responsible for taking on the persona of their assigned delegate and accurately representing his views. (**Note:** Delegates' views on these issues have been simplified but are historically accurate.)

Visual 8

Student Handout 8A

5 **Have students create nametags.** Tell students to make nametags that include the delegate's name in large letters, his state, and a simple visual that represents an aspect of the delegate's personal background and character. If you decide to have students wear masks, pass out *Student Handout 8B: Delegate Masks*. Have students cut out the masks and affix them using masking tape so they can breathe, see, and speak through them.

6 **Assume the role of George Washington.** Use a gavel or similar item to call the delegates to order, and explain that you will play the role of George Washington and facilitate the convention. Tell students they must raise their hands and be acknowledged by you before speaking.

7 **Have delegates greet one another.** Explain that the delegates generally greeted each other with formal phrases, such as, "I am heartily glad to see you, Mr. Madison" or "It is my pleasure to be in your company, Doctor Franklin." Tell students to refer to one another in this manner during the convention, and have them circulate through the room to greet delegates from other states. Encourage them to act out any personal characteristics of their assigned delegates.

8 **Have delegates take a vow of secrecy and "secure" the Assembly Room.** Tell students that some delegates have expressed concerns about being able to speak their minds freely at the convention. Have all students raise their right hands and repeat the following: *I promise not to divulge to the public what is discussed at this convention.* Explain that to ensure secrecy during the convention, you are posting a guard at the door and closing the windows. Have one student close the classroom door while another closes any windows or curtains.

9 **Have students read and complete the Reading Notes for Section 8.4.** Use the Guide to Reading Notes to review answers and check for understanding.

Phase 2: Debating at the Convention

1 **Understand the intent of the debate.** In this phase, students will debate how states should be represented in the new government. If they accurately portray their delegates' views, they will fail to reach a resolution. To ensure that students portray their delegates' views, they will be offered extra credit if the proposal they support is passed (as explained on the role cards). When the debate results in a deadlock, you will tell them they will lose 10 points if they cannot reach a compromise. As with the actual convention, when it comes time to compromise, some students will completely change their position on the issue in an effort to keep the convention from falling apart.

2 **Introduce the issue.** Explain to students that today the delegates are working to resolve this issue: *How should states be represented in the new government?* Project the top half of *Information Master 8B: Debating at the Convention* and review the three proposals for how states should be represented.

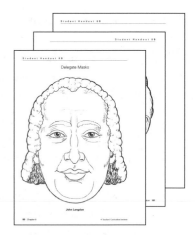

Student Handout 8B

Information Master 8B

3 **Have students read and complete the Reading Notes for Section 8.5.** Use the Guide to Reading Notes to check their answers.

4 **Have students read their role cards to learn about their delegates' views.** Tell students they will defend their delegates' views and try to convince other delegates to join their side during the Constitutional Convention.

5 **Prepare for the debate.** Tell students they will have five minutes to mingle with like-minded delegates and formulate arguments to defend their proposals. Point to one corner of the room and tell delegates who agree with Proposal A to meet there. Do the same for Proposals B and C. Students who agree with more than one proposal should choose one of those corners. As you circulate, quietly remind students of the extra credit points mentioned on their role cards. (**Note:** This step is analogous to the historical fact that delegates would often meet outside of the convention to ally themselves with other delegations and discuss strategies.)

6 **Have state delegations choose a proposal.** Tell students to return to their groups and decide which proposal their delegation will support during the debate. Explain that each state will have one vote. All delegates in a state must agree or the delegation will not be allowed to vote. Instruct groups to prepare arguments in support of their proposal. Tell students to consult the section "Points to Raise During the Convention" on their role cards for ideas.

7 **Conduct the debate.** Call the convention to order. Have delegates make a decision on how to resolve this issue by following these steps:

- Project Information Master 8B and review the steps for discussing how states are to be represented in the new government.

- Have delegates go through the procedure three times, once for each of Proposals A, B, and C.

- Once the convention is deadlocked, announce that the delegates must come up with a compromise or everyone will *lose* 10 points.

- Adjourn the convention. Give delegates a few minutes to brainstorm compromises. (**Note:** The card for Roger Sherman gives the information necessary for the Connecticut delegation to formulate the Great Compromise.)

- Reconvene the convention. Have students follow the procedures on Information Master 8B to attempt to reach a compromise.

8 **Have students read and complete the Reading Notes for Sections 8.6 to 8.10.** Use the Guide to Reading Notes to check their answers.

Phase 3: Signing the Constitution

1 **Announce that it is the last day of the convention.** Have students refer to their role cards to see if their delegates signed the Constitution. Explain that if their delegate did not sign, they must be prepared to share their delegate's reasoning (as given on the role cards). Have the student representing Benjamin Franklin give a speech, as described on his role card, encouraging delegates to sign the Constitution.

2 Have delegates sign the "Constitution." Tell delegates to come forward and trace over their signature on *Student Handout 8C: Facsimile of the Constitution*. If a delegate did not sign the Constitution, have him or her explain the reason to the class. Then have those delegates stand at the back of the room and pretend to watch the ceremony with scorn.

3 Debrief the experience. Ask,

- How did it feel to act as a delegate to the Constitutional Convention?
- What was the most challenging part of being a delegate to the Constitutional Convention? What was the most rewarding part?
- What issues did the delegates have to resolve? How did they resolve them?
- Why was it important for the delegates to compromise on certain issues?
- What compromises emerged from the Constitutional Convention?
- In what ways do you think your experience was different from that of the actual delegates? In what ways do you think your experience was similar?

4 Have students read and complete the Reading Notes for Sections 8.11 and 8.12. Use the Guide to Reading Notes to check their answers.

Student Handout 8B

Processing

Have students complete the Processing activity, in which they will create a poster to encourage Americans to ratify the U.S. Constitution.

Quicker Coverage

Conduct a Shorter Preview Instead of conducting the activity with the radio, have students write a response to this prompt: *You and a large group of friends are spending the afternoon together, but are not sure what to do. Some of you want to see a movie, others want to go to the mall, and others want to go to the park. To make this decision, each friend will cast a vote. The group is not sure how many votes should be required to make this choice. Should you (A) require that an option needs only to get the most votes, even if that's less than half? (B) require that an option get at least half of the votes? (C) require that an option get almost all of the votes? Explain why you think your way of making the decision is the best. Then explain why the other two are poor choices.*

Condense the Activity Consider eliminating the following parts of the Experiential Exercise.

Phase 1: Do not have students use the masks from Student Handout 8B.

Phase 1: Do not have students make nametags or circulate to introduce themselves.

Phase 2: Rather than having students mingle with like-minded delegates, simply have them refer to their role cards for cues on how to defend their positions.

> **Writing: Persuasive Compositions**
>
> Review the structure of a persuasive composition. Guide students to include a clear thesis statement in their introductions, reasoning and explanations to support their propositions in their first body paragraphs, and reasoning and explanations to support their counterarguments in their second and third body paragraphs.

Deeper Coverage

Debate Additional Issues Have delegates follow the procedure in Phase 2 to re-create the debates surrounding two additional issues. Below are the two issues, the four options for addressing each, and the delegates' positions on those issues.

Issue 2: How should slaves be counted?

Option A: Count slaves as property to be taxed like other property.

Option B: Count slaves as people to determine representation in Congress.

Option C: Count slaves as both people for representation in Congress and as property for taxation.

Option D: Do not count slaves as either people for representation or as property for taxation.

Delegates' Positions on Issue 2

- Count slaves for taxes: Dayton, Gerry, Gilman, Langdon, Lansing, Martin
- Count three-fifths of slaves for taxes: Brearley, Ellsworth, Paterson, Yates
- Count slaves for representation: Baldwin, Bedford, Dickinson, Few, Johnson, Pinckney, Read, Rutledge
- Count three-fifths of slaves for representation: Blount, Carroll, Madison, Mason, McHenry, Randolph, Williamson
- Count three-fifths of slaves for both representation and taxes: Gorham, Hamilton, Wilson
- Count slaves for both representation and taxes or for neither: King
- Do not count slaves for representation or taxes: Franklin, Morris, Sherman

Issue 3: How should the chief executive be elected?

Option A: Have the people directly elect the executive.

Option B: Have Congress appoint the executive.

Option C: Have the state legislatures or governors choose the executive.

Option D: Have the people or state legislatures choose electors who will elect the executive.

Delegates' Positions on Issue 3

- The people should elect the executive: Franklin, Bedford, Carroll, Morris, Wilson
- Congress should appoint the executive: Blount, Brearley, Dayton, Dickinson, Few, Gilman, Gorham, Langdon, Lansing, Madison, Mason, Paterson, Pickney, Randolph, Rutledge, Sherman, Yates
- State governors should choose the executive: Gerry
- Electors chosen by the people should choose the executive: Hamilton, King, Read
- Electors chosen by state legislatures should choose the executive: Ellsworth, Johnson, Martin, McHenry, Williamson
- Electors should choose the executive: Baldwin

Assessment

Mastering the Content

1. B	5. B	9. D	13. D
2. B	6. C	10. D	14. C
3. C	7. D	11. A	15. D
4. A	8. C	12. D	16. A

Applying Social Studies Skills

17. C

18. Virginia

19. Maryland; New York

Exploring the Essential Question

20. Answers should include all of the elements requested in the prompt.

Scoring Rubric	
Score	Description
3	Student completes all three parts of the task. Ideas are clearly stated, supported by details, and demonstrate command of standard English conventions.
2	Student responds to most or all parts of the task. Ideas may lack details or not be clearly stated.
1	Student responds to at least one part of the task. Ideas may contain factual or grammatical errors and may lack details.
0	Response does not match the task or is incorrect.

James Madison and the Long, Hot Summer of 1787

1   **Discuss how we learn about the events at important meetings today.** Ask the class how the public learns what takes place at congressional hearings or international conferences. Point out that we take for granted instant access to information via computers, telephones, and television.

2   **Discuss the importance of James Madison in our understanding of the Constitutional Convention.** Explain that without the laboriously written notes of this one man, we would know almost nothing about the debates, negotiations, and compromises that created the system of government that has shaped our nation for more than 200 years. Mention that even these notes were not published until 1840, after Madison's death and more than 50 years after the convention.

3   **Have students read the Chapter 8 Reading Further.** When they have finished, share with them the fact that the Constitutional Convention took place over a total of 88 days. Ask students to imagine what it would have been like to try to record everything the delegates said over 88 days.

4   **Have students complete the Chapter 8 Reading Further in their Interactive Student Notebooks.** Before students begin work on their newspaper articles, you might wish to have them look at the front pages of several newspapers. Have them note the format of the news articles, including headlines, bylines, and datelines. You may want to review the "who, where, what, why, when" structure of a news story.

5   **Invite students to share their articles with the class.** Ask students why they chose particular people to "interview," and have them compare their interpretations of the same people. As a special project, some students may wish to research and share with the class actual articles that appeared in newspapers in 1787.

English Language Learners

Eliminate the Role Cards Have students debate the issue from their own perspective rather than from the perspective of a delegate.

Learners Reading and Writing Below Grade Level

Have Delegates Work in Pairs Divide students into pairs and give each pair one role card. Tell pairs to take turns talking during the convention.

Learners with Special Education Needs

Create Cue Cards Have students create a set of cue cards with key points that they can use during the convention to prompt their memory or to read from directly.

Advanced Learners

Create Delegate Caricatures Tell students to conduct library or Internet research to learn more about their assigned delegates' background. Then have them draw and label caricatures of their delegates that include details about the delegates' backgrounds and reflect what the delegates believe about the issues debated at the convention.

Analyze Murals Have students find, in the library or on the Internet, images of the two Barry Faulkner murals that are displayed above the Charters of Freedom in the Rotunda of the National Archives Building in Washington, D.C. These murals depict the formal presentation of the Declaration of Independence to John Hancock and the presentation of the Constitution to George Washington. Have students analyze the murals and write an essay that addresses these questions:

- Which people in each mural did the artist emphasize? How did the artist do this? Why do you think the artist did this?

- Do you think the artist was present at these events? Why or why not?

- If you were creating murals to represent these events, what would you choose to include in your mural and why?

Enrichment Resources

Find out more about the Constitutional Convention by exploring the following Enrichment Resources for *History Alive! The United States Through Industrialism* at www.teachtci.com.

Enrichment Readings These in-depth readings encourage students to explore selected topics related to the chapter. You may also find readings that relate the chapter's content directly to your state's curriculum.

Internet Connections The recommended Web sites provide useful and engaging content that reinforces skills development and mastery of subjects within the chapter.

Literature Recommendations

The following books offer opportunities to extend the content in this chapter.

Shays' Rebellion and the Constitution in American History by Mary E. Hull (Berkeley Heights, NJ: Enslow Publishers, 2000)

Alexander Hamilton by Stuart A. Kallen (Edina, MN: Abdo and Daughters, 2000)

The Federalist Papers edited by Clinton Rossiter (New York: Signet Classic, 2003)

Section 8.2

1. The Land Ordinance of 1785 addressed the issue of how to divide the western lands acquired by the United States in the Treaty of Paris.

2. When the population reaches 60,000, a territory can apply for statehood. Slavery is banned.

Section 8.3

Possible causes:

- Congress didn't have enough gold or silver to mint coins, which caused a money shortage.

- Farmers had difficulty earning enough to pay their debts and taxes.

- Farmers were required to sell their land and livestock to pay their debts.

Possible effects:

- Many Americans saw these things as signs that the nation was falling apart.

- Congress called for a convention to revise the Articles of Confederation.

- People like Madison concluded that a nation made up of many groups needs a strong central government.

Section 8.4

1. *George Washington:* He presided over the convention and made sure the rules were enforced.

   James Madison: He was the best-prepared delegate and spoke numerous times. His influence was so great that he became known as the "Father of the Constitution." He also kept the best records.

2. Adams, Hancock, and Henry feared that a stronger national government would hurt the rights of the states.

3. Answers will vary. If the student agrees, the focus might be on keeping the public calm or being able to speak freely. If the student disagrees, the focus might be on being able to monitor the proceedings for fairness.

4. Possible answers:

   Delegates for stronger national government: Government should protect "life, liberty, and the pursuit of happiness." The government's powers come from the people. The best way to protect rights is with a republic.

   Delegates for stronger state governments: A strong national government could threaten individual liberty. The state governments are closer to the people's control and so should have more power than the national government.

   Shared beliefs: The national government should have more power so it can do its job of protecting the people's rights. Under the Articles of Confederation, which gives more power to states, the nation is falling apart.

Section 8.5

1. *Articles of Confederation:* The government's power to rule should come from the states.

   James Madison: The government's power to rule should come from the people.

2. Answers:

	Virginia Plan	New Jersey Plan
How many branches of government?	three	three
How was the legislature organized?	two houses: House of Representatives and Senate	one house
Which states did this plan favor? Why?	States with larger populations; they would have more representatives in both houses of Congress.	States with smaller populations; each state would get an equal number of votes in Congress.

Section 8.6

1. Roger Sherman

2. *House of Representatives:* The number of representatives from each state depends on population. This favors the people.

   Senate: Each state has two senators elected by the state's legislature. This favors the states.

Section 8.7

1. Possible answer:

   Delegate from the North: "You treat slaves as property. They should be counted only as property and not for representation."

   Delegate from the South: "Slaves should be counted the same way as every other person is counted."

2. Possible answer:

   Delegate from the North: "Many states have passed laws against slavery, and some Northerners are involved in activities to end slavery."

   Delegate from the South: "The South is not ready to abolish slavery. Our economy is too dependent upon it."

Section 8.8

1. Sketches will vary. Slaves were counted as three-fifths of a person when determining a state's population.

2. Congress could not tax exports to other countries. It could not interfere with the slave trade for 20 years. The fugitive slave clause required that escaped slaves had to be returned to their owners even if captured in a free state.

Section 8.9

1. Possible answer:

   One executive: A single executive can give clear, timely leadership.

   Three-member executive: Three executives can protect against one executive abusing his power.

2. Congress appoints the president. The people elect the president. A specially chosen group of electors from each state elects the president. Opinions about the best proposal will vary.

Section 8.10

1. Each state has as many electors as the number of representatives it sends to Congress.

2. Possible answers:

   - Originally, state legislatures chose the electors in the Electoral College. Today, the people choose their state's electors.

   - Originally, the candidate receiving the most votes became president, and the runner-up became vice-president. Today, the president and vice president run and are elected together.

   - Originally, voters knew little about candidates outside their own states. Today, instant communication has changed the amount of knowledge we can access about candidates.

Section 8.11

Possible answer:

Franklin: "Yes. Even though I don't like everything about this plan, it is as close to perfect as we will get."

Mason: "No. It gives too much power to the national government."

Gerry: "No. It does not protect the rights of the people."

Section 8.12

Possible answer:

In support of ratification: We need a strong central government that can unite our quarreling states. Under the Articles of Confederation, we had a weak central government and the nation was falling apart. This powerful government will not be able to take away the rights of the people as some fear it might. The powers are limited and divided among three branches of power. This is the only way to ensure the survival of our young country. We must give it strength!

Opposing ratification: The Constitution is a horrible plan for government. Congress will ruin our nation with taxes, just like Parliament tried to do two decades ago. The president will rule like a king, and the Supreme Court will swallow up the power of our state courts. Worst of all, this plan does not protect our individual liberties! The Constitution will do nothing but take power from our state governments and its people. It must not be ratified.

The Constitution: A More Perfect Union

How has the Constitution created "a more perfect Union"?

Overview

In a Social Studies Skill Builder, students explore the key features and guiding principles of the U.S. Constitution by assuming the role of law students taking a final exam on the Constitution.

Objectives

In the course of reading this chapter and participating in the classroom activity, students will

Social Studies

- identify the main features of the Constitution and describe the basic lawmaking process.

- analyze how the Constitution divides powers among various levels and branches and preserves individual rights.

- explain how the guiding principles of the Constitution have created "a more perfect Union" and resulted in a government that can adapt to changing times.

Language Arts

- create a composition that has a coherent thesis, supports that thesis, and achieves an effective balance between researched information and original ideas.

Social Studies Vocabulary

Key Content Terms popular sovereignty, legislative branch, executive branch, judicial branch, judicial review, checks and balances, interstate commerce, federalism, majority rule, interest group

Academic Vocabulary ingenious, domestic, diverse, discriminate, function

Materials

History Alive! The United States Through Industrialism

Interactive Student Notebooks

Lesson Masters

- Student Handout 9A (5 copies, cut into cards)
- Student Handout 9B (1 per student)
- Student Handout 9C (cut apart; 1 diploma per student)
- Information Master 9
- Vocabulary Development handout (1 per student, on colored paper)

30 envelopes

Activity	Suggested Time	Materials
Preview	10 minutes	• Interactive Student Notebooks
Vocabulary Development	30–40 minutes	• *History Alive! The United States Through Industrialism* • Interactive Student Notebooks • Vocabulary Development handout
Social Studies Skill Builder	75–100 minutes (1.5–2 regular periods) (0.75–1 block period)	• *History Alive! The United States Through Industrialism* • Interactive Student Notebooks • Student Handouts 9A–9C • Information Master 9 • 30 envelopes
Processing	20 minutes	• Interactive Student Notebooks
Assessment	40 minutes	• Chapter 9 Assessment

Preview

1 **Have students complete the Preview on a separate sheet of paper.** Students will analyze a quotation from James Madison about why governments are necessary.

2 **Have students share their responses in pairs or with the class.**

3 **Explain the connection between the Preview and Chapter 9.** Explain that James Madison believed that government was necessary because humans are imperfect and can be corrupted by power. In 1789, Madison and other leaders sought to create a constitution that protected citizens' rights and ensured that power was not concentrated in the hands of a few. In this chapter, students will examine the guiding principles of the Constitution and analyze how it has created "a more perfect Union."

Vocabulary Development

1 **Introduce the Key Content Terms.** Have students locate the Key Content Terms for the chapter in their Interactive Student Notebooks. These are important terms that will help them understand the main ideas of the chapter. Ask volunteers to identify any familiar terms and how they might be used in a sentence.

2 **Have students complete a Vocabulary Development handout.** Give each student a copy of the Vocabulary Development handout of your choice from the Reading Toolkit at the back of the Lesson Masters. These handouts provide extra practice and support, depending on your students' needs. Review the completed handout by asking volunteers to share one answer for each term.

Reading

1 **Introduce the Essential Question and have students read Section 9.1.** Have students identify the Essential Question: *How has the Constitution created "a more perfect Union"?* Then have them read Section 9.1 and propose some possible answers to the Essential Question.

2 **Have students read and complete the Reading Notes for Section 9.2.** Ask several volunteers to share their responses. Use Guide to Reading Notes 9 to check their answers.

3 **Have students complete the Reading Notes for Chapter 9.** Assign Sections 9.3 to 9.9 during the activity as indicated in the procedures for the Social Studies Skill Builder. Remind students to use the Key Content Terms where appropriate as they complete their Reading Notes.

Vocabulary Development: Word Origins

Explain that because the Roman Empire stretched into what is now Great Britain, many words in the English language have Latin roots or affixes. In particular, English gained many words and word parts related to law and government from Latin. Among these are the roots *jud*, meaning "law" or "right," and *leg*, also meaning "law." The prefix *inter-*, meaning "between," comes from Latin, too. The root *polis* or *polit*, meaning "citizen, city" or "state," however, come from Greek. Have students make connections between these meanings and the relevant vocabulary terms.

Social Studies Skill Builder

1 **Before class, prepare materials and the classroom.**

- Write each of these labels on 5 envelopes (to create 30 envelopes in all): "Legislative Branch (9.3)," "Executive Branch (9.4)," "Judicial Branch (9.5)," "Checks and Balances (9.6)," "Amendment Process (9.7)," "Federal System (9.8)."

- Cut apart five copies of *Student Handout 9A: Constitutional Exam Cards* and place each set of cards into the corresponding envelope. (**Note:** Consider laminating the cards for future use.)

- Designate six areas of the room, either around the perimeter of the room or around a large table, as stations for the six topics. At each area, place the five envelopes and a sign with the name of that topic.

2 **Introduce the activity.** Explain that students will assume the role of law students taking their final class on constitutional law. To pass the class and graduate from law school, they must pass a final exam in which they demonstrate their understanding of the Constitution.

3 **Divide students into pairs.** Give each student a copy of *Student Handout 9B: Constitutional Law Exam.*

4 **Review the procedures for the activity.** Project *Information Master 9: Taking the Constitutional Law Exam* and review the steps for taking the exam. Explain that after pairs complete Sections 9.3 to 9.5, they will follow the same procedures for Sections 9.6 to 9.8.

5 **Conduct the Constitutional Law Exam for Sections 9.3 to 9.5.** Assign each pair one of Sections 9.3, 9.4, or 9.5 to begin with. Then have pairs follow the steps on Information Master 9. When a pair answers all the questions in an envelope, use the Guide to Student Handout 9B in this Lesson Guide to check their answers.

6 **Conduct the Constitutional Law Exam for Sections 9.6 to 9.8.** Tell pairs that they will follow the same steps for Sections 9.6 to 9.8, and assign each pair one of these sections to begin with. When a pair answers all the questions in an envelope, use Guide to Student Handout 9B to check their answers.

7 **Hold a graduation ceremony.** Tell students they have all passed the Constitutional Law Exam and will now graduate from law school. Give a brief speech in which you tell them that as future lawyers, they are charged with upholding the principles of the Constitution. Then hold a mock graduation ceremony by distributing diplomas cut from *Student Handout 9C: Law School Diplomas.*

8 **Debrief the activity.** Ask, *How has the Constitution created "a more perfect Union"?*

9 **Have students read and complete the Reading Notes for Section 9.9.** Have several volunteers share their responses.

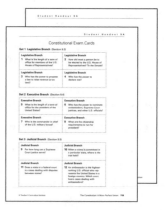

Student Handout 9A

Student Handout 9B

Information Master 9

Law School Diplomas

Student Handout 9C

Processing

Have students complete the Processing activity on a separate sheet of paper. They will write a letter to James Madison describing how the Constitution has created "a more perfect Union." Consider having them share their letters in pairs or with the class.

Quicker Coverage

Condense the Law Exam Use only Sections 9.3 to 9.5 and the corresponding three sets of Constitutional Exam Cards. Alternatively, eliminate two of the cards in each set.

Eliminate the Graduation Ceremony Simply tell students that they passed the law exam and are now lawyers.

Deeper Coverage

Expand the Law Exam After they complete all of the Constitutional Exam Cards, provide pairs with some or all of the following constitutional dilemmas. Have them answer each dilemma in a complete sentence and record the related article and section from the Constitution.

Dilemma 1: Your neighbor was born and raised in France. She moved to the United States five years ago. She would like to hold one of these offices: president, senator, or member of the House of Representatives. Can she? Why or why not? *(No. A representative must have been a citizen for seven years. A senator must have been a citizen for nine years. The president must be a natural-born citizen. Article I, Section 2; Article I Section 3, Article II, Section 1)*

Dilemma 2: The Senate's 100 members cannot agree on a law that forces all fast-food restaurants to sell veggie burgers only. They are split right down the middle: 50 in favor and 50 against. Is it possible to break the tie? If so, how? *(Yes. The vice president can vote to break the tie. Article I, Section 3)*

Dilemma 3: The Senate and House of Representatives have passed a bill requiring all teenagers to shave their heads. Can this law be stopped from taking effect? If so, who can stop it? *(Yes. The president can veto the law. If Congress overrides the veto with a two-thirds vote, the Supreme Court can declare the new law unconstitutional. Article III, Section 2)*

Dilemma 4: It has been revealed that the president has been stealing from the U.S. Treasury. What action should be taken against him? *(The president should be impeached for "high crimes and misdemeanors." Article II, Section 4)*

Dilemma 5: Your client wants to become the U.S. president in 2016. She is 34, and her birthday is on January 16. Can she serve? *(Yes, she can serve, unless you are doing this activity after the year 2016. Article II, Section 1)*

Dilemma 6: A certain senator is tired of living in Washington, D.C. He wants to move back to his home state and run his ranch full-time. He proposes that Congress not meet at all this year. Is his proposal constitutional? Why or why not? *(No. Congress must meet at least once a year. Article I, Section 4)*

Assessment

Mastering the Content

1. A	5. A	9. B	13. B
2. B	6. C	10. D	14. C
3. A	7. C	11. A	15. A
4. A	8. B	12. A	16. B

Applying Social Studies Skills

17. The president can veto bills passed by Congress. Other correct answers are also acceptable, such as that the president may recommend legislation, call special sessions of Congress, or approve bills.

18. The Supreme Court can reject laws and treaties that are unconstitutional.

19. Congress may override the president's veto. Other correct answers are also acceptable, such as that Congress approves presidential appointments or may impeach the president.

Exploring the Essential Question

20. Answers should include all of the elements requested in the prompt.

Scoring Rubric	
Score	Description
3	Student completes both parts of the task. Ideas are clearly stated, supported by details, and demonstrate command of standard English conventions.
2	Student responds to most or all parts of the task. Ideas may lack details or not be clearly stated.
1	Student responds to at least one part of the task. Ideas may contain factual or grammatical errors and may lack details.
0	Response does not match the task or is incorrect.

Who Are "We the People"?

1 **Discuss the meaning of the phrase "We the People."** Write the words "We the people" on the board and ask,

- What does this phrase mean?

- Who are "the people" of the United States?

- What is the significance of having these words at the beginning of the Constitution?

- What does this phrase say about who was creating this system of government?

- Were *all* of the people of the United States included in "We the People"?

2 **Have students read the Chapter 9 Reading Further.** After they have read the first two pages, ask them to reconsider who the framers meant by "We the People." Mention that the United States did not give African Americans and women the right to vote until 1870 and 1920, respectively, and ask, *In what way does the power to vote include someone in "We the People"?*

You may want to mention that the permanent exhibit on the U.S. Constitution at the National Constitution Center in Philadelphia is titled "The Story of We the People." You might encourage students to find out more about the National Constitution Center and its mission at www.constitutioncenter.org.

3 **Have students complete the first page of the Chapter 9 Reading Further in their Interactive Student Notebooks.** Point out that although Abigail Adams warned that women could ignore men's authority, this was easier said than done. It would be almost 150 years before women got the vote.

4 **Have students complete the reading and the second page of the Reading Further.** Remind students to write their letters to the editor as if they lived at the time of Abigail Adams. Their theses should reflect what someone might have thought at the time; for example, "Women can do everything men can do and should have all the same rights." Also, their examples must be chronologically appropriate. You might suggest, for example, that Queen Elizabeth I had ruled England successfully long before the colonies declared their independence.

5 **Have students share their letters to the editor.** Have them compare their theses as well as their examples. You may wish to tell students that they will return to these letters when the class studies the women's rights movement later in the year.

English Language Learners

Condense the Preview In place of the Madison quotation, discuss how students' lives might be different without government. Then have students write a response to this question: *Do you think a country needs a government? Why or why not?*

Provide a Template for the Processing Give students a template, such as the one below, to help them write their letters.

Dear Mr. Madison,

You should be proud that the Constitution you helped write has created "a more perfect Union" within the United States. The structure and principles of the Constitution continue to govern our country smoothly.

For instance, the principle of checks and balances makes sure that . . .

An example of how checks and balances works is . . .

The principle of majority rule makes sure that . . .

An example of majority rule is . . .

Because of your work and the work of the other framers, our government remains strong and effective. Thank you for the time and thought you put into this important document.

Sincerely,

Learners Reading and Writing Below Grade Level

Examine Fewer Cards Require students to complete all of the Reading Notes for the chapter, but have them examine only two or three sets of Constitutional Exam Cards.

Modify the Processing In place of the letter to James Madison, have students write a paragraph in response to this question: *Why do you think the Constitution works?* Require them to include two of the Key Content Terms in their letters and to use two examples to support their position.

Learners with Special Education Needs

Support the Activity Give students the article number for each of the questions from the Constitutional Exam Cards. For some of the more challenging questions, consider giving them both the article and section numbers.

Advanced Learners

Use Only the Constitution Have students use only the Constitution, not the Student Edition or the Reading Notes, to answer the questions on the cards.

Write to a Local Official In place of the Processing activity, have students write a letter to a local official about an issue in their community. The letters should have an introduction, a paragraph with background information about the issue, at least one paragraph with a detailed proposal about what the local government should do about the issue, and a conclusion. Review and comment on students' letters. Then have students revise and send their letters.

Enrichment Resources

Find out more about the Constitution by exploring the following Enrichment Resources for *History Alive! The United States Through Industrialism* at www.teachtci.com.

Enrichment Readings These in-depth readings encourage students to explore selected topics related to the chapter. You may also find readings that relate the chapter's content directly to your state's curriculum.

Internet Connections The recommended Web sites provide useful and engaging content that reinforces skills development and mastery of subjects within the chapter.

Literature Recommendations

The following books offer opportunities to extend the content in this chapter.

A Brilliant Solution: Inventing the American Constitution by Carol Berkin (New York: Harcourt, 2003)

The Words We Live By: Your Annotated Guide to the Constitution by Linda R. Monk (New York: Hyperion, 2004)

A More Perfect Constitution: 23 Proposals to Revitalize Our Constitution and Make America a Fairer Country by Larry J. Sabato (New York: Walker Publishing, 2007)

The answers to the questions on Student Handout 9B appear below. Use them to check student responses to the Constitutional Law Exam.

Set 1: Legislative Branch (Section 9.3)

1. Members of the House of Representatives serve two-year terms. (Article I, Section 2)

2. A person must be 25 to be elected to the House and 30 to be elected to the Senate. (Article I, Sections 2 and 3)

3. The House of Representatives has the power to propose a tax law. (Article I, Section 7)

4. Congress has the power to declare war. (Article I, Section 8)

Set 2: Executive Branch (Section 9.4)

5. The president serves a four-year term. (Article II, Section 1)

6. The president nominates ambassadors, Supreme Court justices, and other U.S. officials. (Article II, Section 2)

7. The president is the commander in chief of the U.S. military forces. (Article II, Section 2)

8. A person running for president must be a natural-born citizen. (Article II, Section 1)

Set 3: Judicial Branch (Section 9.5)

9. Supreme Court justices can serve for life. (Article III, Section 1)

10. Trials are held in the state where the crimes were committed. (Article III, Section 2)

11. Federal courts try cases involving disputes between states. (Article III, Section 2)

12. The Supreme Court hears cases dealing with ambassadors. (Article III, Section 2)

Set 4: Checks and Balances (Section 9.6)

13. Congress can override the veto with a two-thirds vote in each house. (Article I, Section 7)

14. The Senate must approve the president's appointments for ambassadors, judges, and other U.S. officials. (Article II, Section 2)

15. The Senate must approve a treaty made with a foreign country. (Article II, Section 2)

16. The judicial branch has the power to decide whether laws are constitutional. (Article III, Section 2)

Set 5: Amendment Process (Section 9.7)

17. Congress or state legislatures have the power to propose amendments to the Constitution. (Article V)

18. Three-fourths of state legislatures (or three-fourths of special state conventions) approve an amendment. (Article V)

19. The Twenty-second Amendment sets the term limit for the presidency. (Twenty-second Amendment)

20. The Twenty-sixth Amendment gives 18-year-olds the right to vote. (Twenty-sixth Amendment)

Set 6: Federal System (Section 9.8)

21. The Constitution is the supreme law of the land. (Article VI)

22. The full faith and credit clause requires states to accept other states' laws and decisions. (Article IV, Section 1)

23. Congress has the power to regulate interstate commerce. (Article I, Section 8)

24. Congress has the power to print and coin money. (Article 2, Section 8)

Section 9.2

Possible answers:

- "form a more perfect Union": cooperation among the states and a strong relationship between the states and the national government
- "establish Justice": rule by laws, not by the military or a king
- "insure domestic Tranquility": keeping peace and maintaining order within the country
- "provide for the common defence": protecting the nation against foreign enemies
- "promote the general Welfare": supporting an economy and a society in which people can prosper
- "secure the Blessings of Liberty": protecting freedoms gained in the American Revolution and preserving them for future Americans

Sections 9.3 to 9.5

The completed matrix is below. Illustrations of the branches of government will vary.

	9.3 Legislative Branch		9.4 Executive Branch	9.5 Judicial Branch
	Congress		Office of the President	Supreme Court
	House	Senate		
Number of Members	435	100	1	9
Length of Term	2 years	6 years	4 years	life
Are members elected or appointed?	elected	elected	elected	appointed
Age Requirement	25	30	35	none
Citizenship Requirement	7 years	9 years	natural-born citizen	none
Two or More Powers of This Branch of Government	• to decide how to spend tax money • to raise an army and navy • to declare war • to pay government debts • to grant citizenship		• to serve as commander in chief of the military forces • to make treaties • to nominate ambassadors and Supreme Court justices • to grant pardons	• to rule on cases involving a state or an ambassador from another country • to decide whether laws and actions by the other two branches conflict with the Constitution • to protect the "supreme Law of the Land"

Section 9.6

1. The framers developed a system of checks and balances because they wanted to limit the government's power to ensure that one branch did not dominate the others.

2. See diagram at right.

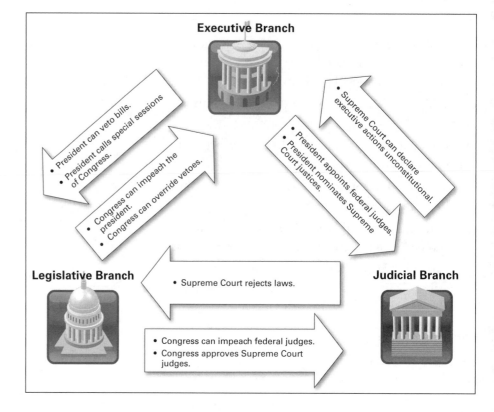

Executive Branch

- President can veto bills.
- President calls special sessions of Congress.

- Congress can impeach the president.
- Congress can override vetoes.

- Supreme Court can declare executive actions unconstitutional.

- President appoints federal judges.
- President nominates Supreme Court justices.

Legislative Branch

- Supreme Court rejects laws.

- Congress can impeach federal judges.
- Congress approves Supreme Court judges.

Judicial Branch

Section 9.7

1. The framers made sure the Constitution could be amended so that it could be responsive to changing times. They made the amendment process difficult, however, so that changes would not be made hastily and without the consent of a large majority of citizens.

2. Flowcharts will vary. An amendment can be proposed by a two-thirds vote of each house of Congress or by a national convention called by Congress at the request of two-thirds of the state legislatures. An amendment can be ratified by at least three-fourths of the state legislatures or by special conventions in at least three-fourths of the states.

Section 9.8

1. The framers wanted a strong national government. At the same time, they wanted the states to have significant powers.

2. The commerce clause gives the national government the power to regulate interstate commerce.

3. With a common market, goods and resources could flow more easily across the country, and large businesses could cross state lines. The common market also helped to create a single national economy.

Section 9.9

1. The principle of majority rule is based on the idea that government actions reflect the popular will. Laws are passed in Congress by majority vote and elections are decided by a majority of voters.

2. Illustrations will vary. Possible answers: People can join political parties or interest groups, vote, and express their interests and concerns to their elected officials.

The Bill of Rights

What rights and freedoms does the Bill of Rights protect and why are they important?

Overview

In a Response Group activity, students learn about the important rights and freedoms protected by the Bill of Rights by analyzing a series of scenarios to determine whether the Bill of Rights protects certain actions taken by citizens.

Objectives

In the course of reading this chapter and participating in the classroom activity, students will

Social Studies

- compare their own desire for rights and the founders' work to add a bill of rights to the Constitution.
- identify key rights and freedoms protected by the Bill of Rights and explain why those freedoms are important in their own lives.
- research news articles that show the functions of a free press in a democracy.
- debate landmark Supreme Court cases to determine whether the rights and freedoms protected by the Bill of Rights relate to the issues involved.

Language Arts

- write a personal narrative that reveals the significance of the events conveyed, employs narrative strategies such as dialogue and specific action, and relates events using well-chosen and interesting details.

Social Studies Vocabulary

Key Content Terms Bill of Rights, warrant, double jeopardy, self-incrimination, due process, defendant

Academic Vocabulary controversial, guarantee, deprive, compensation

Materials

History Alive! The United States Through Industrialism

Interactive Student Notebooks

Visuals 10A–10F

Lesson Masters

- Vocabulary Development handout (1 per student, on colored paper)

Activity	Suggested Time	Materials
Preview	10 minutes	• *History Alive! The United States Through Industrialism* • Interactive Student Notebooks
Vocabulary Development	30–40 minutes	• *History Alive! The United States Through Industrialism* • Interactive Student Notebooks • Vocabulary Development handout
Response Group	50–100 minutes (1–2 regular periods) (0.5–1 block period)	• *History Alive! The United States Through Industrialism* • Interactive Student Notebooks • Visuals 10A–10F
Processing	30 minutes	• Interactive Student Notebooks
Assessment	40 minutes	• Chapter 10 Assessment

Preview

1   **Have students complete the Preview on a separate sheet of paper.** Have students turn to the Preview. Read, or have a volunteer read, the Parents' Constitution aloud. Then have them complete the Preview. (**Note:** This document was adapted from a Parents' Bill of Rights created by parents from the New Haven Unified School District in Union City, California.)

2   **Have students share their responses in pairs or with the class.** Focus the class discussion particularly on Question 3 about parallels between how students feel about the Parents' Constitution and concerns some people felt about the U.S. Constitution when it was first ratified in 1789.

3   **Explain the connection between the Preview and Chapter 9.** Remind students that they found things they would like to change in the Parents' Constitution and identified additional rights they think children should have. Similarly, many Americans in the late 1700s identified important rights and freedoms for individuals that were not protected in the U.S. Constitution. These Americans were determined to make changes, or amendments, to the Constitution to make sure these rights and freedoms were protected. This list of ten amendments is known as the Bill of Rights.

> **Reading Comprehension: Public Documents**
>
> Have students use information in the Parents' Constitution to identify the problems that the parents believed they, their children, or the schools faced and how they sought to solve those problems.

Vocabulary Development

1   **Introduce the Key Content Terms.** Have students locate the Key Content Terms for the chapter in their Interactive Student Notebooks. These are important terms that will help them understand the main ideas of the chapter. Ask volunteers to identify any familiar terms and how they might be used in a sentence.

2   **Have students complete a Vocabulary Development handout.** Give each student a copy of the Vocabulary Development handout of your choice from the Reading Toolkit at the back of the Lesson Masters. These handouts provide extra practice and support, depending on your students' needs. Review the completed handout by asking volunteers to share one answer for each term.

Reading

1 **Introduce the Essential Question and have students read Section 10.1.**
Have students identify the Essential Question: *What rights and freedoms does the Bill of Rights protect and why are they important?* Then have them read Section 10.1. Afterward, ask,

- In Massachusetts, why did opponents object to the Constitution?
- How were supporters of the Constitution able to get it ratified in Massachusetts?
- What rights or freedoms do you think are included in the Bill of Rights?
- Why do you think these rights and freedoms are important?

2 **Have students complete the Reading Notes for Chapter 10.** Have students read and complete the Reading Notes for Section 10.2. Assign Sections 10.3 to 10.6 during the activity as indicated in the procedures for the Response Group. Remind students to use the Key Content Terms where appropriate as they complete their Reading Notes.

Response Group

1 **Introduce the activity.** Explain to students that they will now play a game called *Do They Have the Right?* in which they will read a series of Supreme Court cases related to rights and freedoms protected by the Bill of Rights. For each case, they need to determine whether they think the person or people have that right and justify their position using information from the book and their Reading Notes. They will discuss and debate their ideas with one another before finding out what really happened.

2 **Place students in groups of three.**

3 **Have students read and complete the Reading Notes for Section 10.3.**
Consider reviewing the answers as a class.

4 **Play Round 1 of *Do They Have the Right?*** Project *Visual 10A: Do They Have the Right? First Amendment.* Reveal and follow the steps one at a time. Then project *Visual 10B: Do They Have the Right? First Amendment* and follow the same process. Afterward, ask the class,

- What rights or freedoms does the First Amendment protect?
- Why are these rights and freedoms important to you?

5 **Have students read and complete the Reading Notes for Section 10.4.**
Consider reviewing the answers as a class.

Visuals 10A and 10B

6 **Play Round 2 of** *Do They Have the Right?* Project *Visual 10C: Do They Have the Right? Fourth Amendment.* Reveal and follow the steps one at a time. Then project *Visual 10D: Do They Have the Right? Fourth Amendment* and follow the same process. Afterward, ask the class,

- What rights or freedoms do the Second, Third, and Fourth Amendments protect?
- Why are these rights and freedoms important to you?

7 **Have students read and complete the Reading Notes for Section 10.5.** Consider reviewing the answers as a class.

8 **Play Round 3 of** *Do They Have the Right?* Project *Visual 10E: Do They Have the Right? Sixth Amendment.* Reveal and follow the steps one at a time. Then project *Visual 10F: Do They Have the Right? Fifth and Sixth Amendments* and follow the same process. Afterward, ask the class,

- What rights or freedoms do the Fifth, Sixth, Seventh, and Eighth Amendments protect?
- Why are these rights and freedoms important to you?

9 **Have students read and complete the Reading Notes for Section 10.6.** Consider reviewing the answers as a class.

Processing

Have students complete the Processing activity on a separate sheet of paper. They will select one of the ten amendments in the Bill of Rights that they think has the greatest impact on daily life and write a short story describing what a day in their life might be like without the rights and freedoms that particular amendment protects.

Quicker Coverage

Conduct Just One Round Conduct just a single round of *Do They Have the Right?* using Visuals 10A and 10B. Skip Rounds 2 and 3 (Visuals 10C–10F).

Discuss Just One Case For each round of *Do They Have the Right?* select just one of the two cases to discuss and debate.

Visuals 10C and 10D

Visuals 10E and 10F

Deeper Coverage

Add More Cases Select additional current or controversial cases related to the Bill of Rights for students to discuss during the activity. Follow the format of Visuals 10A–10F to write a short, hypothetical description of the case, followed by a brief description of how the Supreme Court decided the case. The site www.oyez.org is an excellent resource, or you might use one of the three landmark cases described below.

Round 1: First Amendment

- *Case:* Students write an article for their public school newspaper. The principal removes the article without informing the student editors, because, in her opinion, the content of the article is too controversial.

- *Issue:* Do students have the right to print what they think is appropriate in the school newspaper, without censorship from the principal?

- *Outcome:* In the 1988 case of *Hazelwood School District v. Kuhlmeier,* the Supreme Court voted 5–3 against the students. The Court held that the principal did not violate the First Amendment by exercising editorial control over the content of the student newspaper as long as those actions were "reasonably related to legitimate pedagogical concerns."

Round 2: Fourth Amendment

- *Case:* A police officer observes someone acting "suspiciously" in front of a store. The officer suspects the person may be planning a robbery. He stops the person, searches him, and finds he is carrying a weapon.

- *Issue:* Does a citizen have the right to not be searched if a police officer does not have a search warrant?

- *Outcome:* In the 1967 case *Terry v. Ohio,* the Supreme Court held 8–1 that the search undertaken by the police officer was reasonable under the Fourth Amendment. The Court found that "a reasonably prudent man would have been warranted in believing [Terry] was armed and thus presented a threat to the officer's safety while he was investigating his suspicious behavior."

Round 3: Eighth Amendment

- *Case:* A 17-year-old is found guilty of first-degree murder and sentenced to death. His lawyers appeal the death sentence, arguing that because their defendant is not legally an adult, the death sentence constitutes "cruel and unusual punishment."

- *Issue:* Does this convicted criminal have the right to not receive a death sentence?

- *Outcome:* In the 2004 case of *Roper v. Simmons,* the Supreme Court voted 5–4 in favor of Simmons, the convicted murderer. The Court held that standards of decency have evolved so that executing minors is "cruel and unusual punishment" prohibited by the Eighth Amendment. The majority cited a consensus against the juvenile death penalty among state legislatures and overwhelming international opinion against the juvenile death penalty.

Assessment

Mastering the Content

1. A	5. A	9. B	13. B
2. B	6. C	10. D	14. A
3. B	7. A	11. D	15. A
4. B	8. C	12. A	16. A

Applying Social Studies Skills

17. C

18. It is not factual, because even people found guilty of a crime have rights that protect them from unjust punishments and excessive fines.

19. Answers should include the phrase "you are protected from a search of your property without a search warrant."

Exploring the Essential Question

20. Answers should include all of the elements requested in the prompt.

Scoring Rubric	
Score	Description
3	Student completes all three parts of the task. Ideas are clearly stated, supported by details, and demonstrate command of standard English conventions.
2	Student responds to most or all parts of the task. Ideas may lack details or not be clearly stated.
1	Student responds to at least one part of the task. Ideas may contain factual or grammatical errors and may lack details.
0	Response does not match the task or is incorrect.

What Is Religious Freedom?

1 **Discuss First Amendment rights with the class.** Point out that the first ten amendments to the Constitution all give Americans rights, but that the rights we often first think of when someone says "the Bill of Rights" are the five freedoms of the First Amendment. Ask students to name those five freedoms. Have a student read the text of the First Amendment, and then ask,

- Which right is listed first?

- What does this tell you about the importance that the framers of the Bill of Rights placed on religious freedom?

2 **Have students read the Chapter 10 Reading Further up to the subhead "Religious Liberty in the Colonies."** When they have finished reading, ask them,

- What were the issues in the Santa Fe story?

- How did Marian Ward feel about public prayer on school grounds?

- What was Amanda Bruce's position on this issue?

You may wish to point out that two courts are named in the description: a federal court that declared public prayer on school grounds against the First Amendment (that is, unconstitutional) and, later, the Supreme Court, which ruled the same way. Be sure students understand that the process of challenging something on constitutional grounds involves bringing legal action in federal courts. If a lower court decision is appealed, it may go to the Supreme Court.

3 **Have students finish the reading.**

4 **Discuss the origins of the Bill of Rights.** Talk with the class about the fact that the rights protected in the Bill of Rights had their roots in the ideas and experiences of men like Thomas Jefferson and James Madison. The work of Jefferson and Madison on the Statute of Religious Freedom reflects this.

5 **Have students complete the Chapter 10 Reading Further in their Interactive Student Notebooks.** After students have "deconstructed" the sentence from the statute, discuss the differences in wording between this statement and the clause on religious freedom in the First Amendment. Have students read this and other amendments in the Bill of Rights. Ask, *Which is clearer and easier for the average citizen to understand: the statute or the Bill of Rights?*

6 **Have students share their statutes.** You may wish to take a class vote on the statutes and discuss whether to present those that receive the most votes to the school's student government.

English Language Learners

Annotate the Cases Provide a copy of each case with important facts highlighted and vocabulary words annotated; for example:

Case 1: The United States is involved in a controversial (debatable) war. To show their opposition to the war, two students wear black armbands to their public school, even though the school has a policy (rule) against wearing them. School officials say the policy against armbands is to avoid arguments or fights between students who support the war and those who oppose the war.

Learners Reading and Writing Below Grade Level

Brainstorm Arguments as a Class After reading each case, clarify any challenging vocabulary. As a class, brainstorm arguments in favor of the person in the case having the right or freedom and arguments against. Note the arguments on a transparency or the board. Then have students discuss in their groups which side—for or against—is most strongly supported by the cited amendment(s).

Learners with Special Education Needs

Provide an Alternative Processing Have students choose the amendment in the Bill of Rights that they think is most important or has the greatest impact on their daily life. Then have them list at least two ways their daily life would be different without that amendment. Or, have them create a drawing or cartoon showing how their daily lives would be different without that amendment.

Advanced Learners

Write a New Amendment Have students propose their own amendments to the Constitution. Their proposed amendments should protect important rights or freedoms they think people should have. Then have students write one or two paragraphs explaining why their proposed amendment is important, including supporting evidence. If students need ideas, they can conduct an Internet search on proposed amendments to the Constitution.

Enrichment Resources

Find out more about Bill of Rights and the freedoms and rights protected by it by exploring the following Enrichment Resources for *History Alive! The United States Through Industrialism* at www.teachtci.com.

Enrichment Readings These in-depth readings encourage students to explore selected topics related to the chapter. You may also find readings that relate the chapter's content directly to your state's curriculum.

Internet Connections The recommended Web sites provide useful and engaging content that reinforces skills development and mastery of subjects within the chapter.

Literature Recommendations

The following books offer opportunities to extend the content in this chapter.

The Bill of Rights: Creation and Reconstruction by Akhil Reed Amar (New Haven, CT: Yale University Press, 2000)

In Defense of Liberty: The Story of America's Bill of Rights by Russell Freedman (New York: Holiday House, 2003)

The Bill of Rights: A History in Documents by John J. Patrick (New York: Oxford University Press, 2003)

Section 10.2

1. The Bill of Rights contains the first ten amendments to the U.S. Constitution.

2. James Madison took the lead in making sure the Bill of Rights was eventually included in the Constitution.

Section 10.3

1. The five basic freedoms protected by the First Amendment are freedom of religion, speech, the press, and assembly, and the right to petition the government. Explanations of why a selected freedom is important to students will vary.

2. Drawings should indicate that Jefferson supported a separation between religion (church) and government (state).

3. Opinions and explanations will vary.

4. News articles and explanations of the role they represent will vary.

5. Possible example of symbolic speech: burning an American flag. Opinions and explanations will vary.

Section 10.4

1. The Second Amendment protects the right of citizens to bear arms. The Third Amendment prohibits the government from housing troops in citizen's homes.

2. Opinions will vary. Students should support their opinions.

3. Police show a judge that they have a good reason for the search. → If the judge agrees, he or she issues a warrant saying who or what can be searched. → Police present the warrant and conduct the search.

Section 10.5

1. The Fifth Amendment guarantees the right to a grand jury, protects citizens from double jeopardy, prohibits self-incrimination, guarantees due process of law, and prohibits the government from taking private property without fair compensation. Explanations of why students think one of these rights is important will vary.

2. Possible answers: The right to a speedy and public trial, the right to be judged by an impartial jury, the right to hear charges, the right to hear and question witnesses at a trial, and the right to an attorney. Symbols and opinions will vary.

3. Political cartoons will vary.

Section 10.6

1. According to the Ninth Amendment, rights not specially listed in the Constitution belong to the people or the states.

2. Possible answer: One example of a reserved power that affects daily life is the power states have to set speed limits.

Forming a New Nation

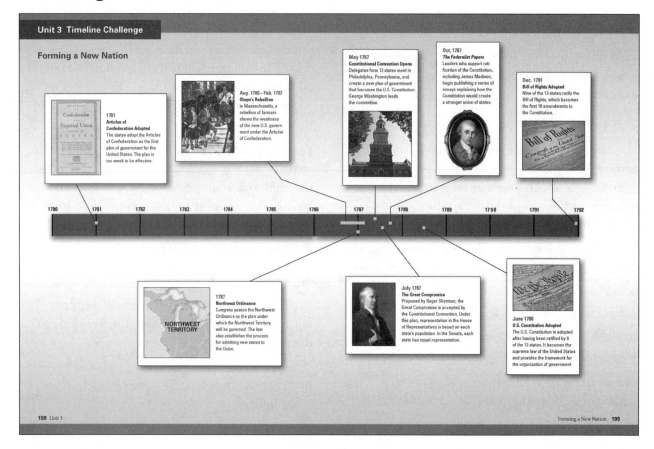

Overview

This Timeline Challenge helps students review the main events and ideas of this unit while providing practice in reading and interpreting timelines. You can vary and expand the activity according to students' needs and the amount of time available.

Basic Procedure

1 **Introduce the timeline in the Student Edition.** Direct students to the Forming a New Nation timeline at the end of Unit 3 in the Student Edition. You may wish to have students read aloud and discuss the timeline entries.

2 **Introduce the Timeline Challenge in the Interactive Student Notebook.** Direct students to the Unit 3 Timeline Challenge in their notebooks. Point out the two types of questions, "Timeline Skills" and "Critical Thinking," and model how to answer each type.

3 **Have students complete the Timeline Challenge.** Monitor students as they work. Use the Guide to Unit 3 Timeline Challenge to check their answers. You may wish to project a transparency of this page as you work through the questions with the class and conduct a discussion of the "Critical Thinking" questions.

4 **Complete the KWL chart.** Return to the KWL chart created at the beginning of the unit, and ask students to list the key information they have learned.

Classroom Timeline

1 **Prepare the Timeline Challenge Cards.** Copy and cut the cards from *Student Handout TC3: Unit 3 Timeline Challenge Cards.* You may wish to laminate the cards for future use.

2 **Create a timeline on a classroom wall.** On an empty wall or a large bulletin board, make a timeline with masking tape or colored paper. Mark off the time intervals in advance, or ask students to do so in class.

3 **Have students place the Timeline Challenge Cards.** Distribute cards to individual students or pairs and have them tape the cards to the timeline in the correct locations. Call on students to provide more information on the timeline topics to review main events and issues.

Student Handout TC3

Internet Research

1 **Review students' suggestions for additional timeline entries.** Have students share their answers to the last question of the Timeline Challenge.

2 **Have students conduct Internet research.** Ask students to choose and research one of their suggested events.

3 **Have students create additional Timeline Challenge Cards.** Direct students to research an appropriate image for their cards and then use the computer to create an illustrated card, complete with timeline entry.

Timeline Skills

Score 1 point for each correct answer.

1. the Articles of Confederation

2. The Northwest Ordinance was the plan under which the Northwest Territory would be governed.

3. George Washington was selected to preside over the Constitutional Convention.

4. Madison, Hamilton, and Jay were the authors of *The Federalist Papers*.

5. 3 years

6. The principle of freedom of speech most closely relates to the Bill of Rights.

Critical Thinking

Score 1 to 3 points for each answer, depending on the thoroughness of the response.

7. The weakness of the central government under the Articles of Confederation led to a money shortage. Farmers found it very hard to pay their debts and taxes, and judges in Massachusetts began to order them to sell their farms. Daniel Shays and his followers used force to close down the courthouses. Under the Articles, there was no national army that could be sent to put down the rebellion.

8. Possible answer: In the Three-Fifths Compromise, representatives from Southern and Northern states agreed that for taxation and representation purposes, each slave would be counted as three-fifths of a person.

9. *The Federalist Papers* had a direct influence on the ratification of the U.S. Constitution, because the essays addressed the fears that many Americans had that a stronger central government would threaten their freedom or take away their rights.

10. Answers will vary. Students must explain why the events they chose merit inclusion.

Using Scores to Inform Instruction

Timeline Skills A score of 4 out of 6 indicates that students understand most of the key events of this unit.

Critical Thinking A score of 8 out of 12 indicates that students are able to think critically about most of the key issues of this unit.

If students score below these levels, consider reviewing timeline and critical thinking skills.

Launching the New Republic

Geography Challenge

**Chapter 11: Political Developments
in the Early Republic**
*How did the Federalist and Republican visions
for the United States differ?*
Experiential Exercise

Chapter 12: Foreign Affairs in the Young Nation
*To what extent should the United States have become
involved in world affairs in the early 1800s?*
Response Group

Chapter 13: A Growing Sense of Nationhood
What did it mean to be an American in the early 1800s?
Writing for Understanding

**Chapter 14: Andrew Jackson and the
Growth of American Democracy**
*How well did President Andrew Jackson promote
democracy?*
Visual Discovery

Timeline Challenge

Launching the New Republic

Overview

This activity introduces geographic information essential to Unit 4. Students read and interpret a map to learn about key events in the growth and change of the republic from 1789 to 1838. They annotate a map showing growth of the United States during this period and answer questions in their Interactive Student Notebooks, and then discuss critical thinking questions. Students' comprehension of content and proficiency in map-reading and higher-order thinking skills will help you gauge their readiness for the unit. The pages that follow include a completed map, answers to questions, a scoring guide to inform your teaching, and suggestions for modifications to meet specific student needs.

Essential Geographic Understandings

1. Names and locations of the states added to the nation from 1791 to 1838

2. Location of landmark events in the nation's development from 1789 to 1838

3. Key human features: Baltimore, New York City, New Orleans, Washington, D.C., Erie Canal, Trail of Tears

4. How events during the republic's first 50 years promoted the nation's growth and strengthened Americans' sense of national identity

Procedures

1   **Introduce the unit.** Tell students that they will learn about developments in the United States that changed the nation during its early years. They will also learn how early involvements in foreign affairs affected Americans and the nation.

2   **Create a KWL chart.** Ask students to identify what they know about the United States in the late 1700s and early 1800s and what they want to learn. Use their responses to gauge how much additional background information they will need as you progress through the unit. Students will return to the KWL chart at the end of the unit and add the key information they have learned.

3   **Have students read Unit 4 "Setting the Stage" in the Student Edition.**

4   **Have students complete the Geography Challenge.** Monitor students as they answer the questions and complete the map. You may want to have them work in pairs. Use the guide on the next two pages to check their answers. You may wish to project the map from the Interactive Student Notebook and have students annotate it as the class works through the map-reading questions. Make sure students have grasped Essential Geographic Understandings 1 to 3.

5   **Discuss the "Critical Thinking" questions.** Help students understand the geographic relationships described in Essential Geographic Understanding 4.

The United States, 1838

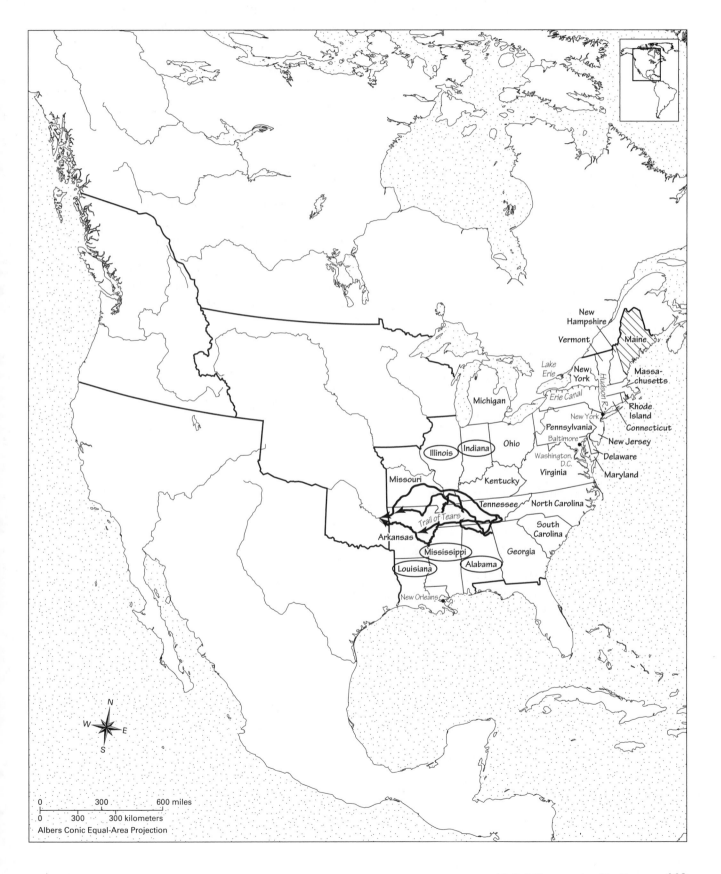

New Hampshire
Vermont
Maine
Lake Erie
New York
Massa- chusetts
Erie Canal
Hudson R.
Michigan
Rhode Island
New York
Connecticut
Pennsylvania
New Jersey
Baltimore
Ohio
Delaware
Washington, D.C.
Illinois
Indiana
Maryland
Missouri
Virginia
Kentucky
Tennessee
North Carolina
Trail of Tears
South Carolina
Arkansas
Mississippi
Georgia
Louisiana
Alabama
New Orleans

0   300   600 miles
0   300   300 kilometers
Albers Conic Equal-Area Projection

Geography Skills

Score 1 point for each correct answer. Use the map on the previous page to check shading and labeling.

1. There were 13 new states added from 1791 to 1838, for a total of 26.

2. Five new states—Louisiana, Indiana, Mississippi, Illinois, and Alabama—were admitted during the 1810s, the most of any decade.

3. Maine was the only state added to the Union in the early 1800s that is not west of the Appalachians.

4. New York City was the nation's capital when Washington became president.

5. These two cities were among the places attacked by the British in the War of 1812. The United States had a problem with Great Britain.

6. The Erie Canal connected Lake Erie and the Hudson River.

7. Tennessee is the home state of Andrew Jackson.

8. The Cherokee were forcibly moved west along the Trail of Tears. It began around northwestern Georgia and ended west of Arkansas.

Critical Thinking

Questions may have more than one correct answer. Score 1 to 3 points for each reasonable answer, depending on the strength of students' geographic reasoning. Possible answers are given here.

9. Possible answer: An event like the War of 1812, with the threats to the homeland that it presented, might serve to unite Americans and increase their sense of patriotism.

10. Jackson was the nation's first president not from an eastern state. His election might not have succeeded without the support of a growing population in the West.

11. Answers and opinions will vary. The Cherokee were removed to free up the land for white settlers.

Using Scores to Inform Instruction

Geography Skills A score of 6 out of 8 or better indicates that students have acquired sufficient geographic information to proceed with the unit.

Critical Thinking A score of 6 out of 9 or better indicates that students are beginning to understand the relationships between physical geography and the different ways in which people live.

Modifying Instruction

ELL or Learners with Special Education Needs Consider focusing on map-reading questions or limiting the number of "Critical Thinking" questions.

Students with Weak Map or Critical Thinking Skills Assign appropriate pages from the Social Studies Skills Toolkit in the back of the Lesson Masters.

Political Developments in the Early Republic

How did the Federalist and Republican visions for the United States differ?

Overview

In an Experiential Exercise, students compare Federalist and Republican visions for the United States by taking on the roles of Alexander Hamilton and Thomas Jefferson to debate the main issues that divided the two groups.

Objectives

In the course of reading this chapter and participating in the classroom activity, students will

Social Studies

- represent the key positions of Federalists and Republicans in a debate, taking on the roles of Alexander Hamilton and Thomas Jefferson.

- analyze Washington's attitude toward the role of the federal government in the Whiskey Rebellion and in his Farewell Address.

- identify the positions of Federalists and Republicans in the election of 1800.

Language Arts

- deliver oral presentations that include important ideas, concepts, and direct quotations and that paraphrase and summarize the relevant perspectives on the topic.

- participate in a dialogue.

Social Studies Vocabulary

Key Content Terms Whiskey Rebellion, Washington's Farewell Address, loose construction, strict construction, sedition, nullify, states' rights theory

Academic Vocabulary reluctant, finance, accumulate, eloquent, resolution

Materials

History Alive! The United States Through Industrialism

Interactive Student Notebooks

CD Tracks 1–4

Lesson Masters

- Information Masters 11A and 11B (1 transparency of each)
- Student Handout 11 (1 for every 2 students)
- Vocabulary Development handout (1 per student, on colored paper)

Activity	Suggested Time	Materials
Preview	15 minutes	• Interactive Student Notebooks • CD Tracks 1 and 2 • Information Master 11A
Vocabulary Development	30–40 minutes	• *History Alive! The United States Through Industrialism* • Interactive Student Notebooks • Vocabulary Development handout
Experiential Exercise	50–75 minutes (1–1.5 regular periods) (0.5–0.75 block period)	• *History Alive! The United States Through Industrialism* • Interactive Student Notebooks • Information Master 11B • Student Handout 11
Processing	20 minutes	• Interactive Student Notebooks • CD Tracks 3 and 4
Assessment	40 minutes	• Chapter 11 Assessment

Preview

1 **Introduce "Hail, Columbia."** Tell students that the song "Hail, Columbia" was first performed at George Washington's inauguration. The song reflects the optimism of the period and Americans' hope that the country and government would remain unified. The song soon became known as the "President's March" and was used to introduce the president at formal events. It is played today to introduce the vice president.

2 **Analyze "Hail, Columbia."** Project *Information Master 11A: Preview Songs* and reveal the lyrics to the first song. Play CD Track 1, "Hail, Columbia," and instruct students to follow along with the lyrics as they listen. Then ask,

- What are three adjectives that describe the song's mood?

- How do you think Washington's swearing in as president united the country?

3 **Have students answer the corresponding Preview questions on a separate sheet of paper.**

4 **Analyze "Fair and Free Elections."** Tell students they will now listen to a campaign song from the 1800 presidential election. Explain that this song was sung by members of the Republican Party, one of the nation's first political parties. Project the lyrics to this song on Information Master 11A and play CD Track 2, "Fair and Free Elections." Then ask,

- What are three adjectives that describe the song's mood?

- According to the lyrics, what were some of the issues of the 1800 presidential election?

- In what ways do you think the nation changed between Washington's inauguration in 1789 and the election of 1800?

5 **Have students answer the remaining Preview questions.**

6 **Explain the connection between the Preview and Chapter 11.** Explain that, as shown by the two songs, the nation changed greatly in its first decade. U.S. cities were more interconnected and the nation faced new foreign threats. One of the most notable changes was the emergence of the first political parties, the Republicans and the Federalists. In this chapter, students will learn about the different visions for the United States held by Republicans and Federalists.

Information Master 11A

Vocabulary Development

1 **Introduce the Key Content Terms.** Have students locate the Key Content Terms for the chapter in their Interactive Student Notebooks. These are important terms that will help them understand the main ideas of the chapter. Ask volunteers to identify any familiar terms and how they might be used in a sentence.

2 **Have students complete a Vocabulary Development handout.** Give each student a copy of the Vocabulary Development handout of your choice from the Reading Toolkit at the back of the Lesson Masters. These handouts provide extra practice and support, depending on your students' needs. Review the completed handout by asking volunteers to share one answer for each term.

Reading

1 **Introduce the Essential Question and have students read Section 11.1.** Have students identify the Essential Question: *How did the Federalist and Republican visions for the United States differ?* Then have them read Section 11.1 and carefully analyze the painting that opens the chapter. Afterward, ask,

  • Why might George Washington have been reluctant to become president?

  • Why did George Washington choose Alexander Hamilton and Thomas Jefferson to serve in his cabinet?

  • Why do you think Hamilton and Jefferson became political rivals?

2 **Have students complete the Reading Notes for Sections 11.2 and 11.3.** Have several volunteers share their responses. Use Guide to Reading Notes 11 to check their answers.

3 **Have students complete the remaining Reading Notes for Chapter 11.** Assign Sections 11.4 to 11.8 during the activity as indicated in the procedures for the Experiential Exercise. Remind students to use the Key Content Terms where appropriate as they complete their Reading Notes.

Experiential Exercise

1 **Set up the classroom.**

  • Arrange the desks in two rows so that pairs of desks directly face each other.

  • Write these slogans on the board:
    Federalists: "Born to rule, we know what we need! With a strong central government, we will succeed!"
    Republicans: "We know what we need from day to day! Don't try to rule us from far away!"

2 **Place students in pairs and have them sit across from one another.**

3 **Assign roles and introduce the activity.** Assign one row of students the role of Alexander Hamilton and the other row the role of Thomas Jefferson. Explain to pairs that they will represent Hamilton and Jefferson in a talk-it-out debate on key issues that divided Federalists and Republicans.

4 **Have students read and complete the Reading Notes for Sections 11.4 and 11.5.** Use the Guide to Reading Notes to review the answers as a class.

5 **Distribute materials.** Distribute *Student Handout 11: Hamilton and Jefferson Masks* to each pair. Have students cut out the masks and cut holes in the eyes and mouth so that they can easily see, speak, and breathe.

6 **Conduct the talk-it-out debate.**

   • Tell pairs that they will debate four issues from the perspective of their assigned character. Encourage students to use their Reading Notes from Sections 11.4 and 11.5 to assist them.

   • Instruct students to put on their masks. Have students representing Hamilton stand up and recite the Federalist slogan together. Then have those representing Jefferson stand up and recite the Republican slogan together.

   • Project *Information Master 11B: Talk-It-Out Prompts* and reveal Issue 1 and the corresponding prompts. Have students representing the first speaker, Hamilton in this case, read their prompt with you aloud. Then have students representing Jefferson read their prompt with you aloud. Tell pairs to continue the debate, discussing the issue for one to two minutes.

   • Reveal the next issue, and repeat the procedure until pairs have debated all four issues.

7 **Debrief the activity.** Ask,

   • How did it feel to represent Alexander Hamilton? Thomas Jefferson?

   • What was the Federalists' vision for the nation? What was the Republicans' vision for the nation?

   • If you were living in 1800, do you think you would have been a Federalist or a Republican? Why?

8 **Have students read and complete the Reading Notes for Sections 11.6 to 11.8.** Use the Guide to Reading Notes to review the answers as a class.

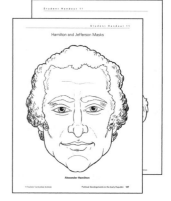

Student Handout 11

Information Master 11B

Processing

Have students complete the Processing activity, in which they will write a campaign song for the 1800 presidential election. Tell students that if they use the tune of "Hail, Columbia" or "Fair and Free Elections," they can use the instrumental versions of these songs on CD Tracks 3 and 4. Consider having volunteers perform their songs for the class.

Quicker Coverage

Shorten the Debate Reduce the time required for the talk-it-out debate by eliminating one or more of the prompts.

Deeper Coverage

Add Prompts for Sections 11.6 and 11.7 Use these issues and the corresponding prompts to continue the talk-it-out debate after students read Sections 11.6 and 11.7.

- **Section 11.6, Issue 5: Alien and Sedition Acts**

  Hamilton: "The Alien and Sedition Acts are needed to protect the country!"

  Jefferson: "Mr. Hamilton, the real purpose of the acts is to . . ."

- **Section 11.7, Issue 6: Election of 1800**

  Jefferson: "Americans should elect me as their next president! I promise to run a simple government."

  Hamilton: "We don't need a simple government, Mr. Jefferson. What we need is . . ."

Expand the Processing To expand the Processing activity, place students in groups and have them create and present a one-minute campaign commercial for one of the candidates in the 1800 presidential election. In addition to using the campaign song from the current Processing requirements, require that groups include a slogan and props in their presentations. Consider allowing groups to videotape their presentations and show them during class.

Host a Political Conference Create eight groups. Assign four groups the role of Federalists and four groups the role of Republicans. Tell groups that they will attend a political conference where party leaders Alexander Hamilton and Thomas Jefferson will debate four issues. Assign one group of Federalists and one group of Republicans to create each of the following:

- a political banner that includes a slogan and an illustration of the party's leader

- a political song that describes the party's beliefs and the qualities of the party's leader

- a keynote speech that outlines the party's main ideas. Have one person be prepared to give the speech.

- debate points for each of these issues: view of human nature, best form of government, ideal economy, relations with Britain and France. Have one person be prepared to take on the role of Hamilton or Jefferson in the debate.

When groups are ready, welcome students to the political conference. Have groups display their banners, chant their slogans, and perform their songs. Then have speakers deliver the keynote speeches. Finally, project Information Master 11B and have "Hamilton" and "Jefferson" use the prompts to debate the four issues.

> ### Writing: Writing Strategies
>
> For deeper coverage, you might also have students write a focused essay, with a formal introduction and conclusion, in which they create a controlling impression of either Hamilton or Jefferson and support that impression with evidence, comparison and contrast, and similar devices. Be sure students also revise their writing for word choice, organization, point of view, and transitions.

Assessment

Mastering the Content

1. D	5. D	9. C	13. C
2. C	6. C	10. A	14. A
3. A	7. D	11. B	15. A
4. C	8. A	12. B	16. C

Applying Social Studies Skills

17. Possible answer: Jefferson hoped to unite the nation by pointing out what people of both parties have in common.

18. Answers should mention the election of 1800.

19. D

Exploring the Essential Question

20. *Republican:* Farmer, supports the French Revolution. *Federalist:* Believes the wealthy should rule; believes in a strong national government. Descriptions should include all of the elements requested in the prompt.

Scoring Rubric

Score	Description
3	Student completes all three parts of the task. Ideas are clearly stated, supported by details, and demonstrate command of standard English conventions.
2	Student responds to most or all parts of the task. Ideas may lack details or not be clearly stated.
1	Student responds to at least one part of the task. Ideas may contain factual or grammatical errors and may lack details.
0	Response does not match the task or is incorrect.

The President's House

1 **Discuss the symbols of the presidency.** Ask students to name things that symbolize the U.S. presidency. The White House will likely be among the first things named.

2 **Have students read the Chapter 11 Reading Further.** If possible, obtain a DVD of Part 6, "Unnecessary War," of the 2008 HBO miniseries *John Adams*. Show the class the memorable scenes of the Adamses' 1800 arrival at the White House and their first days in the chilly, unfinished house.

3 **Have students complete the Chapter 11 Reading Further in their Interactive Student Notebooks.** Point out that for both George Washington and Thomas Jefferson, the design of the president's house reflected its symbolic importance, just as it does for Americans today.

4 **Have students share their house designs.** Give students an opportunity to present their "contest entries." You may even wish to hold a class contest, with outside judges reviewing the entries.

5 **Invite interested students to create a "virtual tour" of the White House.** As an optional project, students can research specific rooms in the White House and create virtual tours based on the extensive resources available on the Internet. Have them explore the Internet Connections for Chapter 11 available through the Enrichment Resources for *History Alive! The United States Through Industrialism*.

English Language Learners

Provide Definitions for the Preview Songs Before playing the songs, provide students with the definitions below. As they listen to the songs, have students jot down any additional unfamiliar words. Afterward, define the words and play the songs once more.

"Hail, Columbia"

Columbia: another name for the United States of America

band: a group of people

valor: the qualities of a hero

rallying: to come together

immortal: something that never dies

patriot: someone who is loyal to his or her country

foe: enemy

impious: without respect

toil: hard work

"Fair and Free Elections"

reflection: your image in a mirror

ballot box: box where votes are placed in an election

thwart: threaten

schemes: plans

traitor disaffections: a person who is unhappy about the conditions in a country

fierce complexions: mean faces

undaunted: not discouraged

forsakes: abandons

Learners Reading and Writing Below Grade Level

Support the Reading and the Processing Give students photocopies of the chapter, and have them highlight information relating to the Federalists in one color and information relating to the Republicans in a second color. Students can refer to the highlighted portions as they complete the Reading Notes and the Processing activity.

Learners with Special Education Needs

Give Students Talk-It-Out Prompts The day before the activity, assign students a role and give them a copy of Information Master 11B. Instruct students to prepare possible responses to each set of prompts on an index card, and allow them to use the cards during the debate.

Advanced Learners

Write a Dialogue In place of the Processing activity, have students write a dialogue that might have occurred between Alexander Hamilton and Thomas Jefferson. The dialogue should revolve around this question: *What is your vision for the nation?* Require students to highlight four differences between Federalists and Republicans and to incorporate all of the Key Content Terms in their dialogue. In addition, require them to include two quotations from both Hamilton and Jefferson (from the chapter or from other sources).

Enrichment Resources

Find out more about the political developments in the early republic by exploring the following Enrichment Resources for *History Alive! The United States Through Industrialism* at www.teachtci.com.

Enrichment Readings These in-depth readings encourage students to explore selected topics related to the chapter. You may also find readings that relate the chapter's content directly to your state's curriculum.

Internet Connections The recommended Web sites provide useful and engaging content that reinforces skills development and mastery of subjects within the chapter.

Literature Recommendations

The following books offer opportunities to extend the content in this chapter.

Alexander Hamilton: America's Bold Lion by John M. Rosenburg (Breckenridge, CO: Twenty-first Century Books, 2000)

Democracy in America by Alexis de Tocqueville (New York: Signet Classic, 2001)

Thomas Jefferson: Philosopher and President by Nancy Whitelaw (Greensboro, NC: Morgan Reynolds, Inc., 2001)

Section 11.2

1. Some members of Congress were eager to build a strong national government while others wanted to limit the power of the new government.

2. *Department of State:* To handle relations with other countries, headed by Thomas Jefferson.

   Treasury Department: To oversee the nation's finances, headed by Alexander Hamilton.

   Department of War: Headed by Henry Knox.

   Symbols will vary.

Section 11.3

1. Answers will vary.

2. In Washington's Farewell Address, the threat of the "spirit of party" referred to the passionate loyalty of Americans to political parties. Washington worried that fighting between parties could tear the nation apart.

Sections 11.4 and 11.5

Possible answers:

1. *Hamilton:* I believe that most people are basically selfish and out for themselves. A government that gives too much power to the common people cannot be trusted.

   Jefferson: Informed citizens can make good decisions for themselves and the country. I have faith in peoples' goodness and wisdom.

2. *Hamilton:* Wealthy, educated, public-spirited men should lead the country.

   Jefferson: Farmers and planters like myself should lead the country.

3. *Hamilton:* We should have a strong national government that unites the states and keeps order among the people.

   Jefferson: The national government should be small, with limited powers.

4. *Hamilton:* The ideal economy is based on business, manufacturing, and trade.

   Jefferson: The ideal economy is based on agriculture.

5. *Hamilton:* Yes. I believe the creation of a national bank is constitutional. I believe in the loose construction of the Constitution. The elastic clause allows Congress to make any necessary laws, such as the establishment of a bank.

   Jefferson: No. The Constitution says nothing about a national bank and therefore Congress cannot create one. I believe in the strict construction of the Constitution. It means what it says and nothing more.

6. *Hamilton:* In the war between France and Great Britain, the United States should side with Great Britain. We should respect Britain's ability to keep order and to defend itself.

   Jefferson: We should support France despite the bloodshed caused by the French Revolution. The bloodshed was necessary to pay for freedom.

Section 11.6

Possible reasons for nullification: The Alien and Sedition Acts were an attack on the rights of free speech and free press. The acts were an attack on Republicans. Congress went beyond the Constitution by passing the acts. According to the states' right theory, the federal government was using its powers improperly.

Section 11.7

Slogans will vary.

Section 11.8

1. The Twelfth Amendment was added to the Constitution to prevent ties in presidential races.

2. The amendment prevents a tie by establishing separate ballots for president and vice president.

CHAPTER

12

Foreign Affairs in the Young Nation

To what extent should the United States have become involved in world affairs in the early 1800s?

Overview

In a Response Group activity, students assume the roles of foreign policy advisers to early presidents to evaluate the extent to which the country should have become involved in world affairs.

Objectives

In the course of reading this chapter and participating in the classroom activity, students will

Social Studies

- propose solutions to early U.S. foreign policy challenges, then compare with real decisions and evaluate them.
- identify major events of the War of 1812 and sequence on a timeline.
- explain the intent of the Monroe Doctrine.

Language Arts

- deliver persuasive presentations that make clear and knowledgeable judgments.
- support arguments with detailed evidence, examples, and reasoning.
- anticipate and answer listener concerns and counterarguments effectively.

Social Studies Vocabulary

Key Content Terms neutrality, isolationism, embargo, blockade, Monroe Doctrine

Academic Vocabulary signify, pursue, cease, liberate

Materials

History Alive! The United States Through Industrialism

Interactive Student Notebooks

Visuals 12A–12E

Lesson Masters

- Vocabulary Development handout (1 per student, on colored paper)

Activity	Suggested Time	Materials
Preview	20 minutes	• Interactive Student Notebooks • Visual 12A
Vocabulary Development	30–40 minutes	• *History Alive! The United States Through Industrialism* • Interactive Student Notebooks • Vocabulary Development handout
Response Group	100–150 minutes (2–3 class periods) (1–1.5 block periods)	• *History Alive! The United States Through Industrialism* • Interactive Student Notebooks • Visuals 12B–12E
Processing	20 minutes	• Interactive Student Notebooks
Assessment	40 minutes	• Chapter 12 Assessment

Preview

1 **Project *Visual 12A: Preview* and have students examine the map.**

2 **Have students answer the Preview questions on another sheet of paper.** Have them share their responses in pairs or with the class.

3 **Explain the connection between the Preview and Chapter 12.** The geographic location of the United States played a significant role in the development of the nation's early foreign policy. In this chapter, students will examine how the United States responded to early foreign policy challenges and assess the extent to which the nation should have become involved in world affairs.

Visual 12A

Vocabulary Development

1 **Introduce the Key Content Terms.** Have students locate the Key Content Terms for the chapter in their Interactive Student Notebooks. These are important terms that will help them understand the main ideas of the chapter. Ask volunteers to identify any familiar terms and how they might be used in a sentence.

2 **Have students complete a Vocabulary Development handout.** Give each student a copy of the Vocabulary Development handout of your choice from the Reading Toolkit at the back of the Lesson Masters. These handouts provide extra practice and support, depending on your students' needs. Review the completed handout by asking volunteers to share one answer for each term.

Reading

1 **Introduce the Essential Question and have students read Section 12.1.** Have students identify the Essential Question: *Should the United States have become involved in world affairs in the early 1800s?* Then have them read Section 12.1. Afterward, have them use information from the reading to propose some possible answers to the Essential Question.

2 **Have students complete the Reading Notes for Section 12.2.** Have several volunteers share their responses. Use Guide to Reading Notes 12 to check their answers.

3 **Have students complete the remaining Reading Notes for Chapter 12.** Assign Sections 12.3 to 12.10 during the activity as indicated in the procedures for the Response Group activity. Remind students to use the Key Content Terms where appropriate as they complete their Reading Notes.

Response Group

1 **Place students in groups of three and introduce the activity.** Tell students they will be assuming the roles of foreign policy advisers to the president. They will make recommendations on how to respond to four foreign policy dilemmas faced by the United States from the 1790s to the 1820s.

2 **Have students read and complete the Reading Notes for Section 12.3.** Use Guide to Reading Notes 12 to review the answers as a class.

3 **Have groups prepare their recommendations.** Tell students that they are now foreign policy advisers to President John Adams. Project *Visual 12B: President Adams's Foreign Policy Dilemma* and review the dilemma and foreign policy options. Instruct groups to prepare arguments in support of one option and arguments in opposition to the other options. Then tell groups to choose and prepare a spokesperson to present their group's recommendation to the president. (**Note:** If it looks like the majority of groups are supporting just one or two options, you may want to assign the remaining options to particular groups to represent.)

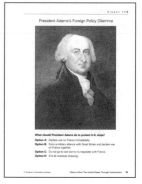

Visual 12B

4 **Facilitate a foreign policy meeting.** You will assume the role of President Adams for the meeting.

- Begin the meeting by saying, "Esteemed advisers, thank you for meeting with me. I am interested in hearing your recommendations about how I should respond to this foreign policy dilemma. We will discuss each option in turn, starting with Option A."

- Call on all spokespersons who support Option A to stand and defend their positions. After they have all presented, call on other advisers to share their arguments in opposition to the option. Repeat for Options B, C, and D.

- When most ideas have been shared, end the meeting by saying, "Thank you, advisers. I will take your recommendations into account as I make my decision."

5 **Have students read and complete the Reading Notes for Section 12.4.** Use the Guide to Reading Notes to review the answers.

6 **Repeat Steps 2 to 6 for the remaining three dilemmas.** Have groups rotate the role of spokesperson for each dilemma.

- *Dilemma 2:* Use Sections 12.5 and 12.6 and *Visual 12C: President Jefferson's Foreign Policy Dilemma.*

- *Dilemma 3:* Use Section 12.7 and 12.8 and *Visual 12D: President Madison's Foreign Policy Dilemma.*

- *Dilemma 4:* Use Sections 12.9 and 12.10 and *Visual 12E: President Monroe's Foreign Policy Dilemma.*

7 **Debrief the activity.** Ask students, *To what extent should the United States have become involved in world affairs in the early 1800s?*

Visuals 12C–12E

Processing

Have students complete the Processing activity, in which they will create tombstones reflecting on the foreign policy decisions of the first five U.S. presidents. Consider having students share their tombstones with the class.

Quicker Coverage

Shorten the Activity Reduce the time required for the Response Group activity by eliminating debate of one or more of the dilemmas.

Deeper Coverage

Debate an Additional Dilemma Prior to having students read Section 12.2, have them debate how President Washington should respond to the war between France and Great Britain in 1793. Give students a brief background of the situation. Then have them prepare their recommendations and facilitate a foreign policy meeting to debate the following dilemma and options:

Dilemma: How should President Washington deal with the war between Great Britain and France?

Option A: Honor the U.S. alliance with France and go to war against Great Britain.

Option B: Do not go to war against Great Britain but assist France by providing the nation with war supplies.

Option C: Support Great Britain in the war by providing the nation with war supplies.

Option D: Do nothing to aid either Great Britain or France.

Dramatize the Dilemmas After students have read Section 12.3, form groups of six students and have them create one-minute minidramas about the dilemma. Require groups to have at least six characters in their dramas and to include simple props. Then choose several groups to perform their minidramas. Repeat for Sections 12.5, 12.7, and 12.9.

Assessment

Mastering the Content

1. B	5. D	9. B	13. D
2. A	6. A	10. B	14. D
3. D	7. D	11. C	15. D
4. C	8. D	12. A	16. A

Applying Social Studies Skills

17. The olive branch represents peace; the arrows represent war.

18. The United States was formed from 13 separate colonies that united as one country.

19. The seal is used to mark the U.S. government approval of documents or to indicate that a document is an official U.S. government document.

Exploring the Essential Question

20. Answers should include all of the elements requested in the prompt.

Scoring Rubric

Score	Description
3	Student completes all five parts of the task. Ideas are clearly stated, supported by details, and demonstrate command of standard English conventions.
2	Student responds to most or all parts of the task. Ideas may lack details or not be clearly stated.
1	Student responds to at least one part of the task. Ideas may contain factual or grammatical errors and may lack details.
0	Response does not match the task or is incorrect.

Tecumseh, the Shooting Star

1 **Have students read the Chapter 12 Reading Further.** To review the patterns of white settlement since 1609, you may wish to have them look at a map of the continental United States. Have a student point out the extent of white settlement in the early 1600s (the coastline of Virginia and Massachusetts), and discuss the fact that 200 years later, white settlers were pushing toward the Mississippi.

2 **Discuss the Northwest Territory.** Have students locate the Northwest Territory on a map, such as the map in Section 8.2 of the Student Edition. Remind students that this land was made part of the British colonial holdings after the French and Indian War. It had become the Northwest Territory under the Articles of Confederation, when it was opened up to settlement. People in the United States believed it was their land to settle—legally.

3 **Have students complete the Chapter 12 Reading Further in their Interactive Student Notebooks.** If possible, play a recording of "This Land Is Your Land" for the class, and discuss the meaning of Guthrie's lyrics. Ask,

- What did Woody Guthrie have to say about sharing the land that we call the United States?

- How is this the same as or different from Tecumseh's concept of land ownership?

4 **Invite students to share their point-of-view statements.**

English Language Learners

Create Cue Cards During the Response Group activity, have students create cue cards like the one below to use when they are the spokespersons for their groups. On their cue cards, have students outline key points to bring up during the debate.

> Our group believes that Option X is the best option for the president to pursue. We feel this way because . . .
>
> Others may disagree with us because . . .
>
> Despite these other opinions, we believe this option is the best for our country because . . .

Learners Reading and Writing Below Grade Level

Modify the Reading Notes In place of the Reading Notes for Sections 12.3 to 12.10, have students create and complete a graphic organizer like the following for each pair of sections (Sections 12.3 and 12.4; 12.5 and 12.6; 12.7 and 12.8; and 12.9 and 12.10).

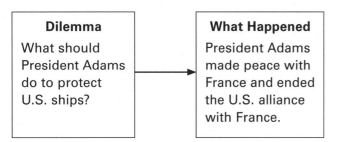

Dilemma	What Happened
What should President Adams do to protect U.S. ships?	President Adams made peace with France and ended the U.S. alliance with France.

Introduce the Foreign Policy Spectrum Prior to having students complete the Reading Notes for Section 12.4, introduce physical movements that reflect the ideas of isolationism (hands held up in a "stop" gesture) and total involvement (hands beckoning as if to draw someone closer).

Learners with Special Education Needs

Reduce the Options for Each Dilemma Provide only two or three foreign policy options for each dilemma on Visuals 12B to 12E. Make sure to retain the option that was actually pursued (Visual 12B: Option C; Visual 12C: Option C; Visual 12D: Option A; Visual 12E: Option D).

Advanced Learners

Write a Eulogy Expand the Processing activity by having students write a eulogy for one of the presidents discussed in the chapter. The eulogy should include

- basic historical facts about the president's personal background.
- a response to this question: *To what extent should the president have been involved in world affairs?*
- at least one direct quotation from the president.

Enrichment Resources

Find out more about foreign affairs in the early United States by exploring the following Enrichment Resources for *History Alive! The United States Through Industrialism* at www.teachtci.com.

Enrichment Readings These in-depth readings encourage students to explore selected topics related to the chapter. You may also find readings that relate the chapter's content directly to your state's curriculum.

Internet Connections The recommended Web sites provide useful and engaging content that reinforces skills development and mastery of subjects within the chapter.

Literature Recommendations

The following books offer opportunities to extend the content in this chapter.

Crossing the Panther's Path by Elizabeth Alder (New York: Farrar, Straus, and Giroux, 2002)

James Monroe: American Statesman by Brent P. Kelley (New York: Chelsea House, 2000)

The War of 1812 by Don Nardo (Farmington Hills, MI: Gale Group, 2000)

Section 12.2

1. Foreign threats to the United States in 1789: The British refused to abandon the Ohio Valley. The United States was still allied with France, which was at war with Great Britain.

2. This means we will stay out of the affairs of other nations and avoid forming alliances.

Section 12.3

1. In the Jay Treaty, the British agreed to pull their troops from the Ohio Valley. The French viewed the Jay Treaty as a violation of its own treaty with the United States and began to attack U.S. ships.

2. Drawings will vary. Congress recruited an army, built new ships for the navy, and authorized warships and privateers to launch a "half war" on the seas.

Section 12.4

1. President Adams sent a peace mission to France. French leader Napoleon made peace with the United States and ended France's alliance with the United States. Students' opinions of whether Adams pursued the best option will vary.

2. Answers will vary. Students should adequately justify their placement.

Section 12.5

1. Great Britain impressed U.S. sailors to serve in the British navy. They claimed the men were British deserters.

2. Drawings will vary. Jefferson had to decide whether to pay tribute to the ruler of Tripoli or to go to war with the Barbary States.

Section 12.6

1. Jefferson sent warships to the Mediterranean to protect U.S. shipping. Tripoli and the United States eventually signed a peace treaty. Jefferson negotiated with both Great Britain and France. When that failed, he imposed an embargo on all nations trading with the United States.

2. Answers will vary. Students should adequately justify their placement.

Section 12.7

Reasons for going to war in 1812: impressments of U.S. sailors, national pride, making the frontier safe for settlement

Section 12.8

1. *July 1812:* Congress declares war on Great Britain.

   Sep. 1813: U.S. naval force captures a British fleet on Lake Erie.

   Aug. 1814: British army invades Washington, D.C.

   Dec. 1814: U.S. and British diplomats sign a peace treaty in Belgium.

   Jan. 1815: Battle of New Orleans

2. Answers will vary. Students should adequately justify their placement.

Section 12.9

Possible answers: The United States was genuinely concerned for the well-being of the new nations. The United States wanted to establish beneficial trade with Latin America. The United States wanted Europe to stay out of the affairs of the American continents.

Section 12.10

1. The Monroe Doctrine said that Europe should not colonize any Latin American nations and that any attempts at colonization would be seen as a threat to the United States. Students' opinions of whether Monroe pursued the best option will vary.

2. Answers will vary. Students should adequately justify their placement.

A Growing Sense of Nationhood

What did it mean to be an American in the early 1800s?

Overview

In a Writing for Understanding activity, students visit an art exhibit, cotillion, and literary gathering to experience American culture in the early 1800s. They then create a chapter of a book describing what it meant to be an American in this period.

Objectives

In the course of reading this chapter and participating in the classroom activity, students will

Social Studies

- describe Henry Clay's American System.

- identify themes in American art, music, and literature including works by Washington Irving, James Fenimore Cooper, and Henry Wadsworth Longfellow.

- identify ways in which politics and popular culture reflected America's growing national identity.

Language Arts

- write and revise a tightly argued essay that includes a coherent thesis, supporting evidence, and well-supported conclusion.

- support a thesis or conclusions with paraphrases, opinions, and comparisons.

- Read and respond to historically or culturally significant works of literature and identify and analyze recurring themes.

- Revise writing for content, appropriate organization, and transitions between paragraphs, passages, and ideas.

Materials

History Alive! The United States Through Industrialism

Interactive Student Notebooks

CD Tracks 5 and 6

Placards 13A–13E (2 sets; create additional sets as needed)

Visual 13

Lesson Masters

- Information Masters 13A–13C (1 transparency of each)
- Student Handout 13A (1 copy, cut apart)
- Student Handout 13B (1 for every 4 students)
- Student Handout 13C (1 per student)
- Vocabulary Development handout (1 per student, on colored paper)

Social Studies Vocabulary

Key Content Terms frontier, capitalism, American System, folk art, spiritual

Academic Vocabulary proclaim, emerge, distinct, stereotype

Activity	Suggested Time	Materials
Preview	15 minutes	• Interactive Student Notebooks • CD Track 5 • Visual 13
Vocabulary Development	30–40 minutes	• *History Alive! The United States Through Industrialism* • Interactive Student Notebooks • Vocabulary Development handout
Writing for Understanding	150–200 minutes (3–4 class periods) (1.5–2 block periods)	• *History Alive! The United States Through Industrialism* • CD Track 6 • Placards 13A–13E (2 sets) • Information Masters 13A–13C • Student Handouts 13A–13C
Processing (optional)	20 minutes	• Interactive Student Notebooks
Assessment	40 minutes	• Chapter 13 Assessment

Preview

1 **Project *Visual 13: Flag at Fort McHenry* and play CD Track 5, "The Star-Spangled Banner."** Ask students to stand while they listen to the song, and encourage them to sing along.

2 **Have students answer the Preview questions on a separate sheet of paper.** Have them share their responses in pairs or with the class.

3 **Explain the connection between the Preview and Chapter 13.** Explain to students that these lyrics were written by Francis Scott Key after the American victory at Fort McHenry during the War of 1812. His lyrics were printed in newspapers around the country and were soon set to music, eventually to become the nation's national anthem. In this chapter, students will examine the growing sense of nationhood in the early 1800s and explore what it meant to be an American in this period.

Visual 13

Vocabulary Development

1 **Introduce the Key Content Terms.** Have students locate the Key Content Terms for the chapter in their Interactive Student Notebooks. These are important terms that will help them understand the main ideas of the chapter. Ask volunteers to identify any familiar terms and how they might be used in a sentence.

2 **Have students complete a Vocabulary Development handout.** Give each student a copy of the Vocabulary Development handout of your choice from the Reading Toolkit at the back of the Lesson Masters. These handouts provide extra practice and support, depending on your students' needs. Review the completed handout by asking volunteers to share one answer for each term.

Reading

1 **Introduce the Essential Question and have students read Section 13.1.** Have students identify the Essential Question: *What did it mean to be an American in the early 1800s?* Then have them read Section 13.1. Afterward, have them use information from the reading and the image that opens the chapter to propose some possible answers to the Essential Question.

2 **Have students complete the Reading Notes for Sections 13.2 and 13.3.** Have several volunteers share their responses. Use Guide to Reading Notes 13 to check their answers.

3 **Have students complete the remaining Reading Notes for Chapter 13.** Assign Sections 13.4 to 13.6 during the activity as indicated in the procedures for the Writing for Understanding activity. Remind students to use the Key Content Terms where appropriate as they complete their Reading Notes.

> Vocabulary Development: Meanings in Context
>
> As students use the Key Content Terms within the context of a growing sense of nationhood, ask them to supply context clues that clarify the meanings of the terms by means of restatement, examples, comparison, or contrast. For example, context clues include settled areas in contrast to frontier, fine art in comparison with folk art, and "Follow the Drinking Gourd" as an example of a spiritual.

Writing for Understanding

1 **Prepare the classroom.** Post the two sets of *Placards 13A–13E: Art of the Early 1800s* on the walls. (**Note:** Create additional sets as needed. For larger classes, consider using three sets.)

2 **Place students in pairs and introduce the activity.** Tell pairs they will visit an art exhibit, a ball, and a literary gathering to explore what it meant to be an American in the early 1800s.

3 **Have pairs visit the art exhibit.** Welcome students to the art exhibit, and explain that the placards around the room each represent a different artist or artistic style described in Section 13.4. Project *Information Master 13A: Visiting an Art Exhibit in the Early 1800s* and reveal only Step 1. After students have read and completed the Reading Notes for Section 13.4, review Steps 2 to 5. Then assign one or two pairs to each placard to begin, and give pairs adequate time to analyze the placards and complete their Reading Notes.

4 **Debrief the placards.** As volunteers share their responses to the Reading Notes for Section 13.4, share the following information about the corresponding placards:

- **Placard 13A: John James Audubon** *Snowy Heron or White Egret* is a hand-colored etching from 1832. Audubon's assistant, George Lehman, painted the background. This work is characteristic of Audubon's finely detailed, realistic portrayals of birds.

- **Placard 13B: Hudson River School** Thomas Cole painted *The Oxbow* in 1836. It is a view from Mount Holyoke, Massachusetts, of an oxbow (a curve in a stream) after a thunderstorm. Infused with light and celebrating natural beauty, it is typical of the Hudson River School style.

- **Placard 13C: George Catlin** *Buffalo Hunt, Chase No. 6* shows a buffalo run in Missouri in the 1830s. Catlin's work is characterized by images of American Indians that highlight their exceptional bravery and skill.

- **Placard 13D: Folk Art** This 1830 fire bucket, painted with a portrait of George Washington, is characteristic of the folk art of the period. Images of Washington were drawn on many common objects as expressions of national pride.

- **Placard 13E: Portrait** *Abigail Smith Adams (Mrs. John Adams)* is a portrait of President Adams's wife painted in 1815 by Gilbert Stuart.

5 **Have students attend a cotillion.**

- Tell students that they are now at a cotillion in the early 1800s. Project *Information Master 13B: Attending a Cotillion in the Early 1800s,* and reveal one step at a time.

- In Step 2, give each group a strip cut from *Student Handout 13A: Dance Steps to the Cotillion.*

- In Step 4, play CD Track 6, "Cotillion Music," and call the number of groups in turn, 1 to 9, to indicate when they should perform their dance steps.

Placards 13A–13E

Information Master 13A

Information Master 13B

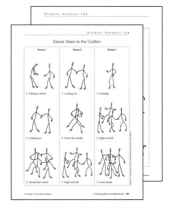

Student Handout 13A

6 Have students attend a literary gathering.

- Tell students that they are now at a literary gathering in a house of a wealthy urban family. Explain that, since contemporary books were expensive and often hard to acquire, wealthy families hosted such gatherings to read and discuss literary works.

- Project *Information Master 13C: Attending a Literary Gathering in the Early 1800s* and reveal only Step 1.

- After students read the section and complete the first two columns of the matrix in their Reading Notes, have pairs join to form groups of four (Step 2 on the Information Master). Distribute a copy of *Student Handout 13B: Excerpts from Literature of the Early 1800s* to each group.

- Review the remaining steps, and give groups adequate time to read the excerpts and complete their Reading Notes. When most groups are finished, quickly debrief their answers.

7 Explain the writing assignment. Tell students that they will now write a chapter of a book by Alexis de Tocqueville describing what it means to be an American in the early 1800s. Distribute *Student Handout 13C: Creating a Chapter of a Book* and review the directions.

8 Have students create their first drafts. Have students write the first drafts of their chapters neatly, in pencil, using every other line to facilitate the peer-checking step that follows.

9 Have students peer-check the first drafts. Have students exchange drafts with a partner. Using Student Handout 13C, have them find each required item in their partner's paragraphs and note any items they do not find. Also, have pairs make suggestions for improving word choice and organizational structure.

10 Have students create their final chapters. Remind students to incorporate the feedback from the peer-review.

Processing (optional)

The chapter-writing assignment serves as this chapter's Processing activity. Should you choose not to have students do the writing assignment, you might use the optional Processing activity in the Interactive Student Notebook.

Information Master 13C

Student Handout 13B

Student Handout 13C

Quicker Coverage

Simplify the Activity Eliminate one or more of the venues in the activity. Instruct students which parts of their Reading Notes to leave unanswered.

Shorten the Activity Eliminate the writing assignment. Instead, debrief the activity by having students answer this question: *In what ways did the art, music, and literature of the early 1800s reflect what it meant to be an American?*

Deeper Coverage

Add Additional Placards Make additional placards of art pieces from some of the artists or artistic styles described in Section 13.4. Label the additional placards, starting with Placard 13F, and post them around the room with Placards 13A–13E. Have students reflect on these placards in their Reading Notes matrix.

Add Additional Literary Excerpts Find additional literary excerpts from one of the four authors described in Section 13.6. Label the additional excerpts, starting with Excerpt E, and distribute copies of them with Student Handout 13B. Have students reflect on these excerpts in their Reading Notes matrix.

Assessment

Mastering the Content

1. D	5. C	9. D	13. D
2. C	6. B	10. B	14. D
3. A	7. D	11. A	15. D
4. B	8. D	12. B	16. B

Applying Social Studies Skills

17. Mississippi River

18. Possible answer: It grew in size. States were added.

19. Possible answer: The area west of the Appalachians was unsettled frontier, so the people who lived there had to build their own trails and clear the land, among other things.

Exploring the Essential Question

20. Answers should include all of the elements requested in the prompt.

Scoring Rubric

Score	Description
3	Student completes all four parts of the task. Ideas are clearly stated, supported by details, and demonstrate command of standard English conventions.
2	Student responds to most or all parts of the task. Ideas may lack details or not be clearly stated.
1	Student responds to at least one part of the task. Ideas may contain factual or grammatical errors and may lack details.
0	Response does not match the task or is incorrect.

A New Literature Celebrates a New Nation

1 **Discuss how and why nations change.** Initiate a discussion on ways in which students feel that the United States is changing today. Ask them, *Imagine that you are living in the early 1800s. How has the nation changed in the approximately 50 years since independence?*

2 **Have students read the first two pages of the Chapter 13 Reading Further.** When they have finished, discuss what they have read. Ask, *If you were to fall asleep tonight and wake up 20 years from now, what changes do you think you might see?*

3 **Have students finish the reading.** After students complete the reading, ask them,

- How would you feel about seeing the pigeon shoot?

- What was Natty Bumppo's position?

- What was Billy Kirby's position?

4 **Have students complete the first page of the Reading Further in their Interactive Student Notebooks.** You may wish to have them use their adjectives in sentences about Rip Van Winkle. After students complete the first page, ask them to compare the changes faced by the two characters.

5 **Have students complete the second page of the Reading Further.** Invite students to share their descriptions with the class.

English Language Learners

Provide Key Definitions For the Preview activity, give students the following definitions for words in the "The Star-Spangled Banner":

twilight: the time of day following sunset

gleaming: a flash of light

perilous: dangerous

ramparts: large banks of earth or stones forming a defensive site

gallantly: proudly

star-spangled banner: the American flag

Choose One Excerpt During the literary gathering, have students read and interpret only one literary excerpt. Provide each student a copy of the excerpt, and have them annotate it by defining the challenging words and then paraphrasing the excerpt. Check for understanding before having students complete the Reading Notes matrix.

Learners Reading and Writing Below Grade Level

Condense the Writing Assignment For the book chapter, have students use the first thesis on Student Handout 13C and provide them with these topic sentences for their body paragraphs:

The works of the Hudson River School reflected Americans' pride in their nation. The growth of patriotic anthems of the period highlighted Americans' pride in their country. In his poem "Paul Revere's Ride," Henry Wadsworth Longfellow illustrated Americans' pride in their nation.

Learners with Special Education Needs

Appoint a Caller During the cotillion, have a student take on the roll of "caller" and announce each group's number in turn, 1 to 9, at your prompting.

Have Students Make Instruments Instead of having students prepare dance steps for the cotillion, have them make simple instruments using materials around the room. During the dance, have students play their instruments.

Advanced Learners

Expand the Writing Assignment Require that students incorporate two or three quotations from Alexis de Tocqueville into their book chapters. They can use the quotations from the Student Edition or find their own quotations online from de Tocqueville's *Democracy in America.*

Enrichment Resources

Find out more about the nation's growing sense of nationhood by exploring the following Enrichment Resources for *History Alive! The United States Through Industrialism* at www.teachtci.com.

Enrichment Readings These in-depth readings encourage students to explore selected topics related to the chapter. You may also find readings that relate the chapter's content directly to your state's curriculum.

Internet Connections The recommended Web sites provide useful and engaging content that reinforces skills development and mastery of subjects within the chapter.

Literature Recommendations

The following books offer opportunities to extend the content in this chapter:

Canals by Raymond Bial (Tarrytown, NY: Marshall Cavendish Corporation, 2001)

Through the Lock by Carol Otis Hurst (Boston: Houghton Mifflin, 2001)

Paul Revere's Ride: The Landlord's Tale by Henry Wadsworth Longfellow, illustrator Charles Santore (New York: Harper Collins, 2003)

Section 13.2

1. Possible answers: Two out of every three Americans lived within 50 miles of the Atlantic Coast. Fewer than one in ten lived west of the Appalachians. Travel between east and west was difficult. News traveled slowly. Distinct regional lifestyles developed.

2. Illustrations and explanations will vary.

Section 13.3

1. taxes on imports to protect industry, new national bank to standardize currency and provide credit.

2. Possible answers: In *McCulloch v. Maryland*, the Court confirmed Congress's power to create a national bank free from state interference. In another case, the Court held that business contracts could not be broken. In *Gibbons v. Ogden*, the Court held that Congress had the authority to regulate interstate commerce.

Section 13.4

Possible answers (symbols and explanations will vary):

- **Folk Art** (Placard 13D)
  Characteristics: Created by ordinary people. Examples included signs, murals, and national symbols. Art was simple, direct, and colorful.

- **Portraits** (Placard 13E)
  Characteristics: Most professional artists made portraits. Gilbert Stuart was the best-known portrait artist.

- **Hudson River School** (Placard 13B)
  Characteristics: Focus on nature more than people. Broad, scenic vistas. Celebrated the country's natural beauty.

- **John James Audubon** (Placard 13A)
  Created detailed portraits of birds. Paintings were highly realistic, the work of a naturalist.

- **George Catlin** (Placard 13C)
  Characteristics: Recorded the lives of American Indians in the West. Showed villages, hunts, and rituals.

Section 13.5

1. Possible answers:

   Classical music: From Europe. Played by orchestras. Used for the cotillion.

   Spirituals: Church hymns that slaves set to African musical styles.

   Patriotic anthems: Became popular. Included songs like "America."

   Minstrel songs: Written by white composers. Mimicked the music of African Americans.

2. Possible answer: The painting shows a cotillion, a ball where couples danced to an orchestra. These balls were elegant. Men wore tuxedos and women wore floor-length dresses.

Section 13.6

Possible answers (explanations will vary):

- **Washington Irving** (Excerpt D)
  Works: "Rip Van Winkle," "The Legend of Sleepy Hollow"
  Characteristics: Drew on German folklore. Set in upstate New York.

- **James Fenimore Cooper** (Excerpt A)
  Works: The Pioneers, The Last of the Mohicans

  Characteristics: Wrote about the adventures of frontier settlers. Described American Indian life.

- **Davy Crockett** (Excerpt B)
  Works: The *Crockett Almanac 1841*
  Characteristics: Plain, backwoods speech and rough humor. Wrote about his life as a hunter, scout, soldier, and explorer.

- **Henry Wadsworth Longfellow** (Excerpt C)
  Works: The Song of Hiawatha, "Paul Revere's Ride," "The Building of the Ship"
  Characteristics: Wrote America's first epic poem. Touched on patriotic themes.

Andrew Jackson and the Growth of American Democracy

How well did President Andrew Jackson promote democracy?

Overview

In a Visual Discovery activity, students analyze and bring to life images of key events in the presidency of Andrew Jackson to evaluate how well he promoted democracy.

Objectives

In the course of reading this chapter and participating in the classroom activity, students will

Social Studies

- describe the perspectives of various groups of people in response to Jackson and his key policies.

- assess the impact of Jackson's policies on the outcome of events.

- evaluate how well Jackson promoted democracy, citing both his positive and negative contributions.

Language Arts

- deliver narrative presentations that relate a clear, coherent event by using well-chosen details and employing strategies such as relevant dialogue.

Social Studies Vocabulary

Key Content Terms Jacksonian Democracy, civil servant, spoils system, tariff, secede, Trail of Tears

Academic Vocabulary ignorant, dispute, voluntarily

Materials

History Alive! The United States Through Industrialism

Interactive Student Notebooks

CD Tracks 1 and 7

Visuals 14A–14F

Lesson Masters

- Student Handout 14 (1 per group)
- Vocabulary Development handout (1 per student, on colored paper)

sheet of white poster board or large piece of paper

Activity	Suggested Time	Materials
Preview	15 minutes	• Interactive Student Notebooks • CD Tracks 1 and 7 • Visual 14A
Vocabulary Development	30–40 minutes	• *History Alive! The United States Through Industrialism* • Interactive Student Notebooks • Vocabulary Development handout
Visual Discovery	100–150 minutes (2–3 regular periods) (1–1.5 block periods)	• *History Alive! The United States Through Industrialism* • Interactive Student Notebooks • Visuals 14B–14F • Student Handout 14 • sheet of white poster board
Processing	20 minutes	• Interactive Student Notebooks
Assessment	40 minutes	• Chapter 14 Assessment

Preview

1 **Play CD Track 1, "Hail Columbia" and project the top half of *Visual 14A: The Elections of Washington and Jackson*.** Remind students that this song was first played at Washington's 1789 inauguration, and explain that the painting shows him on the way to his inauguration. Ask,

- What are two adjectives that describe the song's mood? *(serious, formal, optimistic)*
- How would you describe the people that attended Washington's inauguration? *(wealthy, well-dressed, formal, serious)*

2 **Play CD Track 7, "The Hunters of Kentucky," and project the lower half of Visual 14A.** Explain that this song was written for Jackson's presidential campaign and celebrates his military leadership in the War of 1812. The image shows Andrew Jackson stopping to greet people after winning the 1828 election. Have students follow along with the lyrics in their Interactive Student Notebooks as they listen. Then ask,

- What are two adjectives that describe the song's mood? *(fast, fun, folksy)*
- How would you describe the people in the image who supported Andrew Jackson? *(excited, eager, common people)*
- Judging from the images and songs you have analyzed, how do you think the presidencies of Andrew Jackson and George Washington differed? *(Jackson's presidency was more inclusive, livelier, and more responsive to the needs of ordinary people.)*

3 **Have students complete the Preview questions on a separate sheet of paper.**

4 **Explain the connection between the Preview and Chapter 14.** Tell students that the election of Andrew Jackson ushered in a new era in U.S. politics. Not only had the nation elected a war hero, but it had elected a self-made man— a "hunter from Kentucky" who proclaimed that the common people should control their government. In this chapter, students will examine the presidency of Andrew Jackson to evaluate how well he promoted democracy.

Vocabulary Development

1 **Introduce the Key Content Terms.** Have students locate the Key Content Terms for the chapter in their Interactive Student Notebooks. These are important terms that will help them understand the main ideas of the chapter. Ask volunteers to identify any familiar terms and how they might be used in a sentence.

2 **Have students complete a Vocabulary Development handout.** Give each student a copy of the Vocabulary Development handout of your choice from the Reading Toolkit at the back of the Lesson Masters. These handouts provide extra practice and support, depending on your students' needs. Review the completed handout by asking volunteers to share one answer for each term.

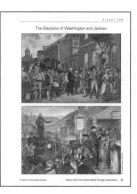

Visual 14A

Vocabulary Development: Figurative Language

Explain that the phrase "Trail of Tears" is a metaphor. Have students infer the literal meaning of the phrase, and then go on to explore the figurative meaning. Next, help students brainstorm possible literal terms for the "Trail of Tears" journey, experience, or resettlement. Discuss why the metaphor has more emotional power or resonance than many or all of the proposed literal terms.

Reading

1 **Introduce the Essential Question and have students read Section 14.1.**
Have students identify the Essential Question: *How well did President Andrew Jackson promote democracy?* Then have them read Section 14.1. Afterward, ask,

- Why was the election of 1828 considered one of the dirtiest in U.S. history?

- What groups of people voted for Adams? Who voted for Jackson?

- In what ways do you think President Jackson might have promoted democracy during his presidency?

2 **Have students read and complete the Reading Notes for Sections 14.2.**
Have several volunteers share their responses. Use Guide to Reading Notes 14 to check their answers.

3 **Have students complete the remaining Reading Notes for Chapter 14.**
Assign Sections 14.3 to 14.7 during the activity as indicated in the procedures for the Visual Discovery activity. Remind students to use the Key Content Terms where appropriate as they complete their Reading Notes.

Visual Discovery

1 **Place students in pairs and introduce the activity.** Tell students they will analyze images relating to the presidency of Andrew Jackson to assess how well he promoted democracy. They will bring two of these images to life in act-it-outs.

2 **Introduce Section 14.3 by projecting *Visual 14B: Jackson's Inauguration*.**
Tell pairs to find three interesting and unique details in the image. After a few minutes, have five to eight volunteers form a line near the projection screen. Hold up the sheet of white poster board, and explain that this "magic paper" can be held about a foot in front of the screen to enlarge a detail from the image. Have the first volunteer use the magic paper to point out a detail. Then have the other volunteers point out their details.

3 **Have students read and complete the Reading Notes for Sections 14.3.**
Review the main points with the class.

4 **Have students prepare to bring the image to life.** Have pairs form groups of four. Distribute a copy of *Student Handout 14: Creating Act-It-Outs About Jackson's Presidency* to each group. Assign each group one of these characters for the first act-it-out: Farmer on the Frontier, Banker from Philadelphia. Then review the directions and give groups about five minutes to prepare.

5 **Conduct the act-it-out.** Call up two farmers and two bankers to stand in front of the projected image, taking on an appropriate character's posture and facial expression. Acting as the on-scene reporter, ask the characters some of the questions from Student Handout 14. (**Note:** Consider conducting the act-it-out a second time with new actors.)

Visual 14B

Student Handout 14

6 Introduce Section 14.4 by projecting *Visual 14C: Jackson's Approach to Governing.* Ask,

- What do you see in this cartoon?
- What is Jackson being shown as?
- Why do you think Jackson is pictured in this way?

7 **Have students read and complete the Reading Notes for Section 14.4.** Review the main points with the class.

8 **Have students reexamine Visual 14C.** Encourage students to use what they learned in Section 14.4 to answer these questions:

- Who are the people trying to grab the objects attached to the strings?
- What do you think is the cartoonist's opinion of the people seeking political office?
- Would the cartoonist think that Jackson's approach to governing promoted democracy? Why or why not?
- Do you agree with the cartoonist? Why or why not?

Visual 14C

9 **Introduce Section 14.5 by projecting *Visual 14D: The Nullification Crisis.*** Ask,

- What do you see in this cartoon?
- What might the man near the top of the staircase be doing?
- Why might the man on the far right be pulling on the coattails of another?

10 **Have students read and complete the Reading Notes for Section 14.5.** Review the main points with the class.

11 **Have students reexamine Visual 14D.** Draw students' attention to the word *DESPOTISM* at the top of the cartoon, and explain that despotism is a form of government in which the ruler is an absolute dictator. Make sure students understand the words on the stairs: *nullification, treason, civil war, deception,* and *disunion.* Also make sure they know that John C. Calhoun, Jackson's vice president, is the figure at the top of the stairs, and that Jackson is the figure pulling on the coattails of a Calhoun supporter. Then ask,

Visual 14D

- What does the cartoonist imply that Calhoun wants?
- Would the cartoonist think that Jackson's response to the nullification crisis promoted democracy? Why or why not?
- Do you agree with the cartoonist? Why or why not?

12 Introduce Section 14.6 by projecting *Visual 14E: Jackson Battles the Bank.* Ask,

- What do you see in this cartoon?
- Andrew Jackson is pictured on the left. What is he doing?
- What might the many-headed monster symbolize?

Visual 14E

13 **Have students read and complete the Reading Notes for Section 14.6.** Review the main points with the class.

14 **Have students reexamine Visual 14E.** Explain that Nicholas Biddle is pictured in a top hat and that the monster's heads represent the 24 state directors of the bank. Then ask,

- What dangers does the cartoonist think this monster will bring?
- Would the cartoonist think that the dismantling of the bank promoted U.S. democracy? How can you tell?
- Do you agree with the cartoonist? Why or why not?

15 **Introduce Section 14.7 by projecting** *Visual 14F: The Trail of Tears.* Ask,

- What do you see?
- How do you think these people feel? How can you tell?
- Where might they be going? Why?

Visual 14F

16 **Have students read and complete the Reading Notes for Section 14.7.** Review the main points with the class.

17 **Have students prepare to bring the image to life.** Have pairs form groups of four. Assign each group one of these characters for the second act-it-out on Student Handout 14: Armed Soldier, Elderly Cherokee Woman, Cherokee Warrior, Cherokee Mother, Cherokee Boy, Cherokee Father Driving Wagon, Georgian Settler, Andrew Jackson. Then review the directions and give groups about five minutes to prepare.

18 **Conduct the act-it-out.** Call up one actor from each group to stand in the appropriate location in front of the projected image, taking on that character's posture and facial expression. Place the settler and Andrew Jackson on opposite sides. Acting as the on-scene reporter, ask the characters some of the questions from Student Handout 14.

Processing

Have students complete the Processing activity, in which they will create a commemorative plaque and a "wanted" poster to evaluate how well Andrew Jackson promoted democracy.

Quicker Coverage

Shorten the Activity Eliminate one or more of the act-it-outs or one or more of the visuals from the activity.

Deeper Coverage

Analyze Additional Images Prior to having students read Section 14.2, have them examine the images in the section. Ask, *What do you see in these images? These images tell part of the story of how Andrew Jackson became president. If you were to tell the story, what other important events would you include? Judging from these images, do you think Jackson was qualified to be president? Why or why not?*

Create Additional Act-It-Outs Add an act-it-out to one or more of the images by selecting characters for students to represent and creating questions for the characters.

Assessment

Mastering the Content

1. B	5. D	9. A	13. A
2. D	6. B	10. D	14. A
3. C	7. A	11. B	15. D
4. D	8. A	12. B	16. A

Applying Social Studies Skills

17. the common man (Students might use other words to describe this group.)

18. Possible answer: "Hero," "Man of the People," "Military Chieftain," "Old Hickory"

19. Possible answers: War of 1812, Battle of New Orleans, Election of 1828

Exploring the Essential Question

20. Answers should include all of the elements requested in the prompt.

Scoring Rubric

Score	Description
3	Student completes all three parts of the task. Ideas are clearly stated, supported by details, and demonstrate command of standard English conventions.
2	Student responds to most or all parts of the task. Ideas may lack details or not be clearly stated.
1	Student responds to at least one part of the task. Ideas may contain factual or grammatical errors and may lack details.
0	Response does not match the task or is incorrect.

The Trail Where They Cried

1 **Have students read the Chapter 14 Reading Further.** To reinforce the geographical realities of the Trail of Tears, have students look at a map of the United States and trace the route from the states where the Cherokees lived—North Carolina, Georgia, Tennessee, and Alabama—to present-day Oklahoma, which was then Indian Territory. Tell students that much of Indian Territory was prairie land with long, hot summers. Ask,

- Based on the photograph of the Cherokee homeland in the reading, how different was the Cherokees' new home from what they were used to?

- How might this have added to the hardships of the removal?

2 **Discuss the importance of first-person accounts in our understanding of the Cherokee removal.** Ask, *Why would John G. Burnett want to record his experiences with the Cherokees for his family?* Read aloud and discuss this Cherokee account from an unnamed survivor of the removal:

> *Long time we travel on way to new land. People feel bad when they leave Old Nation. Womens cry and make sad wails. Children cry and many men cry, and all look sad like when friends die, but they say nothing and just put heads down and keep on go towards West. Many days pass and people die very much. We bury close by Trail.*

3 **Discuss the Cherokee Nation today.** Ask students, *In what ways might an experience such as the Trail of Tears strengthen the identity of a group?* Explain that when Oklahoma was in the process of becoming a state, the Cherokees attempted unsuccessfully to establish their own separate state, called the State of Sequoya. Students can research the State of Sequoya online.

4 **Have students complete the Chapter 14 Reading Further in their Interactive Student Notebooks.** The correct order of the six statements is 4, 2, 5, 1, 6, 3. Invite students to share their letters with the class.

English Language Learners

Introduce Key Groups Prior to the activity, review with students the following terms: *common people, states' rights supporters, upper class, American Indians.* Consider creating poster-size descriptive representations of these individuals, incorporating illustrations and text, to serve as a reference.

Prepare Students in Advance Give students photocopies of the visuals and corresponding questions the night before you conduct the activity. Have students prepare possible answers to the questions.

Learners Reading and Writing Below Grade Level

Highlight Key Information Give students photocopies of the chapter. For the Reading Notes for Sections 14.3, 14.4, and 14.6, have them highlight information pertaining to *common people* in one color and to the *upper class* in a second color. For Section 14.5, have them use different colors to highlight information pertaining to *northerners* and *southerners.* Finally, in Section 14.7, have them highlight information pertaining to how Indians felt about the Indian Removal Act.

Learners with Special Education Needs

Support the Act-It-Outs Consider these tips:

- Have students prepare a script by answering the questions on Student Handout 14. Allow them to read from that script during the act-it-out.
- A few days in advance, tell students which role they will be playing so that they can practice their parts.
- Place students in nonspeaking roles for the act-it-out. For instance, have them take on the roles of the American Indian man driving a wagon, the man leading a horse, or the boy carrying a dog.

Advanced Learners

Brainstorm Other Heroes and Villains After students complete the Processing activity, have them brainstorm other people—historical or contemporary—who are considered heroes by some people and villains by others.

Enrichment Resources

Find out more about Andrew Jackson and growth of American democracy by exploring the following Enrichment Resources for *History Alive! The United States Through Industrialism* at www.teachtci.com.

Enrichment Readings These in-depth readings encourage students to explore selected topics related to the chapter. You may also find readings that relate the chapter's content directly to your state's curriculum.

Internet Connections The recommended Web sites provide useful and engaging content that reinforces skills development and mastery of subjects within the chapter.

Literature Recommendations

The following books offer opportunities to extend the content in this chapter.

The Trail of Tears: A Primary Source History of the Forced Relocation of the Cherokee Nation by Ann Byers (New York: The Rosen Publishing Group, 2003)

Andrew Jackson: Our Seventh President by Ann Gaines (Mankato, MN: The Child's World, 2001)

Andrew Jackson: Frontier President by Nancy Whitelaw (Greensboro, NC: Morgan Reynolds, 2000)

Section 14.2

1. Symbols will vary.

   1767: Jackson was born into poverty on the South Carolina frontier.

   1780: Jackson joined a local militia to fight in the American Revolution.

   1788: Jackson moved to Tennessee to practice law.

   1814: Jackson became a national hero for his defense of New Orleans during the War of 1812.

   1824: Jackson ran for president but did not have enough electoral votes to win a majority.

   1828: Jackson ran for president a second time and won.

2. Possible answers:

   Common people: The people want Jacksonian Democracy. The new Democratic Party will represent the ordinary people of this country like farmers, workers, and the poor.

   Upper class: Jackson is unfit to be president. He's not well educated, and he has a hot temper.

Section 14.3

1. Possible answers:

   Common people: Finally, one of us has been elected president! We have rescued the country from being taken over by the rich!

   Upper class: Is Jackson really the best this country has to offer? He represents the uneducated commoners—look how they behaved after his inauguration!

2. Jackson promised to throw out the monied interests and return the government to the people.

Section 14.4

1. Possible answers:

   Common people: Jackson is a strong leader who does what he thinks is right. We agree with his decision to replace civil servants. Rotating them is more democratic than lifetime service.

   Upper class: The men in Jackson's kitchen cabinet are not the proper sort to be running the country. And Jackson has created a spoils system that rewards his supporters, not the most qualified.

2. Answers will vary.

Section 14.5

1. Possible answers:

   Northerners: We support the new tariff law. Higher prices for imported factory goods means we can sell the products made in our own factories.

   Southerners: The new tariff law is unconstitutional. The tariffs hurt our cotton sales to other countries. We will secede if the government tries to enforce the law.

2. Answers will vary.

Section 14.6

1. Possible answers:

   Common people: President Jackson's dismantling of the bank shows he is a champion of the people! The bank is an unconstitutional monopoly that makes the rich richer at the expense of farmers and workers.

   Upper class: The bank is important to our economy. It supports businesspeople who depend on it for loans. Jackson has overstepped his authority by dismantling the bank and putting federal deposits in his "pet banks."

2. Answers will vary.

Section 14.7

1. Possible answers: Jackson has cheated us of our land by making treaties he never intended to keep. We have been dragged from our homes and forced to move. On the Trail of Tears, 4,000 of us died.

2. Answers will vary.

Launching the New Republic

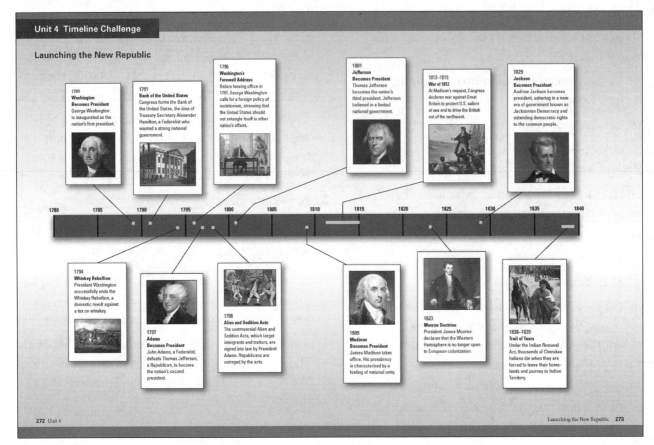

Unit 4 Timeline Challenge

Launching the New Republic

1789
Washington Becomes President
George Washington is inaugurated as the nation's first president.

1791
Bank of the United States
Congress forms the Bank of the United States, the idea of Treasury Secretary Alexander Hamilton, a Federalist who wanted a strong national government.

1796
Washington's Farewell Address
Before leaving office in 1797, George Washington calls for a foreign policy of isolationism, stressing that the United States should not entangle itself in other nation's affairs.

1801
Jefferson Becomes President
Thomas Jefferson becomes the nation's third president. Jefferson believed in a limited national government.

1812–1815
War of 1812
At Madison's request, Congress declares war against Great Britain to protect U.S. sailors at sea and to drive the British out of the northwest.

1829
Jackson Becomes President
Andrew Jackson becomes president, ushering in a new era of government known as Jacksonian Democracy and extending democratic rights to the common people.

1794
Whiskey Rebellion
President Washington successfully ends the Whiskey Rebellion, a domestic revolt against a tax on whiskey.

1797
Adams Becomes President
John Adams, a Federalist, defeats Thomas Jefferson, a Republican, to become the nation's second president.

1798
Alien and Sedition Acts
The controversial Alien and Sedition Acts, which target immigrants and traitors, are signed into law by President Adams. Republicans are outraged by the acts.

1809
Madison Becomes President
James Madison takes office. His presidency is characterized by a feeling of national unity.

1823
Monroe Doctrine
President James Monroe declares that the Western Hemisphere is no longer open to European colonization.

1838–1839
Trail of Tears
Under the Indian Removal Act, thousands of Cherokee Indians die when they are forced to leave their homelands and journey to Indian Territory.

272 Unit 4

Launching the New Republic **273**

Overview

This Timeline Challenge provides students with a review of the main events and ideas of this unit, as well as practice in reading and interpreting timelines. You can vary and expand the activity according to students' needs and the amount of time available.

Basic Procedure

1 **Introduce the timeline in the Student Edition.** Direct students to the Launching the New Republic timeline at the end of Unit 4 in the Student Edition. You may wish to have students read aloud and discuss the timeline entries.

2 **Introduce the Timeline Challenge in the Interactive Student Notebook.** Direct students to the Unit 4 Timeline Challenge in their notebooks. Point out the two types of questions, "Timeline Skills" and "Critical Thinking," and model how to answer each type.

3 **Have students complete the Timeline Challenge.** Monitor students as they work. Use the Guide to Unit 4 Timeline Challenge to check their answers. You may wish to project a transparency of this page as you work through the questions with the class and conduct a discussion of the "Critical Thinking" questions.

4 **Complete the KWL chart.** Return to the KWL chart created at the beginning of the unit, and ask students to list the key information they have learned.

Classroom Timeline

1 **Prepare the Timeline Challenge Cards.** Copy and cut the cards from *Student Handout TC4: Unit 4 Timeline Challenge Cards.* You may wish to laminate the cards for future use.

2 **Create a timeline on a classroom wall.** On an empty wall or a large bulletin board, make a timeline with masking tape or colored paper. Mark off the time intervals in advance, or ask students to do so in class.

3 **Have students place the Timeline Challenge Cards.** Distribute cards to individual students or pairs and have them tape the cards to the timeline in the correct locations. Call on students to provide more information on the timeline topics to review main events and issues.

Student Handout TC4

Internet Research

1 **Review students' suggestions for additional timeline entries.** Have students share their answers to the last question of the Timeline Challenge.

2 **Have students conduct Internet research.** Ask students to choose and research one of their suggested events.

3 **Have students create additional Timeline Challenge Cards.** Direct students to research an appropriate image for their cards and then use the computer to create an illustrated card, complete with timeline entry.

Timeline Skills

Score 1 point for each correct answer.

1. 8 years

2. Washington served two terms. He set the model for future presidents of only two terms.

3. The Alien and Sedition Acts were passed during the presidency of John Adams.

4. 29 years

5. The United States fought the War of 1812 to protect U.S. sailors at sea and to drive the British out of the northwest.

6. The Monroe Doctrine told the world that the Western Hemisphere was no longer open to European colonization.

7. Jacksonian Democracy began when Andrew Jackson took office in 1829. He championed the common citizen instead of the elite.

8. In 1838, the federal government forced the Cherokee nation to relocate to Indian Territory.

Critical Thinking

Score 1 to 3 points for each answer, depending on the thoroughness of the response.

9. Possible answer: The problem was the government's lack of funds to pay off the debt that Congress and the states had accumulated during the revolution. The government imposed a tax to raise money. It also set up a national bank to collect taxes, keep funds safe, and print paper money to give the nation a stable currency. The bank could also make loans to businesspeople to build new factories and ships and expand business and trade.

10. Possible answer: Federalists like Alexander Hamilton believed in a strong central government, run by "the best people." They believed people were driven by self-interest, and they wanted the economy to grow through industry and trade. Republicans like Thomas Jefferson believed in states' rights and a small government. Because they believed people were basically good and wise, they believed in more democratic government, not one conducted by the elite. They also wanted the economy to be based on agriculture.

11. Washington believed in isolationism. He did not think the new nation was strong enough to get involved in foreign affairs. Madison took the country into the War of 1812, responding to public outrage and pressure from members of Congress.

12. Answers will vary. Students must explain why the events they chose merit inclusion.

Using Scores to Inform Instruction

Timeline Skills A score of 6 out of 8 indicates that students understand most of the key events of this unit.

Critical Thinking A score of 8 out of 12 indicates that students are able to think critically about most of the key issues of this unit.

If students score below these levels, consider reviewing timeline and critical thinking skills.

UNIT **5**

An Expanding Nation

An Expanding Nation

Overview

This activity introduces geographic information essential to Unit 5. Students read and interpret a map to learn about U.S. expansion and population in the mid-1800s. They annotate a contiguous, continental U.S. map and answer questions in their Interactive Student Notebooks, and then discuss critical thinking questions. Their comprehension of content and proficiency in map-reading and higher-order thinking skills will help you gauge their readiness for the unit. The pages that follow include a completed map, answers to questions, a scoring guide to inform your teaching, and suggestions for modifications to meet specific student needs.

Essential Geographic Understandings

1. The steps by which the United States expanded its boundaries

2. Key physical features: Arkansas River, Columbia River, Colorado River, Missouri River, North Platte River, Rio Grande, Snake River, Great Plains, Great Salt Lake, Cascade Range, Rocky Mountains, Sierra Nevada, South Pass

3. Key human features: Gadsden Purchase, Louisiana Territory, Mexican Cession, Oregon Country, Texas, California Trail, Mormon Trail, Old Spanish Trail, Oregon Trail, Santa Fe Trail, Fort Hall, Independence, Los Angeles, Portland, Sacramento

4. The role physical geography played in western expansion

5. The role westward migration played in the nation's growth

Procedures

1 **Introduce the unit.** Tell students they will learn how the United States grew to reach the Pacific Ocean, as well as about the settlement of the West.

2 **Create a KWL chart.** Ask students to identify what they know about the nation's westward expansion and what they want to learn. Use their responses to gauge how much additional background information they will need as you progress through the unit. Students will return to the KWL chart at the end of the unit and add the key information they have learned.

3 **Have students read Unit 5 "Setting the Stage" in the Student Edition.**

4 **Have students complete the Geography Challenge.** Monitor students as they answer the questions and complete the map. You may want to have them work in pairs. Use the guide on the next two pages to check their answers. You may wish to project the map from the Interactive Student Notebook and have students annotate it as the class works through the map-reading questions. Make sure students have grasped Essential Geographic Understandings 1 to 3.

5 **Discuss the "Critical Thinking" questions.** Help students understand the geographic relationships in Essential Geographic Understandings 4 and 5.

U.S. Territorial Acquisitions, 1803–1853

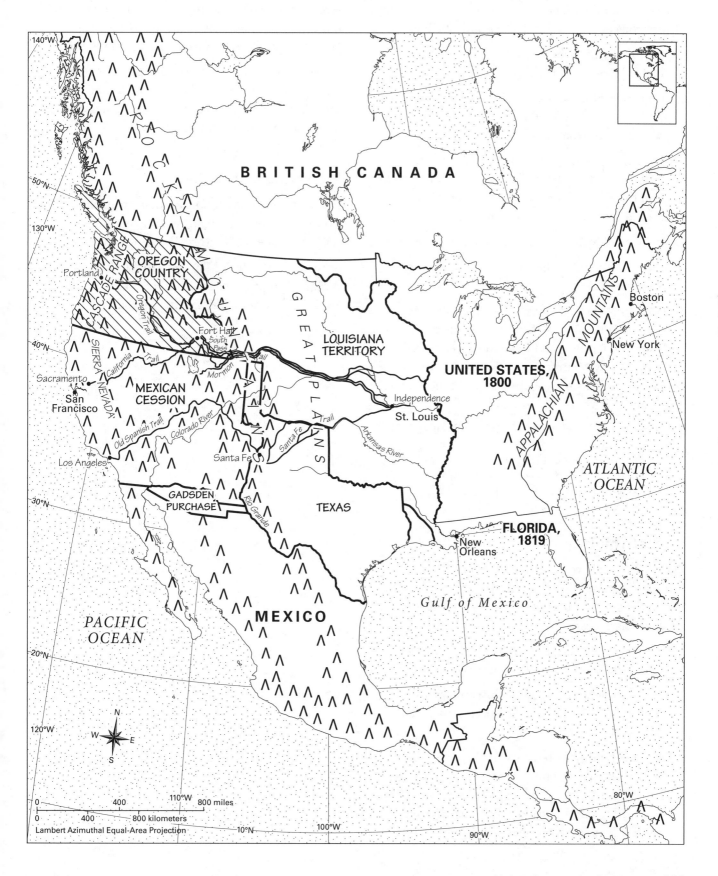

Geography Skills

Score 1 point for each correct answer. Use the map on the previous page to check shading and labeling.

1. Adding the Louisiana Territory in 1803 about doubled the size of the United States.

2. Texas was added in 1845 and the Mexican Cession in 1848. The Gadsden Purchase was the other territory acquired from Mexico.

3. The Oregon Trail crossed the Louisiana Territory on the way to Portland. The Santa Fe Trail crossed it on the way to Santa Fe. The California Trail crossed it on the way to Sacramento.

4. The United States added Oregon Country in 1846.

5. The western end of the Old Spanish Trail was Los Angeles.

6. Following the Santa Fe and Old Spanish trails to California required settlers to cross the Arkansas River, Rio Grande, and Colorado River as well as the Rocky Mountains and Sierra Nevada. (**Note:** Students may not be certain about the Arkansas River.)

7. The California Trail left the Oregon Trail at Fort Hall.

8. The Mormon, Santa Fe, and Oregon trails crossed the Rocky Mountains at South Pass.

Critical Thinking

Questions may have more than one correct answer. Score 1 to 3 points for each reasonable answer, depending on the strength of students' geographic reasoning. Possible answers are given here.

9. By following rivers, the trails provided travelers with a source of water along much of their journey.

10. Moving wagons over mountains, and with snow and cold weather, would have been slower than riding over flat land.

11. Had the Louisiana Territory not become part of the United States, Americans traveling to Oregon and California would have had to cross land that belonged to another nation. This might have discouraged Americans from settling in these regions.

Using Scores to Inform Instruction

Geography Skills A score of 6 out of 9 or better indicates that students have acquired sufficient geographic information to proceed with the unit.

Critical Thinking A score of 6 out of 9 or better indicates that students are beginning to understand the relationships between physical geography and the different ways in which people live.

Modifying Instruction

ELL or Learners with Special Education Needs Consider focusing on map-reading questions or limiting the number of "Critical Thinking" questions.

Students with Weak Map or Critical Thinking Skills Assign appropriate pages from the Social Studies Skills Toolkit in the back of the Lesson Masters.

Manifest Destiny and the Growing Nation

How justifiable was U.S. expansion in the 1800s?

Overview

In a Response Group activity, students re-create each territorial acquisition of the 1800s and then evaluate whether the nation's actions were justifiable.

Objectives

In the course of reading this chapter and participating in the classroom activity, students will

Social Studies

- describe the changing boundaries of the United States throughout the 1800s.

- analyze the causes, events, and effects of the Texas War for Independence and the Mexican-American War.

- determine the effects of manifest destiny on westward expansion in the 1800s.

- evaluate the incentives for territorial expansion and the methods used to acquire these lands in the 1800s.

Language Arts

- deliver details, reasons, and examples to support their positions.

- anticipate and answer listener concerns.

Social Studies Vocabulary

Key Content Terms territory, diplomacy, Texas War for Independence, annex, manifest destiny, Mexican-American War

Academic Vocabulary divine, justifiable, dictator

Materials

History Alive! The United States Through Industrialism

Interactive Student Notebooks

Visual 15

Lesson Masters

- Information Masters 15A–15F (1 transparency of each)

- Vocabulary Development handout (1 per student, on colored paper)

Activity	Suggested Time	Materials
Preview	15 minutes	• *History Alive! The United States Through Industrialism* • Interactive Student Notebooks • Visual 15
Vocabulary Development	30–40 minutes	• *History Alive! The United States Through Industrialism* • Interactive Student Notebooks • Vocabulary Development handout
Response Group	100 minutes (2 regular periods) (1 block period)	• *History Alive! The United States Through Industrialism* • Interactive Student Notebooks • Information Masters 15A–15F
Processing	25 minutes	• *History Alive! The United States Through Industrialism* • Interactive Student Notebooks
Assessment	40 minutes	• Chapter 15 Assessment

Preview

1 Introduce *American Progress*. Project *Visual 15: American Progress by John Gast*. Ask students, *What do you see?* Have them point out objects, people, and actions they think are significant.

2 Have students work with a partner to complete the Preview activity. Afterward, have volunteers come up to the image, point out key details, and share their answers with the class. If students don't identify these details, identify them yourself:

- The United States is portrayed as a woman floating above North America and moving westward.

- The United States carries symbols of progress and modernization: a schoolbook and telegraph wires.

- The right side of the painting (east) is lighter than the left side (west).

- American Indians and wild buffalo are fleeing to or being pushed to the West.

3 Explain the connection between the Preview and Chapter 15. Explain that the painting *American Progress* illustrates manifest destiny, a perspective that favored the westward expansion of the United States in the 1800s. In this chapter, students will examine this concept and its impact on the acquisition of five territories that extended the nation from the Atlantic Ocean to the Pacific Ocean.

Vocabulary Development

1 Introduce the Key Content Terms. Have students locate the Key Content Terms for the chapter in their Interactive Student Notebooks. These are important terms that will help them understand the main ideas of the chapter. Ask volunteers to identify any familiar terms and how they might be used in a sentence.

2 Have students complete a Vocabulary Development handout. Give each student a copy of the Vocabulary Development handout of your choice from the Reading Toolkit at the back of the Lesson Masters. These handouts provide extra practice and support, depending on your students' needs. Review the completed handout by asking volunteers to share one answer for each term.

Visual 15

Listening and Speaking: Media Communications

One way to expand the Preview is by having students work in pairs or groups to discuss and then deliver oral evaluations of the ways in which the image maker affects their impressions or opinions of manifest destiny. In their interpretations, students might focus on the effect on the intended audience of various details (are they mainly positive?), the use of line and color (is it pleasing or harsh?), and the selection of a woman to embody the idea of manifest destiny.

Reading

1 **Introduce the Essential Question and have students read Section 15.1.**
Have students identify the Essential Question for the chapter: *How justifiable was U.S. expansion in the 1800s?* Then have them read Section 15.1. Afterward, have students respond to these questions:

- Who coined the term manifest destiny? What does it mean?

- According to this person, what was the nation's manifest destiny?

- In addition to gaining land, what else did the United States have a duty to do according to manifest destiny?

- What were some of the forms that manifest destiny took during the 1800s?

- Which of these forms do you think are justifiable ways to acquire territory? Explain.

2 **Have students complete the Reading Notes for Chapter 15.** Assign Sections 15.2 to 15.6 during the activity as indicated in the procedures for the Response Group activity. Remind students to use the Key Content Terms where appropriate as they complete the Reading Notes.

Response Group

1 **Prepare the classroom.**
Create a large, open space in the middle of the room. On the floor, use masking tape to create the map shown at right, as large as possible. Alternatively, draw or tape the map on a white, king-size bed sheet and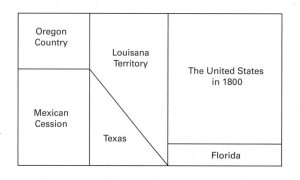
spread the sheet out on the floor. Place desks, in groups of three, around the perimeter of the floor map.

2 **Place students in groups of three and introduce the activity.** Tell students that the floor map is an abstract outline of U.S. territorial acquisitions in the 1800s. Using this map, the class will re-create important events of U.S. expansion and then decide whether the nation's actions were justifiable.

3 **Introduce the narrated act-it-outs.** Tell students they will complete a series of narrated act-it-outs, one for each territorial acquisition, in which volunteer actors will play historical characters. When the teacher says "Action!" the actors will move, act, and speak as described in the narration. Actors can embellish their performances with appropriate movements, facial expressions, and accents. The students in the audience will participate by performing an assigned action when prompted by the teacher. Students do not need to rehearse or prepare for these act-it-outs.

4 Conduct the act-it-out for the Louisiana Territory.

- Project *Information Master 15A: The Louisiana Territory Act-It-Out* and reveal the information above the narration. (**Note:** Alternatively, present all of the material orally, without projecting the Information Masters.) Point out the historical locations on the floor map as indicated on the Information Master.

- Choose volunteers to be the actors and have them take their starting positions. Explain and practice the audience action.

- Reveal and read the narration, one bullet point at a time. After each item, say "Action!" to cue the actors or "Audience!" to cue the class.

5 Have students read and complete the Reading Notes for Section 15.2.

6 Have the class decide whether U.S. expansion into the Louisiana Territory was justifiable. Project *Information Master 15B: Discussing U.S. Expansion* and reveal only Question A under Part 1. Give groups two minutes to discuss the question and then take a class vote. If the vote is yes, write "justifiable" in the corresponding space on the map of U.S. expansion on the Information Master.

7 Repeat Steps 4 to 6 for the remaining territorial acquisitions. Adjust the materials for each new round as follows:

- Florida: Use *Information Master 15C: Florida Act-It-Out*, Section 15.3, and Question B on Information Master 15B.

- Texas: Use *Information Master 15D: Texas Act-It-Out*, Section 15.4, and Question C on Information Master 15B.

- Oregon Country: Use *Information Master 15E: Oregon Country Act-It-Out*, Section 15.5, and Question D on Information Master 15B.

- Mexican-American War: Use *Information Master 15F: Mexican-American War Act-It-Out*, Section 15.6, and Question E on Information Master 15B.

8 Have students judge U.S. expansion in the 1800s. Project Part 2 on Information Master 15B, and have groups follow the procedure to prepare for the final discussion. When groups are ready, call on them one by one to mark the spectrum with their answer and present their position. Encourage students to debate opposing viewpoints and defend their positions.

Processing

Have students complete the Processing activity. Students will annotate the painting *American Progress* to explain how justifiable they believe U.S. expansion was in the 1800s.

Information Master 15A

Information Master 15B

Information Masters 15C–15F

Quicker Coverage

Reduce the Number of Act-It-Outs Conduct the narrated act-it-outs for just two or three territories, prioritizing those that are most important in your state standards. For the remaining territories, have students only complete Reading Notes.

Deeper Coverage

Discuss Each Territorial Acquisition Before the class votes on whether U.S. expansion into a territory was justifiable, have groups select a spokesperson to argue their group's position in a class discussion. Encourage spokespersons to debate and defend their positions.

Assessment

Mastering the Content

1. A	5. B	9. C	13. C
2. D	6. A	10. B	14. B
3. A	7. B	11. A	15. B
4. B	8. B	12. D	16. A

Applying Social Studies Skills

17. The United States purchased the land from France.

18. 3, 5

19. Mississippi River

Exploring the Essential Question

20. Answers should include all of the elements requested in the prompt.

Scoring Rubric

Score	Description
3	Student completes all four parts of the task. Ideas are clearly stated, supported by details, and demonstrate command of standard English conventions.
2	Student responds to most or all parts of the task. Ideas may lack details or not be clearly stated.
1	Student responds to at least one part of the task. Ideas may contain factual or grammatical errors and may lack details.
0	Response does not match the task or is incorrect.

Westward on the Santa Fe Trail

1 **Have students inspect a map of the Santa Fe Trail.** Provide maps of the Santa Fe Trail, either historical maps or contemporary maps that show the route. (You may wish to explore the maps suggested in the Internet Connections for Chapter 15 available through the Enrichment Resources for *History Alive! The United States Through Industrialism*.)

2 **Have students read the first page of the Chapter 15 Reading Further.** When they have finished, review the chronology of Santa Fe's transition from a Spanish colony to being part of the United States. Explain that the Magoffin trip occurred at the beginning of the Mexican War, a conflict that would result in, among other things, the acquisition of New Mexico by the United States.

3 **Have students finish the reading.** Then, on a map of the Santa Fe Trail, have students trace the Magoffins's route. Note that the travelers stopped at Bent's Fort, which means they took the northern route rather than the more dangerous Cimarron Cutoff.

4 **Have students complete the Chapter 15 Reading Further in their Interactive Student Notebooks.** Have students share their postcards. Ask volunteers to describe who they were, their reasons for going on the Santa Fe Trail, and how they feel about the grand style in which the Magoffins traveled.

5 **Invite interested students to create actual postcards, drawing scenes of the trail on the reverse side.**

English Language Learners

Give Extra Vocabulary Support Ensure that students fully understand the terms *justifiable* and *acquire*. Consider adding these terms to the list of Key Content Terms so students will practice their meanings on the Vocabulary Development handout.

Create Cue Cards Have spokespersons create cue cards that include important points they can refer to during the final discussion. Allow students to read their cue cards when they present.

Learners Reading and Writing Below Grade Level

Use Labels During the Act-It-Outs Help students make connections between the performances and the reading by labeling each historical location and having actors make and wear name tags for their historical characters.

Highlight Main Ideas Make copies of Sections 15.2 to 15.6 and highlight or circle main ideas to help students focus their attention and complete their Reading Notes. Alternatively, provide highlighted copies of lengthier readings, such as Sections 15.4 and 15.6, and have students highlight the main ideas in other, shorter sections.

Learners with Special Education Needs

Create Cloze Reading Notes Give students a copy of Reading Notes 15 with partial answers. For example, fill in some of the answers on the timeline in Section 15.4. Or, for Question 2 in Section 15.3, fill in "Spain gave Florida to the United States for a payment of _____" and have students finish the answer.

Modify the Processing Activity Rather than requiring students to write a paragraph for each element they identify in the painting, have them write just a sentence or two for each.

Advanced Learners

Assign a More In-Depth Processing Have students create an original and detailed allegorical image to express their opinion of westward expansion in the 1800s. Students should annotate their images with four to six thought or speech bubbles, as in the original Processing activity, citing at least three pieces of historical evidence to support their position and using as many of the Key Content Terms as possible.

Enrichment Resources

Find out more about manifest destiny by exploring the following Enrichment Resources for *History Alive! The United States Through Industrialism* at www.teachtci.com.

Enrichment Readings These in-depth readings encourage students to explore selected topics related to the chapter. You may also find readings that relate the chapter's content directly to your state's curriculum.

Internet Connections The recommended Web sites provide useful and engaging content that reinforces skills development and mastery of subjects within the chapter.

Literature Recommendations

The following books offer opportunities to extend the content in this chapter.

James Polk: Our Eleventh President by Ann Gaines (Mankato, MN: Child's World, 2002)

In the Shadow of the Alamo by Sherry Garland (Orlando, FL: Harcourt Brace, 2001)

James Monroe by Stuart Kallen (Edina, MN: ABDO Publishing, 2002)

Section 15.2

1. Farmers depended on the river to get their crops to the port in New Orleans, where they would load them onto ships bound for markets in Europe and on the East Coast.

2. Napoleon wanted to settle the territory with French farmers, who would supply food for the slaves that worked in the Caribbean. American farmers feared that if the port of New Orleans were closed to Americans, they would not be able to get their crops to market.

3. The United States agreed to buy the Louisiana Territory for $15 million. Napoleon no longer needed the territory because slaves had revolted in Haiti and overthrown the government. Also, France was about to enter into war with the British and might lose the territory anyway.

4. Possible answers:

Pros of the Louisiana Purchase	Cons of the Louisiana Purchase
• doubled the country's size at a cheap price • secured the free navigation of the Mississippi River • gained lands without bloodshed	• impossible to govern such a large piece of land • some easterners feared they would lose power in Congress to new western states • too expensive when the country had little money • unconstitutional

Section 15.3

1. President Monroe order Jackson to chase raiding Seminole Indians back into Florida, but not to invade Florida. Instead, Jackson invaded Florida, captured military forts, executed two British subjects for stirring up Indian attacks, and replaced the Spanish governor.

2. Spain agreed to leave Florida. The United States agreed to pay $5 million in settlers' claims and to honor Spain's claim to Texas.

Section 15.4

1. Possible answers:

   American settlers: Americans were used to governing themselves and did not want to take orders from the Mexican government. All official documents had to be in Spanish. Mexico outlawed slavery in 1829 and many Americans in Texas were slaveholders.

   Tejanos: Tejanos were upset that many Americans had settled in Texas illegally. Americans showed little respect for Mexican culture. Many Americans had no intention of becoming citizens.

2. Possible answers (terms from the Word Bank are underlined):

   • 1829: Slavery is outlawed in Texas and the rest of Mexico.

   • 1830: 25,000 Americans live in Texas, compared to 4,000 Tejanos.

   • 1833: Stephen F. Austin travels to Mexico City to try to convince the government to reopen Texas to immigration and make it a separate Mexican state. General Santa Anna throws him in jail.

   • 1835: Texas revolts against the government. General Santa Anna marches 6,000 troops into Texas to crush the rebels.

   • March 1836: The Texans are defeated at the Alamo, with no survivors.

   • April 1836: Texans yell "Remember the Alamo!" as they surprise attack and defeat the Mexican army near the San Jacinto River. Santa Anna is captured.

   • 1836–1845: Texas is a free and independent country known as the Lone Star Republic.

3. Texas became a part of the United States.

   Possible arguments against: Annexation might lead to war with Mexico. Some Northerners did not want to add another slave state to the nation.

   Possible arguments in favor: Annexing Texas was our manifest destiny. Some Southerners were eager to add another slave state.

Section 15.5

1. Great Britain and the United States agreed to a peaceful joint occupation of Oregon.

2. Possible answers: fertile soil, towering forests, sunny weather, no disease, free farms

3. Polk wanted the United States to have the entire Oregon Country and was willing to fight Britain for it. He did not follow through with this promise, but instead used diplomacy to reach a compromise that gave half of Oregon to the United States and half to Britain.

Section 15.6

1. Polk thought the Mexican government might sell California and New Mexico because they were thinly settled and neglected by the Mexican government.

2. Possible annotations: Texas claimed the Rio Grande was the border; Mexico wanted the Nueces River to be the border. April 25, 1846: Mexican troops fire on U.S. soldiers patrolling the Rio Grande. President Polk claims Mexico had invaded the United States.

3. Possible headlines for the five battles:

   New Mexico: (U.S.) "Unable to Fight the Spread of Democracy, New Mexico Surrenders Without a Shot"; (Mexico) "New Mexico Surrenders to American Bullies"

   California: (U.S.) "California Revolts! Chooses to Join Forces and Link Its Manifest Destiny with America's!"; (Mexico) "Californian Traitors Join Forces with the Americans"

   Monterrey: (U.S.) "American Forces Take Monterrey, But Santa Anna Slows Their Progress"; (Mexico) "Lawless Americans Invade Mexico— Santa Anna Halts Invasion Outside Monterrey!"

   Buena Vista: (U.S.) "Brutal Fighting Near Buena Vista Leads to Capture of Northern Mexico and One Step Closer to Our Manifest Destiny!"; (Mexico) "Santa Anna's Forces Fight Off the Americans and Return to the South"

   Chapultepec: (U.S.) "Mexico City Captured! Liberty Prevails!"; (Mexico) "Soldiers and Cadets Fight Bravely But Can't Defeat Yankee Tyrants!"

4. *Details of the Treaty of Guadalupe Hildalgo:* Mexico gave up Texas and the Mexican Cession, which included the present-day states of California, Nevada, Utah, Arizona, and New Mexico and parts of Colorado and Wyoming. The United States agreed to pay Mexico $15 million. The United States promised to protect Mexican citizens living in Texas and the Mexican Cession.

   Opposition: Some senators opposed the treaty because they felt the United States only had a right to Texas, not the Mexican Cession. Others opposed the treaty because they also wanted it to cede parts of northern Mexico.

5. Railroad builders wanted this flat piece of land to build a new route across the nation.

Life in the West

What were the motives, hardships, and legacies of the groups that moved west in the 1800s?

Overview

In a Problem Solving Groupwork activity, students create and perform mini-dramas about eight groups of people who moved to the West in the 1800s. Students explore these people's motives for moving, the hardships they faced, and the legacies they left behind for future generations.

Objectives

In the course of reading this chapter and participating in the classroom activity, students will

Social Studies

- analyze the motives, hardships, and economic incentives associated with westward expansion.
- describe the role of pioneer women and the new status that western women achieved.

Language Arts

- employ narrative and descriptive strategies in a dramatization.

Social Studies Vocabulary

Key Content Terms Lewis and Clark expedition, legacy, rancho, Oregon Trail, Mormons, forty-niners

Academic Vocabulary motive, stimulate, status, prospect, persecuted

Materials

History Alive! The United States Through Industrialism

Interactive Student Notebooks

CD Track 8

Visuals 16A–16I

Lesson Masters

- Information Master 16 (1 transparency)
- Student Handout 16 (1 per group)
- Vocabulary Development handout (1 per student, on colored paper)

Activity	Suggested Time	Materials
Preview	15 minutes	• Interactive Student Notebooks • CD Track 8 • Visual 16A • Information Master 16
Vocabulary Development	30–40 minutes	• *History Alive! The United States Through Industrialism* • Interactive Student Notebooks • Vocabulary Development handout
Problem Solving Groupwork	150 minutes (3 regular periods) (1.5 block periods)	• *History Alive! The United States Through Industrialism* • Interactive Student Notebooks • Visuals 16B–16I • Student Handout 16
Processing	30 minutes	• *History Alive! The United States Through Industrialism* • Interactive Student Notebooks
Assessment	40 minutes	• Chapter 16 Assessment

Preview

1 Have students analyze 19th-century primary sources of the journey west. Play CD Track 8, "Sweet Betsy from Pike," while projecting *Information Master 16: Sweet Betsy from Pike* and have students follow along with the lyrics as they listen. Then project *Visual 16A: Westward the Course of Empire Takes Its Way* or direct students to the painting that opens Chapter 16. Ask student to point out features in the painting that are mentioned in the song.

2 Have students work with a partner to complete the Preview activity. Students will answer questions to further analyze these two primary sources.

3 Have students share their responses with the class.

4 Explain the connection between the Preview and Chapter 16. Explain that in the early to mid-1800s, people were lured to the West by the promise of land and new opportunities. "Sweet Betsy from Pike" and the painting *Westward the Course of Empire Takes Its Way* glorify those who took the risk and journeyed to the frontier. In this chapter, students will learn about the motives of eight groups of people that decided to move west, the hardships they faced, and the legacies they left behind for future generations.

Vocabulary Development

1 Introduce the Key Content Terms. Have students locate the Key Content Terms for the chapter in their Interactive Student Notebooks. These are important terms that will help them understand the main ideas of the chapter. Ask volunteers to identify any familiar terms and how they might be used in a sentence.

2 Have students complete a Vocabulary Development handout. Give each student a copy of the Vocabulary Development handout of your choice from the Reading Toolkit at the back of the Lesson Masters. These handouts provide extra practice and support, depending on your students' needs. Review the completed handout by asking volunteers to share one answer for each term.

Reading

1 Introduce the Essential Question and have students read Section 16.1. Have students identify the Essential Question for the chapter, *What were the motives, hardships, and legacies of the groups that moved west in the 1800s?* Then have them read Section 16.1. Afterward, have them use information from the reading and the painting that opens the chapter to propose possible answers to the Essential Question.

2 Have students complete the Reading Notes for Chapter 16. Assign Sections 16.2 to 16.9 during the activity as indicated in the procedures for the Problem Solving Groupwork activity. Remind students to use the Key Content Terms where appropriate as they complete their Reading Notes.

Information Master 16

Visual 16A

Problem Solving Groupwork

1 **Place students in groups of four and introduce the activity.** Tell students that each group of four will create a three-scene minidrama about a group of people that moved to the West in the 1800s. Assign settlers' groups by distributing one of *Visuals 16B–16I: Groups Who Moved West in the 1800s* to each group of students. Also give each group a copy of *Student Handout 16: Preparing a Minidrama About Life in the West*. Explain that students will use these materials and information in their books to create their minidramas.

2 **Assign roles and review the steps for creating the minidramas.** Review the four roles listed in Step 1 on Student Handout 16, and assign each student a role. Then review Steps 2 through 6 on Student Handout 16, and answer any questions students have.

3 **Monitor groups as they create their minidramas.** Allow groups adequate time to prepare. Check their work and initial Student Handout 16 as they complete each of the six steps.

4 **Arrange the room for the presentations.** When students are ready to present their minidramas, arrange the classroom with a stage area in front and the projector centrally located, as shown in the diagram.

Student Handout 16

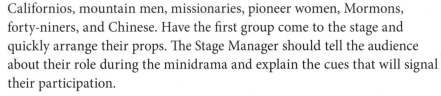

5 **Have the first group set up for their minidrama.** Have groups present in this sequence: explorers, Californios, mountain men, missionaries, pioneer women, Mormons, forty-niners, and Chinese. Have the first group come to the stage and quickly arrange their props. The Stage Manager should tell the audience about their role during the minidrama and explain the cues that will signal their participation.

6 **Have the first group perform their minidrama.** Project the group's image. Remind performers to speak loudly so that they can be easily heard, and encourage everyone to be supportive, respectful, and attentive during the presentation.

7 **After the performance, have students in the audience read and complete the Reading Notes for the corresponding section.** While the audience completes their Reading Notes, have the students who just performed clean up the stage. Then have them write a two-paragraph reflection on their minidrama, explaining what they believe worked well and how they might improve their presentation.

8 **Repeat Steps 5 to 7 for the remaining minidramas.**

Student Handout 16

> **Listening and Speaking: Use Precise Language**
>
> As students create their minidramas, remind them of the power of action verbs, precise language, sensory details, appropriate and colorful modifiers, and the active voice in creating and enlivening dramatic scenes, as well as for maintaining audience interest.

9 **Debrief the activity.** Ask,

- What were the motives of the groups of settlers that moved west in the 1800s?

- If you lived during this time, which of these reasons may have caused you to move to the West?

- What hardships did these groups face?

- Do you think the lives of each of these groups improved as a result of moving to the West? Why or why not?

- What are some important legacies of these groups? How do the histories of these groups in the West affect our lives today?

Processing

Have students complete the Processing activity. They will compose a song with lyrics that describe the experience of four groups that moved to the West.

Quicker Coverage

Streamline the Activity Post two paper sets of Visuals 16B–16I on the walls. Put students in pairs and have them follow the steps below. Consider projecting these steps as students work.

Step 1: Go to an image with your partner.

Step 2: Discuss these questions with your partner: *What interesting details do you see? What are some possible motives, or reasons, for these people to move west? What are some hardships they faced? What are some legacies they left behind?*

Step 3: Return to your desks. Read the corresponding section in your book, and complete your Reading Notes for that section.

Simplify the Presentations Instead of having groups prepare minidramas, have them create a simple presentation about their group of settlers.

- Distribute one of Visuals 16B–16I to each group.

- Have students examine their image and complete the Reading Notes for their group.

- Assign students in each group to one of these topics: *reasons your group moved to the West, hardships your group faced* (assign two students to this topic), and *legacies your group left behind.*

- Have students create a presentation of their topic that is no longer than one minute and includes a prop to illustrate one of their points.

- Have groups project their image and refer to it at least once during their presentation.

Deeper Coverage

Conduct Additional Research Have students gather information from the library or Internet to add to their presentations. Ask them to create a bibliography of their sources.

Assessment

Mastering the Content

1. C	5. C	9. B	13. D
2. C	6. A	10. C	14. D
3. A	7. A	11. B	15. C
4. D	8. B	12. C	16. D

Applying Social Studies Skills

17. mountains

18. Salt Lake City, Utah

19. Possible answer: The trails had different starting points. People traveling along the Oregon Trail had more hardships and a longer trip.

Exploring the Essential Question

20. Answers should include all of the elements requested in the prompt.

Scoring Rubric

Score	Description
3	Student completes all three parts of the task. Ideas are clearly stated, supported by details, and demonstrate command of standard English conventions.
2	Student responds to most or all parts of the task. Ideas may lack details or not be clearly stated.
1	Student responds to at least one part of the task. Ideas may contain factual or grammatical errors and may lack details.
0	Response does not match the task or is incorrect.

Gold Rush Pioneers

1 **Discuss motivations for emigration.** Talk about the various motivations for making a major life change. Ask students what it would take for their families to decide to move to a new place that was far away and hard to get to.

2 **Have students read the Chapter 16 Reading Further.** Discuss the reasons for going to California during the gold rush for each of the people profiled in the reading.

3 **Discuss the gold rush and California statehood.** Ask students to think about how Vicente Pérez Rosales's description of the election points to the heart of the democratic process. The majority decision was accepted as valid by all of the voters.

4 **Have students complete the first page of the Chapter 16 Reading Further in their Interactive Student Notebooks.** Discuss the differences and similarities in the push factors and pull factors for the four people. The opportunity for wealth was part of the attraction for all four pioneers. But for Alvin Coffey, there was an even stronger motivation: freedom.

5 **Have students complete the second page of the Reading Further.** Invite students to share their human-interest articles with the class.

English Language Learners

Eliminate Dialogue in the Minidramas Allow English language learners to use actions instead of words to perform their parts.

Support the Processing Place students in pairs to compose their song lyrics. You may also want to reduce the number of stanzas required.

Learners Reading and Writing Below Grade Level

Complete Reading Notes During the Minidramas As each group stages its minidrama, have students fill in any answers they can in the related Reading Notes.

Provide an Example of the Processing Create an example of the Processing activity that students can refer to for format and wording as they compose their lyrics.

Learners with Special Education Needs

Modify the Reading Notes Replace the Reading Notes with a chart as shown below, and have students draw or write down answers they learn from the minidramas. If any cells remain blank, have students find one answer in their books for each of those cells.

	Reasons for Moving West	Hardships Faced	Legacies Left Behind
Explorers			
Californios			
Mountain Men			
Missionaries			
Pioneer women			
Mormons			
Forty-niners			
Chinese			

Change the Processing Activity Instead of having students write a song, have them create a collage of four groups of settlers. Their collages must show the reasons these groups moved to the West, the hardships they faced, and the legacies they left behind.

Advanced Learners

Lengthen the Processing Have students write a stanza for each of the eight groups they learned about.

Annotate "Sweet Betsy from Pike" Give students a copy of Information Master 16 and challenge them to highlight lyrics that relate to information in the chapter and to explain the connections. For example, they might highlight "They stopped in Salt Lake to inquire the way" and write, *Salt Lake is the Great Salt Lake where the Mormons settled.*

Enrichment Resources

Find out more about life in the West by exploring the following Enrichment Resources for *History Alive! The United States Through Industrialism* at www.teachtci.com.

Enrichment Readings These in-depth readings encourage students to explore selected topics related to the chapter. You may also find readings that relate the chapter's content directly to your state's curriculum.

Internet Connections The recommended Web sites provide useful and engaging content that reinforces skills development and mastery of subjects within the chapter.

Literature Recommendations

The following books offer opportunities to extend the content in this chapter.

Lewis and Clark: Explorers of the Louisiana Purchase by Richard Kozar (New York: Chelsea House, 2000)

When Esther Morris Headed West: Women, Wyoming, and the Right to Vote by Connie Nordhielm Wooldridge (New York: Holiday House, 2001)

Journal of Wong Ming-Chung: A Chinese Miner, California, 1852 by Laurence Yep (New York: Scholastic, 2000)

Section 16.2

1. The Lewis and Clark expedition explored the West to make friendly contact with Indian groups that might want to trade, to find a water route across North America, and to explore the territory the United States had just purchased.

2. Possible answers: sunburn, mosquitoes, blistered hands, sore muscles, rivers and waterfalls, cacti, grizzlies, lack of food

3. Possible answers: Lewis and Clark mapped a route to the Pacific, established good relations with western Indians, and brought back information about the West and its peoples.

4. *Zebulon Pike:* He explored southern Louisiana Territory and made reports of the wealth of Spanish towns along the Rio Grande and Red River, which brought American traders to the region.

   John C. Frémont: He mapped much of the territory between the Mississippi Valley and the Pacific Ocean and inspired many families to move west.

Section 16.3

1. Settlers and soldiers; the government wanted to attract people to settle in California and wanted to reward soldiers.

2. Possible answers: Growing food, raising cattle, fiestas, displays of horsemanship

3. Possible answers: Californios lived far from neighbors and the Mexican government, faced raids by soldier, and were often governed by unskilled and dishonest officials.

4. Possible answers: The Californios' legacy includes Spanish place names, new food crops, and opening California to other settlers.

Section 16.4

1. Manuel Lisa hoped to find beaver in the Rocky Mountains.

2. Possible answers: Mountain men faced attack by fur thieves, Indians, wolves, and bears; accidents; and disease.

3. Answers will vary.

4. Possible answers: The mountain men's legacy includes exploring the West, establishing the Oregon and California Trails, setting up trading posts that later became supply stations for settlers, and recording their stories in personal journals.

Section 16.5

1. Missionaries moved west to convert American Indians to Christianity.

2. The sketch should show Marcus Whitman convincing or leading whites to move to the West. The speech bubble should highlight his belief that whites should settle Oregon and establish their religion there.

3. Possible answers: Many Indians died of the diseases that missionaries, and the settlers that followed them, brought to the West. Missionaries helped open the West to settlement.

Section 16.6

1. Some single women moved west in search of homesteads, husbands, or other new opportunities.

2. Possible answers: Women faced having to leave possessions behind on the trail, the daily drudgery of chores, disease, accidents, drowning, rare Indian attacks, buffalo stampedes, prairie fires, and freezing temperatures.

3. *Biddy Mason:* She was a slave who sued for her freedom and won. She settled in Los Angeles and became a community leader.

   Annie Bidwell: She settled in Chico, California, where she taught sewing to Indian women and English to their children. Her actions helped establish the city's first church.

   Wyoming Territory: This was the first U.S. territory that allowed women the right to vote.

Section 16.7

1. Mormons had views that offended some people in the 1800s, and they were driven from their homes in the East.

2. Many Mormons died on the journey west. When those who survived finally settled, they had to learn how to farm in a very dry environment.

3. Possible answers: The Mormons pioneered new farming methods for dry regions, helped many settlers on their journey west, and established a large Mormon community in the West.

Section 16.8

1. People moved to California after 1848 to mine for gold.

2. Possible answers: Forty-niners faced a difficult journey west, high prices, no law enforcement, the hard work of mining, and gold that was soon gone, leaving many with nothing.

3. Possible answers:

   California Indian: Most of my people have died from the disease and war brought by the settlers.

   Californio: I lost my land to American settlers.

   Forty-niner: We now have enough people in California to make it the first state in the West!

Section 16.9

1. Reports that they would have great pay, large houses, and fine food and clothing motivated Chinese to travel to California.

2. Many Americans abused the Chinese to cause them to leave the mines. Some Chinese moved into California's growing cities to open restaurants and laundries. Others began farming in California's Central Valley.

3. Possible answers: The Chinese helped build such industries as mining and farming in California, and they introduced their rich culture to the West.

Mexicano Contributions to the Southwest

How have Mexicano contributions influenced life in the United States?

Overview

In a Social Studies Skill Builder, students examine important Mexicano contributions and determine how they have influenced life in the United States.

Objectives

In the course of reading this chapter and participating in the classroom activity, students will

Social Studies

- identify the effects of the Mexican-American War on Mexicanos.
- analyze the influence of Mexicano contributions on the culture and economy of the Southwest in the 1800s and the United States today.
- demonstrate an understanding of Mexicano contributions in their communities.

Language Arts

- use word meanings within an appropriate context.

Social Studies Vocabulary

Key Content Terms Mexicanos, irrigation

Academic Vocabulary tradition, accompaniment, procession

Materials

History Alive! The United States Through Industrialism

Interactive Student Notebooks

Visual 17

Placards 17A–17I (2 sets; create additional placards as needed)

Lesson Masters

- Information Master 17 (1 transparency)
- Vocabulary Development handout (1 per student, on colored paper)

Activity	Suggested Time	Materials
Preview	10 minutes	• Interactive Student Notebooks
Vocabulary Development	30–40 minutes	• *History Alive! The United States Through Industrialism* • Interactive Student Notebooks • Vocabulary Development handout
Social Studies Skill Builder	100 minutes (2 regular periods) (1 block period)	• *History Alive! The United States Through Industrialism* • Interactive Student Notebooks • Visual 17 • Placards 17A–17I (2 sets) • Information Master 17
Processing	30 minutes	• Interactive Student Notebooks
Assessment	40 minutes	• Chapter 17 Assessment

Preview

1 **Have students complete the Preview activity.** Students will identify items that they believe are Mexicano contributions to the Southwest.

2 **Have students share their responses with the class.** Reveal one by one that each item is indeed a Mexicano contribution.

3 **Explain the connection between the Preview and Chapter 17.** Tell students that when the United States acquired Texas and the Mexican Cession, they gained much more than a vast holding of diverse land to settle. These territories, which became known as the Southwest, were home to many Mexicanos that had already shaped the culture and economy of the region. In this chapter, students will learn about several Mexicano contributions that not only shaped the region, but also influenced settlers in the 1800s and life in the United States today.

Vocabulary Development

1 **Introduce the Key Content Terms.** Have students locate the Key Content Terms for the chapter in their Interactive Student Notebooks. These are important terms that will help them understand the main ideas of the chapter. Ask volunteers to identify any familiar terms and how they might be used in a sentence.

2 **Have students complete a Vocabulary Development handout.** Give each student a copy of the Vocabulary Development handout of your choice from the Reading Toolkit at the back of the Lesson Masters. These handouts provide extra practice and support, depending on your students' needs. Review the completed handout by asking volunteers to share one answer for each term.

Reading

1 **Introduce the Essential Question and have students read Section 17.1.** Have students identify the Essential Question, *How have Mexicano contributions influenced life in the United States?* Then have them read Section 17.1. Afterward, have them respond to these questions:

   • What promises did the United States make to Mexicanos in the Treaty of Guadalupe Hidalgo? Did the United States keep these promises?

   • Describe how most white settlers felt about Mexicanos in the 1800s.

   • In what areas have Mexicanos made contributions to life in the United States?

2 **Have students complete the Reading Notes for Chapter 17.** Assign Sections 17.2 to 17.10 during the activity as indicated in the procedures for the Social Studies Skill Builder. Remind students to use the Key Content Terms where appropriate as they complete their Reading Notes.

Social Studies Skill Builder

1 **Prepare the classroom.** Post two sets of *Placards 17A–17I: Mexicano Contributions* on the walls, spacing them a few feet apart. (**Note:** Create additional placards as needed.) Tape only the top corners to the wall, as students will flip the placards up during the activity to read the information on the back.

2 **Introduce the activity.** Tell students that they will work with a partner to discover a variety of Mexicano contributions to the Southwest and how those contributions have influenced life in the United States.

3 **Practice the process as a class.** Before pairs work on their own, project *Visual 17: Packing for the Mule Train* and have students hypothesize about the image by responding to the questions listed. Tell students that this image shows preparing a mule train for travel and that the answer to Question 2 is mule packing.

4 **Discuss information about mule trains.** Tell students that Mexicanos improved transportation in the Southwest with the use of the mule train, and ask them to share any knowledge they may have about mule trains before you reveal these facts:

- The *atajo,* or mule train, was used by Mexicanos in the Valley of Mexico, and its use eventually spread north.

- Mules are able to carry up to 400 pounds over dangerous, steep trails on which horses cannot travel.

- Up to 200 mules can be used in a single atajo. Even when loaded down with packs, these sturdy animals can travel close to 15 miles per day.

5 **Place students in pairs and review the steps for the activity.** Project and review the steps on *Information Master 17: Examining Mexicano Contributions*. Explain that the same questions that were used to hypothesize about the mule train image will be asked about each placard image.

6 **Conduct the activity.** Monitor student progress and check each pair's Reading Notes at least once early in the activity. Continue the activity until most pairs have examined most of the placards and completed the corresponding Reading Notes.

7 **Review the contributions.**

- Remove the placards from the wall and distribute one to each pair.

- Give pairs a few minutes to prepare a one-minute presentation that highlights the information in their Reading Notes about the contribution shown on their placard.

- Ask volunteers to come to the front of the room and present their Mexicano contribution to the class.

Placards 17A–17I

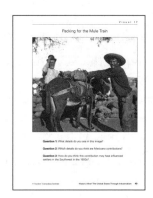

Visual 17

Information Master 17

8 Debrief the activity by creating a human spectrum.

- Draw a horizontal line along the board and label the ends "Strong Influence Today" and "No Influence Today."

- Give pairs a few minutes to discuss where on the spectrum they would place the contribution on their placard.

- Have one student from each pair come forward, stand where the pair determined the contribution belongs, and hold up the placard.

- Ask seated students to identify contributions they believe are misplaced. Encourage discussion of where the contributions should be placed.

Processing

Have students complete the Processing activity in their Interactive Student Notebooks or on a separate sheet of paper. Students will create a collage of Mexicano contributions found in their own community.

Quicker Coverage

Use Fewer Placards Choose just four or five placards for students to examine in class and assign the remaining Reading Notes for homework. Consider choosing placards that reflect Mexicano contributions in your community.

Eliminate the Spectrum Instead of creating a human spectrum to debrief the activity, simply ask the class these questions:

- Which of these contributions were familiar to you? Unfamiliar to you?
- Which contribution do you think was the most important to settlers in the Southwest in the 1800s? Why?
- How have Mexicano contributions influenced life in the United States?

Deeper Coverage

Map the Contribution Symbols Give students a simple outline map of the United States and have them go back to the reading, identify appropriate locations for their symbols, and place them on the map. Students should then create a key and title for their maps. Finally, ask students to write a one-paragraph answer to these questions below the map: *Where are Mexicano contributions concentrated in this map? Why do you think they are concentrated there?*

Create a Spectrum of Contributions Have students draw a line in their notebooks and label the ends "Strong Influence Today" and "No Influence Today." Ask students to place their symbols for each contribution on the spectrum according to their own opinions. Then have them write a paragraph justifying their placement of the two contributions they put closest to the "Strong" end of the spectrum.

Assessment

Mastering the Content

1. A	5. A	9. B	13. D
2. B	6. C	10. C	14. A
3. A	7. A	11. B	15. D
4. D	8. C	12. B	16. A

Applying Social Studies Skills

17. Answers will vary and may include the idea that parts of the United States were once territories of Mexico.

18. A

19. Answers will vary.

Exploring the Essential Question

20. Answers should include all of the elements requested in the prompt.

Scoring Rubric

Score	Description
3	Student completes all three parts of the task. Ideas are clearly stated, supported by details, and demonstrate command of standard English conventions.
2	Student responds to most or all parts of the task. Ideas may lack details or not be clearly stated.
1	Student responds to at least one part of the task. Ideas may contain factual or grammatical errors and may lack details.
0	Response does not match the task or is incorrect.

Mexicano Culture Today

1 **Talk about ways in which visual arts and performances can convey culture.** Engage the class in a discussion of how culture is conveyed through various media. Ask students to describe a song, painting, or performance that tells a story or gives a sense of contemporary American culture. If there are any public murals in your community, bring those into the discussion.

2 **Have students read the Chapter 17 Reading Further.** Ask students what similarities they see in the purposes behind the murals, the farmworkers' theater, Charro Days, and ballet folklórico. Also discuss the cultural pride that each form of art reflects. (**Note:** Encourage interested students to conduct further research about *The Great Wall of Los Angeles*. You may want to have them explore the Internet Connections for Chapter 17 available through the Enrichment Resources for *History Alive! The United States Through Industrialism*.)

3 **Have students complete the first page of the Chapter 17 Reading Further in their Interactive Student Notebooks.** When they are finished, discuss the careful planning and cooperation that are involved in a project such as a public mural.

4 **Have students complete the second page of the Reading Further.** Invite students to share their design proposals with the class. Encourage students who wish to add sketches to their proposals to do so.

English Language Learners

Give Extra Vocabulary Support Ensure that students understand the terms *contribution, influence,* and *adapt.* Consider adding these terms to the list of Key Content Terms so students will work with them on the Vocabulary Development handout.

Learners Reading and Writing Below Grade Level

Illustrate the Reading Notes Rather than requiring them to answer in complete sentences, allow students to make and label sketches in their Reading Notes.

Simplify the Processing Activity In place of having them write paragraphs, have students write a one-sentence summary explaining how each item has influenced or enhanced their lives.

Learners with Special Education Needs

Highlight the Reading Provide students with copies of Sections 17.2 to 17.10 to use for their Reading Notes. Have students highlight the reading in three colors, using one color for examples of contributions, another for ways those contributions influenced settlers in the 1800s, and a third for ways those contributions have influenced life in the United States. Consider highlighting one or two sections in this manner as a model for students.

Make the Placards Accessible Hang placards at a level where they can be viewed by all students. Or, have students remain seated during the activity and pass placards from pair to pair.

Advanced Learners

Write a New Chapter Section Challenge students to find and research another important Mexicano contribution to the United States and write a new section for Chapter 17. The section must have a section title, subsections with titles, and an image with a caption. The text must adequately describe the contribution with examples and explain its influence on the United States.

Enrichment Resources

Find out more about Mexicano contributions to the Southwest by exploring the following Enrichment Resources for *History Alive! The United States Through Industrialism* at www.teachtci.com.

Enrichment Readings These in-depth readings encourage students to explore selected topics related to the chapter. You may also find readings that relate the chapter's content directly to your state's curriculum.

Internet Connections The recommended Web sites provide useful and engaging content that reinforces skills development and mastery of subjects within the chapter.

Literature Recommendations

The following books offer opportunities to extend the content in this chapter.

In the Days of the Vaqueros: America's First True Cowboys by Russell Freedman (New York: Clarion Books, 2001)

Mexico: The People by Bobbie Kalman (New York: Crabtree Publishing, 2002)

Culture and Customs of Mexico by Peter Standish (Westport, CT: Greenwood Press, 2003)

Possible answers to the matrix questions. Symbols will vary.

Mexicano Contributions to the Southwest

Topic	List details you think are Mexicano contributions.	Give three or more examples or details of Mexicano contributions from this section.
Mining Placard 17A Section 17.2	gold pan riffle box	• Gold pans (bateas) and riffle boxes were introduced to extract gold from streams. • Arrastras, or grinding mills, were used to mine gold from rocks. • Mexicano miners helped discover and mine silver and copper.
Cattle Ranching Placard 17B Section 17.3	cattle brand vaquero roundup cattle	• Spanish cattle adapted well to the Southwest's dry climate and soon there were millions of cattle in the region. • The main products of ranches were meat, hides, and tallow. • Vaqueros were hired to care for cattle. • The roundup, or rodeo, was used to brand cattle.
The Cowboy Placard 17C Section 17.4	lariat ten-gallon hat chaps boots western saddle	• Special clothing made cowboys' work easier. • The western saddle, with its horn, made roping easier. • The lariat, or rope, was used to rope cattle. • Cowboys adopted many words, such as bronco, canyon, and ranch.
Sheep Raising Placard 17D Section 17.5	large-scale sheep- raising pastor	• Sheep were used to feed, clothe, and support Mexicanos. • Churro sheep from Spain thrived in New Mexico's dry climate. • Mexicanos ran large, well-organized businesses with managers, range bosses, and pastors watching the herds.
Irrigated Farming Placard 17E Section 17.6	Spanish system of irrigation fruit trees	• Mexicanos used irrigation techniques from Spain, North Africa, and Pueblo Indians. • Irrigation ditches brought water to fields. • The Mexican system allowed water to be saved as one field was watered at a time.

Describe how these contributions influenced settlers in the Southwest in the 1800s.	Describe how these contributions influenced life in the United States.
Mexicanos gave settlers the tools and techniques needed to mine gold, silver, and copper.	Copper is used in electrical and telephone wires across the U.S.
Settlers were used to small dairy farms in the East. They learned how to run huge cattle ranches from Mexicanos.	Cowboys, the rodeo, and branding are still part of life in the West.
American cowboys learned how to do their job from vaqueros.	All of these contributions, including words taken from the vaqueros, are still in use today.
American settlers learned from the Mexican sheep-raising industry that raising sheep could be profitable.	Californians crossed merinos and churros to create a better wool. Wool production soared from 1862 to 1880 due to Mexicano sheep-raising advancements.
Settlers, who had little knowledge of irrigation because of the plentiful water in the East, learned irrigation techniques from Mexicanos.	Mexicano irrigation techniques enabled Americans to turn the Southwest into America's fruit basket and introduced many unknown fruits to the U.S.

Mexicano Contributions to the Southwest

Topic	List details you think are Mexicano contributions.	Give three or more examples or details of Mexicano contributions from this section.
Food Placard 17F Section 17.7	chili peppers beans chili (stew)	• Mexican cooking is a result of one of the greatest food revolutions in history. • It uses ingredients from Europe such as beef, rice, oranges, and potatoes. • It also uses Indian foods such as avocados, beans, chilis, and chocolate.
Architecture Placard 17G Section 17.8	thick walls red-tile roof rounded arches	• Adobe was created from local materials. • Spanish-style architecture was suited to the Southwest climate. • Patios and verandas allowed people to spend time outdoors. • Red-tiled roofs protected people from fire and rain.
Laws Placard 17H Section 17.9	mining laws	• Mining law regulated the mining industry. • "Pueblo law" said water should be shared. • Community property law gave women half the couple's property if they divorced.
Entertainment Placard 17I Section 17.10	lariat cowboy rodeo	• Dramatic stories called corridos are accompanied by guitars. • Colorful and energetic dances such as the fandango and la bamba were part of fiestas. • Religious fiestas honored saints. • Rodeos featured competitions in calf roping and bull riding.

Describe how these contributions influenced settlers in the Southwest in the 1800s.	Describe how these contributions influenced life in the United States.
Settlers were introduced to new flavors and borrowed recipes.	The mixing of American and Mexicano foods gave us chili and Tex-Mex cooking.
Settlers saw the advantages of Spanish-style architecture and quickly adopted it to build homes, government offices, and other buildings.	The style was adapted to newer building materials such as stucco and concrete and can be seen in millions of Spanish-style homes today.
Settlers, who knew little about dealing with mining conflicts and water scarcity, adopted Mexicano laws. They also adopted Mexicano property laws.	Many states, like Texas and California, are community property states today.
Americans who settled in the Southwest shared in Mexicano entertainments.	Rodeos are still an exciting sport for many Americans. Cinco de Mayo is widely celebrated.

An Expanding Nation

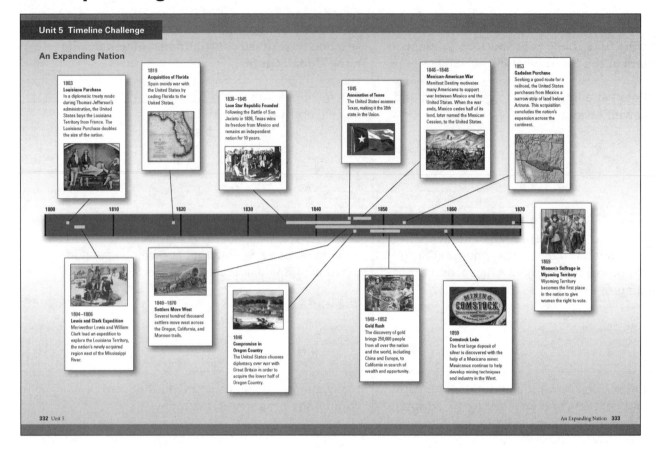

An Expanding Nation

1803
Louisiana Purchase
In a diplomatic treaty made during Thomas Jefferson's administration, the United States buys the Louisiana Territory from France. The Louisiana Purchase doubles the size of the nation.

1819
Acquisition of Florida
Spain avoids war with the United States by ceding Florida to the United States.

1836–1845
Lone Star Republic Founded
Following the Battle of San Jacinto in 1836, Texas wins its freedom from Mexico and remains an independent nation for 10 years.

1845
Annexation of Texas
The United States annexes Texas, making it the 28th state in the Union.

1846–1848
Mexican-American War
Manifest Destiny motivates many Americans to support war between Mexico and the United States. When the war ends, Mexico cedes half of its land, later named the Mexican Cession, to the United States.

1853
Gadsden Purchase
Seeking a good route for a railroad, the United States purchases from Mexico a narrow strip of land below Arizona. This acquisition concludes the nation's expansion across the continent.

1800 1810 1820 1830 1840 1850 1860 1870

1804–1806
Lewis and Clark Expedition
Meriwether Lewis and William Clark lead an expedition to explore the Louisiana Territory, the nation's newly acquired region east of the Mississippi River.

1840–1870
Settlers Move West
Several hundred thousand settlers move west across the Oregon, California, and Mormon trails.

1846
Compromise in Oregon Country
The United States chooses diplomacy over war with Great Britain in order to acquire the lower half of Oregon Country.

1848–1852
Gold Rush
The discovery of gold brings 250,000 people from all over the nation and the world, including China and Europe, to California in search of wealth and opportunity.

1859
Comstock Lode
The first large deposit of silver is discovered with the help of a Mexicano miner. Mexicanos continue to help develop mining techniques and industry in the West.

1869
Women's Suffrage in Wyoming Territory
Wyoming Territory becomes the first place in the nation to give women the right to vote.

332 Unit 5

An Expanding Nation 333

Overview

This Timeline Challenge provides students with a review of the main events and ideas of this unit, as well as practice in reading and interpreting timelines. You can vary and expand the activity according to students' needs and the amount of time available.

Basic Procedure

1 **Introduce the timeline in the Student Edition.** Direct students to the An Expanding Nation timeline at the end of Unit 5 in the Student Edition. You may wish to have students read aloud and discuss the timeline entries.

2 **Introduce the Timeline Challenge in the Interactive Student Notebook.** Direct students to the Unit 5 Timeline Challenge in their notebooks. Point out the two types of questions, "Timeline Skills" and "Critical Thinking," and model how to answer each type.

3 **Have students complete the Timeline Challenge.** Monitor students as they work. Use the Guide to Unit 5 Timeline Challenge to check their answers. You may wish to project a transparency of this page as you work through the questions with the class and conduct a discussion of the "Critical Thinking" questions.

4 **Complete the KWL chart.** Return to the KWL chart created at the beginning of the unit, and ask students to list the key information they have learned.

Classroom Timeline

1 **Prepare the Timeline Challenge Cards.** Copy and cut the cards from *Student Handout TC5: Unit 5 Timeline Challenge Cards.* You may wish to laminate the cards for future use.

2 **Create a timeline on a classroom wall.** On an empty wall or a large bulletin board, make a timeline with masking tape or colored paper. Mark off the time intervals in advance, or ask students to do so in class.

3 **Have students place the Timeline Challenge Cards.** Distribute cards to individual students or pairs and have them tape the cards to the timeline in the correct locations. Call on students to provide more information on the timeline topics to review main events and issues.

Student Handout TC5

Internet Research

1 **Review students' suggestions for additional timeline entries.** Have students share their answers to the last question of the Timeline Challenge.

2 **Have students conduct Internet research.** Ask students to choose and research one of their suggested events.

3 **Have students create additional Timeline Challenge Cards.** Direct students to research an appropriate image for their cards and then use the computer to create an illustrated card, complete with timeline entry.

Timeline Skills

Score 1 point for each correct answer.

1. The Louisiana Territory was purchased from France. Florida was ceded by Spain to avoid war. Texas was annexed while it was an independent nation. The lower half of Oregon Country was acquired through a diplomatic agreement. The Mexican Cession was ceded by Mexico after the Mexican-American War. The Gadsden Purchase was bought from Mexico.

2. to explore the Louisiana Territory; more than 2 years

3. to acquire wealth and new opportunity

4. Possible answer: missionaries, forty-niners, Mormons, Mexicanos, Chinese

5. The gold rush lasted 4 years. It brought more than 250,000 people to California.

6. 50 years

7. Texas was an independent nation known as the Lone Star Republic. It lasted 10 years.

8. Manifest destiny motivated many Americans to support the war.

9. It became the first place in the United States to give women the right to vote.

Critical Thinking

Score 1 to 3 points for each answer, depending on the thoroughness of the response.

10. Possible answer: Manifest destiny was the idea that the United States should possess all the land across North America. This idea influenced many Americans to support any measure, even war, to acquire these territories.

11. Possible answer:

   • Mexicanos may have believed that the United States acquired their territory unfairly and therefore felt resentful about U.S. expansion.

   • Mormons may have felt positive about expansion because it gave them religious freedom.

   • Missionaries may have felt positive about expansion because it gave them an opportunity to spread their religion.

   • Forty-niners may have felt excited about the opportunity to gain wealth.

   • Women may have felt hopeful about new opportunities in the West, such as voting.

   • The Chinese may have had mixed feelings. They had new opportunities to gain wealth but also faced discrimination.

12. Answers will vary. Students must include an explanation of why they chose their contribution.

13. Answers will vary. Students must explain why the events they chose merit inclusion.

Using Scores to Inform Instruction

Timeline Skills A score of 6 out of 9 indicates that students understand most of the key events of this unit.

Critical Thinking A score of 8 out of 12 indicates that students are able to think critically about most of the key issues of this unit.

If students score below these levels, consider reviewing timeline and critical thinking skills.

UNIT **6**

Americans in the Mid-1800s

Geography Challenge

Chapter 18: An Era of Reform
To what extent did the reform movements of the mid-1800s improve life for Americans?
Response Group

Chapter 19: The Worlds of North and South
How was life in the North different from life in the South?
Visual Discovery

Chapter 20: African Americans in the Mid-1800s
How did African Americans face slavery and discrimination in the mid-1800s?
Writing for Understanding

Timeline Challenge

Americans in the Mid-1800s

Overview

This activity introduces geographic information essential to Unit 6. Students read and interpret maps to learn about the movement and distribution of the slave population by 1860. They annotate a map and answer questions in their Interactive Student Notebooks, and then discuss critical thinking questions. Students' comprehension of content and proficiency in map-reading and higher-order thinking skills will help you gauge their readiness for the unit. The pages that follow include a completed map, answers to questions, a scoring guide to inform your teaching, and suggestions for modifications to meet specific student needs.

Essential Geographic Understandings

1. The development and regional patterns of the domestic slave trade from the early 1800s to 1860

2. The distribution of the South's slave population by 1860

3. Key physical features: Gulf of Mexico, Atlantic Ocean, Ohio River

4. Key human features: Virginia, South Carolina, Tennessee, Alabama, Mississippi, Louisiana

5. Why geographic factors made ending slavery such a difficult reform

Procedures

1 **Introduce the unit.** Tell students they will learn about the economy and society of the North and the South, including what life was like for the each region's African American population. They will also learn about efforts to reform American society, including efforts to end slavery.

2 **Create a KWL chart.** Ask students to identify what they know about the North and South in the decades before the Civil War and what they want to learn. Use their responses to gauge how much additional background information they will need as you progress through the unit. Students will return to the KWL chart at the end of the unit and add key information they have learned.

3 **Have students read Unit 6 "Setting the Stage" in the Student Edition.**

4 **Have students complete the Geography Challenge.** Monitor students as they answer the questions and complete the map. You may want to have them work in pairs. Use the guide on the next two pages to check their answers. You may wish to project the map from the Interactive Student Notebook and have students annotate it as the class works through the map-reading questions. Make sure students have grasped Essential Geographic Understandings 1 to 4.

5 **Discuss the "Critical Thinking" questions.** Help students understand the geographic relationships described in Essential Geographic Understanding 5.

The Slave Trade in the United States

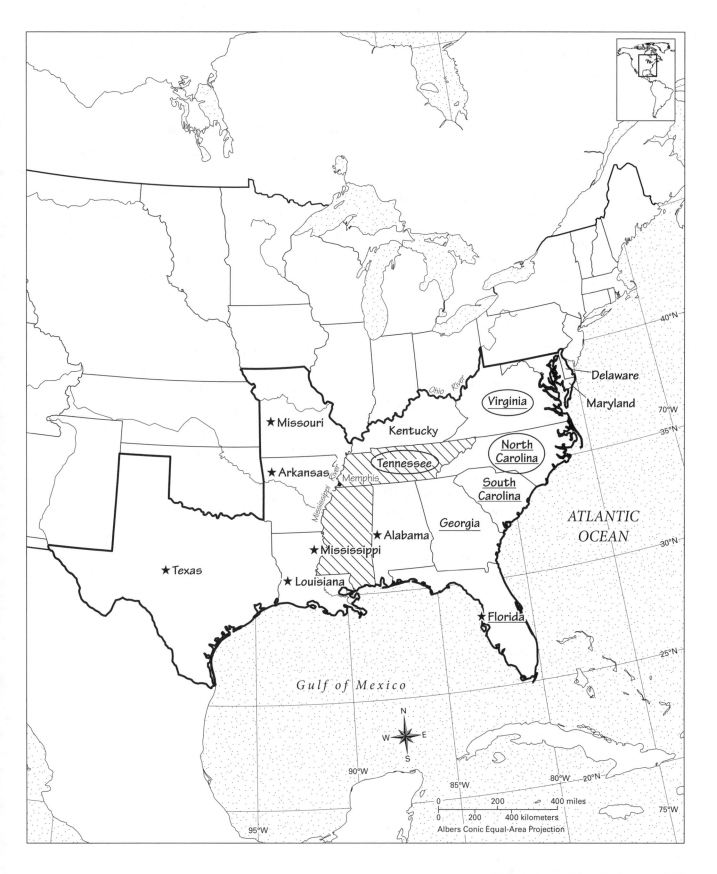

Delaware

Maryland

Virginia

Ohio River

Missouri

Kentucky

North Carolina

Arkansas

Tennessee

Memphis

Mississippi River

South Carolina

Georgia

ATLANTIC OCEAN

Alabama

Mississippi

Texas

Louisiana

Florida

Gulf of Mexico

N
W   E
S

90°W

85°W

95°W

80°W

75°W

40°N

70°W

35°N

30°N

25°N

20°N

0   200   400 miles

0   200   400 kilometers

Albers Conic Equal-Area Projection

Geography Skills

Score 1 point for each correct answer. Use the map on the previous page to check shading and labeling.

1. The Ohio and Mississippi rivers were along the border between slaves and free states.

2. South Carolina had the largest slave population in 1860, and Delaware had the smallest. The map key tells this information.

3. Slave trade centers were cities where large numbers of slaves were bought and sold. New York and Philadelphia were slave trade centers outside the slave states.

4. Missouri, Louisiana, Mississippi, Alabama, Arkansas, Florida, and Texas entered the Union between 1812 and 1845.

5. Mississippi, Louisiana, and Alabama were most important to slavery's expansion and growth. This is shown by their high numbers of slaves on the slave population map.

6. Slaves sold in the slave market at Montgomery came largely from Virginia, North Carolina, and Tennessee.

7. Slaves from Kentucky were most likely to end up in Tennessee and Mississippi.

8. Slaves arrived in ships by sea from Virginia, North Carolina, South Carolina, Georgia, and elsewhere in Florida.

9. Memphis was probably the main source for Arkansas slaveholders to purchase slaves.

Critical Thinking

Questions may have more than one correct answer. Score 1 to 3 points for each reasonable answer, depending on the strength of students' geographic reasoning. Possible answers are given here.

10. Most slaves sold to Texas probably arrived by sea because of the distances involved and the relative difficulty and challenges of transporting slaves over land.

11. Areas with greater population or more agriculture probably had more slaves than other areas.

12. Possible answer: Transporting slaves by sea from the Atlantic coast through the Gulf of Mexico could allow ships carrying slaves from the Caribbean to mix in with ships carrying U.S. slaves to sell in Gulf coast slave markets like Pensacola and New Orleans.

Using Scores to Inform Instruction

Geography Skills A score of 6 out of 9 or better indicates that students have acquired sufficient geographic information to proceed with the unit.

Critical Thinking A score of 6 out of 9 or better indicates that students are beginning to understand the relationships between physical geography and the different ways in which people live.

Modifying Instruction

ELL or Learners with Special Education Needs Consider focusing on map-reading questions or limiting the number of "Critical Thinking" questions.

Students with Weak Map or Critical Thinking Skills Assign appropriate pages from the Social Studies Skills Toolkit in the back of the Lesson Masters

An Era of Reform

To what extent did the reform movements of the mid-1800s improve life for Americans?

Overview

Students examine the reform movements of the mid-1800s to evaluate to what extent they improved life for Americans. In a Response Group activity, they debate the extent to which grievances from the Declaration of Sentiments have been redressed today.

Objectives

In the course of reading this chapter and participating in the classroom activity, students will

Social Studies

- analyze how transcendentalism contributed to the spirit of reform.

- describe the conditions in prisons, in schools, for slaves, and for women in the mid-1800s, and identify the reform movements that resulted.

- evaluate how well reform movements improved life for Americans.

- explain the contributions of such reformers as Horace Mann, William Lloyd Garrison, Frederick Douglas, and Elizabeth Cady Stanton.

- debate the degree to which the grievances from the Declaration of Sentiments have been redressed today.

Language Arts

- deliver persuasive presentations.

Social Studies Vocabulary

Key Content Terms reform, Second Great Awakening, transcendentalism, abolitionist, Seneca Falls Convention, Declaration of Sentiments

Academic Vocabulary intuition, conform, individualism, devote

Materials

History Alive! The United States Through Industrialism

Interactive Student Notebooks

Visual 18

Lesson Masters

- Student Handouts 18A and 18B (1 of each for every 3 students)
- Information Master 18 (1 transparency)
- Vocabulary Development handout (1 per student, on colored paper)

Activity	Suggested Time	Materials
Preview	15 minutes	• Interactive Student Notebooks • Visual 18
Vocabulary Development	30–40 minutes	• *History Alive! The United States Through Industrialism* • Interactive Student Notebooks • Vocabulary Development handout
Response Group	75 minutes (1.5 regular periods) (0.75 block period)	• *History Alive! The United States Through Industrialism* • Student Handouts 18A and 18B • Information Master 18
Processing	20 minutes	• Interactive Student Notebooks
Assessment	40 minutes	• Chapter 18 Assessment

Preview

1 **Have students analyze a reform song.** Project *Visual 18: Let Us All Speak Our Minds* and have a volunteer read the lyrics aloud. Then have students complete the Preview questions.

2 **Have students share their responses in pairs or with the class.**

3 **Explain the connection between the Preview and Chapter 18.** Tell students that this song was written in the 1800s to protest the unequal treatment of women. During this period, reformers—people who work to improve and correct injustices—strove not only to end slavery and improve education, but also to promote equal rights for women. In this chapter, students will examine the reform movements of the period to evaluate the extent to which they improved life for Americans.

Visual 18

Vocabulary Development

1 **Introduce the Key Content Terms.** Have students locate the Key Content Terms for the chapter in their Interactive Student Notebooks. These are important terms that will help them understand the main ideas of the chapter. Ask volunteers to identify any familiar terms and how they might be used in a sentence.

2 **Have students complete a Vocabulary Development handout.** Give each student a copy of the Vocabulary Development handout of your choice from the Reading Toolkit at the back of the Lesson Masters. These handouts provide extra practice and support, depending on your students' needs. Review the completed handout by asking volunteers to share one answer for each term.

Reading

1 **Introduce the Essential Question and have students read Section 18.1.** Have students identify the Essential Question: *To what extent did the reform movements of the mid-1800s improve life for Americans?* Then have them read Section 18.1. Afterward, have them use information from the reading and the image that opens the chapter to propose some possible answers to the Essential Question.

2 **Have students complete the Reading Notes for Sections 18.2 to 18.6.** Remind them to use the Key Content Terms where appropriate as they complete their Reading Notes. Have several volunteers share their responses, and use Guide to Reading Notes 18 to check their answers.

> **Vocabulary Development: Metaphors**
>
> Have students analyze the term Second Great Awakening as a metaphor. Begin by contrasting the literal and figurative senses of the word *awakening*. Guide students to consider how the modifier *great* elevates the idea of an awakening and helps intensify the term's positive connotations.

Response Group

1   **Place students in groups of three and introduce the activity.** Explain that they will examine and discuss three excerpts from the Declaration of Sentiments and then debate the extent to which women have achieved equal rights today.

2   **Prepare groups for the activity.** Distribute *Student Handout 18A: Reflecting on the Declaration of Sentiments* to each group and review the steps. Make sure groups understand the terms *grievance* (formal complaint) and *redress* (correction of an unfair condition). Then distribute *Student Handout 18B: Fact Sheet on Women in the United States Today* to each group and explain that groups will use these facts to defend their placements on a spectrum.

3   **Have students work with Excerpt A on Student Handout 18A.** After about five minutes, have a few groups share their rephrased excerpts. Then give groups time to mark the spectrum and find supporting evidence to defend their placements. Remind them to prepare a spokesperson for the upcoming discussion.

4   **Have groups mark the class spectrum.** Place *Information Master 18: Class Spectrum* on the projector, but do not turn the projector on. Assign each group a number. Then have the spokespersons come up to the projector and mark the spectrum using their group numbers.

5   **Facilitate a class discussion.** Turn on the projector, and call on the first spokesperson to defend his or her group's placement. Then call on other spokespersons to share their placements. Require each to begin by saying, *"(Name of previous spokesperson), our group agrees/disagrees with your group's placement because . . ."* End the discussion when all new ideas have been voiced.

6   **Repeat Steps 3 to 5 with Excerpts B and C.** Before having groups mark the class spectrum, erase the previous marks.

7   **Debrief the activity.** Ask,

  • In what areas have women made the most progress since the Seneca Falls Convention? Why do you think so?

  • In what areas have women made the least progress since the Seneca Falls Convention? Why do you think so?

  • What actions are women and men taking today to continue to redress the grievances in the Declaration of Sentiments?

  • To what extent did the reform movements of the mid-1800s improve life for prisoners? Schoolchildren? African Americans?

Student Handout 18A

Student Handout 18B

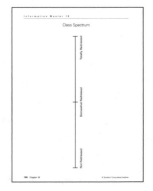

Information Master 18

Processing

Have students complete the Processing activity. Students will create a "report card" evaluating the reform movements of the period. Consider having students share their evaluations with a partner or the class.

Quicker Coverage

Shorten the Activity Eliminate one or two of the excerpts from Student Handout 18A.

Deeper Coverage

Analyze More Excerpts Choose additional excerpts from the Declaration of Sentiments, such as those below, for groups to analyze and discuss following the procedure from the activity. Depending on the excerpts, you may want to give students additional statistics as well.

- "He has denied her the facilities for obtaining a thorough education, all colleges being closed against her."
- "He closes against her all the avenues to wealth and distinction, which he considers most honorable to himself. As a teacher of theology, medicine, or law, she is not known."
- "He has taken from her all right in property, even to the wages she earns."

Research Additional Facts Restructure the activity by having students analyze all three excerpts at one time. For each excerpt, ask them to research additional facts to support their placements on the spectrum. Then facilitate a discussion for each excerpt.

Assessment

Mastering the Content

1. D	5. B	9. A	13. D
2. C	6. B	10. A	14. A
3. A	7. A	11. C	15. C
4. D	8. D	12. C	16. C

Applying Social Studies Skills

17. A

18. Possible answer: More people were given their rights.

19. C

Exploring the Essential Question

20. Answers should include all of the elements requested in the prompt.

Scoring Rubric

Score	Description
3	Student completes all three parts of the task. Ideas are clearly stated, supported by details, and demonstrate command of standard English conventions.
2	Student responds to most or all parts of the task. Ideas may lack details or not be clearly stated.
1	Student responds to at least one part of the task. Ideas may contain factual or grammatical errors and may lack details.
0	Response does not match the task or is incorrect.

Brook Farm and the Utopian Dream

1 **Discuss the ideal of creating a "perfect" community.** Ask a volunteer to read aloud the Preamble to the U.S. Constitution. Talk about the fact that people have a long history of trying to create the best society possible— whether on a national level or as a community.

2 **Have students read the Chapter 18 Reading Further.** Ask students to summarize George Ripley's goals for Brook Farm. Ask, *Why do you think writer Nathaniel Hawthorne enjoyed physical labor at first? Why do you think he eventually changed his mind?*

3 **Compare Brook Farm to communes in the 1960s.** Tell the class that in the 1960s, many people formed communes with the idea of creating more ideal communities than they found in mainstream society. Talk about ways in which the young people filled with the spirit of "newness" in the 1860s were similar to the hippie culture of the 1960s.

4 **Discuss life at Brook Farm.** Ask, *Would you have liked to have lived at Brook Farm? Why or why not?*

5 **Have students complete the Chapter 18 Reading Further in their Interactive Student Notebooks.** Invite students to share their storyboards. If possible, post them in a classroom display. Encourage students to describe and compare their utopian communities. Discuss how the utopias reflect differences from the society in which students live.

English Language Learners

Provide an Alternative Preview Have students write responses to the following questions, and discuss their responses as a class.

- Do you think girls and boys are treated equally in the classroom? In the workplace?

- Do you think women in the United States have the same rights as men? Why or why not?

- How do you think male and female roles in the United States have changed since the mid-1800s?

Provide Paraphrased Excerpts For the activity, provide students with the following rewordings for the Declaration of Sentiments excerpts.

- Excerpt A: Men do not allow women to vote. Women have no say in the creation of laws.

- Excerpt B: Men have the jobs that pay the most. Women's jobs pay very little.

- Excerpt C: Men expect women to have different morals than men.

Learners Reading and Writing Below Grade Level

Highlight Main Ideas Give students photocopies of the chapter. For the Reading Notes for Section 18.2, have students highlight information about transcendentalism. For Sections 18.3, 18.4, and 18.6, have them highlight information pertaining to conditions in one color and reforms in a second color. For Section 18.5, have them highlight information about William Lloyd Garrison in one color, Frederick Douglas in a second color, and Sojourner Truth in a third color.

Learners with Special Education Needs

Support the Activity Consider these tips:

- Give students copies of Student Handouts 18A and 18B ahead of time to familiarize them with the activity.

- Assign students to be the spokesperson for Excerpt B. Highlight some of the facts on Student Handout 18B that may help them determine where to mark the spectrum.

- Have students prepare cue cards to use during the class discussions. Encourage them to outline what they might say to the class and to include at least one statistic from Student Handout 18B.

- Appoint one student as the facilitator for each round. Have this student call on spokespersons.

Advanced Learners

Write a Letter to a Reformer In lieu of the Processing activity, have students write a letter to one of the reformers discussed in the chapter. The letter should contain

- an introduction that reviews some of the reformer's accomplishments.

- two paragraphs that describe the extent to which the related reform movement improved life for Americans.

- a conclusion that discusses whether the issues of the reform movement have been totally redressed today.

Students will need to do additional research to address some of these points.

Enrichment Resources

Find out more about the reform movements of the mid-1800s by exploring the following resources for *History Alive! The United States Through Industrialism* at www.teachtci.com.

Enrichment Readings These in-depth readings encourage students to explore selected topics related to the chapter. You may also find readings that relate the chapter's content directly to your state's curriculum.

Internet Resources These recommended Web sites provide useful and engaging content that reinforces skills development and mastery of subjects within the chapter.

Literature Recommendations

The following books offer opportunities to extend the content in this chapter.

Sojourner Truth: Abolitionist and Women's Rights Activist by Catherine Bernard (Berkeley Heights, NJ: Enslow Publishers, 2001)

A Journey into the Transcendentalists' New England by R. Todd Felton (Berkeley, CA: Roaring Forties Press, 2006)

Time for Courage by Kathryn Lasky (New York: Scholastic, 2001)

Section 18.2

1. People could be saved by doing good works.

2. Possible answer: Thoreau's quotation reflects transcendentalism by urging people not to conform to others' expectations and to be true to themselves.

3. Transcendentalists added to the spirit of reform by urging people to question society's rules and institutions.

Section 18.3

1. Possible answers:

   Conditions: Prisoners were locked in cages. Children were jailed with adults. Debtors were imprisoned for years. The mentally ill were locked away in crowded prisons.

   Reforms: Massachusetts and other states created public asylums for the mentally ill. State governments stopped putting debtors in prison. Most states created special justice systems for children. Many states outlawed cruel punishments.

2. Possible answer: With my eyes, I see dirty, overcrowded jails. With my heart, I feel resolved to fight for the rights of the mentally ill. With my hands, I write detailed reports of the conditions of state prisons.

Section 18.4

1. Possible answers:

   Conditions: Schools were often only part time and a single room. Teachers had limited education and received little pay.

   Reforms: In Massachusetts, citizens voted to pay teachers higher salaries and to establish special training schools for teachers. By 1850, white boys in many states attended free public schools. In the 1860s, most public universities accepted female students.

2. Possible answer: With my eyes, I see poor children stealing and destroying property when they should be in school. With my mouth, I speak out for the need for public schools. With my heart, I believe that women and African Americans should have more educational opportunities.

Section 18.5

Possible answers:

William Lloyd Garrison: With my heart, I feel outrage at the institution of slavery. With my ears, I hear proslavery groups destroying my printing press and burning my house. With my hands, I write about the abolitionist movement in my newspaper, *The Liberator*.

Frederick Douglass: With my eyes, I see slave children being treated cruelly. With my hands, I write about the injustices of slavery in my newspaper, the *North Star*. With my mouth, I speak to abolitionist groups about the conditions of slavery.

Sojourner Truth: With my eyes, I see women and African Americans being treated as inferior. With my mouth, I preach and speak out about injustices my people face. With my heart, I feel optimistic that God will end slavery peacefully.

Section 18.6

1. Possible answers:

   Conditions: Men control their wives' money and property. Husbands can discipline wives however they want. Women cannot speak in public. Women have no representation in government.

   Reforms: Massachusetts and Indiana passed more liberal divorce laws. Elizabeth Blackwell started her own hospital and medical school. Eventually, women gained the right to vote.

2. Possible answer: With my eyes, I see women not being allowed to vote and being treated like slaves by their husbands. With my heart, I feel compelled to speak out that all men and women are created equal and deserve equal rights. With my hands, I write speeches that call for women to be given the right to own property, to practice professions, and to vote.

The Worlds of North and South

How was life in the North different from life in the South?

Overview

In a Visual Discovery activity, students analyze and bring to life images from the mid-1800s to compare the different ways of life in the North and the South.

Objectives

In the course of reading this chapter and participating in the classroom activity, students will

Social Studies

- analyze images to hypothesize how the geographies, economies, types of transportation, and societies differed in the North and South.

- compare the economies and societies of the North and South by re-creating scenes from the two regions.

- explain the effects of new inventions and manufacturing methods on the North and South.

- examine the geographic, economic, and political factors involved in building a network of roads, canals, and railroads.

Language Arts

- interpret analogies.

- write a narrative that employs descriptive strategies.

Social Studies Vocabulary

Key Content Terms deforestation, agrarian, plantation, cotton gin, Industrial Revolution, industrialist, immigrant

Academic Vocabulary manual, innovation, drastic, internal, hostility

Materials

History Alive! The United States Through Industrialism

Interactive Student Notebooks

Visuals 19A–19E

CD Tracks 9 and 10

Lesson Masters

- Student Handout 19 (1 per group)

- Vocabulary Development handout (1 per student, on colored paper)

Activity	Suggested Time	Materials
Preview	15 minutes	• Interactive Student Notebooks • Visual 19A
Vocabulary Development	30–40 minutes	• *History Alive! The United States Through Industrialism* • Interactive Student Notebooks • Vocabulary Development handout
Visual Discovery	100 minutes (2 regular periods) (1 block period)	• *History Alive! The United States Through Industrialism* • Interactive Student Notebooks • Visuals 19B–19E • CD Tracks 9 and 10 • Student Handout 19
Processing	20 minutes	• Interactive Student Notebooks
Assessment	40 minutes	• Chapter 19 Assessment

Preview

1 **Have students complete the Preview in their Interactive Student Notebooks.** Students will complete a spoke diagram highlighting the main features of their community. Afterward, have several volunteers share some of their entries. Then ask, *How might your spoke diagram look different if you lived in another part of the country?*

2 **Have students compare images of the North and the South.** Project the top image *Visual 19A: The North and the South*, and explain that it shows the city of Pittsburgh in the mid-1800s. Ask students to identify features of the area's geography, economy, transportation, and society. For example, they might notice the river, ironworks, steamships, and factory workers. Then display the bottom image, of a Mississippi plantation, and ask them to do the same. Students may comment on the flat farmland, cotton fields, carts, and slaves.

3 **Explain the connection between the Preview and Chapter 19.** Explain to students that the geographies, economies, types of transportation, and societies of the North and South varied greatly in the mid-1800s. In this chapter, they will explore how these factors led to different ways of life in the North and South.

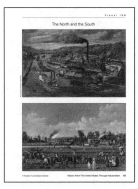

Visual 19A

Vocabulary

1 **Introduce the Key Content Terms.** Have students locate the Key Content Terms for the chapter in their Interactive Student Notebooks. These are important terms that will help them understand the main ideas of the chapter. Ask volunteers to identify any familiar terms and how they might be used in a sentence.

2 **Have students complete a Vocabulary Development handout.** Give each student a copy of the Vocabulary Development handout of your choice from the Reading Toolkit at the back of the Lesson Masters. These handouts provide extra practice and support, depending on your students' needs. Review the completed handout by asking volunteers to share one answer for each term.

Reading

1 **Introduce the Essential Question and have students read Section 19.1.** Have students identify the Essential Question on the first page of the chapter: *How was life in the North different from life in the South?* Then have them read Section 19.1. Afterward, have them use information from the reading and from the image that opens the chapter to propose some possible answers to the Essential Question.

2 **Have students complete the Reading Notes for Chapter 19.** Assign Sections 19.2 to 19.9 during the activity as indicated in the procedures for the Visual Discovery activity. Remind students to use the Key Content Terms where appropriate as they complete their Reading Notes.

Visual Discovery

1 **Place students in groups of four and introduce the activity.** Tell groups that they will analyze and bring to life images depicting the different ways of life in the North and the South in the mid-1800s.

2 **Introduce Sections 19.2 and 19.3 by projecting** *Visual 19B: Geographies of the North and South.* Ask,

   • What do you see here?

   • How would you describe the land in each area? Climate? Natural resources?

   • Which image shows the North and which shows the South? *(The top image shows the North; the bottom shows the South.)* How can you tell?

   • How do you think geography influenced life in the North during this period? Life in the South?

Visual 19B

3 **Have students read and complete the Reading Notes for Sections 19.2 and 19.3.** Use Guide to Reading Notes 19 to review the main points with the class.

4 **Introduce Sections 19.4 and 19.5 by projecting** *Visual 19C: Economies of the North and South.* Ask,

   • What do you see?

   • What are the workers in each image doing?

   • Which image shows the North and which shows the South? *(The top image shows the North; the bottom shows the South.)* How can you tell?

   • How do you think the economy of the North differed from the economy of the South?

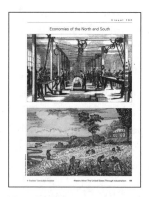

Visual 19B

5 **Have students read and complete the Reading Notes for Sections 19.4 and 19.5.** Use the Guide to Reading Notes to review the main points.

6 **Have students prepare to bring the images to life.** Choose four characters in each image on Visual 19C and assign each of those eight characters to a different group. Then distribute *Student Handout 19: North and South Act-It-Outs* to each group and review the directions for Act-It-Out 1. Make sure groups understand that they are only responsible for portraying their assigned character. Give groups about five minutes to prepare.

7 **Conduct the first act-it-out.** Project the top image on Visual 19C. Call up one actor for each character to stand in the appropriate location in front of the projected image, taking on that character's posture and facial expression. Softly play CD Track 9, "Factory Sounds." Then, acting as the on-scene reporter, ask the characters some of the questions from Student Handout 19. Repeat this procedure with the bottom image and CD Track 10, "Moses."

Student Handout 19

8 Introduce Sections 19.6 and 19.7 by projecting *Visual 19D: Transportation in the North and South.* Ask,

- What do you see here?

- What types of transportation are depicted in each image?

- Which image shows the North and which shows the South? (*The bottom image shows the North; the top shows the South.*) How can you tell?

- Why do you think the main types of transportation in the North differed from those in the South?

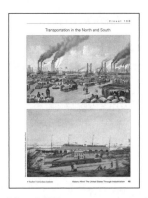

Visual 19D

9 Have students read and complete the Reading Notes for Sections 19.6 and 19.7. Use the Guide to Reading Notes to review the main points.

10 Introduce Sections 19.8 and 19.9 by projecting *Visual 19E: Societies of the North and South.* Ask,

- What do you see here?

- How would you describe the way of life in the top image? In the bottom image?

- Which image shows the North and which shows the South? (*The top image shows the North; the bottom shows the South.*) How can you tell?

- Why do you think society in the North differed from society in the South?

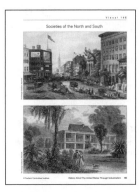

Visual 19E

11 Have students read and complete the Reading Notes for Sections 19.8 and 19.9. Use the Guide to Reading Notes to review the main points.

12 Conduct the second act-it-out. Repeat Step 7 using Visual 19E and the directions for Act-It-Out 2 on Student Handout 19. (There are no CD tracks for this act-it-out.)

Processing

Have students complete the Processing activity. They will draw and annotate images to illustrate how life in the North was different from life in the South. Consider having students share their finished drawings with one another.

Quicker Coverage

Shorten the Activity Eliminate one or both of the act-it-outs.

Condense the Preview In place of having students complete the spoke diagram, project Visual 19A and have students note interesting details about the images in their notebooks. Then have volunteers share their responses.

Deeper Coverage

Analyze Additional Images Find additional images depicting the geographies, economies, types of transportation, and societies of the North and South from the mid-1800s. Post the images around the room. After students have completed the Reading Notes for the chapter, have pairs determine whether each image reflects life in the North or the South and cite evidence for their decision. When all pairs have examined all of the images, have pairs share their responses.

Assessment

Mastering the Content

1. C	5. D	9. A	13. B
2. C	6. C	10. D	14. A
3. D	7. A	11. A	15. A
4. B	8. B	12. C	16. B

Applying Social Studies Skills

17. B

18. A

19. Answers will vary.

Exploring the Essential Question

20. Answers should include all of the elements requested in the prompt.

Scoring Rubric

Score	Description
3	Student completes all four parts of the task. Ideas are clearly stated, supported by details, and demonstrate command of standard English conventions.
2	Student responds to most or all parts of the task. Ideas may lack details or not be clearly stated.
1	Student responds to at least one part of the task. Ideas may contain factual or grammatical errors and may lack details.
0	Response does not match the task or is incorrect.

The Mill Girls of Lowell

1 **Have volunteers read aloud the first page of the Chapter 19 Reading Further.** You may want to read the introductory paragraph to the class and then ask a different volunteer to read each subsequent paragraph. Try to create a sense of the vibrant, bustling scene in 1850 Lowell, Massachusetts.

2 **Explain the distinction between a factory and a mill.** Point out that the words *factory* and *mill* are often used interchangeably. A factory is any building or group of buildings in which goods are manufactured. A mill is a particular kind of factory, usually one in which raw materials are turned into processed goods—such as a textile mill.

3 **Have students finish the reading.** Focus students' attention on the quotations from the mill girls. Ask students whether they think they themselves would have left their farm homes to go to Lowell.

4 **Discuss the pros and cons of life in Lowell.** Point out the song lyrics in the caption at the end of the reading. Ask,

- What would have made some of the mill girls say they felt like slaves?

- What were the crucial differences between enslaved African Americans and the mill girls?

5 **Have students complete the Chapter 19 Reading Further in their Interactive Student Notebooks.** Invite students to share their diary entries. Discuss any differences they indicated in their feelings about Lowell at the beginning and after a year.

English Language Learners

Offer Additional Support for the Activity Consider these tips:

- Provide students with a written copy of the spiral questions for Visuals 19B to 19E.

- Place students in nonspeaking roles for the act-it-outs. For instance, they might be factory or plantation workers in Visual 19C and dockworkers or passengers in Visual 19E.

- Have students prepare a cue card to use during the act-it-outs that contains the answers to the questions on Student Handout 19.

Learners Reading and Writing Below Grade Level

Supply Partially Completed Reading Notes Provide students with two examples from the Guide to Reading Notes for each hub of each spoke diagram.

Model How to Complete a Spoke Diagram After students have read Section 19.2, complete the corresponding spoke diagram as a class, using the Guide to Reading Notes to provide examples.

Learners with Special Education Needs

Annotate Visual 19A Support the Processing activity by placing students in pairs and giving each pair four sticky notes. Project Visual 19A and assign half the pairs the top image and the remaining pairs the bottom image. Have pairs find one example of each of the following in their image: geography, economy, transportation, and society. Then have pairs place their sticky notes on the appropriate places on the projected image and explain their placements. As students work on the Processing activity, keep the images (and sticky notes) projected.

Advanced Learners

Create a Venn Diagram As a more challenging Processing activity, have students create a Venn diagram highlighting the similarities and differences between the North and the South. Require that students include at least two examples from each of these aspects of life—geography, economy, transportation, and society—using a different color for each aspect.

Enrichment Resources

Find out more about the North and the South in the mid-1800s by exploring the following resources for *History Alive! The United States Through Industrialism* at www.teachtci.com.

Enrichment Readings These in-depth readings encourage students to explore selected topics related to the chapter. You may also find readings that relate the chapter's content directly to your state's curriculum.

Internet Connections These recommended Web sites provide useful and engaging content that reinforces skills development and mastery of subjects within the chapter.

Literature Recommendations

The following books offer opportunities to extend the content in this chapter.

The Transcontinental Railroad: Tracks Across America by Jil Fine (New York: Children's Press, 2005)

Eli Whitney and the Cotton Gin by Jessica Gunderson (Mankato, MN: Capstone Press, 2007)

Canals by Robert J. Kapsch (New York: W.W. Norton and Company, 2004)

Possible answers are given for each section.

Section 19.2

- four distinct seasons
- jagged New England coast with rocky soil
- thick forests in New England
- plains with rich soil in New York, Pennsylvania, and New Jersey
- a large, forested region in the Central Plains
- region is undergoing deforestation

Section 19.3

- mild winters and long, hot, humid summers
- fertile coastal plains with swamps and marshes
- rolling hills and mountain hollows
- thick pine forests in North Carolina
- broad, flat rivers

Section 19.4

- economy based on agriculture
- Agrarians favored a way of life based on farming and policies that supported agricultural interests.
- Most whites worked their own small farms.
- Plantations used slaves to raise cash crops, especially cotton.
- With Eli Whitney's cotton gin, cotton became the South's most important crop.

Section 19.5

- center of the Industrial Revolution, the shift from hand manufacturing to machines
- The economy was spurred by industrialists, people who owned large factories and other businesses based on manufacturing.
- New inventions and manufacturing methods, like steam-powered engines, made goods cheaper and more plentiful.
- Industrialists favored a strong national government.

Section 19.6

- The National Road connected the new western states with the East.
- Steamboats made river travel faster and cheaper.
- The Erie Canal linked the Central Plains to East Coast cities.
- 20,000 miles of rail linked Northern factories to cities hundreds of miles away.

Section 19.7

- River travel was the main form of transportation.
- Cities sprang up along waterways.
- Southerners opposed federal funding for internal improvements.
- In 1860, the South had 10,000 miles of rail.

Section 19.8

- Wealth was measured in terms of land and slaves.
- a rigid social structure with rich plantation owners at the top, white farmers and workers in the middle, and blacks at the bottom
- Wealthy plantation owners dominated the economy and politics.
- Most white families worked their own fields.
- Free blacks worked as craftspeople, servants, and laborers.
- Most blacks in the South were slaves.

Section 19.9

- More Northerners were moving to towns and cities.
- Cities lacked sewers and paved streets.
- African Americans were free but not equal.
- Immigrants settled in cities.

African Americans in the Mid-1800s

How did African Americans face slavery and discrimination in the mid-1800s?

Overview

In a Writing for Understanding activity, students analyze quotations and examine images to discover how African Americans faced slavery and discrimination in the mid-1800s. They then create a journal describing some of the experiences of a slave in the period.

Objectives

In the course of reading this chapter and participating in the classroom activity, students will

Social Studies

- compare the lives and opportunities of free blacks in the North with those of free blacks in the South.
- describe aspects of slave life and forms of resistance to slavery.
- describe and illustrate how slaves faced slavery and discrimination.

Language Arts

- interpret an analogy.
- write a narrative that employs descriptive strategies.

Social Studies Vocabulary

Key Content Terms racism, discrimination, segregation, Underground Railroad, Nat Turner's Rebellion, oppression

Academic Vocabulary reformer, passive, sympathetic, evident

Materials

History Alive! The United States Through Industrialism

Interactive Student Notebooks

CD Track 10

Placards 20A–20H (2 sets; create additional placards as needed)

Visual 20

Lesson Masters

- Information Master 20
- Student Handout 20A (3 copies, cut apart)
- Student Handout 20B (1 per student)
- Vocabulary Development handout (1 per student, on colored paper)

Activity	Suggested Time	Materials
Preview	15 minutes	• Interactive Student Notebooks • Visual 20 • CD Track 10
Vocabulary Development	30–40 minutes	• *History Alive! The United States Through Industrialism* • Placards 20A–20H • Interactive Student Notebooks • Vocabulary Development handout
Writing for Understanding	150–200 minutes (3–4 regular periods) (1.5–2 block periods)	• *History Alive! The United States Through Industrialism* • Interactive Student Notebooks • Information Master 20 • Student Handouts 20A and 20B
Processing (optional)	20 minutes	• Interactive Student Notebooks
Assessment	40 minutes	• Chapter 20 Assessment

Preview

1 **As a class, analyze a quilt block.** Project only the photograph on *Visual 20: Moses* and explain that this is a quilt block from a quilt sewed by an enslaved woman in the 1800s. Tell students that while quilts served as bed coverings, they also often told biblical stories. This one tells the story of Moses leading slaves out of bondage. Ask,

Visual 20

- Which figure represents Moses? How can you tell? *(The central figure. He is holding a staff that turns into a serpent.)*

- Why do you think the woman who sewed this quilt chose to tell the story of Moses? *(The story provided hope that slaves in the United States, like Moses and his people, would eventually be led out of bondage.)*

2 **Analyze the song "Moses."** Reveal the lyrics on Visual 20 and play CD Track 10, "Moses." Then have students answer the Preview questions. Have volunteers share their responses by asking,

- What words describe the song's mood? *(defiant, hopeful, inspiring)*

- Who might King Pharaoh represent? *(a slave owner)* What might the river Jordan represent? *(the border between North and South)*

- What does the song tell us about how African Americans faced slavery? *(They remained hopeful that one day they would escape bondage.)*

3 **Explain the connection between the Preview and Chapter 20.** Explain that biblical stories gave enslaved African Americans hope and inspired them to fight for their freedom. In this chapter, students will explore how African Americans faced slavery and discrimination in the mid-1800s.

Vocabulary

1 **Introduce the Key Content Terms.** Have students locate the Key Content Terms for the chapter in their Interactive Student Notebooks. These are important terms that will help them understand the main ideas of the chapter. Ask volunteers to identify any familiar terms and how they might be used in a sentence.

2 **Have students complete a Vocabulary Development handout.** Give each student a copy of the Vocabulary Development handout of your choice from the Reading Toolkit at the back of the Lesson Masters. These handouts provide extra practice and support, depending on your students' needs. Review the completed handout by asking volunteers to share one answer for each term.

Reading

1 Introduce the Essential Question and have students read Section 20.1.
Have students identify the Essential Question: *How did African Americans face slavery and discrimination in the mid-1800s?* Then have them read Section 20.1. Afterward, ask,

- What kinds of messages were contained in slave quilts?

- What were the three gifts that W. E. B. Du Bois said African Americans brought to the United States?

- What are some ways that African Americans might have faced slavery and discrimination in the period?

Placards 20A–20H

2 Have students complete the Reading Notes for Sections 20.2 and 20.3.
Have several volunteers share their responses. Use Guide to Reading Notes 20 to check their answers.

3 Have students complete the Reading Notes for Chapter 20. Assign Sections 20.4 to 20.11 as indicated in the procedures for the Writing for Understanding activity. Remind students to use the Key Content Terms where appropriate as they complete their Reading Notes.

Student Handout 20A

Writing for Understanding

1 Prepare the classroom. Post two sets of *Placards 20A–20H: Images of Slavery* on the walls of the room. (**Note**: Create additional sets of placards as needed. For larger classes, consider making a third set.) Place the quotations cut from *Student Handout 20A: Quotations from Slaves* in a pile.

2 Place students in pairs and introduce the activity. Explain that pairs will match quotations and images describing how African Americans faced slavery in the mid-1800s. Students will then create a journal describing how African Americans faced slavery and discrimination.

3 Project *Information Master 20: Analyzing Quotations and Images* and review the steps. Show students the quotations. Point out that the title of each placard matches the title of the corresponding section in their books.

Information Master 20

4 Have students match quotations and images. Give each pair one quotation to begin with. Have them follow the steps on Information Master 20 to match the quotation to an image and then read and complete the Reading Notes for the corresponding section in their books. When pairs indicate they are ready for you to check their work, verify their answers using the Guide to Reading Notes.

5 Introduce the writing assignment. Tell students they will be creating "slave journals" describing how an African American might have faced slavery and discrimination in the mid-1800s. Distribute *Student Handout 20B: Writing a Slave Journal* to each student and review the instructions.

6 Have students create their journals. Give students at least one class period to create their journals, or have them create them as homework.

Student Handout 20B

Processing (optional)

The journal-writing assignment serves as this chapter's Processing activity. Should you choose not to have students do the writing assignment, you might use the optional Processing activity in the Interactive Student Notebook.

Quicker Coverage

Use Fewer Placards Choose just four to six placards for students to review, and assign the remaining topics and reading sections for homework. Consider making three or four sets of the selected placards to help the activity proceed quickly.

Shorten the Activity Eliminate the writing assignment. Instead, debrief the activity by asking students these questions: *What were the most difficult aspects of slave life? In what ways did slaves cope with their situation? Why do you think slavery lasted so long in the United States?*

Conduct a Jigsaw Modify the activity by having each pair join three other pairs to form groups of eight. Then have each pair choose two placards to analyze and complete the corresponding Reading Notes. Finally, convene the original groups of eight, and have students share their answers to the Reading Notes.

Deeper Coverage

Create a Class Quilt Have each student copy the illustration from the quilt block in the Reading Notes for one of Sections 20.4 to 20.11 onto a piece of white paper, using at least three colors. Then have them assemble the blocks on a wall to resemble a completed quilt. Ask volunteers to share their symbols.

Read Excerpts from Frederick Douglass's Autobiography Before students create their slave journals, read excerpts from *Narrative of the Life of Frederick Douglass* aloud. Alternatively, create a handout with excerpts, divide students into groups, and have group members take turns reading the excerpts aloud.

Writing: Create Coherence

Before students write their journals, remind them of methods for creating coherence. These methods include linking ideas within and between sentences and paragraphs with transitions, as well as making sure that all pronouns clearly refer to appropriate antecedents. You might also review simple parallel structures that help create coherence, such as parallel items in a series joined by coordinating conjunctions.

Assessment

Mastering the Content

1. A	5. C	9. A	13. D
2. B	6. B	10. B	14. B
3. C	7. C	11. C	15. B
4. B	8. D	12. C	16. C

Applying Social Studies Skills

17. B

18. Answers will vary.

19. B

Exploring the Essential Question

20. Answers should include all of the elements requested in the prompt.

Scoring Rubric

Score	Description
3	Student completes all four parts of the task. Ideas are clearly stated, supported by details, and demonstrate command of standard English conventions.
2	Student responds to most or all parts of the task. Ideas may lack details or not be clearly stated.
1	Student responds to at least one part of the task. Ideas may contain factual or grammatical errors and may lack details.
0	Response does not match the task or is incorrect.

Harriet Tubman, Moses of the Underground Railroad

1 **Have students read the title and introductory paragraph of the Chapter 20 Reading Further.** Be sure they understand the implications of describing Harriet Tubman as "Moses." Explain that the Bible tells of Moses leading the Hebrews out of slavery.

2 **Have students finish the reading.** Ask them to try to imagine the bravery it must have taken for enslaved people to flee slavery as Harriet Tubman did. Ask, *Would you have followed Harriet Tubman on the Underground Railroad? Why or why not?*

3 **Discuss historians' sources of information about Harriet Tubman and the Underground Railroad.** Point out the picture of William Still and have students read the caption. In addition to interviewing almost all of the many fugitives who passed through Philadelphia, Still collected letters from famous "conductors" such as Thomas Garrett. The book he published in 1872 is an invaluable source of documentation on the Underground Railroad.

4 **Discuss the importance of the Underground Railroad.** Explain that no one knows exactly how many people escaped slavery through the Underground Railroad. Sources such as the National Underground Railroad Freedom Center, however, estimate the number at more than 100,000 men, women, and children. Although this was only a small fraction of the slave population, the Underground Railroad played an important role as a symbol of both slave rebellion and interracial collaboration.

5 **Have students complete the Chapter 20 Reading Further in their Interactive Student Notebooks.** Invite students to read their biographies aloud. They may wish to compare their biographies with ones they find online.

English Language Learners

Supply Paraphrased Quotations During the activity, give students the following paraphrased quotations.

Quotation 1: Our huts were ragged. Our beds were hard. Still, we were so tired after working that it was nice to sleep.

Quotation 2: My slave master was cruel. He once attached a plow to a slave's back and made him work like a horse. He beat the slave every day. After the slave died, the slave master was haunted by the groans of the slave.

Quotation 3: Slavery will end one day. God will free us. We will be happy when we are free and the slave masters will drown.

Quotation 4: My father was sold and had to leave our family. We did not worry about being separated from our mother, since mothers and children stay together. We missed our father and he missed us. Sometimes, he would visit us at night. We would crawl on his lap and he would tickle us. When he got caught, his master would beat him.

Quotation 5: At night, most men rested or helped the women. Young slaves sang or visited each other. On Saturday nights, slaves got together. George played an instrument and the slaves danced. On Sundays, slaves went to church and visited each other.

Quotation 6: On Sundays, some slaves went to secret places to pray. If some whites saw slaves praying or singing a hymn, the whites would kill the slaves before the slaves' masters could save them.

Quotation 7: I had a vision. I saw white and black ghosts fighting. There was blood in the rivers and on the corn. On May 12, 1828, I heard a voice from heaven and it said that I should fight against the Serpent. It told me to get ready and kill my enemies.

Quotation 8: Uncle Big Jake worked the slaves all day. You must work hard in the field whether it is raining or snowing. The women with little children don't have to work as hard.

Learners Reading and Writing Below Grade Level

Support the Processing Activity Have students complete only one of the three journal entries. Have them write a first draft so that you can provide feedback.

Learners with Special Education Needs

Model How to Analyze a Quotation and an Image Before class, copy one of the quotations onto a transparency or the board, and make a transparency of the matching placard. Before conducting the activity, project the quotation and analyze it as a class. Then project the corresponding placard and have students describe what it shows. Finally, have students explain how the quotation matches the placard.

Advanced Learners

Analyze Additional Quilt Blocks Challenge students to interpret the quilt blocks shown in the photograph in Section 20.10. Ask, *what images and symbols do you see in the quilt? Do you recognize any biblical stories? What do the quilt blocks tell us about how African Americans faced slavery and discrimination?*

Watch "Africans in America" Have students watch the 90-minute segment "Brotherly Love (1791–1831)" from the PBS documentary "Africans in America" and then have them create a collage highlighting the key events and people of the period. Require them to include two key events, two key people, one quotation, and two illustrations. Allow them to use the resources on the accompanying PBS Web site.

Enrichment Resources

Find out more about African Americans in the mid-1800s by exploring the following resources for *History Alive! The United States Through Industrialism* at www.teachtci.com.

Enrichment Readings These in-depth readings encourage students to explore selected topics related to the chapter. You may also find readings that relate the chapter's content directly to your state's curriculum.

Internet Connections These recommended Web sites provide useful and engaging content that reinforces skills development and mastery of subjects within the chapter.

Literature Recommendations

The following books offer opportunities to extend the content in this chapter.

Stealing South: A Story of the Underground Railroad by Katherine Ayres (New York: Delacorte, 2001)

Frederick Douglass by Helaine Becker (Farmington Hills, MI: Gale Group, 2001)

Stealing Freedom by Elisa Carbone (New York: Bantam Doubleday Dell, 2001)

Section 20.2

Possible answers:

Slaves: Were considered legal property. Could be bought and sold. Could not own or buy anything. Worked mostly on farms and plantations and were sometimes hired out to factories or mills.

Free blacks in the South: Worked as laborers, craftspeople, or household servants. Were forbidden to own guns. Could not travel freely. Were not allowed to work certain jobs.

Free blacks in the North: Experienced discrimination. Were denied the right to vote. Had trouble finding good jobs. Had to live under policies of segregation. Started their own churches, schools, and self-help organizations.

Section 20.3

The economy of the South depended on cotton, and cotton planters depended on slave labor to grow their crops.

Section 20.4

1. Placard 20A matches Quotation 8. Explanations will vary.

2. Answers will vary.

3. Possible answer: Slaves worked from morning to late at night. Some slaves worked in the fields, while others worked in the house. Some were skilled seamstresses, carpenters, or blacksmiths. Slaves started working at the age of six.

4. Sketches will vary.

Section 20.5

1. Placard 20B matches Quotation 1. Explanations will vary.

2. Answers will vary.

3. Possible answer: Slaves lived crowded together in crude cabins. They ate cornmeal, bacon, molasses, and food from gardens and hunting. Slaves wore coarse linen called "Negro cloth." Slaves received some medical treatment, but it was poor.

4. Sketches will vary.

Section 20.6

1. Placard 20C matches Quotation 2. Explanations will vary.

2. Answers will vary.

3. Slave owners' methods included beating, whipping, and branding slaves; keeping slaves ignorant and dependent; and instilling fear in them.

4. Sketches will vary.

Section 20.7

1. Placard 20D matches Quotation 7. Explanations will vary.

2. Answers will vary.

3. Possible answers: Slaves broke tools, worked sloppily, acted dumb or sick, refused orders, ran away with the help of the Underground Railroad, or revolted, as in the case of Nat Turner's Rebellion.

4. Sketches will vary.

Section 20.8

1. Placard 20E matches Quotation 4. Explanations will vary.

2. Responses will vary.

3. Possible answer: Most slave families were headed by a mother and father. Parents taught children lessons they needed for survival. Children learned to respect themselves and other members of the slave community, especially elders.

4. Sketches will vary.

Section 20.9

1. Placard 20F matches Quotation 5. Explanations will vary.

2. Answers will vary.

3. Possible answers: Leisure activities included quilting bees, corn-husking parties, singing and dancing, telling tales, hunting, fishing, going to church, and playing games.

4. Sketches will vary.

Section 20.10

1. Placard 20G matches Quotation 6. Explanations will vary.

2. Answers will vary.

3. Possible answer: Being invisible was important because slave churches were the one place where slaves could come together to share in their hardships without being watched by their masters. Slave churches gave voice to slaves' longings, sorrows, and desire for freedom.

4. Sketches will vary.

Section 20.11

1. Placard 20H matches Quotation 3. Explanations will vary.

2. Answers will vary.

3. Possible answers: Quilts contained African images, such as animals. Spirituals used African rhythms and harmonies to express oppression. Slave dances were based on African traditions. Stories incorporated African legends and folktales.

4. Sketches will vary.

Americans in the Mid-1800s

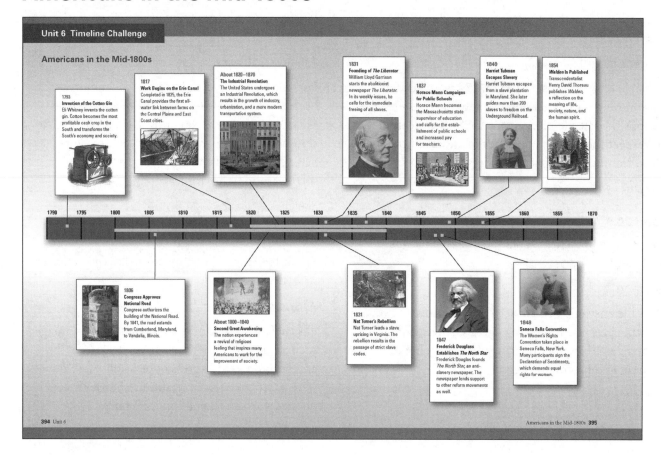

Overview

This Timeline Challenge provides students with a review of the main events and ideas of this unit, as well as practice in reading and interpreting timelines. You can vary and expand the activity according to students' needs and the amount of time available.

Basic Procedure

1 **Introduce the timeline in the Student Edition.** Direct students to the Americans in the Mid-1800s timeline at the end of Unit 6 in the Student Edition. You may wish to have students read aloud and discuss the timeline entries.

2 **Introduce the Timeline Challenge in the Interactive Student Notebook.** Direct students to the Unit 6 Timeline Challenge in their notebooks. Point out the two types of questions, "Timeline Skills" and "Critical Thinking," and model how to answer each type.

3 **Have students complete the Timeline Challenge.** Monitor students as they work. Use the Guide to Unit 6 Timeline Challenge to check their answers. You may wish to project a transparency of this page as you work through the questions with the class and conduct a discussion of the "Critical Thinking" questions.

4 **Complete the KWL chart.** Return to the KWL chart created at the beginning of the unit, and ask students to list the key information they have learned.

Classroom Timeline

1 **Prepare the Timeline Challenge Cards.** Copy and cut the cards from *Student Handout TC6: Unit 6 Timeline Challenge Cards.* You may wish to laminate the cards for future use.

2 **Create a timeline on a classroom wall.** On an empty wall or a large bulletin board, make a timeline with masking tape or colored paper. Mark off the time intervals in advance, or ask students to do so in class.

3 **Have students place the Timeline Challenge Cards.** Distribute cards to individual students or pairs and have them tape the cards to the timeline in the correct locations. Call on students to provide more information on the timeline topics to review main events and issues.

Student Handout TC6

Internet Research

1 **Review students' suggestions for additional timeline entries.** Have students share their answers to the last question of the Timeline Challenge.

2 **Have students conduct Internet research.** Ask students to choose and research one of their suggested events.

3 **Have students create additional Timeline Challenge Cards.** Direct students to research an appropriate image for their cards and then use the computer to create an illustrated card, complete with timeline entry.

Timeline Skills

Score 1 point for each correct answer.

1. The cotton gin was invented in 1793 by Eli Whitney.

2. By 1841, the National Road extended from Maryland to Illinois.

3. The Erie Canal provided the first all-water link between farms on the Central Plains and East Coast cities.

4. Henry David Thoreau; the book reflects the transcendentalist philosophy.

5. about 1800 to 1840; the Second Great Awakening

6. *The Liberator* (William Lloyd Garrison) and *The North Star* (Frederick Douglass)

7. 1831; The rebellion resulted in the passage of strict slave codes.

8. the establishment of public schools and increased pay for teachers

9. 1849; more than 200 slaves

10. 1848 in Seneca Falls, New York

Critical Thinking

Score 1 to 3 points for each answer, depending on the thoroughness of the response.

11. Possible answer: The cotton gin made it much easier to clean cotton and enabled cotton to be produced on a much larger scale. As a result, more planters across the South began growing cotton. Within a decade, cotton was the South's most important crop and, by 1860, brought in more money than all other U.S. exports combined.

12. Possible answer: During the Second Great Awakening, preachers taught that people could be saved by doing good works. This message inspired people to work for the improvement of society. Many Americans devoted themselves to such causes as ending slavery, promoting women's rights, and improving education.

13. Possible answer: The Industrial Revolution created a new class of wealthy industrialists who owned large factories and other businesses. It made goods cheaper and more plentiful. It shifted work from skilled craftspeople to less-skilled laborers and made agriculture more efficient. It also led to the rapid growth of the Northern economy and to the building of better roads and faster ships and trains.

14. Answers will vary. Students must explain why the events they chose merit inclusion.

Using Scores to Inform Instruction

Timeline Skills A score of 7 out of 10 indicates that students understand most of the key events of this unit.

Critical Thinking A score of 8 out of 12 indicates that students are able to think critically about most of the key issues of this unit.

If students score below these levels, consider reviewing timeline and critical thinking skills.

The Union Challenged

The Union Challenged

Overview

This activity introduces geographic information essential to Unit 7. Students read and interpret maps to learn about the distribution of political power between the North and the South from the early 1800s until 1850. They annotate a map of the United States in 1850 and answer questions in their Interactive Student Notebooks, and then discuss critical thinking questions. Students' comprehension of content and proficiency in map-reading and higher-order thinking skills will help you gauge their readiness for the unit. The pages that follow include a completed map, answers to questions, a scoring guide to inform your teaching, and suggestions for modifications to meet specific student needs.

Essential Geographic Understandings

1. The order in which free states and slave states were added to the Union

2. How the nation's growth and expansion affected the balance of power between free and slave states in both houses of Congress

3. Key human features: Indiana, Mississippi, Illinois, Alabama, Maine, Missouri, Arkansas, Michigan, Florida, Texas, Iowa, Wisconsin, Mexican Cession, California

4. Why the expansion of slavery was such an important issue to the South

Procedures

1   **Introduce the unit.** Tell students they will learn about the issues and events that divided North and South and led to the Civil War. They will also learn about the war itself, its aftermath, and the changes it brought to the South and the nation.

2   **Create a KWL chart.** Ask students to identify what they already know about the causes and consequences of the Civil War and what they want to learn. Use their responses to gauge how much additional background information they will need as you progress through the unit. Students will return to the KWL chart at the end of the unit and add the key information they have learned.

3   **Have students read Unit 7 "Setting the Stage" in the Student Edition.**

4   **Have students complete the Geography Challenge.** Monitor students as they answer the questions and complete the map. You may want to have them work in pairs. Use the guide on the next two pages to check their answers. You may wish to project the map from the Interactive Student Notebook and have students annotate it as the class works through the map-reading questions. Make sure students have grasped Essential Geographic Understandings 1 to 3.

5   **Discuss the "Critical Thinking" questions.** Help students understand the geographic relationships described in Essential Geographic Understanding 4.

The United States, Mid-1850

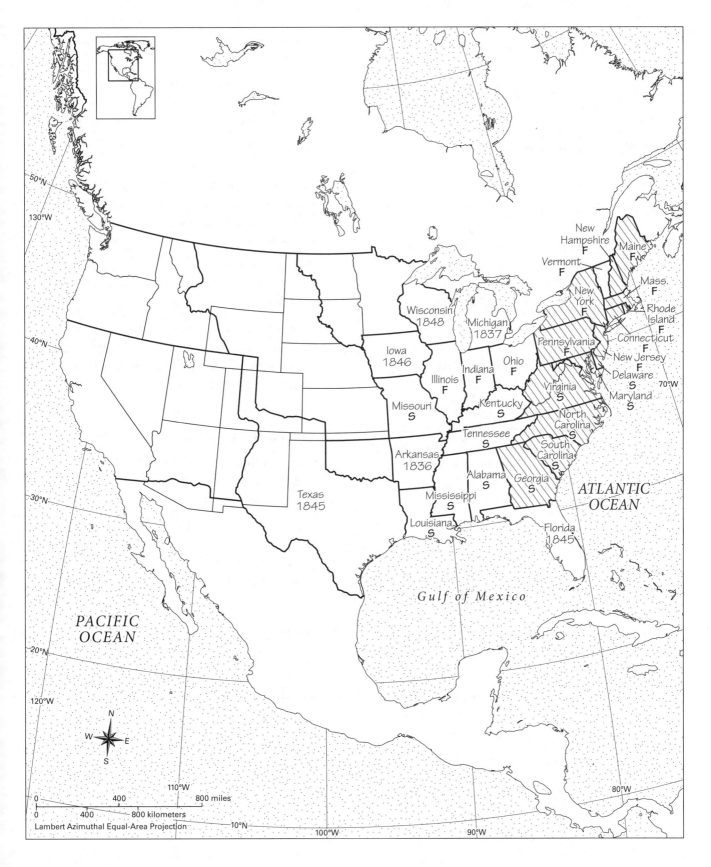

New Hampshire
F

Maine
F

Vermont
F

Mass.
F

New York
F

Rhode Island
F

Connecticut
F

Pennsylvania
F

New Jersey
F

Delaware
S

Maryland
S

Wisconsin
1848

Michigan
1837

Iowa
1846

Ohio
F

Indiana
F

Illinois
F

Virginia
S

Missouri
S

Kentucky
S

North Carolina
S

Tennessee
S

South Carolina
S

Arkansas
1836

Alabama
S

Georgia
S

Texas
1845

Mississippi
S

Louisiana
S

Florida
1845

ATLANTIC OCEAN

Gulf of Mexico

PACIFIC OCEAN

N
W E
S

0   400   800 miles
0   400   800 kilometers
Lambert Azimuthal Equal-Area Projection

50°N
130°W
40°N
30°N
120°W
20°N
110°W
10°N
100°W
90°W
80°W
70°W

Geography Skills

Score 1 point for each correct answer. Use the map on the previous page to check shading and labeling.

1. There were 30 states in mid-1850: 15 slave states and 15 free states.

2. Of the original 13 states, 6 (Delaware, Georgia, Maryland, North Carolina, South Carolina, Virginia) were slave states and 7 (Connecticut, Massachusetts, Rhode Island, New Hampshire, New Jersey, New York, Pennsylvania) were free states.

3. Of the first 5 states added to the Union following the original 13 states, 3 (Kentucky, Tennessee, Louisiana) were slave states and 2 (Vermont and Ohio) were free states. This made 9 slave states and 9 free states in 1812.

4. The next 6 states were Indiana (1816), Mississippi (1817), Illinois (1818), Alabama (1819), Maine (1820), and Missouri (1821). Indiana, Illinois, and Maine were free states; Mississippi, Alabama, and Missouri were slave states.

5. Students should notice that Congress was either alternating between free and slave states or admitting states in pairs—one free state followed by one slave state. This kept the free and slave states equal in number and gave the North and South the same number of votes in the Senate.

6. The admission of Arkansas and Michigan did follow the pattern set between 1816 and 1821, because one was a slave state and the other was a free state.

7. Two states (Florida and Texas) were slave states and two (Iowa and Wisconsin) were free states.

8. The Senate remained balanced, with 30 senators from the 15 slave states and 30 senators from the 15 free states.

9. Of the slave states, Virginia had the most votes (15). Three free states (New York, Pennsylvania, and Ohio) had more votes than Virginia.

10. The North controlled the House of Representatives in mid-1850.

Critical Thinking

Questions may have more than one correct answer. Score 1 to 3 points for each reasonable answer, depending on the strength of students' geographic reasoning. Possible answers are given here.

11. Because the numbers of free and slave states were balanced at 15 each, California's admission would give either the free states or the slave states control of the Senate.

12. If California became a free state, the South would not control either house of Congress. If California became a slave state, the South would control the Senate, but the North would still control the House of Representatives.

13. The admission of Kansas would either restore the balance between free and slave states in the Senate or widen the gap between them.

14. The election of 1860 added control of the presidency to the free states' existing control of Congress. Southerners would fear government action against slavery in such a situation.

Using Scores to Inform Instruction

Geography Skills A score of 7 out of 10 or better indicates that students have acquired sufficient geographic information to proceed with the unit.

Critical Thinking A score of 9 out of 12 or better indicates that students are beginning to understand the relationships between physical geography and the different ways in which people live.

Modifying Instruction

ELL or Learners with Special Education Needs Consider focusing on map-reading questions or limiting the number of "Critical Thinking" questions.

Students with Weak Map or Critical Thinking Skills Assign appropriate pages from the Social Studies Skills Toolkit in the back of the Lesson Masters.

A Dividing Nation

Which events of the mid-1800s kept the nation together and which events pulled it apart?

Overview

In a Visual Discovery activity, students analyze and bring to life images depicting the growing conflict between the North and the South to understand why the nation could not prevent civil war.

Objectives

In the course of reading this chapter and participating in the classroom activity, students will

Social Studies

- identify the regulations on slavery in the Northwest Ordinance.

- trace the effects of territorial expansion on the debate over slavery.

- analyze the impact of key events on the antislavery movement and on the Union.

Language Arts

- participate in simulated historical debate.

Social Studies Vocabulary

Key Content Terms Union, Missouri Compromise, fugitive, Wilmot Proviso, Compromise of 1850, Kansas-Nebraska Act, Dred Scott decision, Lincoln-Douglas debates

Academic Vocabulary confront, ensure, faction

Materials

History Alive! The United States Through Industrialism

Interactive Student Notebooks

Visuals 21A–21G

Lesson Masters

- Student Handout 21 (1 per every 4 students)

- Vocabulary Development handout (1 per student, on colored paper)

Activity	Suggested Time	Materials
Preview	10 minutes	• Interactive Student Notebooks
Vocabulary Development	30–40 minutes	• *History Alive! The United States Through Industrialism* • Interactive Student Notebooks • Vocabulary Development handout
Visual Discovery	150–200 minutes (3–4 regular periods) (1.5–2 block periods)	• *History Alive! The United States Through Industrialism* • Interactive Student Notebooks • Visuals 21A–21G • Student Handout 21
Processing	25 minutes	• Interactive Student Notebooks
Assessment	40 minutes	• Chapter 21 Assessment

Preview

1 Have students complete the Preview in their Interactive Student Notebooks. Students will interpret a metaphor used by Abraham Lincoln to warn of the potential end of the Union.

2 Have students share their responses in pairs or with the class.

3 Explain the connection between the Preview and Chapter 21. Tell students that Lincoln's warning reveals the tensions that developed between the North and the South throughout the 1800s. The "house" symbolized the Union; the issue dividing the house was slavery. The nation's attempts to keep from dividing ultimately failed. In this chapter, students will discover which events of the mid-1800s kept the Union together for a time and which pulled it apart.

Vocabulary Development

1 Introduce the Key Content Terms. Have students locate the Key Content Terms for the chapter in their Interactive Student Notebooks. These are important terms that will help them understand the main ideas of the chapter. Ask volunteers to identify any familiar terms and how they might be used in a sentence.

2 Have students complete a Vocabulary Development handout. Give each student a copy of the Vocabulary Development handout of your choice from the Reading Toolkit at the back of the Lesson Masters. These handouts provide extra practice and support, depending on your students' needs. Review the completed handout by asking volunteers to share one answer for each term.

Reading

1 Introduce the Essential Question and have students read Section 21.1. Have students identify the Essential Question on the first page of the chapter: *Which events of the mid-1800s kept the nation together and which events pulled it apart?* Then have them read Section 21.1 Afterward, ask,

- What was the troubling question that the nation tried to avoid?
- Why could this question no longer be ignored?
- Why were new problems created when the nation attempted to compromise on this question?

2 Have students complete the Reading Notes for Chapter 21. Assign Sections 21.2 to 21.9 during the activity as indicated in the procedures for the Visual Discovery activity. Remind students to use the Key Content Terms where appropriate as they complete their Reading Notes.

Visual Discovery

1 **Introduce the activity.** Explain that students will analyze maps and bring to life images to understand how tensions developed between the North and the South in the mid-1800s. Then they will decide which events of the mid-1800s kept the nation together and which events pulled it apart.

2 **Have students read and complete the Reading Notes for Section 21.2.**

3 **Introduce the Missouri Compromise.** Project *Visual 21A: The United States in 1819 and 1821*. Reveal only the top map, "The United States, 1819," and ask,

- What do you see on this map?

- How many free states are there? How many slave states?

- Why did the issue of Missouri statehood pull the nation apart?

- How would you have solved this problem? Why or why not?

Reveal the bottom map and ask,

- How does this map differ from the first one?

- According to this map, what compromises might have been made to keep the nation together in 1820?

- How might Northerners have reacted to these compromises? How might Southerners have reacted?

- Do you think these compromises will keep the nation together or pull it apart? Why or why not?

4 **Have students read and complete the Reading Notes for Sections 21.3 and 21.4.**

5 **Have students prepare to bring to life an image about California statehood.** Project *Visual 21B: The Senate Debates California Statehood* and tell students that this image shows the Senate debating California statehood and slavery in 1850. Place students in groups of four and give a copy of *Student Handout 21: Creating Act-It-Outs About a Dividing Nation* to each group. Assign each group one of the characters in the first act-it-out: Northern Senator, Southern Senator, Abolitionist in the Gallery, Slave Owner in the Gallery. Then review the directions and give groups five to ten minutes to prepare.

6 **Conduct the act-it-out.** Call up four actors to stand in front of the projected image, taking on an appropriate character's posture and facial expression. Acting as the on-scene reporter, ask the characters some of the questions from Student Handout 21. (**Note:** Consider conducting the act-it-out a second time with new actors.)

Visual 21A

Visual 21B

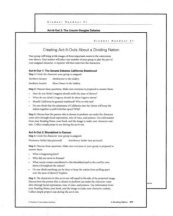

Student Handout 21

7   **Introduce the Compromise of 1850 by projecting *Visual 21C: The United States in 1821 and 1850.*** Reveal both maps and ask,

- How do the two maps differ? What changed between 1821 and 1850?

- According to the bottom map, what compromises might have been made to keep the nation together in 1850?

- How might Northerners have reacted to these compromises? How might Southerners have reacted?

- Do you think these compromises will keep the nation together or pull it apart? Why or why not?

Visual 21C

8   **Have students read and complete the Reading Notes for Sections 21.5 and 21.6.**

9   **Have students prepare to bring to life an image of Lawrence, Kansas.** Project *Visual 21D: Bloodshed in Kansas* and tell students that this image depicts the raid on Lawrence, Kansas, in 1856. Place students in groups of four and assign each group one of the characters in the second act-it-out on Student Handout 21: Proslavery Settler or Antislavery Settler. Then review the directions and give groups five to ten minutes to prepare.

10 **Conduct the act-it-out.** Call up two sets of actors (four students in all) to stand to the sides of the projected image, taking on appropriate postures and facial expressions. Acting as the on-scene reporter, ask the characters some of the questions from Student Handout 21. (**Note:** Consider conducting the act-it-out a second time with new actors.)

Visual 21D

11 **Introduce the Dred Scott decision by projecting *Visual 21E: The United States in 1850 and 1857.*** Reveal both maps and ask,

- How do the two maps differ? What changed between 1850 and 1857?

- According to the bottom map, what decision might have been made to settle the controversy over slavery?

- How might Northerners have reacted to this decision? How might Southerners have reacted?

- Do you think this decision will keep the nation together or pull it apart? Why or why not?

Visual 21E

12 **Have students read and complete the Reading Notes for Section 21.7 and 21.8.**

13 **Have students prepare to bring to life an image of the Lincoln-Douglas debates.** Project *Visual 21F: The Lincoln-Douglas Debates* and tell students that this image depicts one of the seven Illinois senatorial debates between Abraham Lincoln and Stephen Douglas in 1858. Place students in groups of four. Assign each group one of the characters in the third act-it-out on Student Handout 21: Abraham Lincoln or Stephen Douglas. Then review the directions and give groups approximately ten minutes to prepare.

Visual 21F

14 Conduct the act-it-out. Tell the class that these debates gained national attention and drew large, enthusiastic crowds, with one debate having an audience of more than 10,000 people. Call up two actors to stand in front of the projected image, taking on an appropriate character's posture and facial expression, and have them perform the debate. Instruct half of the audience to cheer loudly after each statement made by Lincoln and the other half to cheer after each statement made by Douglas. Afterward, acting as the on-scene reporter, randomly ask audience members one of the questions from Student Handout 21.

15 Introduce the election of 1860 by projecting *Visual 21G: The United States in 1860.* Ask,

- What do you see on this map?

- What does this map tell you about the nation in 1860?

- How might Northerners have reacted to these election results? How might Southerners have reacted?

- Do you think these results will keep the nation together or pull it apart? Why?

16 Have students read and complete the Reading Notes for Section 21.9.

17 Have students reflect on what they have learned. Ask, *Several compromises were made to try to keep the United States united. Why were they ultimately unsuccessful in holding the nation together?*

Visual 21G

Processing

Have students complete the Processing activity, in which they will choose the event of the mid-1800s that they believe pulled the nation the furthest apart and discuss it in a letter to the editor. Consider distributing letters to the editor from your local newspaper as examples.

Quicker Coverage

Eliminate One or More Act-It-Outs Consider performing only the act-it-outs that pertain to your state standards.

Jigsaw the Topics for Section 21.6 Count students off from 1 to 5. Assign the 1s "The Fugitive Slave Act," the 2s *"Uncle Tom's Cabin,"* the 3s "The Ostend Manifesto and the Kansas-Nebraska Act," the 4s "Bloodshed in Kansas," and the 5s "Violence in Congress." Have groups complete the Reading Notes for their assigned section. Then call on volunteers to share their answers with the class as the other groups take notes.

> **Writing: Sentence Structure**
>
> Remind students to vary sentence types in their letters to the editor by using simple, compound, and complex sentences, as well as sentences of different lengths. Also demonstrate ways to vary sentence openings, such as by using verb phrases, prepositional phrases, and various forms of clauses, including absolutes. As needed, contrast various phrases and other fragments with short, dramatic, and correct sentences.

Deeper Coverage

Analyze the Act-It-Out Images To help students preview Sections 21.4, 21.6, and 21.8, project Visual 21B before students complete the Reading Notes for Section 21.4, Visual 21D before Section 21.6, and Visual 21F before Section 21.8. Ask these questions for each image:

- What details do you see in this image?
- What do you think is happening here? Cite evidence from the image.
- Do you think the event depicted here might keep the nation together or pull it apart? Why?

Add Characters to Act-It-Out 2 Expand the list of characters on Student Handout 21 by adding Northerner, Southerner, and Charles Sumner. Have groups that are assigned one of these added characters use the questions below to prepare. During the act-it-out, have these students remain seated. After interviewing the actors in the image, move into the audience and randomly call on students to answer the questions below from the perspective of their characters.

- What is your opinion of the recent events in Kansas? Explain.
- What is your opinion of other political events such as the Fugitive Slave Act, the Ostend Manifesto, and the Kansas-Nebraska Act? Explain.
- Have you read *Uncle Tom's Cabin*? What do you think of its message?

Create an Illustrated Timeline Have students create a timeline on a large sheet of paper that contains a summary sentence for each of the major events from Chapter 21. Tell students to organize the information by placing events that kept the nation together on one side of the timeline and events that pulled the nation apart on the other. Also have them create a small illustration or symbol to represent each event.

Assessment

Mastering the Content

1. D	5. D	9. B	13. A
2. C	6. C	10. C	14. B
3. A	7. A	11. A	15. A
4. D	8. D	12. C	16. B

Applying Social Studies Skills

17. B

18. the United States or the country

19. C

Exploring the Essential Question

20. Answers should include all of the elements requested in the prompt.

Scoring Rubric

Score	Description
3	Student completes all four parts of the task. Ideas are clearly stated, supported by details, and demonstrate command of standard English conventions.
2	Student responds to most or all parts of the task. Ideas may lack details or not be clearly stated.
1	Student responds to at least one part of the task. Ideas may contain factual or grammatical errors and may lack details.
0	Response does not match the task or is incorrect.

Slavery Divides Boston

1   **Have students read the first page of the Chapter 21 Reading Further.** Ask the class to speculate why Anthony Burns was being returned to slavery and why people were so upset.

2   **Have students finish the reading.** Point out that, in addition to increasing the conflict between North and South and between abolitionists and others, the Fugitive Slave Act overruled the state antislavery law.

3   **Discuss how laws affect our lives.** Ask, *How did the Fugitive Slave Act change the lives of escaped slaves? Of Northerners?* Point out that laws are not simply words on paper, but can influence our lives in powerful ways. Ask students to name some laws that affect their lives.

4   **Ask students to compare Boston as a center of abolition with Boston a century earlier.** Point out the quotation from William Lloyd Garrison and ask, *How did William Lloyd Garrison link the two periods?*

5   **Have students complete the Chapter 21 Reading Further in their Interactive Student Notebooks.** Invite students to share their handbills with the class.

English Language Learners

Preview the Images Give students photocopies of Visuals 21A to 21G and corresponding questions the night before you conduct the activity, and have them prepare possible answers to the questions.

Complete the Processing in Pairs Have students partner with other students who chose the same event for their letter to the editor and write their letters together.

Learners Reading and Writing Below Grade Level

Draw the Preview Have students draw a picture of Lincoln's warning to the nation. When the class discusses the Preview questions, have students label the drawing with their answers.

Provide an Example of the Processing Create a sample letter to the editor for students to use as a reference. Consider choosing an event that students are not likely to use, such as the Missouri Compromise or the Wilmot Proviso.

Learners with Special Education Needs

Provide Additional Support for the Act-It-Outs Consider these tips:

- Have students prepare a script by answering the questions on Student Handout 21. Allow them to read from the script during the act-it-out.

- Tell students which role they will be playing a few days in advance so they can practice their parts.

Advanced Learners

Assign Historical Roles in Act-It-Out 1 Instead of using the characters listed on Student Handout 21, assign each group a historical senator in the debate over California statehood, such as Henry Clay, Daniel Webster, John C. Calhoun, Stephen A. Douglas, David Wilmot, John Bell, Jefferson Davis, or William H. Seward. Have students research each senator's viewpoint and use their findings to answer the questions for the performance.

Expand Act-It-Out 3 Divide the class into seven groups. Give each group a transcript of one of the seven Lincoln-Douglas debates, which can be found on the Internet. Have groups write paraphrased versions of their assigned debate and then use the guidelines on Student Handout 21 to perform it for the class.

Enrichment Resources

Find out more about the dividing nation by exploring the following resources for *History Alive! The United States Through Industrialism* at www.teachtci.com.

Enrichment Readings These in-depth readings encourage students to explore selected topics related to the chapter. You may also find readings that relate the chapter's content directly to your state's curriculum.

Internet Connections These recommended Web sites provide useful and engaging content that reinforces skills development and mastery of subjects within the chapter.

Literature Recommendations

The following books offer opportunities to extend the content in this chapter.

Meet Abraham Lincoln by Barbara Cary (New York: Random House, 2001)

Harriet Beecher Stowe by LeeAnne Gelletly (New York: Chelsea House, 2000)

John Brown's Raid on Harpers Ferry by Brendan January (Danbury, CT: Children's Press, 2000)

Section 21.2

1. Sketches should show that slavery was illegal in states north of the Ohio River and legal in states south of the Ohio River.

2. Possible answer:

   Northerner: The ban against slavery should extend across the Mississippi River. Missouri should not be a slave state.

   Southerner: Congress does not have the right to decide if slavery should be allowed in a new state. The people of that state should decide.

3. Southerners were outnumbered in the House of Representatives. If the South and North had an equal number of senators, the South would hold onto some power in Congress. For example, Southerners did not want the Tallmadge Amendment because it would have made Missouri a free state. They did not have enough votes to stop it in the House, but they did in the Senate—so they were able to keep the amendment from becoming law.

Section 21.3

1. Missouri became a slave state. Maine became a free state. Congress drew an imaginary line across the Louisiana Territory and declared slavery to be banned north of the line and allowed south of it.

2. Possible answer: I have decided to support the Missouri Compromise because I believe it is the best solution we can create under the Constitution. I am not willing to endanger the Union and possibly cause it to split. However, if the Union does split, slavery will be the cause. For now, the controversy is at rest.

Section 21.4

1. Adams proposed a constitutional amendment stating that no one could be born into slavery after 1845. The gag rule kept Congress from debating slavery for ten years, so Congress refused to consider his proposal.

2. *Fugitive slave issue*: Northerners often helped runaway slaves to freedom. This angered Southerners, who regarded these Northerners as thieves.

   Wilmot Proviso: When President Polk asked for funding for the Mexican-American War, Representative Wilmot put a provision in the bill stating that if we gained any land from Mexico, slavery could never be allowed there. Southerners opposed this provision.

3. Northerners in Congress accepted California's application for statehood and Southerners rejected it because California had applied as a free state.

Section 21.5

1. California would be admitted as a free state. New Mexico and Utah would be territories open to slavery. The slave trade would end in Washington D.C., but slave owners could keep their slaves. A strong fugitive slave law would be passed.

2. Possible answer: It took nine months of argument to pass the Compromise of 1850, and many Southerners were still wary of it.

Section 21.6

Possible answers:

Events After the Compromise of 1850	Two Key Details	How the Event Pulled the Nation Apart
Fugitive Slave Act passed	Captured runaway slaves had almost no legal rights. Anyone caught helping runaway slaves could be jailed.	Many Northerners openly defied the law, which angered Southerners.
Uncle Tom's Cabin published	Harriet Beecher Stowe wrote this novel after having a vision about the abuses of slavery. It was first published in a newspaper and later as a novel.	The book made millions of people in the North even more angry about slavery.
Kansas-Nebraska Act passed	Southerners in Congress agreed to support the bill only if a few changes were made to it. The act abolished the Missouri Compromise and allowed the settlers to decide whether to allow slavery.	Northerners were outraged and feared more territory would be open to slavery.
Raid on Lawrence, Kansas	Pro- and antislavery settlers poured into Kansas to protect their interests in the new territory. Proslavery settlers raided and attacked the city of Lawrence, the headquarters of the antislavery movement in Kansas.	Northerners raised money to send more antislavery settlers into the region.
Beating of Senator Sumner	Senator Charles Sumner protested the violence in Kansas in a speech criticizing prominent proslavery leaders. A nephew of one of the men he criticized beat Sumner into unconsciousness with a cane.	Southerners applauded the attack while Northerners were outraged.

Section 21.7

1. Dred Scott's owner had taken him to Wisconsin, a free state. Scott argued that his stay in a state where slavery was outlawed made him free.

2. Possible answers: Slaves were not citizens. No African American, slave or free, could become a citizen. The Missouri Compromise was unconstitutional. Banning slavery in a territory was the same as taking property from slaveholders. Congress had a constitutional responsibility to protect the property of slaveholders in territories.

3. Possible answers:

   Northerner: This verdict is outrageous and immoral! I will not obey it!

   Southerner: The question of slavery is finally settled, and in our favor. No one—especially not Congress—can take our property without just cause!

Section 21.8

1. The debates made Abraham Lincoln famous nationwide and brought the moral issue of slavery into sharp focus.

2. John Brown wanted to arm slaves and begin a rebellion to end slavery.

Section 21.9

1. Possible answer: "Lincoln Wins! South Is Powerless!"

2. *December 20, 1860:* South Carolina seceded from the Union.

   February 1861: Seven states that have seceded form the Confederate States of America.

3. Lincoln stated that secession is wrong and unconstitutional. He appealed to the rebellious Southern states to return in peace.

4. Possible answer: "Rebels Attack Fort Sumter! War Will Restore the Union!"

The Civil War

What factors and events influenced the outcome of the Civil War?

Overview

In an Experiential Exercise, students take on the role of soldiers at the Battle of Gettysburg and encounter key aspects of what it was like to be a soldier in the Civil War and then write about their experiences.

Objectives

In the course of reading this chapter and participating in the classroom activity, students will

Social Studies

- compare the strengths and weaknesses of the Union and Confederacy at the outbreak of the Civil War to predict the outcome of the war.
- draw connections between significant writings and speeches of Abraham Lincoln and the Declaration of Independence.
- identify the views of leaders on both sides and compare and contrast the experiences of white and black Union soldiers.
- examine critical battles and events of the war and connect them to the Union's Anaconda Plan.
- explain how key events of the Civil War, like the Battle of Gettysburg, affected soldiers and civilians.

Language Arts

- write a journal entry describing life during the Civil War.

Social Studies Vocabulary

Key Content Terms Confederacy, civil war, Emancipation Proclamation, habeas corpus, Gettysburg Address, Appomattox Court House

Academic Vocabulary technological, perpetual, crisis, assert, reinforcements

Materials

History Alive! The United States Through Industrialism

Interactive Student Notebooks

CD Tracks 11–13

Visuals 22A–22E

Lesson Masters

- Student Handouts 22A and 22B (2 copies of each)
- Student Handout 22C (1 copy, cut apart)
- Student Handout 22D (3 copies, cut apart)
- Vocabulary Development handout (1 per student, on colored paper)

Activity	Suggested Time	Materials
Preview	20 minutes	• Interactive Student Notebooks • Visuals 22A and 22B
Vocabulary Development	30–40 minutes	• *History Alive! The United States Through Industrialism* • Interactive Student Notebooks • Vocabulary Development handout
Experiential Exercise	50 minutes (1 regular period) (0.5 block period)	• *History Alive! The United States Through Industrialism* • Interactive Student Notebooks • CD Tracks 11–13 • Visuals 22C–22E • Student Handouts 22A–22D
Processing	20 minutes	• *History Alive! The United States Through Industrialism* • Interactive Student Notebooks
Assessment	40 minutes	• Chapter 22 Assessment

Preview

1 **Assign roles.** Assign students on one side of the classroom to be Union soldiers and students on other side to be Confederate soldiers.

2 **Have students respond to images and music.** Follow these steps:

   • Project *Visual 22A: Union Soldiers Marching Off to War.* Ask students to identify significant details in the image.

   • Tell Union students to picture themselves in this scene, and ask them how they might feel.

   • Project *Visual 22B: Confederate Soldiers Marching Off to War.* Ask students to identify significant details in the image, including any differences between this image and the previous image.

   • Tell Confederate students to picture themselves in this scene, and ask them how they might feel.

3 **Have students answer the Preview questions given in the Interactive Student Notebooks.** Afterward, have volunteers from both sides share their answers.

4 **Explain the connection between the Preview and Chapter 22.** Explain that the mood at the beginning of the Civil War, in both the North and the South, was optimistic and defiant. Most people on both sides did not expect the war to be long or bloody, but they were wrong. In this chapter, students will learn how key events and battles of the Civil War affected soldiers and civilians and how attitudes toward the war changed as the war progressed.

Visual 22A

Visual 22B

Vocabulary Development

1 **Introduce the Key Content Terms.** Have students locate the Key Content Terms for the chapter in their Interactive Student Notebooks. These are important terms that will help them understand the main ideas of the chapter. Ask volunteers to identify any familiar terms and how they might be used in a sentence.

2 **Have students complete a Vocabulary Development handout.** Give each student a copy of the Vocabulary Development handout of your choice from the Reading Toolkit at the back of the Lesson Masters. These handouts provide extra practice and support, depending on your students' needs. Review the completed handout by asking volunteers to share one answer for each term.

Reading

1 **Introduce the Essential Question and have students read Section 22.1.**
Have students identify the Essential Question on the first page of the chapter: *What factors and events influenced the outcome of the Civil War?* Then have them read Section 22.1. Afterward, ask,

- At the start of the war, what were Southerners fighting for? Northerners?

- What were the attitudes of people on both sides at the beginning of the war?

- How might those attitudes have changed as the war went on for several years?

- How do you think events and battles of the Civil War might have affected soldiers? How might they have affected civilians back home?

2 **Have students complete the Reading Notes for Chapter 22.** Have students read and complete the Reading Notes for Sections 22.2 to 22.4. Use Guide to Reading Notes 22 to review their answers as a class. Assign Sections 22.5 to 22.8 at the end of the activity as indicated in the procedures for the Experiential Exercise. Remind students to use the Key Content Terms where appropriate as they complete their Reading Notes.

Experiential Exercise

1 **Prepare the classroom.** Before class, arrange the classroom into two opposing "camps." Designate half of the room as the Confederate camp and the other half as the Union camp. Set up the projector so that images can be seen clearly by students in both camps.

2 **Assign students to camps and introduce the Battle of Gettysburg.** When students enter the room, have them go to their assigned camp—Confederate or Union. Tell them to take paper and pencils with them. Then read the following background information about the Battle of Gettysburg.

In May 1863, the Confederate commander, Robert E. Lee, made the decision to invade Union territory. By invading the North, Lee knew he could feed his hungry army by taking food from Northern farms that had been untouched by the war. Lee had just led his army to several key victories and was extremely confident that his soldiers could defeat the demoralized Union army. He also hoped that a decisive victory on Union soil would convince Northerners that it was useless to continue fighting and pressure President Lincoln into signing a peace treaty.

By mid-June, Confederate forces had marched into Northern territory. Two weeks later, the Confederate and Union armies finally faced off at the small town of Gettysburg, Pennsylvania.

3 **Select Union and Confederate officers and give them their orders.**
Promote two soldiers in each camp to become the Captain and First
Lieutenant of their company. Select officers who will take the role seriously, give orders loudly and clearly, and have the respect of the soldiers
in their company. Then give a copy of *Student Handout 22A: Orders for
Union Officers* or *Student Handout 22B: Orders for Confederate Officers*
to the Captain and First Lieutenant of the respective camps. Briefly
review the handout with the officers.

Student Handouts 22A and 22B

4 **Conduct Gettysburg Experience 1.** Tell soldiers that it is the morning of
the most important battle of the Civil War. Remind them to stay in character throughout the activity. Project *Visual 22C: Waiting for Battle* and follow
these steps:

- Tell the Union Captain to give Order 1. Then tell the Confederate Captain
  to give Order 1.

- Play CD Track 11, "The Battle of Gettysburg: Days One and Two."

- When the recording ends, tell the Confederate Captain to give Order 2.
  Then tell the Union Captain to give Order 2. Give soldiers two to three
  minutes to write their letters home.

Visual 22C

5 **Conduct Gettysburg Experience 2.** Project *Visual 22D: Marching into Battle*,
and follow these steps:

- Tell the Union Captain to give Order 3. Then tell the Confederate Captain
  to give Order 3.

- Play CD Track 12, "The Battle of Gettysburg: Day Three."

- When the recording ends, tell the Union Captain to carry out Order 4.
  Then tell the Confederate Captain to carry out Order 4. Encourage soldiers
  on both sides to cheer.

Visual 22D

6 **Conduct Gettysburg Experience 3.** Post a sign at the back of each camp that
reads "Field Hospital." *Project Visual 22E: The Aftermath of the Battle*, and
follow these steps:

- Tell the Union Captain to give Order 5. Then tell the Confederate Captain
  to give Order 5.

- Play CD Track 13, "The Aftermath of the Battle of Gettysburg."

Visual 22E

- Select two soldiers from the Union side to be a Union doctor and stretcher bearer and two soldiers from the Confederate side to be a Confederate doctor and stretcher bearer. Give each of these four soldiers the appropriate role card cut from *Student Handout 22C: Civil War Experience 3 Role Cards*.

- Give all other soldiers and officers a card cut from *Student Handout 22D: Civil War Experience 3 Casualty Cards*.

- Have all soldiers read their cards carefully. Make sure doctors and stretcher bearers clearly understand their roles.

- Tell wounded soldiers to follow the directions on their cards.

- Tell doctors and stretcher bearers to follow the directions on their cards and to attend to their wounded soldiers *as quickly as possible*. Give them two to three minutes to attend to the wounded.

- After all wounded soldiers have been attended to, tell them to look at the bottom of their cards and raise their hands if they see an X there. Tell these soldiers they have just died—not from their battle wounds but from infections they contracted while receiving medical care.

Student Handout 22C

Student Handout 22D

7 **Debrief the activity.** After Civil War Experience 3, or the next day, ask students the following questions:

- What did you write in the letters to your family or friends back home? What do you think soldiers wrote about in these kinds of letters? *(Many wrote about how much they loved their families or how proud they were to be able to fight for their ideals, even if they died.)*

- How did you feel as you were preparing for battle? What do you think soldiers worried about just before going into battle? *(Many worried about whether they would be injured or die. New soldiers often worried about how they would react in a real battle.)*

- How did it feel to be waiting on the battlefield for medical attention? How did it feel to be a doctor or stretcher bearer attending to wounded soldiers? Why do you think the number of casualties (dead and wounded) during the Civil War was so high? *(New weapons were more efficient at causing casualties among soldiers, but unsanitary conditions caused many more soldiers to die of infections they received during medical treatment.)*

- Based on your experiences, how do you think events like the Battle of Gettysburg affected soldiers? How might they have affected civilians?

8 **Have students read and complete the Reading Notes for Sections 22.5 to 22.8.** Use the Guide to Reading Notes to review their answers.

Processing

Have students complete the Processing activity, in which they will write a journal entry from the perspective of a Civil War soldier or civilian.

> **Writing: Use Parallelism**
>
> As students write their journal entries, encourage them to include items in a series—such as three modified nouns, three verb phrases, or three prepositional phrases. Also ask them to check that each group of words is parallel, as in "to load the stretcher, to lift the wounded, and to carry the men to the field hospital."

Quicker Coverage

Condense Gettysburg Experience 3 Play CD Track 13 and then distribute role cards. Explain that students will use these cards to gather information, rather than acting out a field hospital. Ask the doctors and stretcher bearers to summarize their responsibilities. Call on various students to describe their wounds. Ask which students have an X on their cards, and explain that these represent soldiers who will die. Discuss conditions at the field hospital with students. Then ask, *What generalizations can you make from this information?*

Deeper Coverage

Create Civil War Journals After the Preview activity and after each of the three Gettysburg experiences, have students create a journal entry from the perspective of a Union or Confederate soldier. Each entry should include

- a historically accurate date and appropriate location.
- one or two paragraphs describing what that particular aspect of the Civil War —marching off to war, waiting for battle, marching into battle, caring for the wounded—was like from the perspective of a soldier.
- a sketch or photograph that relates to that aspect of the war. Students should refer to the visual somewhere in the entry.

Assessment

Mastering the Content

1. B	5. C	9. C	13. C
2. B	6. D	10. C	14. A
3. B	7. A	11. C	15. A
4. C	8. B	12. D	16. B

Applying Social Studies Skills

17. Possible answers: The North was able to produce more food to feed the civilian and military populations. The South used most of their farmland to produce cotton and other products for export, while the North used their land to produce food for soldiers.

18. Possible answers: The North had a greater population from which to draw soldiers. The North had a better transportation system to move soldiers and equipment. The North had more financial resources. The North had a greater manufacturing ability to produce war resources.

19. C

Exploring the Essential Question

20. Answers should include all of the elements requested in the prompt.

Scoring Rubric

Score	Description
3	Student completes all six parts of the task. Ideas are clearly stated, supported by details, and demonstrate command of standard English conventions.
2	Student responds to most or all parts of the task. Ideas may lack details or not be clearly stated.
1	Student responds to at least one part of the task. Ideas may contain factual or grammatical errors and may lack details.
0	Response does not match the task or is incorrect.

Divided House, Divided Families

1   **Have students consider how they feel when they take a position different from ones that others hold.** Ask, *What emotions do you feel when you are in an argument with close friends or family members that involves strong disagreements?* Have them imagine how powerful such emotions would be in a life-and-death situation such as a civil war.

2   **Have students read the Chapter 22 Reading Further.** After they have finished, ask,

   • Why was Kentucky a symbol of the divided nation?

   • Why did Lincoln feel that it was crucial to keep Kentucky in the Union?

3   **Have students complete the first page of the Chapter 22 Reading Further in their Interactive Student Notebooks.** Introduce the activity by discussing how emotions are described in the reading. Ask students to point out adjectives in the reading that describe Benjamin Hardin Helm's decision, such as "hopeful dreams," a "bitter struggle," and "the most painful moment of my life." Then ask them to put themselves in Helm's shoes and describe the emotions they might have experienced.

4   **Have students complete the Reading Further.** Invite students to share their personal letters with the class.

English Language Learners

Make Connections to the Preview Explain that many Union soldiers were recent immigrants to the United States, some speaking very little English. Have these students respond to the following questions, instead of those given in the Interactive Student Notebook:

- How do you think recent immigrants might have felt as they marched off to war in a parade like this?

- Why do you think so many recent immigrants were willing to join the Union army?

- How do you think events and battles during the war might have affected these soldiers and their feelings toward their new country?

Learners Reading and Writing Below Grade Level

Revise the Processing Activity Have students write a journal entry from the perspective of a soldier at the Battle of Gettysburg. The journal entry should include

- the date and location: July 3, 1863; Gettysburg, Pennsylvania.

- one or two paragraphs describing their experiences as a soldier during the battle and how it affected them. Tell them to use details from the classroom activity.

- a sketch or photograph that relates to something they write about in the entry. Tell them to refer to this visual somewhere in their entry.

Learners with Special Education Needs

Take the Role of Civil War Photographer Assign the role of photographer to any students for whom participating in the Civil War experiences might be too challenging. Explain that the Civil War was the first war documented by photographers, the most famous of whom was Mathew Brady. Provide a camera for students to use to take pictures during the three experiences. Make sure they understand that they need to take their role seriously and take pictures that capture what the war was like for soldiers. You may wish to make the pictures available for students to print out and use in the Processing activity.

Advanced Learners

Write Letters to Civil War Soldiers Have students research a primary source journal or letter from a Civil War soldier. The source should discuss at least one aspect of the war that students experienced in the activity. Then have students write a letter to that soldier from the perspective of their own experience as a soldier in the classroom activity. In their letters, they should express to the soldier how their respective experiences were similar and different.

Enrichment Resources

Find out more about the Civil War by exploring the following resources for *History Alive! The United States Through Industrialism* at www.teachtci.com.

Enrichment Readings These in-depth readings encourage students to explore selected topics related to the chapter. You may also find readings that relate the chapter's content directly to your state's curriculum.

Internet Connections These recommended Web sites provide useful and engaging content that reinforces skills development and mastery of subjects within the chapter.

Literature Recommendations

The following books offer opportunities to extend the content in this chapter.

The Civil War Soldier: A Photographic Journey by Ray M. Carson and James L. Robertson (Mechanicsburg, PA: Stackpole Books, 2000)

Retreat from Gettysburg by Kathleen Ernst (Shippensburg, PA: White Mane Publishing, 2000)

Promises of the Dead by Mary Downing Hahn (New York: Harper Trophy, 2002)

Section 22.2

1. Possible answers:

	Strengths	**Weaknesses**
North	larger population controlled 90% of the nation's manufacturing controlled most of the banks ✓ more farms to provide food for troops ✓ land contained most of the nation's iron, coal, copper, and gold ✓ controlled the seas ✓ extensive railroad lines to transport troops and supplies Abraham Lincoln's leadership	lacked good military leadership
South	excellent military leadership ✓ large territory made it difficult to invade and conquer Southerners were defending their liberty, homes, and traditions	✓ the Confederacy could easily be split in two if the North took control of the Mississippi few factories to produce guns or other military supplies limited transportation for troops and supplies

2. Most students will identify the North as more likely to win because it had more strengths and fewer weaknesses than the South.

3. *Lincoln:* In his first inaugural address, Lincoln said his goal was to preserve the Union, a Union begun by the revolution and "matured and continued" by the Declaration of Independence.

    Davis: In his inaugural address, Davis said the South was fighting for the same freedom that was asserted by the founders in the Declaration of Independence.

Section 22.3

1. *Step 1:* Surround the South by sea to cut off its trade.

    Step 2: Divide the Confederacy into sections.

    Step 3: Capture Richmond and destroy the Confederate government.

2. The South won the Battle of Bull Run. Rose Greenhow was a spy who warned Southern military leaders of the Union plan to attack. "Stonewall" Jackson and his men refused to give way to the Union attack and held strong until reinforcements arrived.

3. Possible answers: running farms or businesses, factory work, nurses, teachers, government workers, messengers, guides, scouts, smugglers, soldiers, spies, tending sick and wounded soldiers.

Section 22.4

1. *Step 1:* By the end of 1861, the Union had blocked most Southern ports.

    Step 2: In 1862, the Union navy captured New Orleans and General Grant won victories in Kentucky and Tennessee.

    Step 3: In 1862, the Union attempted to capture Richmond, but failed.

2. Many soldiers called Antietam a defeat for both armies because of the numbers of dead and wounded. About 2,100 Union soldiers died, and about 10,300 were wounded or missing. For the Confederates, 2,770 died and 11,000 were wounded or missing.

3. Improved weapons made it easier to kill. Doctors operated in unsanitary conditions and infections spread rapidly. Unsanitary conditions in camps led to high rates of death from disease. (Students should circle the third reason.)

Section 22.5

1. *Reasons for:* Declaring an end to slavery would discourage Europeans opposed to slavery from supporting the Confederacy. Freeing slaves would take away a large part of the South's workforce.

Effects of: No slaves are freed immediately. But the war becomes a crusade for freedom and living up to the ideals of the Declaration of Independence.

2. Possible answers:

Before Gettysburg: "If I can capture a Northern city, it might convince the North to end the war and seek peace. I know my boys are up to it."

After Gettysburg: "Gettysburg is a horrible loss for our boys. One-third of my men have been killed. We must retreat to Virginia."

3. Some Northerners were more interested in saving the Union than stopping slavery, while others were sympathetic to the Confederate cause. Lincoln sent troops to restore order when opposition turned violent and even suspended the right of habeas corpus.

4. Possible answer: "Dedicated to the proposition that all men are created equal"; Lincoln wanted Americans to rededicate themselves to the ideals of liberty and equality in the Declaration so that soldiers killed at Gettysburg would have died for a worthy cause.

Section 22.6

1. Possible entries:
   - Railroads were used to transport supplies and troops.
   - Telegraphs were used to communicate with distant armies.
   - Photographs were used to record events.
   - Combat occurred between iron-plated steamships.

2. *Step 1:* The Union built enough iron-clad ships, like the Monitor, to maintain a naval blockade of the Confederacy.

   Step 2: On July 4, 1863, the city of Vicksburg surrendered and Union forces finally took complete control of the Mississippi, dividing the Confederacy in two.

3. Letters should include the following information: Life in the South is very difficult for civilians. Goods are scarce due to the blockade at sea and very expensive. Invading Union forces cut railroad lines and destroy crops. Many people have little or nothing to eat.

Section 22.7

White Union Soldiers: Encouraged to enlist at the start of the war. Received regular pay. If captured in battle, would be treated as prisoners. Received regular training and equipment.

African American Soldiers: Were not allowed to enlist until 1862. Often received less pay. If captured in battle, could be killed or sold into slavery. Received less training and poorer equipment.

Similarities: Both fought bravely in Civil War. Both suffered high casualties.

Section 22.8

1. By total war, General Grant meant to wage war on the enemy's will to fight and ability to support an army. Answers about whether this is an appropriate strategy will vary.

2. *Step 3:* Grant battered Lee's army at Petersburg for nine months, finally breaking through and capturing Richmond.

3. Possible answer: Lee Surrenders to Grant—War Finally Over! On April 9, 1865, in Appomattox Court House, Virginia, General Robert E. Lee formally surrendered to General Ulysses S. Grant. Grant ordered his men to treat the defeated Confederates with respect now that they were all countrymen again. Lee accepted Grant's terms.

4. Possible answers:
   - It was the first modern war, using technologies of the Industrial Revolution such as railroads, the telegraph, and iron-clad ships.
   - It introduced the concept of total war—war between entire societies, not just armies.
   - It devastated the economy and environment of the South for generations.
   - It ended slavery in the United States.
   - It affirmed that the United States was a single nation, not a collection of sovereign states.

The Reconstruction Era

To what extent did Reconstruction bring African Americans closer to full citizenship?

Overview

In a Visual Discovery activity, students analyze primary source images to evaluate how close African Americans came to full citizenship during Reconstruction.

Objectives

In the course of reading this chapter and participating in the classroom activity, students will

Social Studies

- cite purposes and examples of black codes.
- identify the effects of the Freedmen's Bureau.
- examine the Thirteenth, Fourteenth, and Fifteenth Amendments and their role in Reconstruction.
- trace the relationship between President Johnson and Congress.
- illustrate the effects of Reconstruction on African Americans' pursuit of full citizenship.
- identify the factors that caused African Americans to leave the South.

Language Arts

- create a metaphor.

Social Studies Vocabulary

Key Content Terms Reconstruction, Thirteenth Amendment, Freedmen's Bureau, black codes, civil rights, Fourteenth Amendment, Fifteenth Amendment, Jim Crow laws

Academic Vocabulary resolve, so-called, tolerate

Materials

History Alive! The United States Through Industrialism

Interactive Student Notebooks

Visuals 23A–23D

Lesson Masters

- Student Handout 23 (1 for every 4 students)
- Vocabulary Development handout (1 per student, on colored paper)

small sticky notes

Activity	Suggested Time	Materials
Preview	10 minutes	• Interactive Student Notebooks
Vocabulary Development	30–40 minutes	• *History Alive! The United States Through Industrialism* • Interactive Student Notebooks • Vocabulary Development handout
Visual Discovery	150 minutes (3 regular periods) (1.5 block periods)	• *History Alive! The United States Through Industrialism* • Interactive Student Notebooks • Visuals 23A–23D • Student Handout 23 • small sticky notes
Processing	25 minutes	• *History Alive! The United States Through Industrialism* • Interactive Student Notebooks
Assessment	40 minutes	• Chapter 23 Assessment

Preview

1 **Have students complete the Preview activity.** They will take the perspective of emancipated slaves at the end of the Civil War and project their hopes for their life as freedmen.

2 **Have students share their responses in pairs or with the class.**

3 **Explain the connection between the Preview and Chapter 23.** Tell students that as the nation emerged from the Civil War, many African Americans considered the meaning of their new status as freedmen. Integrating former slaves into American society as citizens became one of the most difficult and controversial aims of the era. In this chapter, students will learn how the nation was able to rebuild after the Civil War and to what extent the events of this era brought African Americans closer to full citizenship.

Vocabulary Development

1 **Introduce the Key Content Terms.** Have students locate the Key Content Terms for the chapter in their Interactive Student Notebooks. These are important terms that will help them understand the main ideas of the chapter. Ask volunteers to identify any familiar terms and how they might be used in a sentence.

2 **Have students complete a Vocabulary Development handout.** Give each student a copy of the Vocabulary Development handout of your choice from the Reading Toolkit at the back of the Lesson Masters. These handouts provide extra practice and support, depending on your students' needs. Review the completed handout by asking volunteers to share one answer for each term.

Reading

1 **Introduce the Essential Question and have students read Section 23.1.** Have students identify the Essential Question on the first page of the chapter: *To what extent did Reconstruction bring African Americans closer to full citizenship?* Then have them read Section 23.1. Afterward, ask,

   - Give an example from Lincoln's second inaugural address that shows what hopes he had for the nation after the Civil War.
   - What happened on April 14, 1865?
   - Do you think that African Americans gained full citizenship rights after the Civil War? Why or why not?

2 **Have students complete the Reading Notes for Chapter 23.** Assign Sections 23.2 to 23.7 during the activity as indicated in the procedures for the Visual Discovery activity. Remind students to use the Key Content Terms where appropriate as they complete their Reading Notes.

Vocabulary Development: Word Origins

Note that words have entered the English language in many ways. Point out that several Key Content Terms come from Latin (*Reconstruction, amendment,* and *civil*). In addition, several words or word parts in these terms come from Old English, including *free, right, thirteen, fourteen,* and *fifteen.* Furthermore, words can be coined in various ways: *Jim Crow* (a prejudicial term) comes from the name of a black character in a popular song-and-dance act during the era of minstrel shows.

Visual Discovery

1 **Introduce the activity.** Tell students they will analyze four images to evaluate how close African Americans came to full citizenship during Reconstruction. They will then bring to life one of these images.

2 **Introduce Section 23.2 by projecting *Visual 23A: Emancipation.*** Ask,

- What details do you see on the left side of this image? The center? The right?

- What seems to be happening in the scenes on the left? The center? The right?

- This political cartoon was published in 1863, shortly after President Lincoln issued the Emancipation Proclamation. What types of changes does the artist envision for slaves after emancipation?

Visual 23A

3 **Have students read and complete the Reading Notes for Sections 23.2.** Review the main points with the class.

4 **Have students reexamine Visual 23A.** Encourage them to use what they learned in Section 23.2 to answer these questions:

- Which, if any, of the changes envisioned by the artist became a reality during this period of Reconstruction?

- What government agency assisted former slaves and made some of the changes depicted in the cartoon a reality?

- What activities of the Freedmen's Bureau are not shown in this cartoon?

- Overall, do you believe this period of Reconstruction brought African Americans closer to full citizenship? Explain.

5 **Introduce Section 23.3 by projecting *Visual 23B: Collision on the Grand Trunk Columbia Railroad.*** Ask,

- What details do you see in this image?

- What seems to be happening here?

- What or who might each of these men represent?

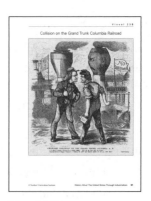

Visual 23B

6 **Have students read and complete the Reading Notes for Sections 23.3.** Review the main points with the class.

7 **Have students reexamine Visual 23B.** Encourage them to use what they learned in Section 23.3 to answer these questions:

- Who is each of these men? How can you tell?

- How does this political cartoon illustrate the relationship between Congress and the president during this period of Reconstruction? Give examples of this relationship from Section 23.3.

- Overall, do you believe this period of Reconstruction brought African Americans closer to full citizenship? Explain.

8 **Introduce Section 23.4 by projecting *Visual 23C: "The First Vote."*** Ask,

- What details do you see in this image?

- What seems to be happening here?

- How do these men differ from one another? How do you think each of these men feels about what is happening here?

- Overall, do you believe what is happening in this scene led African Americans closer to full citizenship? Explain.

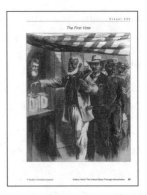

Visual 23C

9 **Have students read and complete the Reading Notes for Sections 23.4.** Review the main points with the class.

10 **Have students prepare to bring the image to life.** Place students in groups of four and distribute a copy of *Student Handout 23: Creating an Act-It-Out for "The First Vote"* to each group. Assign each group one of these characters for the act-it-out: Poll Worker (white man), Skilled Craftsman (black man), City Dweller (black man), Union Army Veteran (black man), Southern Democrat (not pictured). Then review the directions and give groups about five minutes to prepare.

Student Handout 23

11 **Conduct the act-it-out.** Call up five actors to stand in front of the projected image, taking on their appropriate characters' postures and facial expressions. Acting as the on-scene reporter, ask the characters some of the questions from Student Handout 23. (**Note:** Consider conducting the act-it-out a second time with new actors.)

12 **Introduce Section 23.5 by projecting *Visual 23D: "Worse Than Slavery."*** Ask,

- What details do you see in this image?

- What seems to be happening here?

- What are the goals of the two figures shaking hands? What tactics are they using to fulfill their goals?

Visual 23D

13 **Have students read and complete the Reading Notes for Sections 23.5.** Review the main points with the class.

14 **Have students reexamine Visual 23D.** Place students in pairs and have them review Section 23.5 to find information that helps them further understand the cartoon. Ask four or five volunteers to come forward and place a sticky note over a significant detail in the image. Remove the notes one by one, each time asking the volunteer to use evidence from the reading to explain that detail. Finally, ask the class,

- What is the artist's message in this cartoon?

- Overall, do you believe this period of Reconstruction brought African Americans closer to full citizenship? Explain.

15 Have students read and complete Reading Notes for Sections 23.6 and 23.7. Review the main points with the class.

16 Debrief the activity. Ask,

- Which events brought African Americans closer to full citizenship during Reconstruction?

- Which events brought African Americans further from full citizenship during Reconstruction?

- To what extent did Reconstruction bring African Americans closer to full citizenship? Explain.

Processing

Have students complete the Processing activity. They will create an illustration of a road that represents how the events of Reconstruction affected African Americans' journey toward full citizenship.

Quicker Coverage

Shorten the Activity Eliminate the act-it-out from the activity, or, alternatively eliminate one or more of Visuals 23A to 23D.

Condense the Processing Activity Instead of having students create an illustration of a road, have them write a paragraph answering the Essential Question. They must cite at least two pieces of evidence to support their answer.

Deeper Coverage

Analyze Additional Images Use one of the image-analysis strategies in the activity (spiral questions with reexamination, act-it-out, or marking the image with sticky notes) to analyze the images in Sections 23.6 and 23.7 of the book.

Assessment

Mastering the Content

1. B	5. A	9. A	13. D
2. D	6. C	10. D	14. A
3. D	7. C	11. C	15. C
4. A	8. D	12. C	16. B

Applying Social Studies Skills

17. the dates the states were readmitted to the Union

18. D

19. B

Exploring the Essential Question

20. Answers should include all of the elements requested in the prompt.

Scoring Rubric

Score	Description
3	Student completes all six parts of the task. Ideas are clearly stated, supported by details, and demonstrate command of standard English conventions.
2	Student responds to most or all parts of the task. Ideas may lack details or not be clearly stated.
1	Student responds to at least one part of the task. Ideas may contain factual or grammatical errors and may lack details.
0	Response does not match the task or is incorrect.

The Long Road to Equal Rights

1 **Have students define *civil rights*.** Explain that the word *civil* comes from the ancient word for "citizen" and that civil rights are all the legal rights due to a citizen. Although students may associate the term with the movement to gain equal rights for African Americans, explain that the quest for civil rights has been part of human history for as long as there have been governments.

2 **Have students read the Chapter 23 Reading Further.** When they have finished, focus their attention on the fact that in the school integration and voting rights movements, African Americans were asking for the ability to *exercise* rights that the Constitution had given them 100 years earlier. Local, state, and—in the case of "separate but equal" facilities—national rulings and customs had prevented them from exercising the rights granted in the Reconstruction amendments.

3 **Discuss how our values affect our actions.** Ask students to define *values* and to give examples of personal values (such as being loyal to friends) and national values (such as in a democracy, everyone's voice should be heard). Then discuss how these values might affect people's actions.

4 **Have students complete the Chapter 23 Reading Further in their Interactive Student Notebooks.** When they have finished, encourage discussion of the values expressed by the Little Rock Nine, Charles Houston, and the Selma marchers. Then invite students to share their personal statements.

English Language Learners

Preview the Images Give students photocopies of Visuals 23A to 23D and the corresponding questions the night before you conduct the activity, and have them prepare possible answers to the questions.

Have Students Work in Pairs For Visuals 23A and 23B, place students in pairs to complete the Reading Notes. Also have them discuss the set of questions used to reexamine the image before you pose the questions to the class.

Learners Reading and Writing Below Grade Level

Highlight the Reading Photocopy the reading and highlight important events in the African American struggle for full citizenship. Use one color to highlight events that brought African Americans closer to full citizenship and another color for events that prevented their progress. Use these highlighted photocopies as an aid during the activity and when students choose events for their Processing activity.

Learners with Special Education Needs

Support the Act-It-Outs Consider these tips:
- Have students prepare a script by answering the questions on Student Handout 23. Allow them to read from that script during the act-it-out.
- Tell students in advance which role they will be playing so they can practice their parts.

Provide an Incomplete Processing Draw a road with twists and turns that correspond to the major events of Reconstruction, and have students complete it with labels and symbols. Consider providing the following Word Bank of events to include on the road: *black codes, Compromise of 1877, Fifteenth Amendment, Fourteenth Amendment, Freedmen's Bureau, Military Reconstruction Act, new state constitutions, Thirteenth Amendment, violence against African Americans.* Alternatively, you may want to place each event from the Word Bank in the correct place on the road and simply have students create symbols for each.

Advanced Learners

Use an Alternate Preview Tell students that African American scholar and reformer W. E. B. Du Bois referred to Reconstruction as a "splendid failure." Ask students to write what they believe he meant by this and then share their answers with the class (do not reveal the meaning of the quotation). During the debriefing at the end of the activity, ask students to revisit the quotation and discuss its meaning. Then explain that many whites expected the supposed inferiority of blacks to cause Reconstruction to fail. Du Bois responded that Reconstruction actually failed African Americans, but did reveal to the nation that African Americans were capable and deserving of full citizenship.

Have Students Research Thomas Nast Mention to students that Thomas Nast's cartoons are prominently featured in this chapter, and challenge them to learn more about his Reconstruction-era cartoons on the Internet or at the library. Then have students synthesize Nast's overall view on Reconstruction in a short essay. As their thesis, ask students to hypothesize Nast's answer to the question, *To what extent did Reconstruction bring African Americans closer to full citizenship?*

Enrichment Resources

Find out more about Reconstruction by exploring the following resources for *History Alive! The United States Through Industrialism* at www.teachtci.com.

Enrichment Readings These in-depth readings encourage students to explore selected topics related to the chapter. You may also find readings that relate the chapter's content directly to your state's curriculum.

Internet Connections These recommended Web sites provide useful and engaging content that reinforces skills development and mastery of subjects within the chapter.

Literature Recommendations

The following books offer opportunities to extend the content in this chapter.

The Andersonville Prison Civil War Crimes Trial: A Headline Court Case by Susan Banfield (Berkeley Heights, NJ: Enslow Publishers, 2000)

Reconstruction: Binding the Wounds by JoAnne W. Deitch, Ed. (Carlisle, MA: Discovery Enterprises, 2001)

When Johnny Went Marching Home: Young Americans Fight the Civil War by G. Clifton Wisler (New York: HarperCollins Juvenile Books, 2001)

Section 23.2

1. Southern states had to create new governments that were loyal to the Union. Slavery had to be abolished (students should circle this answer).

2. Congress established the Freedmen's Bureau to assist former slaves. Possible activities: Provided food, provided medical care, helped freedmen arrange for wages and good working conditions, distributed land, provided public education.

3. Possible answers:

Black Codes Enacted During Presidential Reconstruction

Purpose	Example
To limit the rights of freedmen	Blacks could not vote or serve on juries.
To help planters find workers to replace their slaves	Freedmen were required to work. If they were unemployed they could be arrested and hired out to planters. Freedmen were limited to farmwork and other low-skill jobs.
To keep freedmen at the bottom of the social order in the South	Blacks and whites were segregated in public places.

Section 23.3

1. Radical Republicans wanted freedmen to be granted the full rights of citizenship. Congress extended the life of the Freedmen's Bureau and enacted the Civil Rights Act of 1866, which gave blacks the same civil rights as whites.

2. Possible answer: Difficult. Johnson opposed the Fourteenth Amendment and wanted Republican lawmakers thrown out of office. Congress passed the Military Reconstruction Act over Johnson's veto.

3. President Johnson was impeached because he fired an official who was protected under the Tenure of Office Act and because the House felt he had brought the office of president into disgrace. He was spared removal from office by one vote.

4. Sharecroppers had to borrow money from plantation owners to buy the supplies they needed. Few earned enough money to pay back what they owed.

Section 23.4

1. Students should write *former Confederates* over the first symbol and *freedmen, white Southerners who opposed the war,* and *Northerners who had moved south after the war* over the next three symbols.

2. Republicans learned that for a political party to keep control of the White House, it needed African American votes.

3. Possible answers:

Fifteenth Amendment: This constitutional amendment guaranteed every male citizen the right to vote, regardless of race.

New State Constitutions: New state constitutions were written throughout the South guaranteeing such rights as voting and free public education.

New State Governments: New state governments were composed primarily of Republicans, including many African Americans, who ratified the Fourteenth and Fifteenth Amendments and built roads, hospitals, and schools.

African Americans in Office: African Americans served in every Southern state legislature and in both houses of Congress and held high offices in three states.

Section 23.5

1. Possible answers: Many Southerners hated seeing blacks voting and holding public office. → Southern Democrats tried to use legal means to keep blacks from voting or taking office. → Whites used violence to drive blacks from political life. → Congress passed the Enforcement Acts, making it illegal to prevent someone from voting through bribery, force, or scare tactics. → President Grant sent troops to the South to enforce the acts, but people were still afraid to speak out against the violence being directed at blacks.

2. Republican candidate Hayes received more electoral votes than Democratic candidate Tilden. Twenty electoral votes were in dispute, and Congress awarded these to Hayes, which outraged Democrats.

3. The election was resolved by compromise: Hayes was allowed to take office if he promised to withdraw remaining federal troops from the South. The election was devastating for blacks. Democrats quickly returned the South to "white man's rule."

Section 23.6

1. Possible answers:

   Education: Spending for public schools was cut, many schools closed, and others charged fees.

   Voting rights: Many Southern states required citizens to pay a poll tax and pass a literacy test in order to vote. Both requirements excluded many African Americans from voting.

   Segregation: Democrats reintroduced segregation laws, which kept blacks and whites separate in public.

2. Sketches might show some form of segregation. Possible caption: In *Plessy v. Ferguson,* the Supreme Court ruled that separate facilities, as long as they were equal, did not violate the Constitution. However, these separate facilities often favored whites over blacks.

Section 23.7

1. Possible answers:

   Push factors: attacks and lynching by white mobs; racism; poverty

   Pull factors: better opportunities; more equal treatment

2. *The North:* African Americans still faced racism but could find employment.

   The West: African Americans faced discrimination as they moved west, but found work as cowboys and Indian fighters.

   The South: African Americans relied on families, churches, and communities to build businesses, provide education, and improve their lives.

The Union Challenged

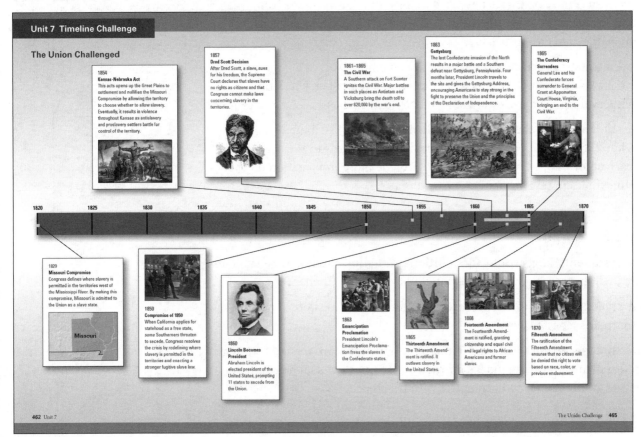

Overview

This Timeline Challenge provides students with a review of the main events and ideas of this unit, as well as practice in reading and interpreting timelines. You can vary and expand the activity according to students' needs and the amount of time available.

Basic Procedure

1 **Introduce the timeline in the Student Edition.** Direct students to The Union Challenged timeline at the end of Unit 7 in the Student Edition. You may wish to have students read aloud and discuss the timeline entries.

2 **Introduce the Timeline Challenge in the Interactive Student Notebook.** Direct students to the Unit 7 Timeline Challenge in their notebooks. Point out the two types of questions, "Timeline Skills" and "Critical Thinking," and model how to answer each type.

3 **Have students complete the Timeline Challenge.** Monitor students as they work. Use the Guide to Unit 7 Timeline Challenge to check their answers. You may wish to project a transparency of this page as you work through the questions with the class and conduct a discussion of the "Critical Thinking" questions.

4 **Complete the KWL chart.** Return to the KWL chart created at the beginning of the unit, and ask students to list the key information they have learned.

Classroom Timeline

1 **Prepare the Timeline Challenge Cards.** Copy and cut the cards from *Student Handout TC7: Unit 7 Timeline Challenge Cards.* You may wish to laminate the cards for future use.

2 **Create a timeline on a classroom wall.** On an empty wall or a large bulletin board, make a timeline with masking tape or colored paper. Mark off the time intervals in advance, or ask students to do so in class.

3 **Have students place the Timeline Challenge Cards.** Distribute cards to individual students or pairs and have them tape the cards to the timeline in the correct locations. Call on students to provide more information on the timeline topics to review main events and issues.

Student Handout TC7

Internet Research

1 **Review students' suggestions for additional timeline entries.** Have students share their answers to the last question of the Timeline Challenge.

2 **Have students conduct Internet research.** Ask students to choose and research one of their suggested events.

3 **Have students create additional Timeline Challenge Cards.** Direct students to research an appropriate image for their cards and then use the computer to create an illustrated card, complete with timeline entry.

Timeline Skills

Score 1 point for each correct answer.

1. The Missouri Compromise defined where slavery was permitted in the territories west of the Mississippi. It was in effect for 34 years.

2. Some Southerners were upset that California applied for statehood as a free state.

3. The Kansas-Nebraska Act opened up the Great Plains for settlement.

4. The Dred Scott decision declared that blacks had no rights as citizens and that Congress could not make decisions about slavery in the territories.

5. 1860; Eleven Southern states seceded from the Union as a result of his election.

6. the attack on Fort Sumter; 4 years

7. 2 years; Lincoln freed slaves in the Confederate states.

8. the Battle of Gettysburg and Lincoln's Gettysburg Address; The battle was a defeat for the South and its last attempt to invade the North. In his Gettysburg Address, Lincoln encouraged the nation to stay strong in the fight to preserve the Union and its principles.

9. 1865; at Appomattox Court House, Virginia

10. The Thirteenth Amendment outlawed slavery. The Fourteenth Amendment granted citizenship and equal civil and legal rights to African Americans and former slaves. The Fifteenth Amendment ensured that no citizen would be denied the right to vote based on race, color, or previous enslavement.

Critical Thinking

Score 1 to 3 points for each answer, depending on the thoroughness of the response.

11. Congress tried to keep the Union together through a series of compromises that kept a balance of power between Northern and Southern states. Opinions will vary, but students might mention that the compromises led to more tension or that compromises would never be able to settle the moral issue of slavery.

12. Possible answer: There were difficulties with Union military leadership as opposed to superior Confederate military leadership. The South only had to succeed in defending their territory, but the North had the larger objective of invading and subduing the vast regions of the South. Southerners fought hard due to their belief that they were defending their liberty, homes, and traditions.

13. If students indicate Reconstruction was successful, they will likely cite the three amendments added to the Constitution and the work of the Freedmen's Bureau. If they indicate Reconstruction was unsuccessful, they will likely cite the emergence of the Ku Klux Klan, poll taxes, and Jim Crow laws.

14. Answers will vary. Students must explain why the events they chose merit inclusion.

Using Scores to Inform Instruction

Timeline Skills A score of 7 out of 10 indicates that students understand most of the key events of this unit.

Critical Thinking A score of 8 out of 12 indicates that students are able to think critically about most of the key issues of this unit.

If students score below these levels, consider reviewing timeline and critical thinking skills.

Migration and Industry

Migration and Industry

Overview

This activity introduces geographic information essential to Unit 8. Students read and interpret maps to learn about the relationship between the development of transportation systems—in this case, the railroad—and patterns of development, migration, and settlement. They annotate a map and answer questions in their Interactive Student Notebooks, and then discuss critical thinking questions. Their comprehension of content and proficiency in map-reading and higher-order thinking skills will help you gauge their readiness for the unit. The pages that follow include a completed map, answers to questions, a scoring guide to inform your teaching, and suggestions for modifications to meet specific student needs.

Essential Geographic Understandings

1. The extent of the nation's rail system in 1870

2. The growth in the nation's rail system between 1870 and 1890

3. Key human features: Albuquerque, Denver, Omaha, Sacramento, Salt Lake City, Seattle, California, Colorado, Kansas, Nebraska, New Mexico, Utah

4. Key physical features: Great Lakes, Great Salt Lake

5. How transportation influenced patterns of western migration, population growth, and development

Procedures

1 **Introduce the unit.** Tell students they will learn about the growth of industry and agriculture after the Civil War and the role played by railroads. They will also learn how these developments impacted western American Indians.

2 **Create a KWL chart.** Ask students to identify what they know about how railroads serve agriculture and industry and what they want to learn. Use their responses to gauge how much additional background information they will need as you progress through the unit. Students will return to the KWL chart at the end of the unit and add the key information they have learned.

3 **Have students read Unit 8 "Setting the Stage" in the Student Edition.**

4 **Have students complete the Geography Challenge.** Monitor students as they answer the questions and complete the map. You may want to have them work in pairs. Use the guide on the next two pages to check their answers. You may wish to project the map from the Interactive Student Notebook and have students annotate it as the class works through the map-reading questions. Make sure students have grasped Essential Geographic Understandings 1 to 4.

5 **Discuss the "Critical Thinking" questions.** Help students understand the geographic relationships described in Essential Geographic Understanding 5.

Major Railroads in the United States, 1870

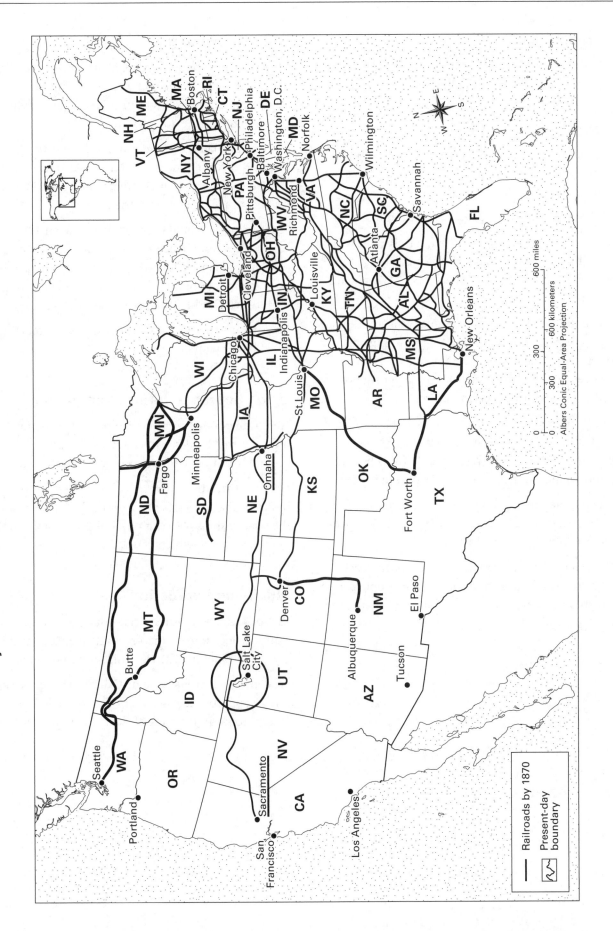

Railroads by 1870

Present-day boundary

600 miles

600 kilometers

0   300

0   300

Albers Conic Equal-Area Projection

Geography Skills

Score 1 point for each correct answer. Use the map on the previous page to check shading and labeling.

1. Eastern end: Omaha, Nebraska; western end: Sacramento, California

2. Population density around Omaha rose from 2–45 people per square mile in 1870 to 18–45 people per square mile in 1890.

3. The connecting point is located in Utah.

4. The southern route passed through Butte and Fargo. Both lines passed through the present-day states of Washington, Idaho, Montana, North Dakota, and Minnesota.

5. The population near Albuquerque went from under 6 people per square mile in 1870 to 6–18 people per square mile in 1890. The population around Denver jumped from under 6 people per square mile to 18–45 people per square mile.

6. The population of eastern South Dakota went from under 6 people per square mile in 1870 to 6–45 people in 1890. At the western end of this line, the population also increased to 6–18 people in 1890.

7. The population around Fort Worth increased from 6–18 people per square mile in 1870 to 18–45 people per square mile in 1890.

8. The populations of western Minnesota and eastern North Dakota went from under 2 people per square mile in 1870 to 6–18 people per square mile in 1890.

Critical Thinking

Questions may have more than one correct answer. Score 1 to 3 points for each reasonable answer, depending on the strength of students' geographic reasoning. Possible answers are given here.

9. The railroad increased economic opportunities and the growth of industries—such as farming, services, and commerce—in Omaha, which would have encouraged people to settle there.

10. Most of the population growth between 1870 and 1890 took place along or near railroad lines. Railroads made it easier to get people and products into and out of the West—which made farming, business, and life in general easier there.

11. Answers should indicate that it was a combination of both factors.

Using Scores to Inform Instruction

Geography Skills A score of 6 out of 8 or better indicates that students have acquired sufficient geographic information to proceed with the unit.

Critical Thinking A score of 6 out of 9 or better indicates that students are beginning to understand the relationships between physical geography and the different ways in which people live.

Modifying Instruction

ELL or Learners with Special Education Needs Consider focusing on map-reading questions or limiting the number of "Critical Thinking" questions.

Students with Weak Map or Critical Thinking Skills Assign appropriate pages from the Social Studies Skills Toolkit in the back of the Lesson Masters.

Tensions in the West

How did settlers change the West and affect American Indians?

Overview

In a Problem Solving Groupwork activity, students create a music video to illustrate how western settlement affected the Nez Perce. They then examine how settlers changed the West and affected other American Indian groups.

Objectives

In the course of reading this chapter and participating in the classroom activity, students will

Social Studies

- identify the groups that came west following the Civil War, the reasons they came, and their roles in changing the West.
- evaluate the effects of western settlement on American Indians.
- describe the clash between American Indians and settlers that resulted from settlement of the frontier.

Language Arts

- analyze analogies and metaphors to infer literal and figurative meanings.
- interpret a ballad and deliver an oral response to it.

Social Studies Vocabulary

Key Content Terms reservation, homesteader, transcontinental railroad, subsidy

Academic Vocabulary acknowledge, civilized

Materials

History Alive! The United States Through Industrialism

Interactive Student Notebooks

CD Track 14

Visuals 24A–24E

Lesson Masters

- Student Handout 24A (1 per group)
- Student Handout 24B (2 copies)
- Vocabulary Development handout (1 per student, on colored paper)

Activity	Suggested Time	Materials
Preview	15 minutes	• Interactive Student Notebooks
Vocabulary Development	30–40 minutes	• *History Alive! The United States Through Industrialism* • Interactive Student Notebooks • Vocabulary Development handout
Problem Solving Groupwork	100–150 minutes (2–3 regular periods) (1–1.5 block periods)	• *History Alive! The United States Through Industrialism* • Interactive Student Notebooks • CD Track 14 • Visuals 24A–24E • Student Handouts 24A and 24B
Processing	20 minutes	• *History Alive! The United States Through Industrialism* • Interactive Student Notebooks
Assessment	40 minutes	• Chapter 24 Assessment

Preview

1 **Have students complete the Preview activity.** Students will reflect on a time when someone broke a promise to them.

2 **Have students share their responses in pairs or with the class.**

3 **Explain the connection between the Preview and Chapter 24.** Explain that from the time the nation was founded, the U.S. government broke many promises to American Indians. In the 1830s, American Indians were promised lands in the West in exchange for giving up their homelands in the East. As more settlers moved west, however, the government forced Indians onto government lands that settlers didn't want. In this chapter, students will examine how settlers changed the West and affected American Indians.

Vocabulary Development

1 **Introduce the Key Content Terms.** Have students locate the Key Content Terms for the chapter in their Interactive Student Notebooks. These are important terms that will help them understand the main ideas of the chapter. Ask volunteers to identify any familiar terms and how they might be used in a sentence.

2 **Have students complete a Vocabulary Development handout.** Give each student a copy of the Vocabulary Development handout of your choice from the Reading Toolkit at the back of the Lesson Masters. These handouts provide extra practice and support, depending on your students' needs. Review the completed handout by asking volunteers to share one answer for each term.

Reading

1 **Introduce the Essential Question and have students read Section 24.1.** Have students identify the Essential Question on the first page of the chapter: *How did settlers change the West and affect American Indians?* Then have them read Section 24.1 and examine the accompanying images. Afterward, ask,

   - Why did the government want to divide the Nez Perce reservation into farm plots?
   - How did the settlers and the Nez Perce differ in their view of land?
   - How do you think western settlers affected American Indians?

2 **Have students complete the Reading Notes for Chapter 24.** Assign Sections 24.2 through 24.8 during the activity as indicated in the procedures for the Problem Solving Groupwork activity. Remind students to use the Key Content Terms where appropriate as they complete their Reading Notes.

Problem Solving Groupwork

1 **Introduce the activity and divide students into groups.** Put students into groups of four, and explain that they will work in their groups to create a music video to a song about the Nez Perce. Each group will then talk about their video in a "Behind the Music Video" interview.

2 **Have students complete the Reading Notes for Section 24.2.** Have several volunteers share their responses. Consult the Guide to Reading Notes 24 for possible answers.

3 **Introduce the song for the music video.** Play CD Track 14, "The Heart of the Appaloosa." At the appropriate time, project the following visuals in order, one for each of the five verses of the song: *Visual 24A: Nez Perce on an Appaloosa, Visual 24B: Lewis and Clark Converse with a Group of American Indians, Visual 24C: Chief Joseph, Visual 24D: Chief Joseph Surrenders*, and *Visual 24E: Nez Perce Using Traditional Fishing Method.*

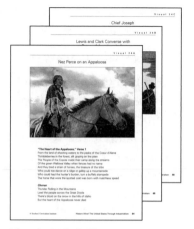

Visuals 24A–24E

4 **Assign roles and review the steps for creating a music video.**

- Distribute *Student Handout 24A: Creating a Music Video* to each group. Assign each group member a role, and review the steps on the handout.

- Assign each group one of the five verses of the song. You will likely have some duplicate groups. Then give each group the appropriate page from *Student Handout 24B: Background Information on "The Heart of the Appaloosa."*

- Explain that as groups perform their music videos, you will project the corresponding visuals to serve as backdrops.

Student Handout 24A

5 **Monitor progress as groups create their music videos.** Give groups at least one class period to create their music videos. Tell groups that when they complete a step, they should raise their hands to have you initial that step before they move on.

6 **Set up the classroom for the performances.** Have students place their desks in a semicircle so that there is room in the center for groups to perform and everyone can see the screen.

7 **Have groups for Verse 1 perform their music videos.** Have one group for Verse 1 come to the center of the room. Project Visual 24A and play CD Track 18, and have the group perform their music video. Pause the CD at the end of the verse. Repeat this step for any additional groups for Verse 1.

Student Handout 24B

8   **Conduct a "Behind the Music Video" interview for Verse 1.** Have all the performers for Verse 1 stand in front of the projector. Interview the performers by asking,

- How did it feel to perform in this music video?

- Why did you choose the props and costumes you did?

- What emotions do the Nez Perce experience in this verse?

- How do you think western settlement affected the Nez Perce?

Finally, call on volunteers to explain each line of Verse 1.

9   **Repeat Steps 7 and 8 with remaining groups.** As you repeat Steps 7 and 8 for the groups performing Verses 2 to 5, project Visuals 24B to 24E and continue to play CD Track 14.

10 **Have students read and complete the Reading Notes for Sections 24.3 to 24.8.** Have several volunteers share their responses.

Processing

Have students complete the Processing activity. Students will create two acrostic poems comparing the perspectives of white settlers and American Indians about the settlement of the West. Consider having students share their poems in pairs or with the class.

Quicker Coverage

Break Up the Reading After students have completed the Reading Notes for Section 24.3, divide them into groups of four. Have each student in each group complete the Reading Notes for one of Sections 24.4, 24.5, 24.6, or 24.7. When they are finished, have them share the information from their Reading Notes with the rest of the group.

Explain the Meaning of the Verses Place students in groups of four and assign each group a verse from "The Heart of the Appaloosa." In lieu of music videos, have groups prepare to explain the meaning behind each line in their assigned verse. Then project Visual 24A and have a corresponding group come forward and explain the verse. Repeat for Verses 2 to 5, using Visuals 24B to 24E.

Listening and Speaking: Recite Poetry

As an alternative Processing activity, have students recite the entire "The Heart of the Appaloosa" ballad. Require students to modulate their tone, pitch, and volume to help convey the meaning of the words and to differentiate the chorus. Also ask them to incorporate gestures and movement to help express the meaning of the ballad.

Deeper Coverage

Create a Sixth Verse Have groups write a sixth verse for "The Heart of the Appaloosa" that provides information about the Nez Perce today. Have groups conduct a search on the official Nez Perce Tribal Web site, and encourage them to include in their verse such information as where the reservation is located, its population, its form of government, and its main sources of income. Have groups read or sing their new verses aloud.

Expand the Music Videos Consider having groups incorporate one or more of the following into their music videos:

- three large visuals that illustrate parts of the song, such as geographic features that are mentioned
- sound effects that involve the audience, such as a horse's neigh or the roar of thunder
- a symbol that captures the essence of the verse, such as a movement, a color, or an object

Assessment

Mastering the Content

1. D	5. B	9. A	13. A
2. C	6. A	10. B	14. B
3. C	7. D	11. A	15. B
4. B	8. D	12. A	16. C

Applying Social Studies Skills

17. D

18. B

19. Possible answers: The U.S. Army forced American Indians off their land. The U.S. government moved American Indians to reservations.

Exploring the Essential Question

20. Answers should include all of the elements requested in the prompt.

Scoring Rubric

Score	Description
3	Student completes all six parts of the task. Ideas are clearly stated, supported by details, and demonstrate command of standard English conventions.
2	Student responds to most or all parts of the task. Ideas may lack details or not be clearly stated.
1	Student responds to at least one part of the task. Ideas may contain factual or grammatical errors and may lack details.
0	Response does not match the task or is incorrect.

Black Exodus

1   **Discuss the meaning of the word *exodus*.** Explain that the word comes from the ancient Greek words *ex,* meaning "out," and *hodos,* meaning "way" or "journey." An *exodus* is a movement or migration of a large number of people out of a place.

2   **Have students consider the motivations for migrations.** Ask, *Describe some examples from history when people chose to move. How did those people feel about moving?* Also discuss the push and pull factors that can lead to a migration. Remind students of what they have learned about the end of Reconstruction and the terrible conditions brought about by black codes and Jim Crow laws. Point out that terrible conditions still lead people to make dramatic changes in their lives today.

3   **Have students read the Chapter 24 Reading Further.** When they have finished, have them use a map of the United States to trace the possible routes black migrants took from states such as Mississippi to Plains states such as Kansas and Nebraska. Mention that most migrants had little or no money. They traveled to the Mississippi River by walking or riding on horseback or in wagons.

4   **Have students complete the Chapter 24 Reading Further in their Interactive Student Notebooks.** Encourage students to choose different moments in time for their diary entries so that all four stages of the exodus are covered: departure, on the way, arrival, and five years later. After students have completed their entries, you may want to have them share their entries in groups—either in groups that chose the same stage or groups including all four stages.

English Language Learners

Paraphrase the Verses Before playing the song, provide students with the paraphrased verses below. After playing each verse, pause the CD track to define any unfamiliar words.

Verse 1: Many years ago, the Nez Perce Indians lived in an area called the Columbia Plateau. At that time, there were no boundaries separating lands. The Nez Perce had a special horse, the Appaloosa.

Verse 2: One winter, the Lewis and Clark explorers came to the Columbia Plateau. The Nez Perce fed and housed the explorers. The explorers showed them the Bible. Soon, Christian groups and farmers moved to the Columbia Plateau. Then the government forced the Nez Perce to move far away to a piece of government land.

Verse 3: Chief Joseph was the leader of the Nez Perce. His Indian name means "Thunder Rolling in the Mountains." He did not want to move his people to the government land because it was poor land that was hard to farm. Chief Joseph tried to lead his people to Canada. The government followed the Nez Perce and fought battles with them.

Verse 4: The Nez Perce traveled hundreds of miles to try to escape the U.S. soldiers. Many of them died. Finally, Chief Joseph decided to surrender.

Verse 5: The Nez Perce were sent to a piece of government land in Oklahoma. Many of them died from sickness and sadness. But the great spirit of the Appaloosa lives on.

Learners Reading and Writing Below Grade Level

Support the Processing Activity Consider these tips:

- Have students write just one of the two acrostics.
- Provide sentence starters, such as these for American Indians' view of the settlement of the West:

  Settlers came from the East.

  Eager to mine or farm, they . . .

  Treaties that were made with us were . . .

  The buffalo . . .

  Land that birthed our grandparents was . . .

  Eventually we . . .

  Moving to a reservation was . . .

  Everyone missed . . .

  Never again will we . . .

  The American Indian spirit remains . . .

Learners with Special Education Needs

Support the Music Video Consider these tips:

- Have students underline the verbs in their assigned verses. Point out that the verbs signal the main actions of the verse and can guide them in creating their pantomimes.
- Add a fifth role of Stage Director. This student will assist the Producer in Step 5, during the rehearsal. During the performance, the Stage Director will be in charge of any set-up tasks, including projecting the image and cueing the music.
- To help students prepare for the interview, assign group members their two lines of the verse ahead of time. Have them prepare a cue card with an explanation of those lines as well as the answers to the interview questions on Student Handout 24A.

Advanced Learners

Create Venn Diagrams After students complete their Reading Notes, have them create a Venn diagram comparing the Nez Perce with the Sioux Indians in such areas as location, leaders, interaction with the government, and reservation life. Have students conduct outside research to complete their diagrams.

Enrichment Resources

Find out more about tensions in the West in the late 1800s by exploring the following resources for *History Alive! The United States Through Industrialism* at www.teachtci.com.

Enrichment Readings These in-depth readings encourage students to explore selected topics related to the chapter. You may also find readings that relate the chapter's content directly to your state's curriculum.

Internet Connections These recommended Web sites provide useful and engaging content that reinforces skills development and mastery of subjects within the chapter.

Literature Recommendations

The following books offer opportunities to extend the content in this chapter.

Golden Quest by Bonnie Bader (New York: Silver Moon Press, 2000)

Sitting Bull and His World by Albert Marrin (New York: Penguin Putnam, 2000)

The Chisholm Trail in American History by William R. Sanford (Berkeley Heights, NJ: Enslow Publishers, 2000)

Section 24.2

Possible answers:

With my eyes, I see the lush mountains and valleys where the Nez Perce have lived for centuries.

With my mouth, I tell the white man that I am tired, my heart is sick and sad, and from where the sun now stands, I will fight no more forever.

With my heart, I feel for my people, who have been forced from our lands onto reservations.

Section 24.3

The Homestead Act gave homesteaders a plot of public land to cultivate. The Pacific Railway Act resulted in the building of a transcontinental railroad, which made it easier for settlers to travel west.

Sections 24.4 and 24.5

Symbols will vary. Possible answers:

	Who the Settlers Were	Reasons for Moving West	Challenges Faced by Settlers	How Settlers Changed the West	Effect on American Indians
Section 24.4 Railroad Builders	Irish, Chinese, and other immigrants; ex-soldiers; Mexicans; freed slaves	to find jobs and adventure	hard and dangerous labor unsafe tent cities attacks from American Indians	brought new settlers to the West encouraged the building of towns and cities encouraged mail and supplies to be shipped to the West	invaded American Indians' homelands destroyed the buffalo, a main source of food for Indians
Section 24.5 Miners	young, white American males; some immigrants	to seek their fortunes	boomtowns had no government, no law, and little order robbery and murder	created boomtowns, some of which became prosperous cities opened the mountains and deserts to other settlers	damaged the land and displaced American Indians

Sections 24.6 and 24.7

Symbols will vary. Possible answers:

	Who the Settlers Were	Reasons for Moving West	Challenges Faced by Settlers	How Settlers Changed the West	Effect on American Indians
Section 24.6 Ranchers and Cowboys	Texans, Mexican Americans, African Americans	to work cattle ranches and transport cattle from Texas to the East	dangerous, low-paying jobs buffalo stampedes cow towns could be dangerous collapse of the cattle industry in 1887	established cow towns, which became ranching centers opened the Great Plains to settlement established the cattle industry	killed almost all the buffalo, which forced Plains Indians onto reservations
Section 24.7 Home-steaders	eastern farm families, former slaves, European immigrants	they wanted land to farm former slaves were looking for a new start Russian Mennonites sought religious freedom	unpredictable rain, locusts, little wood for homes	made the plains the most productive wheat-growing region in the world	displaced American Indians and forced them to move onto reservations

Section 24.8

1. Timeline symbols will vary. Possible answers:

   1830: Under the Indian Removal Act, American Indians were promised lands in the Great Plains in exchange for giving up their homelands in the East.

   1867: Congress tried to separate American Indians and settlers by moving the Indians onto reservations in exchange for food, farm tools, and schools.

   1876: General Custer and his troops clashed with Sioux and Cheyenne Indians in the Battle of the Little Big Horn. Although Custer was defeated, the army tracked down the Indians and moved them onto reservations.

2. Sitting Bull was referring to reservations, where Indians were forced to stay in one place and could no longer hunt.

The Rise of Industry

Did the benefits of industrialization outweigh the costs?

Overview

In an Experiential Exercise, students take on the role of workers on an assembly line to experience the costs and benefits of industrialization.

Objectives

In the course of reading this chapter and participating in the classroom activity, students will

Social Studies

- replicate assembly-line work and describe the working conditions of the period.
- explain how industrialists, with government encouragement, created big businesses.
- compare the costs and benefits of industrialization and urbanization and identify the effects of urbanization on the nation.
- evaluate the success of the labor movement in improving conditions.
- identify inventors and evaluate the impact of their inventions.

Language Arts

- write a dialogue using well-chosen details.

Social Studies Vocabulary

Key Content Terms entrepreneur, laissez-faire, mass production, corporation, trust, monopoly, urbanization, labor union

Academic Vocabulary invest, initial, urban, rural

Materials

History Alive! The United States Through Industrialism

Interactive Student Notebooks

CD Track 9

Lesson Masters

- Information Master 25 (1 transparency)
- Vocabulary Development handout (1 per student, on colored paper

8.5″ × 11″ scrap paper (100 sheets, cut in half)

8.5″ × 11″ plain white paper (300–400 full sheets)

crayons or colored pencils (1 of each per student)

Activity	Suggested Time	Materials
Preview (optional)	15 minutes	• Interactive Student Notebooks
Experiential Exercise	50 minutes (1 regular period) (0.5 block period)	• *History Alive! The United States Through Industrialism* • CD Track 9 • Information Master 25 • 8.5" × 11" scrap paper • 8.5" × 11" plain white paper • crayons and colored pencils
Vocabulary Development	30–40 minutes	• *History Alive! The United States Through Industrialism* • Interactive Student Notebooks • Vocabulary Development handout
Processing	40 minutes	• *History Alive! The United States Through Industrialism* • Interactive Student Notebooks
Assessment	40 minutes	• Chapter 25 Assessment

Preview (optional)

1 **Understand the intent of the Preview.** If you choose not to do the activity, which serves to preview the content of the chapter, consider having students complete the optional Preview activity.

2 **Have students complete the Preview in their Interactive Student Notebooks.** Students sketch a modern innovation and explain how it has affected their lives.

3 **Have students share their responses in pairs or with the class.**

4 **Explain the connection between the Preview and Chapter 25.** Explain that just like modern innovations have influenced students' lives, the inventions of the late 1800s had a dramatic impact on the lives of Americans. In particular, inventions such as the assembly line, electric power, and the telephone spurred rapid industrialization. In this chapter, students will examine the rise of industry in the United States and evaluate whether its benefits outweighed its costs.

Experiential Exercise

1 **Understand the intent of the activity.** In this activity, students experience the working conditions of the early 1900s by taking on the role of workers on an assembly line. You will take on the role of a harsh factory supervisor, criticizing workers and destroying unsatisfactory work. Historical analogies are noted in the steps below. Do not share these analogies with students until after they complete their Reading Notes for the chapter.

The activity has roles for 32 students. If you have more than 32 students, add additional assembly-line workers and additional features to the blouse on Information Master 25. If you have fewer than 32 students, eliminate some of the immigrants or some of the workers, beginning with Worker 14. It is important to assign the same number of students to each assembly line; add or subtract immigrants as needed.

2 **Have students design a woman's blouse.** Distribute a sheet a paper to each student. Give students three minutes to draw a detailed picture of a stylish woman's blouse. After three minutes, have them put their drawings aside. *Historical analogy:* Individual artisans worked in their homes as part of the textile cottage industry.

3   **Set up the classroom and assign roles.** Have students form two assembly lines by arranging the desks in two facing rows, as shown in the diagram. Post a sign reading "Tri Company" at the head of one row and a sign reading "Angle Company" at the head of the other row. Assign three or four students the role of immigrants, and tell them to observe from the side of the room until you give them further instructions. Tell the remaining students that they are factory workers on an assembly line. Have half of them sit along the Tri Company assembly line and the other half sit along the Angle Company assembly line.

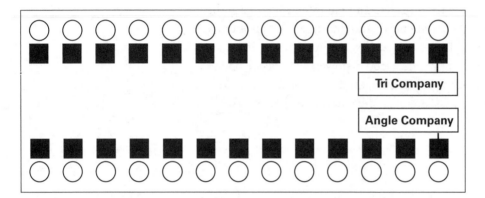

4   **Explain the operation of the assembly line.** Tell students that each assembly line will have 20 minutes to produce as many "blouses" as possible and that workers will specialize in producing one feature of the blouse. Project *Information Master 25: Assignments for Making a Shirtwaist Blouse* and have workers in each company count off from 1 to 14. (**Note:** If you have fewer than 28 students on the assembly line, eliminate workers starting with Worker 14.) Make sure everyone understands which blouse feature to draw. Then assume the role of factory supervisor and read these rules aloud in a stern manner:

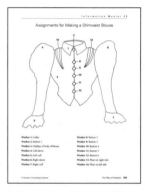

Information Master 25

*   There will be absolutely no talking, laughing, or horseplay during production.

*   Workers who work hard and according to the guidelines will receive 10 points.

*   Workers of the company that creates the most high-quality shirtwaist blouses will receive 5 bonus points.

5   **Have workers begin production.** Distribute a crayon to each worker. Give the first worker from each line approximately 100 half-sheets of scrap paper. Instruct the Worker 1s to begin production by drawing their assigned blouse feature on a piece of paper and passing the sheet to the Worker 2s. Worker 2 will pass the paper to Worker 3, and so on. Walk around the room making frequent loud demands, such as "Keep production moving!" and "Concentrate!" ***Historical analogy:*** The crayons and half-sheets of paper represent the crude materials used by early factories. Workers often worked on assembly lines, where they each specialized in a single task.

6 After 5 minutes, announce that technological advances have been made. Explain that due to these advances, you expect workers to make blouses more efficiently. Distribute a colored pencil to each worker and give each Worker 1 approximately 150 to 200 full sheets of scrap paper. Then tell workers to resume production. *Historical analogy:* Technological advancements, as represented by the colored pencils and larger sheets of paper, allowed factories to be more productive.

7 After 5 more minutes, announce that the Tri and Angle companies are merging. Explain that the companies are merging to increase production, decrease overhead costs, and make more profit. Remove the "Tri" and "Angle" signs and post a new sign reading "Triangle Company" at the front of the room. Tell workers that the assembly line with the greatest number of high-quality shirts at the end of the period will receive 10 additional bonus points. Then tell workers to resume production. *Historical analogy:* Businesses grew during the Industrial Revolution, sometimes through mergers.

8 After 5 more minutes, announce that the Triangle Company is moving to the city. Explain that the city will provide better access to workers, materials, and transportation, but that the new factory space is smaller. Instruct workers in each row to push their desks together so that there is no space between them. Resume production and in a loud voice, tell the immigrants waiting at the side of the room, "These workers cost 10 points but are doing a poor job. I'll fire them if you're willing to work for 5 points." Then randomly replace workers with immigrants. *Historical analogy:* Companies moved their factories to cities for better resources and greater access to labor. Immigrants flocked to cities looking for jobs and were often willing to work for less.

9 Deteriorate the working conditions. Turn off the lights. Play CD Track 9, "Factory Sounds," as loud as possible. Continue to make harsh demands, such as "Work faster!" and "I demand high quality!" Monitor the workers carefully and dispose of any drawings that are messy. Expect students to complain. If they begin talking about a strike, allow this idea to circulate. If necessary, secretly encourage a student or two to yell, "Strike!" *Historical analogy:* Workers were subjected to poor working conditions during the Industrial Revolution. As a result, labor unions gained strength and sometimes organized strikes.

10 After about 20 minutes, stop the assembly lines and debrief the activity. Have workers count the number of finished products. Then ask,

- What feelings did you experience during this activity?

- How do you think your experience on this assembly line reflected the working conditions of the late 1800s?

- Based on this experience, what do you think were the benefits of the assembly line? What do you think were the costs? Do you think the benefits outweighed the costs?

Vocabulary

1 **Introduce the Key Content Terms.** Have students locate the Key Content Terms for the chapter in their Interactive Student Notebooks. These are important terms that will help them understand the main ideas of the chapter. Ask volunteers to identify any familiar terms and how they might be used in a sentence.

2 **Have students complete a Vocabulary Development handout.** Give each student a copy of the Vocabulary Development handout of your choice from the Reading Toolkit at the back of the Lesson Masters. These handouts provide extra practice and support, depending on your students' needs. Review the completed handout by asking volunteers to share one answer for each term.

Reading

1 **Introduce the Essential Question and have students read Section 25.1.** Have students identify the Essential Question on the first page of the chapter: *Did the benefits of industrialization outweigh the costs?* Then have students read Section 25.1. Afterward, have them use information from Section 25.1 and the images that open the chapter to propose some possible answers to the Essential Question.

2 **Have students complete the Reading Notes for Chapter 25.** Assign Sections 25.2 to 25.7. Remind students to use the Key Content Terms where appropriate as they complete their Reading Notes.

3 **Have students complete the matrix in their Reading Notes, comparing the classroom experience to history.** You may want to complete the matrix as a class.

Processing

Have students complete the Processing activity. Students will create a dialogue between a factory owner and worker. Consider having volunteers recite their dialogues in pairs or with the class.

> **Writing: Punctuation and Grammar**
>
> Review the mechanics of dialogue, including creating a new paragraph each time the speaker changes, using quotation marks, capitalizing, and using commas to set off speaker tags. Have students edit or peer-edit their work for punctuation and capitalization, as well as for varied and correct use of past-tense verbs in the speaker tags.

Quicker Coverage

Compare Methods of Production In place of the Experiential Exercise, follow these steps to have students compare production methods in the cottage industry to those of the assembly line.

- Assign half of the students to work in their "homes" (the cottage industry) and the other half to the assembly line. Tell students in the cottage industry that they will create decorative women's blouses. Tell students in the assembly line that they will specialize in producing one feature of a shirtwaist blouse.

- Have students in the assembly line place their desks in one long row. Project Information Master 25 and assign each student one feature of the blouse.

- Give students in the cottage industry crayons and half-sheets of scrap paper. Give the assembly-line workers colored pencils and full sheets of paper. Then give groups 5 minutes to produce as many blouses as possible. During that time, ignore the cottage industry and take on the role of assembly-line factory supervisor.

- After 5 minutes, have both groups count their blouses. Debrief the experience by asking, *How did it feel to work individually, in your homes? On the assembly line? Which group produced the most blouses? Why do you think this is so? Based on this experience, what do you think were the benefits of the assembly line? What do you think were the costs? Do you think the benefits outweighed the costs?*

Deeper Coverage

Conduct a Talk-It-Out Create an Information Master with the prompts below. After students have completed the Reading Notes, place them in pairs with their desks directly facing each other. Assign one student in each pair the role of worker and the other the role of factory owner. Reveal the first prompt, and have the workers read it aloud with you. Then instruct the factory owners to continue the dialogue by responding to the prompt. After one minute, reveal the next prompt and have the factory owners read it aloud with you. Continue until students have discussed all the prompts.

Worker: Why do you pay us such low wages?

Factory owner: Why can't you workers be more productive?

Worker: Why is the work here so boring and repetitive?

Factory owner: Why have you threatened to strike?

Worker: What are you going to do about all the accidents and injuries suffered by workers?

Factory owner: We're over budget. Will you take a pay cut?

Assessment

Mastering the Content

1. A	5. C	9. A	13. C
2. D	6. B	10. A	14. C
3. D	7. D	11. C	15. A
4. B	8. D	12. A	16. C

Applying Social Studies Skills

17. A

18. B

19. Answers will vary.

Exploring the Essential Question

20. Answers should include all of the elements requested in the prompt.

Scoring Rubric

Score	Description
3	Student completes all four parts of the task. Ideas are clearly stated, supported by details, and demonstrate command of standard English conventions.
2	Student responds to most or all parts of the task. Ideas may lack details or not be clearly stated.
1	Student responds to at least one part of the task. Ideas may contain factual or grammatical errors and may lack details.
0	Response does not match the task or is incorrect.

The Celebrity Inventor

1 **Discuss students' prior knowledge of Thomas Edison.** Write *Thomas Edison* on the board and ask students what they associate with this name. Students will most likely mention the electric light bulb first. Tell the class that Edison was one of the most prolific inventors of all time and still holds one of the top world records for inventions, with 1,093 individual patents. If necessary, explain that a patent is issued by the government to protect an inventor's rights to his or her invention.

2 **Have students read the first page of the Chapter 25 Reading Further up to "The Invention that Launched the Legend."** When they have finished, ask,

  - What present-day inventors have had a huge effect on your lives?

  - To whom would you like to write a fan letter, and what would you say?

3 **Have students finish the reading.** Students may be surprised to learn that it was the phonograph, not the electric light bulb, that catapulted Edison into celebrity status. (It was said that by the time Edison was 30, when he invented the phonograph, he was the best-known American in the world.) Note that Edison's first phonograph came out of his interest in improving the telegraph. He was searching for a better way to transcribe and transmit sound signals. So the early phonographs actually recorded sound as well as played it, as the Edward Johnson quotation describes.

4 **Discuss the modern world's dependence on electricity.** Explain that the enormous electrical grids that exist today had their beginnings in the electrical-distribution systems that Thomas Edison invented. Ask students if they have ever experienced a blackout, or a loss of electrical power. If possible, share with them some of the stories of the August 2003 blackout in northeastern North America that are available online.

5 **Have students complete the Chapter 25 Reading Further in their Interactive Student Notebooks.** Invite students to share their paragraphs with the class.

English Language Learners

Provide an Overview of the Activity To prepare students for the activity, provide them with the overview below and a worker number from Information Master 25 ahead of time.

- You will draw a blouse (shirt) on a piece of paper by yourself.

- You will then be assigned to a blouse factory. With your group, you will move your desks into one long row.

- You will be Worker __ and you will specialize in making _____ for blouses. When you get a piece of paper from the worker in front of you, draw your assigned part of the blouse.

- The teacher will play the role of factory supervisor and will walk around and tell the workers to go faster and that you are not doing a good job. At one point, the teacher will tell you to move your desk. The teacher will also play loud music, which will make it difficult to work. Remember that the teacher is only acting.

- Some students may ask you to join a strike. If you choose to join, the teacher will not penalize you.

Learners Reading and Writing Below Grade Level

Simplify the Processing As an alternative Processing activity, have students answer the following questions from the perspective of a worker or factory owner.

Worker: Why do you pay us such low wages?

Factory owner:

Factory owner: Why can't you workers be more productive?

Worker:

Worker: What are you going to do about all the accidents and injuries suffered by workers?

Factory owner:

Factory owner: Why are you workers threatening to strike?

Worker:

Learners with Special Education Needs

Assign an Alternate Role During the activity, assign students the role of factory observer. Provide a transparency with a checklist of emotions including *happy, excited, confident, bored, frustrated, scared,* and *angry.* Each time you change the conditions in the activity, give the observers a different color to circle the words that reflect the factory workers' moods. As the first step of the debriefing process, allow observers to use the transparency to report their findings to the class. Consider having students take pictures during each phase of the activity and share them as well.

Advanced Learners

Write a Reflection of the Triangle Fire Tell students to suppose that they are survivors of the Triangle Factory Fire and have been asked to write a memoir of their experience. Have students research more about the fire by going to the resources Cornell University's "Triangle Factory Fire" Web site at www.ilr.cornell.edu/trianglefire/. Encourage them to listen to the audio recordings of the three survivors. Then have them write a one- to two-page memoir from the perspective of a survivor. Have them include their character's age, background, reasons for working at the factory, whereabouts at the time of the fire, escape route, and reflections on the working and factory conditions.

Enrichment Resources

Find out more about the rise of industry by exploring the following resources for *History Alive! The United States Through Industrialism* at www.teachtci.com.

Enrichment Readings These in-depth readings encourage students to explore selected topics related to the chapter. You may also find readings that relate the chapter's content directly to your state's curriculum.

Internet Connections These recommended Web sites provide useful and engaging content that reinforces skills development and mastery of subjects within the chapter.

Literature Recommendations

The following books offer opportunities to extend the content in this chapter.

The Gilded Age: A History in Documents by Janette Greenwood (New York: Oxford University Press, 2000)

Alexander Graham Bell by Stewart Ross (Austin, TX: Raintree Steck-Vaughn, 2002)

John D. Rockefeller: Anointed with Oil by Grant Segall (New York: Oxford University Press, 2001)

Section 25.2

1. Federal, state, and local governments helped business through favorable laws and subsidies and by passing higher tariffs.

2. Possible answers:

Benefits: Cities grew. Entrepreneurs amassed enormous wealth. Technological inventions improved life. Businesses boomed. A wide range of affordable consumer goods were produced.

Costs: Many workers lived in poverty. Immigrants faced prejudice and discrimination. Workers often lost their jobs. Politicians became corrupt.

Section 25.3

Symbols will vary. Possible answers:

Invention	Inventor	Impact of the Invention
Bessemer process	Henry Bessemer	Steel replaced iron in rails, trains, and bridges. Steel nails, needles, and knives became common household items.
Electrical power station	Thomas Edison	Brought electricity to homes, stores, and factories.
Telephone	Alexander Graham Bell	Allowed Americans to communicate with one another and made industry more efficient and competitive.
Mass production	Several people contributed to this invention.	Enabled workers to produce more goods per day at a lower cost.
Airplane	Orville and Wilbur Wright	Sparked worldwide interest in flying. Started the air travel industry, air mail delivery, the use of planes by the military, and commercial flights.

Section 25.4

1. Rockefeller and Carnegie grew their businesses by setting up corporations and trusts. They also took control of every step of their businesses. For example, Rockefeller bought oil fields along with railroads, pipelines, ships, warehouses, and oil barrels.

2. The newspaper was referring to the influence of trusts on the political process and warning that wealthy entrepreneurs could use their wealth to buy elections and corrupt officials.

Section 25.5

Possible flowcharts:

1. urbanization ⟶ demand for cheap housing ⟶ construction of tenements ⟶ dangerous conditions and quick-spreading disease ⟶ deaths of children

2. urbanization ⟶ increase in cost of land ⟶ building of skyscrapers ⟶ businesspeople rent space in skyscrapers ⟶ by early 1900s, more than half of New York City's workers labored above the seventh floor

Section 25.6

Journal entries will vary.

Section 25.7

1. Labor unions organized workers to fight for better wages and working conditions. Sometimes they negotiated with business owners to achieve their goals. Other times, they used strikers.

2. Labor unions were only somewhat successful at improving working conditions. For instance, although a strike by the International Ladies' Garment Workers' Union resulted in a shorter workweek and better pay, workers' demands for safety improvements were not met.

Sections 25.2 to 25.7

Classroom Experience	Historical Connection
Students created individual shirts.	Craftspeople worked from their homes to produce textiles as part of the cottage industry.
When students worked on the assembly line, they were more productive.	Mass-production techniques, like assembly lines, enabled workers to produce more goods per day at less cost.
Students were more productive when they used pencils and full sheets of paper as opposed to crayons and half-sheets of paper.	Technological advances of the Industrial Revolution made factories more productive.
The Tri and Angle companies merged to form the Triangle Company.	Many businesses merged during the Industrial Revolution to be more productive.
Students worked closer together.	Many companies moved to big cities, where factory space was limited.
Immigrants were willing to replace workers for fewer points.	Immigrants were often willing to work for less.
Students listened to loud noise and worked without light.	Working conditions in factories were usually poor.
Students' bodies and hands hurt from drawing the same part over and over.	Many workers experienced strain and injuries from repetitive work.
Students were resentful of the supervisor's reprimands.	Assembly workers became alienated from their supervisors.
Some students complained and threatened to strike.	Employees formed labor unions and led strikes.

The Great Wave of Immigration

What was life like for immigrants in the early 1900s?

Overview

In a Writing for Understanding activity, students create scrapbooks illustrating what life was like for immigrants in the early 1900s.

Objectives

In the course of reading this chapter and participating in the classroom activity, students will

Social Studies

- compare and contrast experiences of immigrant groups.
- describe the journeys of immigrants to the United States.
- interpret and express what life was like for U.S. immigrants.
- explain why nativism surged in this period and how Congress responded.

Language Arts

- write and edit autobiographical anecdotes that reveal the writer's attitude.

Social Studies Vocabulary

Key Content Terms refugee, assimilation, pogrom, passport, nativism, quota

Academic Vocabulary reinforce, mutual, vital, enrich

Materials

History Alive! The United States Through Industrialism

Interactive Student Notebooks

Lesson Masters

- Student Handout 26 (1 per pair)
- Vocabulary Development handout (1 per student, on colored paper)

masking tape or rope

Activity	Suggested Time	Materials
Preview	15 minutes	• Interactive Student Notebooks • masking tape or a rope
Vocabulary Development	30–40 minutes	• *History Alive! The United States Through Industrialism* • Interactive Student Notebooks • Vocabulary Development handout
Writing for Understanding	100–150 minutes (2–3 regular periods) (1.5–2 block periods)	• *History Alive! The United States Through Industrialism* • Interactive Student Notebooks • Student Handout 26
Processing (optional)	20 minutes	• *History Alive! The United States Through Industrialism* • Interactive Student Notebooks
Assessment	40 minutes	• Chapter 26 Assessment

Preview

1 **Prepare the classroom.** Before class, define an area about 6 feet by 10 feet at the front of the room. Mark a "border" down the middle of the cleared area using masking tape or rope.

2 **Have students take on the roles of immigrants and native citizens.** Divide the class into two groups and have each group stand on a different side of the border. Explain that the tape or rope represents the border between two countries. Instruct one group to cross the border into the other country. Tell that group that they are immigrants, people who move to a new country, and ask them, *Why did you leave your country? How do you feel in your new country?* Tell the other group of students that they are native citizens, and ask them, *How has immigration affected you? How do you feel about immigration?*

3 **Have students complete the Preview activity in their Interactive Student Notebooks.** When they are done, have volunteers share their responses.

4 **Explain the connection between the Preview and Chapter 26.** Explain that people immigrate to the United States for various reasons, including better opportunities, turmoil in their native countries, and to join family members. From 1880 to 1920, more than 23 million immigrants arrived in the United States. In this chapter, students will explore why various groups of immigrants came to the United States and what life was like for them when they arrived.

Vocabulary

1 **Introduce the Key Content Terms.** Have students locate the Key Content Terms for the chapter in their Interactive Student Notebooks. These are important terms that will help them understand the main ideas of the chapter. Ask volunteers to identify any familiar terms and how they might be used in a sentence.

2 **Have students complete a Vocabulary Development handout.** Give each student a copy of the Vocabulary Development handout of your choice from the Reading Toolkit at the back of the Lesson Masters. These handouts provide extra practice and support, depending on your students' needs. Review the completed handout by asking volunteers to share one answer for each term.

Reading

1 **Introduce the Essential Question and have students read Section 26.1.** Have students identify the Essential Question on the first page of the chapter: *What was life like for immigrants in the early 1900s?* Then have students read Section 26.1. Afterward, have them use information from Section 26.1 and the images that open the chapter to propose some possible answers to the Essential Question.

2 **Have students read and complete the Reading Notes for Section 26.2.** Have several volunteers share their responses. Use Guide to Reading Notes 26 to check their answers.

3 **Have students complete the Reading Notes for the remaining reading sections.** Assign Sections 26.3 to 26.7 during the activity as indicated in the procedures for the Writing for Understanding activity. Remind students to use the Key Content Terms where appropriate as they complete their Reading Notes.

4 **Have students complete the matrix comparing the classroom experience to history.** When students have finished the reading of Sections 26.3 to 26.7, have them fill in the matrix in their Reading Notes.

Writing for Understanding

1 **Place students in pairs and introduce the activity.** Tell pairs that they will create a scrapbook illustrating what life was like for an immigrant at the turn of the century.

2 **Have pairs learn about an immigrant group.** Assign each pair one of four immigrant groups: Italian, Jewish, Chinese, or Mexican. Tell pairs to read the section in the book about their immigrant group and to complete the corresponding Reading Notes in their Interactive Student Notebooks.

3 **Explain how to create a scrapbook.** Distribute *Student Handout 26: Creating an Immigrant Scrapbook* to each pair of students and review the steps with the class. Emphasize that the scrapbook should appear to have been created by the immigrant. Encourage students to incorporate such mementos as ticket stubs, coins, and letters from home into their scrapbooks.

Student Handout 26

4 **Monitor pairs as they work.** Give students at least one period to create their scrapbooks.

5 **Have pairs share their scrapbooks.** Have pairs display their scrapbooks on their desks. Then instruct students to walk around and examine at least two scrapbooks from each of the other three immigrant groups. Have them use the information from their classmates' scrapbooks to complete the Reading Notes for Sections 26.3 to 26.6.

6 **Have students verify the information they have recorded.** Have students read Sections 26.3 to 26.6 and compare what they read to the notes they have recorded about the various immigrant groups, adding information as necessary.

7 **Have students read and complete the Reading Notes for Section 26.7.** Ask several volunteers to share their responses. Use the Guide to Reading Notes to check their answers.

8 **Hold a class discussion.** Ask,

- How would you describe life for an immigrant at the turn of the century?

- In what ways were the experiences of the four immigrant groups similar?

- In what ways were the experiences of the four groups different?

- How did the growth of nativism affect immigrants?

- In what ways do you think immigration at the turn of the century might have been similar to immigration today? In what ways do you think it might have been different?

Processing (optional)

1 **Understand the intent of the Processing activity.** The scrapbook serves as this chapter's Processing activity. Should you choose not to have students do that assignment, you might use the optional Processing activity in the Interactive Student Notebook.

2 **Have students complete the Processing activity.** Students will write a letter from the perspective of an immigrant describing the immigrant's journey to and experiences in the United States. Consider having students share their letters in pairs or with the class.

Quicker Coverage

Jigsaw the Reading In lieu of assigning the scrapbook, divide students into eight groups. Assign two groups to each of Sections 26.3 to 26.6. Have groups become "experts" for their assigned section by reading and completing the Reading Notes for that section. Then have students form new groups of four, with one expert on each of Sections 26.3 to 26.6, and share their respective Reading Notes.

Deeper Coverage

Interview an Immigrant Have students conduct an interview with a U.S. immigrant. Have them find out why the person left his or her native country and how he or she traveled to the United States, as well as about his or her experiences in this country. Then have students create a scrapbook from the perspective of the immigrant. Encourage students to take photographs of any artifacts the interviewer might have to incorporate into their scrapbooks.

Learn About Ellis Island or Angel Island Have students research more about immigrants' experiences at Ellis Island or Angel Island and incorporate some of the information into additional pages of their scrapbooks. Require them to include

- at least one written document, such as a letter or a journal entry about the experience at the detention center.

- one artifact from the detention center, such as a poem etched into a wall or a health form.

- at least two visuals showing the conditions at the center.

Writing Applications: Research Reports

As students use both primary and secondary sources, remind them to reflect on the relative value of each. For example, ask them to name ways in which a journal entry or other first-person account might be flawed, slanted, or inaccurate, as well as to name ways in which it might provide details, insights, and an overall perspective that no other account could give.

Assessment

Mastering the Content

1. B	5. D	9. B	13. D
2. D	6. B	10. A	14. B
3. A	7. B	11. B	15. A
4. A	8. C	12. C	16. C

Applying Social Studies Skills

17. The thickness of the arrows relates to the number of immigrants from that particular region; the thicker the arrow, the more immigrants came from that region.

18. A

19. D

Exploring the Essential Question

20. Answers should include all of the elements requested in the prompt.

Scoring Rubric

Score	Description
3	Student completes all three parts of the task. Ideas are clearly stated, supported by details, and demonstrate command of standard English conventions.
2	Student responds to most or all parts of the task. Ideas may lack details or not be clearly stated.
1	Student responds to at least one part of the task. Ideas may contain factual or grammatical errors and may lack details.
0	Response does not match the task or is incorrect.

Young Immigrants Today

1 **Have students read the Chapter 26 Reading Further.** When they have finished, ask them to identify the reasons for immigration in each case. Note that for three of the five young people, escaping the violence of war led them to the United States. For Yulia and Tito, economic opportunities brought their families to this country.

2 **Discuss recent immigration to the United States.** Have students talk about any recent immigrants they know. Depending on the makeup of your class and school, you may want to ask students or invite visitors to describe their experiences and then ask the class, *What parallels do you see with the stories of the immigrants you read about?*

3 **Compare recent immigration to that of earlier times.** Based on what they have learned about earlier waves of immigration, have students note similarities and differences. Interested students may wish to research current immigration laws and compare them with restrictions of earlier times.

4 **Have students complete the Chapter 26 Reading Further in their Interactive Student Notebooks.** After students have written their interview questions, ask volunteers to share and discuss their questions with the class.

5 **Conduct interviews using the questions.** For extra credit, some students may wish to interview recent immigrants using the questions they have developed. Have them share their interviews with the class.

English Language Learners

Create Personal Scrapbooks Since many English language learners come from immigrant families, you might have students create a scrapbook about their own experiences or the experiences of a family member. Encourage students to include actual artifacts, such as photographs and mementos.

Learners Reading and Writing Below Grade Level

Condense the Scrapbook Have students create a simple, one- or two-page scrapbook that includes one artifact about the journey from the immigrant's home country, one written document about the immigrant's experience arriving in the United States, and one visual.

Learners with Special Education Needs

Prepare Students for the Preview Before class, describe the Preview activity to students. Assign them their desired role and have them prepare answers to the questions you will ask.

Show Students a Sample Scrapbook Create or find a sample scrapbook to share with students. After conducting this activity for the first time, take pictures of or save some scrapbooks to show students in subsequent years.

Advanced Learners

Create a Political Cartoon In lieu of having students complete the Reading Notes for Section 26.7, have them create a political cartoon that shows the efforts of the U.S. government to restrict immigration at the turn of the century. Require them to include an appropriate title and date and to write a paragraph describing the cartoon.

Enrichment Resources

Find out more about U.S. immigration at the turn of the century by exploring the following resources for *History Alive! The United States Through Industrialism* at www.teachtci.com.

Enrichment Readings These readings provide additional enrichment opportunities for students. You may also find readings that relate the chapter's content directly to your state's curriculum.

Internet Connections These recommended Web sites provide useful and engaging content that reinforces skills development and mastery of subjects within the chapter.

Literature Recommendations

The following books offer opportunities to extend the content in this chapter.

The Dream of America: Immigration, 1870–1920 by Kevin Hillstrom (Detroit: Omnigraphics, 2009)

Chinese Americans by Michael Martin (Philadelphia: Chelsea House Publishers, 2003)

Bound for America: The Story of the European Immigrants by Milton Meltzer (New York: Benchmark Books, 2001)

Section 26.2

1. Possible answer: With my eyes, I saw violence and poverty in my homeland. With my mouth, I learned to speak English. With my hands, I worked hard to help build the railroad and to mine gold and silver. With my feet, I crossed over mountains and swam across rivers to arrive as a refugee in this country.

2. Possible answer: Immigrants made contributions to the country's industrializing society. For example, they built railroads, mined gold and silver, and worked in oil fields, in factories, and on farms. They also brought diversity to the country through their customs, crafts, languages, and faiths.

Section 26.3

1. Possible answers:

   - Italian immigrants left Italy to escape poverty.

   - On their voyage, they usually traveled in steerage, where sleeping quarters were tight, food was spoiled, and there was nowhere to bathe.

   - At Ellis Island, they had to pass medical exams and answer questions about how they planned to support themselves.

   - Those who did not pass inspection could be sent home, even if this meant separating the family.

2. Possible answers:

   - Many Italian immigrants found unskilled jobs like building sewers, laying bricks, or cleaning streets.

   - They often lived in poor, crowded neighborhoods with other Italians.

   - Some Italian children did not attend school because their families needed them to earn money or feared that learning English would distance them from the family.

   - Other Americans often mistakenly looked on Italians as people who would always remain poor and illiterate.

3. Drawings will vary.

Sections 26.4

1. Possible answers:

   - Many Jewish immigrants left Russia to escape persecution.

   - They often traveled in overcrowded trains with long delays and then by ship in crowded compartments.

   - They landed at New York Harbor, but only wealthy passengers were admitted quickly.

   - Others were taken to Ellis Island, where they were questioned by doctors and inspectors before they could proceed to shore.

2. Possible answers:

   - Many Jews settled in New York City's Lower East Side, where they started synagogues, shops, newspapers, and religious schools.

   - Jewish immigrants were poor but had many skills.

   - They valued education and insisted their children attend school.

   - Other Americans discriminated against Jews and excluded them from private clubs, schools, and places of employment.

3. Drawings will vary.

Sections 26.5

1. Possible answers:

   - Chinese immigrants came to escape poverty and make money.

   - The Chinese Exclusion Act of 1882 banned Chinese laborers from immigrating to the United States and denied Chinese immigrants the right to become citizens.

   - After an earthquake in San Francisco destroyed most birth records, many Chinese men claimed to be native-born citizens and arranged for people in China to immigrate as relatives.

   - The new immigrants were detained for several weeks or longer at Angel Island, where they were questioned about their claims to be related to native U.S. citizens.

2. Possible answers:

- Most Chinese settled in city neighborhoods, where they could find work at Chinese laundries, restaurants, and stores.

- For many years, most Chinese immigrants were male.

- Housing was closed to Chinese in most areas of San Francisco, so when women and children began to arrive, many Chinatowns became crowded.

3. Drawings will vary.

Sections 26.6

1. Possible answers:

- Many Mexican immigrants came to the United States to escape the Mexican Revolution.

- Mexicans traveled by foot, on burros, in two-wheel carts, and by railroad.

- Immigrants could enter the United States freely, without passports or money.

2. Possible answers:

- American employers welcomed Mexican workers because they were willing to work hard for little pay.

- Most Mexican immigrants worked in agriculture and moved from area to area, harvesting crops.

- Farmworkers often lived in temporary shelters that had no running water. After harvest season, some moved into barrios in nearby towns.

- Mexican immigrants often faced strong prejudice, earned low wages, and had little say in their working conditions.

3. Drawings will vary.

Section 26.7

1. Nativism began to rise in the 1880s because of the surge in immigration.

2. Congress banned further immigration from Japan in 1907 and, in 1917, required all immigrants to prove they could read and write before they could enter the country. In the 1920s, Congress established a quota system to limit the number of immigrants allowed to enter each year.

Migration and Industry

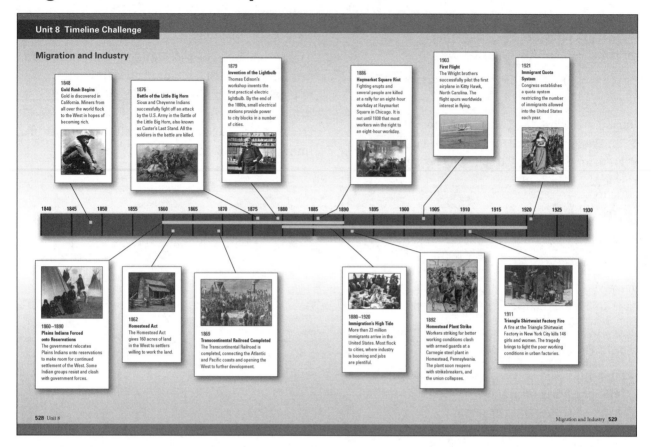

Unit 8 Timeline Challenge

Migration and Industry

1848
Gold Rush Begins
Gold is discovered in California. Miners from all over the world flock to the West in hopes of becoming rich.

1876
Battle of the Little Big Horn
Sioux and Cheyenne Indians successfully fight off an attack by the U.S. Army in the Battle of the Little Big Horn, also known as Custer's Last Stand. All the soldiers in the battle are killed.

1879
Invention of the Lightbulb
Thomas Edison's workshop invents the first practical electric lightbulb. By the end of the 1880s, small electrical stations provide power to city blocks in a number of cities.

1886
Haymarket Square Riot
Fighting erupts and several people are killed at a rally for an eight-hour workday at Haymarket Square in Chicago. It is not until 1938 that most workers win the right to an eight-hour workday.

1903
First Flight
The Wright brothers successfully pilot the first airplane in Kitty Hawk, North Carolina. The flight spurs worldwide interest in flying.

1921
Immigrant Quota System
Congress establishes a quota system restricting the number of immigrants allowed into the United States each year.

1860–1890
Plains Indians Forced onto Reservations
The government relocates Plains Indians onto reservations to make room for continued settlement of the West. Some Indian groups resist and clash with government forces.

1862
Homestead Act
The Homestead Act gives 160 acres of land in the West to settlers willing to work the land.

1869
Transcontinental Railroad Completed
The Transcontinental Railroad is completed, connecting the Atlantic and Pacific coasts and opening the West to further development.

1880–1920
Immigration's High Tide
More than 23 million immigrants arrive in the United States. Most flock to cities, where industry is booming and jobs are plentiful.

1892
Homestead Plant Strike
Workers striking for better working conditions clash with armed guards at a Carnegie steel plant in Homestead, Pennsylvania. The plant soon reopens with strikebreakers, and the union collapses.

1911
Triangle Shirtwaist Factory Fire
A fire at the Triangle Shirtwaist Factory in New York City kills 146 girls and women. The tragedy brings to light the poor working conditions in urban factories.

528 Unit 8

Migration and Industry **529**

Overview

This Timeline Challenge provides students with a review of the main events and ideas of this unit, as well as practice in reading and interpreting timelines. You can vary and expand the activity according to students' needs and the amount of time available.

Basic Procedure

1 **Introduce the timeline in the Student Edition.** Direct students to the Migration and Industry timeline at the end of Unit 8 in the Student Edition. You may wish to have students read aloud and discuss the timeline entries.

2 **Introduce the Timeline Challenge in the Interactive Student Notebook.** Direct students to the Unit 8 Timeline Challenge in their notebooks. Point out the two types of questions, "Timeline Skills" and "Critical Thinking," and model how to answer each type.

3 **Have students complete the Timeline Challenge.** Monitor students as they work. Use the Guide to Unit 8 Timeline Challenge to check their answers. You may wish to project a transparency of this page as you work through the questions with the class and conduct a discussion of the "Critical Thinking" questions.

4 **Complete the KWL chart.** Return to the KWL chart created at the beginning of the unit, and ask students to list the key information they have learned.

Classroom Timeline

1 **Prepare the Timeline Challenge Cards.** Copy and cut the cards from *Student Handout TC8: Unit 8 Timeline Challenge Cards.* You may wish to laminate the cards for future use.

2 **Create a timeline on a classroom wall.** On an empty wall or a large bulletin board, make a timeline with masking tape or colored paper. Mark off the time intervals in advance, or ask students to do so in class.

3 **Have students place the Timeline Challenge Cards.** Distribute cards to individual students or pairs and have them tape the cards to the timeline in the correct locations. Call on students to provide more information on the timeline topics to review main events and issues.

Student Handout TC8

Internet Research

1 **Review students' suggestions for additional timeline entries.** Have students share their answers to the last question of the Timeline Challenge.

2 **Have students conduct Internet research.** Ask students to choose and research one of their suggested events.

3 **Have students create additional Timeline Challenge Cards.** Direct students to research an appropriate image for their cards and then use the computer to create an illustrated card, complete with timeline entry.

Timeline Skills

Score 1 point for each correct answer.

1. 1869; It connected the Atlantic and Pacific coasts and opened the West to continued development.

2. the Homestead Act

3. Sioux and Cheyenne Indians successfully fought off an attack by the U.S. Army.

4. Plains Indians were relocated to reservations between 1860 and 1890 to make room for continued settlement of the West.

5. Most immigrants flocked to cities because industry was booming and jobs were plentiful there.

6. the Haymarket Square riot and the Homestead Plant strike; Strikers did not achieve their aims in either strike.

7. 1921; to restrict the number of immigrants allowed into the United States each year

8. 1879; within a decade

9. in 1903, in Kitty Hawk, North Carolina

Critical Thinking

Score 1 to 3 points for each answer, depending on the thoroughness of the response.

10. Possible answer: The techniques of mass production made businesses more efficient by enabling workers to produce more goods per day at lower costs. Inventions like electric streetcars and vacuum cleaners made life easier for Americans.

11. Possible answer: Immigrants faced many challenges, including learning a new language, finding a job, and discrimination. They overcame such challenges by learning English, living and working in immigrant communities, and sending their children to school in order to give them better opportunities in the future.

12. Possible answer: Western settlement damaged the lands and livelihood of American Indians. The building of the railroad destroyed much of the land of the Plains Indians and resulted in the slaughtering of their main food source, the buffalo. The United States forced the Plains Indians onto reservations in order to separate them from settlers.

13. Answers will vary. Students must explain why the events they chose merit inclusion.

Using Scores to Inform Instruction

Timeline Skills A score of 6 out of 9 indicates that students understand most of the key events of this unit.

Critical Thinking A score of 8 out of 12 indicates that students are able to think critically about most of the key issues of this unit.

If students score below these levels, consider reviewing timeline and critical thinking skills.

UNIT

A Modern Nation Emerges

Geography Challenge

Timeline Challenge

A Modern Nation Emerges

Overview

This activity introduces geographic information essential to Unit 9. Students read and interpret a map and data about U.S. overseas expansion and domestic reform in the late 1800s and early 1900s. They annotate a world map, answer questions in their Interactive Student Notebooks, and discuss critical thinking questions to explore the relationship between the nation's economic growth, expansion, and reform. Their comprehension of content and proficiency in map-reading and higher-order thinking skills will help you gauge their readiness for the unit. The pages that follow include a completed map, answers to questions, a scoring guide to inform your teaching, and suggestions for modifications to meet specific student needs.

Essential Geographic Understandings

1. The extent of U.S. expansion in 1867

2. The extent of U.S. expansion in 1903

3. Key human features: Panama, Panama Canal

4. Key physical features: Alaska, Cuba, Hawaiian Islands, Midway, Philippines, Puerto Rico

5. The effect of overseas expansion on U.S. economic growth and foreign trade

Procedures

1 **Introduce the unit.** Tell students they will learn about U.S. overseas involvement in the late 1800s and early 1900s and about reforms in the nation during that period.

2 **Create a KWL chart.** Ask students to identify what they know about U.S. foreign involvement in the late 1800s and early 1900s and what they want to learn about this subject. Use their responses to gauge how much additional background information they will need as you progress through the unit. Students will return to the KWL chart at the end of the unit and add the key information they have learned.

3 **Have students read Unit 9 "Setting the Stage" in the Student Edition.**

4 **Have students complete the Geography Challenge.** Monitor students as they answer the questions and complete the map. You may want to have them work in pairs. Use the guide on the next two pages to check their answers. You may wish to project the map from the Interactive Student Notebook and have students annotate it as the class works through the map-reading questions. Make sure students have grasped Essential Geographic Understandings 1 to 4.

5 **Discuss the "Critical Thinking" questions.** Help students understand the geographic relationships described in Essential Geographic Understanding 5.

U.S. Territorial Expansion, 1867–1903

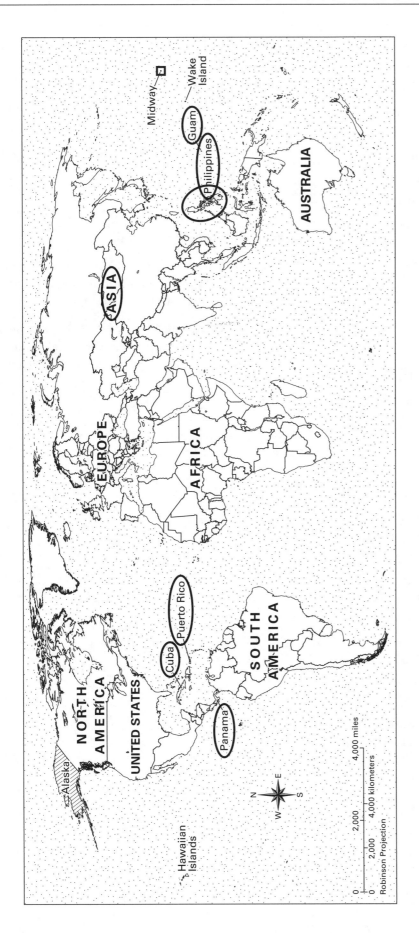

Geography Skills

Score 1 point for each correct answer. Use the map on the previous page to check shading and labeling.

1. The United States obtained Alaska from Russia in 1867.

2. The Philippines was the greatest distance from the United States.

3. Cuba and Panama were not U.S. possessions but were under U.S. control.

4. The United States gained Guam, the Philippines, and Puerto Rico as a result of its war with Spain.

5. Midway is about halfway between North America and Asia.

6. Wake Island is located about 1,000 miles southwest of Midway.

7. Guam is about 1,400 miles east of the Philippines.

8. Americans in the late 1800s were interested in trade with Asia.

Critical Thinking

Questions may have more than one correct answer. Score 1 to 3 points for each reasonable answer, depending on the strength of students' geographic reasoning. Possible answers are given here.

9. Hawaii, the Philippines, and other Pacific islands would provide places where U.S. ships traveling between Asia and the United States could stop for fuel and supplies.

10. A canal would greatly reduce the travel distance between the eastern United States, where most manufacturing was located, and Asia.

11. If the United States controlled Cuba and Puerto Rico, it could put military bases on these islands. Ships and troops on these bases could help to protect the canal.

Using Scores to Inform Instruction

Geography Skills A score of 6 out of 8 or better indicates that students have acquired sufficient geographic information to proceed with the unit.

Critical Thinking A score of 6 out of 9 or better indicates that students are beginning to understand the relationships between physical geography and the different ways in which people live.

Modifying Instruction

ELL or Learners with Special Education Needs Consider focusing on map-reading questions or limiting the number of "Critical Thinking" questions.

Students with Weak Map or Critical Thinking Skills Assign appropriate pages from the Social Studies Skills Toolkit in the back of the Lesson Masters.

The Progressive Era

Did the progressives improve life in the United States?

Overview

In a Response Group activity, students take on the roles of Progressive era leaders in a panel discussion to evaluate whether progressives improved life in the United States.

Objectives

In the course of reading this chapter and participating in the classroom activity, students will

Social Studies

- determine the impact of the National Grange and the Populist Party.
- discuss industrialists' laissez-faire ideals.
- describe the effects of urbanization and industrialization on the environment and society.
- analyze the success of Progressive reforms in the areas of government, child labor, workers' rights, conservation, equal rights for African Americans, and women's suffrage.

Language Arts

- support arguments with examples and reasoning.

Social Studies Vocabulary

Key Content Terms Progressive movement, National Grange, Populist Party, platform, social Darwinism, regulation, conservation, suffrage

Academic Vocabulary dictate, radical, vague, advocate

Materials

History Alive! The United States Through Industrialism

Interactive Student Notebooks

CD Track 15

Lesson Masters

- Student Handouts 27A and 27B (1 biography and 1 mask for each group of 4 students)
- Information Master 27 (1 transparency)
- Vocabulary Development handout (1 per student, on colored paper)

Activity	Suggested Time	Materials
Preview	10–15 minutes	• *History Alive! The United States Through Industrialism* • Interactive Student Notebooks • CD Track 15
Vocabulary Development	30–40 minutes	• *History Alive! The United States Through Industrialism* • Interactive Student Notebooks • Vocabulary Development handout
Response Group	100 minutes (2 regular periods) (1 block period)	• *History Alive! The United States Through Industrialism* • Interactive Student Notebooks • Information Master 27 • Student Handouts 27A and 27B
Processing	20 minutes	• Interactive Student Notebooks
Assessment	40 minutes	• Chapter 27 Assessment

Preview

1 **Analyze a song from the Progressive era.** Play CD Track 15, "Future America," and have students follow or sing along with the lyrics in their Interactive Student Notebooks. Then ask,

- What famous tune is used for this song? What differences are there between this song and "America" (also known as "My Country 'Tis of Thee")?
- What might have been some of the problems in American society at the time this song was written?
- Why do you think the songwriter chose to use the tune of "My Country 'Tis of Thee"?

2 **Have students complete the Preview in their Interactive Student Notebooks.** Students will hypothesize about three problems that existed in American society at the time the song was written.

3 **Have students share their responses in pairs or with the class.**

4 **Explain the connection between the Preview and Chapter 27.** Tell students that at the turn of the 20th century, numerous problems existed in American society. Progressives—political reformers that focused on improving society—proposed a variety of solutions to these problems. In this chapter, students will discover the problems of this era and consider whether the progressives were able to improve life in the United States.

Vocabulary Development

1 **Introduce the Key Content Terms.** Have students locate the Key Content Terms for the chapter in their Interactive Student Notebooks. These are important terms that will help them understand the main ideas of the chapter. Ask volunteers to identify any familiar terms and how they might be used in a sentence.

2 **Have students complete a Vocabulary Development handout.** Give each student a copy of the Vocabulary Development handout of your choice from the Reading Toolkit at the back of the Lesson Masters. These handouts provide extra practice and support, depending on your students' needs. Review the completed handout by asking volunteers to share one answer for each term.

Reading

1 **Introduce the Essential Question and have students read Section 27.1.** Have students identify the Essential Question on the first page of the chapter: *Did the progressives improve life in the United States?* Then have students read Section 27.1. Afterward, have them use information from the reading and the images that open the chapter to propose some possible answers to the Essential Question.

2 Have students read and complete the Reading Notes for Section 27.2. Use Guide to Reading Notes 27 to check for understanding.

3 Have students complete the remaining Reading Notes for Chapter 27. Assign Sections 27.3 to 27.10 during the activity as indicated in the procedures for the Response Group. Remind students to use the Key Content Terms where appropriate as they complete their Reading Notes.

Response Group

1 Place students in groups of four and introduce the activity. Explain to students that they will participate in a Progressive era panel discussion. Students will take turns playing the role of a Progressive era leader assigned to their group.

2 Assign each group a Progressive era leader. Distribute one biography from *Student Handout 27A: Biographies of Progressive Era Leaders* to each group. Have the students in each group read the handout together. Then tell groups to read the section in the book that corresponds to their assigned leader and to complete the corresponding Reading Notes.

3 Have students prepare for Round 1 of the panel discussion.

- Distribute the appropriate mask from *Student Handout 27B: Masks of Progressive Era Leaders* to each group.

- Project *Information Master 27: Progressive Era Panel Discussion*. Review the directions for Round 1, and have groups choose a group member to take on the role of the panelist.

- Instruct panelists to give historically accurate responses during the panel discussion. Panelists must behave in character according to the descriptions in their biographies and the book.

- Give groups adequate time to prepare, including creating props or costumes for their panelists.

4 Conduct Round 1 of the panel discussion. Project Information Master 27 and facilitate the discussion as follows:

- Place nine chairs in a row, facing the audience. Have panelists take their places with their props or costumes and wearing their masks.

- Remind panelists to give historically accurate responses and to act in character. They should address their fellow panelists respectfully and speak clearly so the entire audience can hear. (**Note**: Consider awarding points to groups for giving historically accurate responses and behaving in character.)

- Direct audience members to listen carefully. As they listen, they may begin their Reading Notes by filling in the first column of the matrix with appropriate adjectives.

- Acting as the moderator, ask the panelists to introduce themselves.

Student Handout 27A

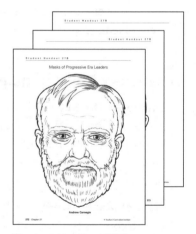

Student Handout 27B

Information Master 27

5   Have students choose one of the remaining sections of Chapter 27, read that section, and complete the corresponding Reading Notes.

6   **Repeat Steps 3 to 5 for Rounds 2, 3, and 4 of the panel discussion.** For each new round, have groups choose a new panelist and discuss the topic given on Information Master 27. Encourage lively debate among the panelists and, when appropriate, allow them to respond directly to one another.

7   **Debrief the activity.** Ask,

- Which panelists' viewpoints or ideas do you agree with most? Which do you disagree with most?

- Did the progressives improve life in the United States? Explain.

- Which of the panelists had the most lasting impact on American society? Explain.

8   **Have students complete their remaining Reading Notes as homework.**

Processing

Have students complete the Processing activity in their Interactive Student Notebook. Students will create a new verse for the song "America."

Quicker Coverage

Shorten the Activity Make one or more of these modifications to the panel discussion.

- Eliminate the masks.
- Do not have groups create costumes or props.
- Combine Rounds 1 and 2.
- Eliminate Round 4.

Deeper Coverage

Conduct Further Research Have students research information using the library or Internet as they prepare for the panel discussion. Consider having students write a biography of their Progressive era leader after the panel discussion.

Apply Learning to Present-Day Issues After the panel discussion, have groups list the tactics the progressives used to improve life in the United States. Next, tell groups to choose a problem in American society today and create a plan to address that problem. The plan should include tactics used during the Progressive era and a rationalization for their use. Have groups create and display posters of their plans. Then conduct a gallery walk with the whole class.

Listening and Speaking: Oral Language Conventions

As students discuss the leaders, require the use of appositives or appositive phrases to identify them, such as "Jane Addams, the social reformer," and "Carrie Chapman Catt, a leader of the suffrage movement." Challenge students to subordinate ideas as they present orally. As needed, provide sentence frames such as the following, model their completion, and use them to review subordination: "Because [the leader did such and such], [independent clause stating lasting influence]."

Assessment

Mastering the Content

1. C	5. B	9. B	13. D
2. C	6. C	10. D	14. A
3. A	7. C	11. B	15. D
4. C	8. A	12. D	16. A

Applying Social Studies Skills

17. A

18. D

19. Answers should reflect that Sinclair is trying to convey the seriousness of the situation or that what he has written is not exaggerated.

Exploring the Essential Question

20. Answers should include all of the elements requested in the prompt.

Scoring Rubric

Score	Description
3	Student completes all four parts of the task. Ideas are clearly stated, supported by details, and demonstrate command of standard English conventions.
2	Student responds to most or all parts of the task. Ideas may lack details or not be clearly stated.
1	Student responds to at least one part of the task. Ideas may contain factual or grammatical errors and may lack details.
0	Response does not match the task or is incorrect.

Children at Work

1 **Discuss child labor today.** To introduce the topic of child labor, show the class images of children at work around the world today. (Photographs are readily available online.) Tell students that the United Nations estimates that 73 million children aged 10 to 14 are working at jobs around the world—the majority of them in Asia. Ask students whether they know anyone who works like this in the United States. Explain that this country now has laws that limit the age that children can work and the kinds of work they can do.

2 **Have students read the Chapter 27 Reading Further.** When they have finished, ask them to think about what it would have been like to work from dawn to dark as a breaker boy, a door boy, or a newsie. Ask,

- What would be the hardest part of such a job?
- What of your present life would you miss the most? Why?

3 **Have students complete the first page of the Chapter 27 Reading Further in their Interactive Student Notebooks.** Discuss the rights of childhood presented in the NCLC declaration. Ask,

- Why do you think the declaration included the rights to play and to dream?
- How do these actions contribute to a child's development?

Also talk about what the reformers saw as the benefits of education.

- How do you think that school helps develop your "mind and heart"?

4 **Have students complete the Reading Further activity.** Invite volunteers to deliver their speeches to the class. Compare and discuss the various rights students selected.

English Language Learners

Allow Extra Preparation Time Give students the instructions and discussion topics for the panel discussion the night before you conduct it in class.

Use Cue Cards Have students create cue cards to use during the panel discussion. You might allow them to read from their cue cards or simply use them as a prompt for more difficult words or concepts.

Learners Reading and Writing Below Grade Level

Alter the Processing Instead of song lyrics, have students write a paragraph that answers the Essential Question: *Did the progressives improve life in the United States?* Tell students to choose between one of the topic sentences below and then write four to five more sentences with details that support their topic sentence.

- The progressives greatly improved life in the United States.
- The progressives did not improve life in the United States.

Learners with Special Education Needs

Assign Students to Specific Rounds Instead of having groups decide who will be the panelist in each round, make assignments ahead of time. Assign students to the rounds that best match their skills and abilities.

Use Illustrations for the Reading Notes For Sections 27.3 to 27.10, have students give their answers by drawing pictures and writing "yes" or "no" in Columns 2 and 3.

Advanced Learners

Increase the Reading Notes Have students read two sections between rounds, rather than one.

Add a Writing Assignment Have students write a fictional article for *McClure's Magazine*. Gather a few muckraking articles from the original magazine and have students read them. Then ask students to choose one of the issues presented in Chapter 27 and write an article about the issue that might have appeared in *McClure's Magazine* during the Progressive era. Encourage them to use a writing style and format similar to that used in the original articles.

Lengthen the Processing Have students write three additional verses to "America."

Enrichment Resources

Find out more about the Progressive era by exploring the following Enrichment Resources for *History Alive! The United States Through Industrialism* at www.teachtci.com.

Enrichment Readings These readings provide additional enrichment opportunities for students. You may also find readings that relate the chapter's content directly to your state's curriculum.

Internet Connections These recommended Web sites provide useful and engaging content that reinforces skills development and mastery of subjects within the chapter.

Literature Recommendations

The following books offer opportunities to extend the content in this chapter.

Andrew Carnegie: Industrial Philanthropist by Laura B. Edge (Minneapolis, MN: Lerner Publications Company, 2004)

Theodore Roosevelt: Champion of the American Spirit by Betsy Harvey Kraft (New York: Clarion Books, 2003)

The Wilderness World of John Muir by John Muir; edited by Edwin Way Teale and Henry Bugbee Kane (New York: Mariner Books/Houghton Mifflin Company, 2001)

Section 27.2

1. 3, 6, 7, 1, 5, 2, 4

2. The Populist Party hoped to form an alliance between farmers and industrial workers.

3. William McKinley drew support for his candidacy from business and financial interests. Winning the presidency meant that fewer people favored reform and that the Populist Party had weakened.

Sections 27.3 to 27.10

Possible answers are given below. Descriptive adjectives and questions to ask the individuals will vary.

Section and Historical Figure	How would this individual answer this question: *Is there something wrong in America?* Explain.	Did this individual improve life in the United States? Give at least one example supporting your opinion.
Section 27.3 Andrew Carnegie, Industrialist	No. Railroads link the towns and cities of the nation. New industries have been established. There are more jobs for immigrants. Ordinary Americans can afford wonderful new products. Competition provides for the survival of the most fit.	Yes. He established a $250 million steel company and used his wealth to build concert halls, universities, hospitals, and libraries.
Section 27.3 John D. Rockefeller, Industrialist	No. Railroads link the towns and cities of the nation. New industries have been established. There are more jobs for immigrants. Ordinary Americans can afford wonderful new products.	Yes. He funded universities, medical research, the arts, and education. He started the Rockefeller Foundation to promote the well-being of people throughout the world.
Section 27.4 Theodore Roosevelt, Progressive	Possible answer: Yes. Business monopolies are using unfair business practices to drive out competition.	Yes. The government began enforcing the Sherman Antitrust Act, which outlawed monopolies, and broke up railroad and oil monopolies.
Section 27.5 Robert La Follette, Progressive	Yes. Political bosses choose candidates for office. These candidates usually represent powerful business interests. Bosses bribe voters and stuff ballot boxes.	Yes. Because of his influence, many states adopted direct primaries, which allow party members to choose the candidates.

Sections 27.3 to 27.10 (continued)

Section and Historical Figure	How would this individual answer this question: *Is there something wrong in America?* Explain.	Did this individual improve life in the United States? Give at least one example supporting your opinion.
Section 27.6 Mother Jones, Progressive	Yes. Young children work long hours in factories under unsafe conditions. Adult workers also have terrible working conditions.	Yes. Because of her work, child labor was outlawed in 43 states by 1909.
Section 27.7 John Muir, Progressive	Yes. The wilderness is being ruined. Loggers are destroying the nation's forests. Miners are scarring mountains and polluting rivers. Many bird and animal species are nearly or already extinct.	Yes. He convinced Congress to create Yosemite National Park. He influenced President Roosevelt to increase the land set aside for national forests, to double the number of national parks, and to outlaw logging and ranching in national parks.
Section 27.8 W. E. B. Du Bois, Progressive	Yes. Racism is everywhere. The South has segregated schools, trains, and parks, and blacks cannot vote. In the North, blacks are discriminated against in housing and jobs. African Americans who fight injustice are often lynched.	Yes. He helped establish the National Association for the Advancement of Colored People, which works for equal rights for African Americans.
Section 27.9 Upton Sinclair, Progressive	Yes. Few safety measures are in place for workers. Meat is packed under very unsanitary conditions.	Yes. His shocking revelations led Congress to pass the Meat Inspection Act and Pure Food and Drug Acts in 1906, which required manufacturers to use safe ingredients in their products and to advertise them truthfully.
Section 27.10 Alice Paul, Progressive	Yes. Women cannot vote.	Yes. Her women's suffrage movement pushed Congress to approve the Nineteenth Amendment, giving women the right to vote.

The United States Becomes a World Power

Should U.S. actions in world affairs around the turn of the 20th century be praised or condemned?

Overview

In a Social Studies Skill Builder, pairs analyze political cartoons about U.S. actions in world affairs around the turn of the 20th century and evaluate the differing viewpoints of those actions.

Objectives

In the course of reading this chapter and participating in the classroom activity, students will

Social Studies

- summarize arguments for and against U.S. expansion.
- identify causes and results of the Spanish-American War.
- explain the process by which the United States gained control of the Panama Canal.
- examine U.S. involvement in World War I and the subsequent peace negotiations.
- analyze political cartoons with differing viewpoints of U.S. actions in world affairs during this era.

Language Arts

- demonstrate how political cartoons communicate information and convey a specific viewpoint.

Social Studies Vocabulary

Key Content Terms imperialism, yellow journalism, nationalism, militarism

Academic Vocabulary derive, exert, coordinate

Materials

History Alive! The United States Through Industrialism

Interactive Student Notebooks

Visuals 28A–28I

Lesson Masters

- Vocabulary Development handout (1 per student, on colored paper)

Activity	Suggested Time	Materials
Preview	20 minutes	• Interactive Student Notebooks • Visual 28A
Vocabulary Development	30–40 minutes	• *History Alive! The United States Through Industrialism* • Interactive Student Notebooks • Vocabulary Development handout
Social Studies Skill Builder	150 minutes (3 regular periods) (1.5 block periods)	• *History Alive! The United States Through Industrialism* • Interactive Student Notebooks • Visuals 28B–28I
Processing	30 minutes	• Interactive Student Notebooks
Assessment	40 minutes	• Chapter 28 Assessment

Preview

1 **Analyze a political cartoon from the turn of the 20th century.** Project *Visual 28A: Cartoon of an Eagle and a Globe.* Have students examine the image and complete the Preview questions in their Interactive Student Notebooks.

Visual 28A

2 **Have students share their responses with the class.** Tell students that this cartoon was created in 1904, at a time when the United States had recently become much more involved in world affairs. Then ask,

- What do you think is the cartoonist's message or viewpoint?

- Do you think the cartoonist is praising or condemning U.S. actions in world affairs around the turn of the 20th century? How can you tell?

3 **Explain the connection between the Preview and Chapter 28.** Tell students that this political cartoon gives one viewpoint of U.S. actions in world affairs around the turn of the 20th century. Many of these actions were praised, while others were condemned. In this chapter, students will learn about the key U.S. actions in world affairs during this era and the differing viewpoints about them.

Vocabulary Development

1 **Introduce the Key Content Terms.** Have students locate the Key Content Terms for the chapter in their Interactive Student Notebooks. These are important terms that will help them understand the main ideas of the chapter. Ask volunteers to identify any familiar terms and how they might be used in a sentence.

2 **Have students complete a Vocabulary Development handout.** Give each student a copy of the Vocabulary Development handout of your choice from the Reading Toolkit at the back of the Lesson Masters. These handouts provide extra practice and support, depending on your students' needs. Review the completed handout by asking volunteers to share one answer for each term.

Reading

1 **Introduce the Essential Question and have students read Section 28.1.** Have students identify the Essential Question on the first page of the chapter: *Should U.S. actions in world affairs around the turn of the 20th century be praised or condemned?* Then have students read Section 28.1 Afterward, ask them,

- Why did some newspapers call Theodore Roosevelt patriotic and others worry he would push the country into war?

- Who were the expansionists? What were their goals?

2   **Have students complete the Reading Notes for Chapter 29.** Assign Sections 28.2 to 28.9 during the activity as indicated in the procedures for the Social Studies Skill Builder. Remind students to use the Key Content Terms where appropriate as they complete their Reading Notes.

Social Studies Skill Builder

1   **Place students in pairs and introduce the activity.** Explain to pairs that they will analyze political cartoons about U.S. actions around the turn of the 20th century. After reading about each action, they will identify the cartoonist's viewpoint and offer their own evaluation of the action.

2   **Introduce the first U.S. action in world affairs.** Project *Visual 28B: Political Cartoon A*, revealing only the left side. Have pairs analyze the image by answering the questions below. Then have volunteers share their answers with the class. (**Note:** Students can refer to the same questions in the Preview.)

Visual 28B

  • What people or symbols do you see in this cartoon? Who or what might they represent?

  • What details, if any, are exaggerated in this cartoon? Why might they be exaggerated?

  • What does the caption say? How might it relate to the cartoon?

3   **Have students read and complete the Reading Notes for Section 28.2.**

4   **Have pairs guess the missing part of the cartoon.** Tell students that the questions at the bottom of Visual 28B provide clues to the missing parts of the cartoon. Have pairs brainstorm possible answers and then share their guesses and reasoning with the class. Consider giving pairs paper on which to create simple, bold drawings of the missing parts. Volunteers can then hold their drawings up to the blank space of the projected cartoon and explain the reasoning behind their guesses.

5   **Reexamine the complete political cartoon.** Reveal the complete cartoon on the right side of Visual 28B, and have pairs discuss these questions:

  • Does the cartoonist think U.S. actions in Hawaii should be praised or condemned? How can you tell?

  • In your opinion, should U.S. actions in Hawaii be praised or condemned? Explain.

6   **Repeat Steps 2 to 5 for the remaining political cartoons.** Make these adjustments:

  • For Political Cartoon B, use *Visual 28C: Political Cartoon B* and Section 28.3, and ask students about U.S. actions in Cuba.

  • For Political Cartoon C, use *Visual 28D: Political Cartoon C* and Section 28.4, and ask students about U.S. actions in the Philippines.

Reading: Compare and Contrast Texts

Have students compare and contrast what they learn about each event or issue in their books with what they learn by studying each cartoon. Suggest these points of comparison: scope of information, point of view, treatment of information, and organization of ideas (such as sequence, main idea and details, or cause-effect). Guide students to consider the concepts of audience and purpose, especially as they relate to primary and secondary sources.

- For Political Cartoon D, use *Visual 28E: Political Cartoon D* and Section 28.5, and ask students about U.S. actions in Panama.

- For Political Cartoon E, use *Visual 28F: Political Cartoon E* and Section 28.6, and ask students about U.S. actions at the outbreak of World War I.

- For Political Cartoon F, use *Visual 28G: Political Cartoon F* and Section 28.7, and ask students about U.S. actions during the early years of World War I.

- For Political Cartoon G, use *Visual 28H: Political Cartoon G* and Section 28.8, and ask students about U.S. actions during the later years of World War I.

- For Political Cartoon H, use *Visual 28I: Political Cartoon H* and Section 28.9, and ask students about U.S. actions after World War I.

Visuals 28C–28I

7 **Wrap up the activity.** Ask the class, *Should U.S. actions in world affairs around the turn of the 20th century be praised or condemned? Explain.*

Processing

Have students complete the Processing activity in their Interactive Student Notebook. Students will create political cartoons to express their viewpoints about U.S. actions in world affairs around the turn of the 20th century.

Quicker Coverage

Decrease the Number of Cartoons Eliminate the analysis of any four political cartoons (perhaps those that do not relate to your state standards) and simply have students complete the Reading Notes for those sections.

Rearrange the Activity Steps Introduce four political cartoons (using the first three analysis questions) and have students begin reading the corresponding sections and completing the Reading Notes in class. Have them complete any remaining Reading Notes that night for homework. In class the next day, have students guess the missing parts and reexamine the cartoons. Use the remaining time to begin the process again for the remaining cartoons.

Eliminate Guessing the Missing Parts For the first set of image-analysis questions, show students the complete cartoon. After students read the section, skip the steps involving guessing the missing parts of the cartoon and move right to the second set of analysis questions.

Deeper Coverage

Write a Newspaper Article Have students take on the role of journalists at the beginning of the 20th century and write a short article about one of the U.S. actions described in this chapter. Tell students to either praise or condemn U.S. actions in their articles. Students should include reasons and a colorful illustration to support their ideas.

Assessment

Mastering the Content

1. C	5. B	9. C	13. A
2. C	6. D	10. B	14. A
3. A	7. A	11. A	15. B
4. D	8. B	12. C	16. B

Applying Social Studies Skills

17. Possible answers: The cartoonist thought Alaska was composed of little more than ice-covered land. The cartoonist was making fun of the purchase; his viewpoint was that the land obtained through the treaty was cold, icy, and worthless.

18. A

19. A

Exploring the Essential Question

20. Answers should include all of the elements requested in the prompt.

Scoring Rubric

Score	Description
3	Student completes all three parts of the task. Ideas are clearly stated, supported by details, and demonstrate command of standard English conventions.
2	Student responds to most or all parts of the task. Ideas may lack details or not be clearly stated.
1	Student responds to at least one part of the task. Ideas may contain factual or grammatical errors and may lack details.
0	Response does not match the task or is incorrect.

The Yellow Press Goes to War

1 **Discuss the idea of journalistic responsibility.** Talk with the class about the traditional rules for responsible journalism and the expected divisions between news and opinion in newspaper, television, and radio reporting.

2 **Discuss bias.** Ask students for a definition of the word *bias*. Discuss the fact that some bias is present in any news outlet simply by virtue of selecting what stories to include. Nonetheless, the expectation is that newspaper and news programs will do their best to report what they believe to be factual information.

3 **Have students read the Chapter 28 Reading Further.** When they have finished, ask how many of them read newspapers with any regularity. Point out that in the 1890s, the role of newspapers was similar to the role of television and the Internet today. They were people's main source of information about anything happening outside their own communities.

4 **Discuss students' reactions to the practices of yellow journalism.** Ask students to point out examples of the differences between news stories and opinion in newspapers or on the Internet. Have them differentiate between the opinion expressed in a blog, for example, and the "straight news" from a news site. Ask, *Do you think it is important to distinguish between news and opinion? Why or why not?*

5 **Have students complete the Chapter 28 Reading Further in their Interactive Student Notebooks.** Interested students may wish to do further research on the *Maine* incident in order to write longer news articles. Invite students to share their articles with the class.

English Language Learners

Build a Schema Before the activity, review the definitions of *praise* and *condemn*. Discuss a recent example of a public figure who has been praised by the press and another who has been condemned by the press. Consider also having students write about a time when they felt praised and a time when they felt condemned.

Learners Reading and Writing Below Grade Level

Jigsaw Each Reading Section Have pairs join with another pair to form groups of four. Divide each of the reading sections into four parts, and assign each group member one part. Have group members read their assigned passages and then discuss the reading and complete the Reading Notes together.

Practice Writing Skills Instead of simply discussing the last two questions used to analyze the political cartoons, have students write short answers to the questions, using complete sentences. Provide students with answer starters, such as these for the cartoon about U.S. actions in Hawaii:

- The cartoonist believes U.S. actions in Hawaii should be praised/condemned. The cartoonist shows his praise/condemnation by . . .
- I believe U.S. actions in Hawaii should be praised/condemned because . . .

Learners with Special Education Needs

Provide Choices for the Missing Pieces Have students refer to the following list when guessing what is missing from each political cartoon.

- a backrest for Uncle Sam labeled "USA"
- a bottle labeled "Anti Expansion Policy"
- a brace
- a buckle labeled "U.S."
- "Europe"
- "Hawaii"
- rebellious
- ships
- a shovel
- "Spain"
- a submarine periscope
- an umbrella labeled "U.S. army"
- "U.S."
- U.S. flags
- "U.S. Patience"
- "War"

Modify the Processing Consider these options:

- Require students to use just two artistic devices in their cartoons.
- Allow students to simply draw a picture that shows their opinion of U.S. expansionism or the U.S. role in World War I, along with a two-sentence explanation.

Advanced Learners

Expand the Processing Have students create two political cartoons about the same topic, from opposite perspectives. One cartoon should praise U.S. actions and the other should condemn U.S. actions.

Create a War Journal Challenge students to research information on daily life for soldiers in either the Spanish-American War or World War I. Have students write three historically accurate journal entries from the viewpoint of a soldier. Topics should include an explanation of why the United States is fighting the war, descriptions of daily life, and a mention of what Americans might gain.

Enrichment Resources

Find out more about U.S. expansion at the turn of the 20th century and World War I by exploring the following Enrichment Resources for *History Alive! The United States Through Industrialism* at www.teachtci.com.

Enrichment Readings These readings provide additional enrichment opportunities for students. You may also find readings that relate the chapter's content directly to your state's curriculum.

Internet Connections These recommended Web sites provide useful and engaging content that reinforces skills development and mastery of subjects within the chapter.

Literature Recommendations

The following books offer opportunities to extend the content in this chapter.

The Panama Canal by Scott Ingram (San Diego, CA: Blackbirch Press, 2004)

Roosevelt's Rough Riders by Andrew Santella (Minneapolis, MN: Compass Point Books, 2006)

Seward's Folly by Melissa Whitcraft (New York: Children's Press, 2002)

Section 28.2

1. *Possible arguments for:* Would open up new places to establish mines and plantations. Would open up new markets for U.S. products. Would follow in line with other great nations of the world that take over other lands.

   Possible arguments against: Expansionism is contrary to American values. It might cause revolutions abroad. Nonwhites could never learn American values. The U.S. could be powerful without taking over other lands.

2. 1887: The United States establishes a naval base at Pearl Harbor on Oahu.

   1891: Queen Liliuokalani gives up her throne.

   1898: The United States annexes Hawaii.

Section 28.3

1. Possible answers: Expansionists pushed to annex Cuba and Puerto Rico to enforce the Monroe Doctrine and keep European powers out of the Western Hemisphere. Americans read news of the suffering of Cubans under Spanish rule and became willing to go to war for Cuba. Many Americans believed that the Spanish sunk the *Maine,* and they called for war.

2. Possible answers: Cuba gained its independence. Puerto Rico came under U.S. rule. Spain also ceded Guam to the United States.

Section 28.4

1. When the United States invaded the Philippines to expel Spain, Filipino fighters were willing to join the Americans because they wanted independence from Spanish rule. They eventually felt betrayed because the United States bought the Philippines from Spain instead of allowing it to become an independent nation.

2. Possible answers:

   Anti-imperialist: The acquisition of the Philippines is wrong! We are once again creating a society with first- and second-class citizens and ignoring our American values.

   U.S. Expansionist: This is a great day for America! We have a grand new harbor, and we will show the Filipinos a superior way of life.

Section 28.5

1. The United States offered Columbia $10 million for land in Panama, but the Columbian government turned down the offer. → President Roosevelt sent troops to Panama to help them gain independence from Columbia. → The U.S. paid $10 million to Panama for control over the "canal zone."

2. Possible answers: bad drinking water, diseases such as yellow fever and malaria, cutting through the mountains and excavating the dirt to create dams

Section 28.6

1. European countries tried to stay safe by building up their military forces and forming alliances with other countries, in which they promised to protect each other in case of attack.

2. The illustration should show the following: Austria-Hungary declared war on Serbia. To defend Serbia, Russia declared war on Austria-Hungary. Next, Germany defended Austria-Hungary by declaring war on Russia. Eventually, France and Great Britain joined Russia and Serbia and were known as the Allied Powers. Germany and its allies were known as the Central Powers.

Section 28.7

1. Drawings should illustrate trench warfare, machine guns, and chemical weapons.

2. Answers:

   - The German navy was unable to use surface ships because Britain mined the North Sea, the Germans' only access to the ocean.

   - Germany planned to blockade British ships by attacking them with U-boats and by threatening to sink any ship, even those from neutral countries.

   - The *Lusitania* was a British luxury liner that the Germans sank on May 17, 1915.

   - Germany promised not to attack merchant and passenger ships without warning. U.S. manufacturers increased their trade with the Allies.

Section 28.8

1. President Wilson asked Congress to declare war on Germany because the Germans again began sinking merchant ships without warning.

2. Possible answers (circled factors will vary): Convoys of U.S. warships escorted cargo vessels safely to Europe. U.S. destroyers helped the British assault U-boats. General Pershing created a plan to drive the Germans out of the trenches. U.S. reinforcements helped protect Paris from capture. One million soldiers joined the Allies in Europe.

Section 28.9

1. Possible answers:

   Wilson's Fourteen Points: freedom of the seas; fair treatment of all countries including Germany

   Treaty of Versailles: Germany was required to disband almost all of its armed forces, give up its colonies, surrender territory in Europe, and pay reparations.

   center: new national boundaries based on self-determination; League of Nations

2. The Senate rejected the Treaty of Versailles and participation in the League of Nations because many senators feared that the U.S. military might be drawn into other international conflicts.

Linking Past to Present

What changes since 1914 have shaped how we live today?

Overview

In a Social Studies Skill Builder, students discover important events of the last century and learn how they have affected society in the United States.

Objectives

In the course of reading this chapter and participating in the classroom activity, students will

Social Studies

- paraphrase the events since 1914 that have shaped life in the United States.
- interview a community member and document how historical events have shaped that person's life.

Language Arts

- summarize main ideas using standard English conventions at an appropriate grade level.

Social Studies Vocabulary

Key Content Terms feminist, mass media, globalization, service sector, knowledge worker, communism

Academic Vocabulary inherent, automation, trend

Materials

History Alive! The United States Through Industrialism

Interactive Student Notebooks

Lesson Masters

- Information Master 29 (1 transparency)
- Student Handout 29 (1 copy, cut into cards)
- Vocabulary Development handout (1 per student, on colored paper)

Activity	Suggested Time	Materials
Preview	10 minutes	• Interactive Student Notebooks
Vocabulary Development	30 minutes	• *History Alive! The United States Through Industrialism* • Interactive Student Notebooks • Vocabulary Development handout
Social Studies Skill Builder	100 minutes (2 regular periods) (1 block periods)	• *History Alive! The United States Through Industrialism* • Interactive Student Notebooks • Information Master 29 • Student Handout 29
Processing	40 minutes	• Interactive Student Notebooks
Assessment	40 minutes	• Chapter 29 Assessment

Preview

1 Have students complete the Preview activity. Students will link a past event to a present-day event or situation in their lives.

2 Have students share their responses in pairs or with the class.

3 Explain the connection between the Preview and Chapter 29. Tell students that just as events in their past shape their lives today, events in our nation's past shape life in the United States today. The eventful years since 1914 have brought significant changes to our nation. In this chapter, students will learn how these changes came about and how they have shaped life in the 21st century.

Vocabulary Development

1 Introduce the Key Content Terms. Have students locate the Key Content Terms for the chapter in their Interactive Student Notebooks. These are important terms that will help them understand the main ideas of the chapter. Ask volunteers to identify any familiar terms and how they might be used in a sentence.

2 Have students complete a Vocabulary Development handout. Give each student a copy of the Vocabulary Development handout of your choice from the Reading Toolkit at the back of the Lesson Masters. These handouts provide extra practice and support depending on your students' needs. Review the completed handout by asking volunteers to share one answer for each term.

Reading

1 Introduce the Essential Question and have students read Section 29.1. Have students identify the Essential Question on the first page of the chapter: *What changes since 1914 have shaped how we live today?* Then have students read Section 29.1. Afterward, have them use information from the reading and the images that open the chapter to propose some possible answers to the Essential Question.

2 Have students complete the Reading Notes for Chapter 29. Remind students to use the Key Content Terms where appropriate as they complete their Reading Notes.

Social Studies Skill Builder

1 **Introduce the activity.** Tell the class that they will now play a game called *Name That Event!* to test their knowledge of events since 1914.

2 **Divide the class into eight teams.** Assign each team a number. To build camaraderie, you might have teams create a team name or chant.

3 **Explain how to play the game.** Project *Information Master 29: How to Play Name That Event!* and review the objective and directions for the game. Place the cards cut from *Students Handout 29: Event Cards* face down in a central location.

4 **Conduct the game.** Follow the directions on Information Master 29 to conduct the game. Give teams adequate time to prepare their pantomimes and answers to the question. Choose one team to perform their pantomime. Allow teams in the audience to use their Reading Notes to help them guess the event. Repeat the process until each team has taken a turn. Then tally the points and declare a winner.

5 **Wrap up the activity.** Ask,

- Which events in this game did you know the least about? Which events did you know the most about?

- What changes since 1914 have shaped how we live today?

- How do you think life in the United States will change in the next 100 years?

Processing

Have students complete the Processing activity. Students will conduct an interview of an older community member and create a timeline of events that have shaped that person's life.

Information Master 29

Student Handout 29

Quicker Coverage

Shorten the Processing Essay Have students write a single paragraph, explaining how just one event shaped their interviewee's life.

Shorten the Processing Activity Instead of having students conduct an interview and annotate a timeline, have them simply write a paragraph addressing the Essential Question, *What changes since 1914 have shaped how we live today?*

Deeper Coverage

Add to the Game Play additional rounds of *Name That Event!* by adding the following cards to the game.

1920 The nation's first commercial radio stations begin broadcasting.

1945 The United Nations is formed.

1954 The Supreme Court decision in *Brown v. Board of Education of Topeka, Kansas* desegregates schools.

1955 The Montgomery Bus Boycott begins with Rosa Parks's refusal to give up her seat.

1965 The Voting Rights Act bans practices that had kept African Americans from voting in many Southern states.

1966 The National Organization for Women is founded.

1991 The Soviet Union collapses and the Cold War ends.

1991 The World Wide Web opens to the public.

Assessment

Mastering the Content

1. D	5. A	9. B	13. D
2. B	6. B	10. D	14. A
3. A	7. D	11. B	15. C
4. C	8. A	12. D	16. C

Applying Social Studies Skills

17. D

18. Possible answers: People were denied fair treatment in public places because of their race. Restaurants, hotels, and other public places had policies denying services to African Americans because of their race.

19. B

Exploring the Essential Question

20. Answers should include all of the elements requested in the prompt.

Scoring Rubric

Score	Description
3	Student completes all three parts of the task. Ideas are clearly stated, supported by details, and demonstrate command of standard English conventions.
2	Student responds to most or all parts of the task. Ideas may lack details or not be clearly stated.
1	Student responds to at least one part of the task. Ideas may contain factual or grammatical errors and may lack details.
0	Response does not match the task or is incorrect.

Questions for the Future

1 **Have students read the beginning of the Chapter 29 Reading Further.** Ask students to read the introduction and the first paragraph. Explain the origin of the title Rachel Carson chose for her book by describing the "Fable for Tomorrow" with which she opened *Silent Spring*. Carson began with a scene in which people in an imaginary town suddenly realize there are no birds. Birdsong no longer fills the air, making springtime silent. The birds—and much else—have died from exposure to pesticides used to destroy the insects that ate crops. If possible, read the opening of *Silent Spring* aloud to the class.

2 **Discuss the power of Carson's message.** The Reading Further asks readers to consider whether a book can change the world. Discuss with students the power of Carson's message. Tell them that incidents occurred around the time of the book's publication that confirmed Carson's message. In late 1963, for example, millions of dead fish appeared in the Mississippi River. They had been killed by a pesticide that had been dumped into the river illegally.

3 **Have students finish the reading.** Ask students to compare what they have read about Rachel Carson with Norman Borlaug's position. "Food is the moral right of all who are born into this world," Borlaug said. Share with the class some information on world hunger from the United Nations:

- Malnutrition and hunger are leading health risks worldwide.
- A child dies of malnutrition or starvation every six seconds somewhere in the world.

Talk about how the realities of world hunger might affect Borlaug's arguments.

4 **Discuss the ongoing debate over how our food is raised and processed.** You might ask students to monitor the debate in the media (including online blogs and the like) for a week and report back to the class.

5 **Have students complete the Chapter 29 Reading Further in their Interactive Student Notebooks.** After students prepare their debate arguments, you may wish to have a class discussion or stage an actual debate. Ask for volunteers for teams to take each position. Follow the rules of debate, including appointing judges to determine the winner.

English Language Learners

Scaffold the Processing Give students a script, such as the one below, to use during the interview.

1. Introduce yourself and the assignment. Say, "Hello, my name is _____. Thank you for allowing me to interview you about how important historical events have shaped your life."

2. Share three of the events you have learned about with the person you are interviewing.

3. Ask the person, "What three historical events have had the greatest effect on your life? How have these events shaped your life?"

4. Finish the interview. Say, "Thank you very much for allowing me to interview you."

Learners Reading and Writing Below Grade Level

Highlight Main Ideas Give students photocopies of the reading, and have them highlight the important dates in each section. (Alternatively, give students photocopies of the reading with the important dates already highlighted.) Students can focus on highlighted portions of the text when completing their Reading Notes.

Learners with Special Education Needs

Record the Interview Have students record their interviews so that they can focus on listening during the interview. They can take notes by listening to the recording later.

Advanced Learners

Write a Futuristic Essay Have students write an essay about U.S. society 100 years in the future. The essay should include an introduction with a thesis, four body paragraphs with supporting details, and a conclusion. Each body paragraph should discuss one of the main topics in the chapter: securing equal rights and opportunities, innovations, the economy, and the United States on the world stage.

Enrichment Resources

Find out more about U.S. society since 1914 by exploring the following Enrichment Resources for *History Alive! The United States Through Industrialism* at www.teachtci.com.

Enrichment Readings These in-depth readings encourage students to explore selected topics related to the chapter. You may also find readings that relate the chapter's content directly to your state's curriculum.

Internet Resources These recommended Web sites provide useful and engaging content that reinforces skills development and mastery of subjects within the chapter.

Literature Recommendations

The following books offer opportunities to extend the content in this chapter.

Cesar Chavez: We Can Do It! by Sunita Apte (New York: Bearport Publishers, 2006)

March On! The Day My Brother Martin Changed the World by Christine King Farris (New York: Scholastic Press, 2008)

Great Women of the Suffrage Movement by Dana Meachen Rau (Minneapolis, MN: Compass Point Books, 2006)

Sections 29.2 to 29.5

Students should have chosen at least three events for each timeline and annotated the timelines with a date, a one-sentence summary, and an illustration for each event. Paragraphs explaining how one of the events has shaped how we live today should be well supported.

A Modern Nation Emerges

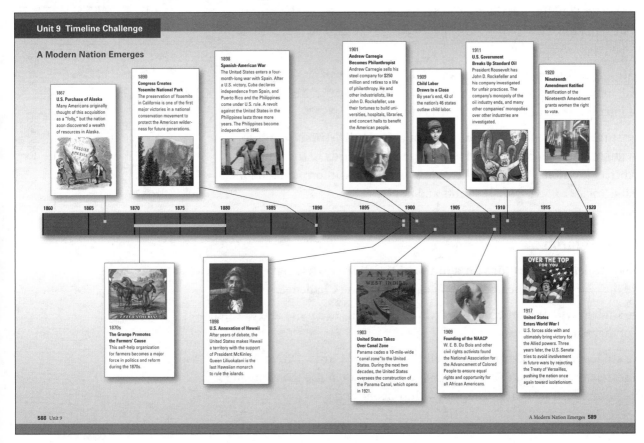

Overview

This Timeline Challenge helps students review the main events and ideas of this unit while providing practice in reading and interpreting timelines. You can vary and expand the activity according to students' needs and the amount of time available.

Basic Procedure

1   **Introduce the timeline in the Student Edition.** Direct students to the A Modern Nation Emerges timeline at the end of Unit 9 in the Student Edition. You may wish to have students read aloud and discuss the timeline entries.

2   **Introduce the Timeline Challenge in the Interactive Student Notebook.** Direct students to the Unit 9 Timeline Challenge in their notebooks. Point out the two types of questions, "Using Timeline Skills" and "Critical Thinking," and model how to answer each type.

3   **Have students complete the Timeline Challenge.** Monitor students as they work. Use the Guide to Unit 9 Timeline Challenge to check their answers. You may wish to project a transparency of this page as you work through the questions with the class and conduct a discussion of the "Critical Thinking" questions.

4   **Complete the KWL chart.** Return to the KWL chart created at the beginning of the unit, and ask students to list the key information they have learned.

Classroom Timeline

1 **Prepare the Timeline Challenge Cards.** Copy and cut the cards from *Student Handout TC9: Unit 9 Timeline Challenge Cards.* You may wish to laminate the cards for future use.

2 **Create a timeline on a classroom wall.** On an empty wall or a large bulletin board, make a timeline with masking tape or colored paper. Mark off the time intervals in advance, or ask students to do so in class.

3 **Have students place the Timeline Challenge Cards.** Distribute cards to individual students or pairs and have them tape the cards to the timeline in the correct locations. Call on students to provide more information on the timeline topics to review main events and issues.

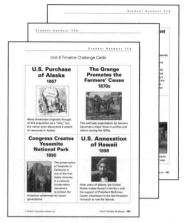

Student Handout TC9

Internet Research

1 **Review students' suggestions for additional timeline entries.** Have students share their answers to the last question of the Timeline Challenge.

2 **Have students conduct Internet research.** Ask students to choose and research one of their suggested events.

3 **Have students create additional Timeline Challenge Cards.** Direct students to research an appropriate image for their cards and then use the computer to create an illustrated card, complete with timeline entry.

Timeline Skills

Score 1 point for each correct answer.

1. Alaska, Hawaii, Puerto Rico, the Philippines, and the Panama Canal Zone; 36 years

2. a self-help organization for farmers; during the 1870s

3. Congress created Yosemite National Park in 1890. By 1909, 43 of 46 states had outlawed child labor.

4. The Spanish-American War lasted four months. The United States acquired the Philippines as a result, but the territory rebelled against U.S. rule. This conflict lasted 3 years.

5. Andrew Carnegie retired from his business and began a career of philanthropy. His many charities provided such institutions as libraries and hospitals for the American people.

6. The United States wanted to build the Panama Canal in this zone.

7. 1909; Its purpose is to secure equal rights and opportunity for all African Americans.

8. Rockefeller used his fortune to benefit the American people. His Standard Oil Company was investigated and broken up by the U.S. government in 1911.

9. The United States entered World War I on the side of the Allied powers in 1917. In 1920, it voted not to sign the Treaty of Versailles, thus isolating itself from the rest of the world.

Critical Thinking

Score 1 to 3 points for each answer, depending on the thoroughness of the response.

10. Students will probably choose one of the following individuals: Andrew Carnegie, John D. Rockefeller, Theodore Roosevelt, Robert La Follette, Mother Jones, John Muir, W. E. B. Du Bois, Upton Sinclair, Alice Paul, or Woodrow Wilson. Students should explain at least one specific example from the person's life to show the person's impact on the United States.

11. Students will likely discuss one of the following: Alaska, Hawaii, Puerto Rico, the Philippines, or the Panama Canal Zone. Specific details about the chosen acquisition should be given to support the opinion.

12. Answers will vary. Students might discuss the nation's need to protect itself as support of the Senate's decision. Students who oppose the Senate's decision may argue the need to be involved in the League of Nations in order to maintain world peace.

13. Answers will vary. Students must explain why the events they chose merit inclusion.

Using Scores to Inform Instruction

Timeline Skills A score of 6 out of 9 indicates that students understand most of the key events of this unit.

Critical Thinking A score of 8 out of 12 indicates that students are able to think critically about most of the key issues of this unit.

If students score below these levels, consider reviewing timeline and critical thinking skills.

This pacing guide suggests how many instructional days to allot to each chapter, including activities and assessment, for teaching the course in 50-minute classes, five times per week.

Unit 1: Our Colonial Heritage	
Geography Challenge	1 day
Chapter 1: The First Americans	4–5 days
Chapter 2: European Exploration and Settlement	4–5 days
Chapter 3: The English Colonies in North America	5 days
Chapter 4: Life in the Colonies	4–5 days
Timeline Challenge	1 day

Unit 2: Revolution in the Colonies	
Geography Challenge	1 day
Chapter 5: Toward Independence	5–6 days
Chapter 6: The Declaration of Independence	5–6 days
Chapter 7: The American Revolution	3 days
Timeline Challenge	1 day

Unit 3: Forming a New Nation	
Geography Challenge	1 day
Chapter 8: Creating the Constitution	5 days
Chapter 9: The Constitution: A More Perfect Union	4 days
Chapter 10: The Bill of Rights	4 days
Timeline Challenge	1 day

Unit 4: Launching the New Republic	
Geography Challenge	1 day
Chapter 11: Political Developments in the Early Republic	3–4 days
Chapter 12: Foreign Affairs in the Young Nation	5–6 days
Chapter 13: A Growing Sense of Nationhood	6 days
Chapter 14: Andrew Jackson and the Growth of American Democracy	4 days
Timeline Challenge	1 day

Unit 5: An Expanding Nation	
Geography Challenge	1 day
Chapter 15: Manifest Destiny and the Growing Nation	5 days
Chapter 16: Life in the West	5–6 days
Chapter 17: Mexicano Contributions to the Southwest	4–5 days
Timeline Challenge	1 day

Unit 6: Americans in the Mid-1800s	
Geography Challenge	1 day
Chapter 18: An Era of Reform	4 days
Chapter 19: The Worlds of North and South	4 days
Chapter 20: African Americans in the Mid-1800s	6 days
Timeline Challenge	1 day

Unit 7: The Union Challenged	
Geography Challenge	1 day
Chapter 21: A Dividing Nation	6 days
Chapter 22: The Civil War	5 days
Chapter 23: The Reconstruction Era	5 days
Timeline Challenge	1 day

Unit 8: Migration and Industry	
Geography Challenge	1 day
Chapter 24: Tensions in the West	5 days
Chapter 25: The Rise of Industry	3–4 days
Chapter 26: The Great Wave of Immigration	5 days
Timeline Challenge	1 day

Unit 9: A Modern Nation Emerges	
Geography Challenge	1 day
Chapter 27: The Progressive Era	4–5 days
Chapter 28: The United States Becomes a World Power	5–6 days
Chapter 29: Linking Past to Present	5 days
Timeline Challenge	1 day

History Alive! The United States Through Industrialism — Skills Correlation

	Map Skills	Comparing and Contrasting	Sequencing Events	Creating a Timeline	Analyzing Cause and Effect	Making Predictions	Recognizing the Role of Chance, Error, and Oversight in History	Framing Questions to Research	Distinguishing Fact from Opinion	Selecting Useful Information	Selecting Credible Sources: Primary Sources	Selecting Credible Sources: Secondary Sources	Drawing Sound Conclusions	Identifying Frame of Reference and Point of View	Identifying Bias, Stereotyping, and Propaganda	Conducting a Cost-Benefit Analysis	Interpreting Political Cartoons
Unit 1: Our Colonial Heritage																	
Geography Challenge	•																
Chapter 1: The First Americans	•		•			•	•	•		•	•	•	•	•	•		
Chapter 2: European Exploration and Settlement	•	•	•		•	•	•		•	•	•		•	•	•		
Chapter 3: The English Colonies in North America	•	•								•	•				•	•	
Chapter 4: Life in the Colonies		•			•	•		•		•	•	•	•				
Timeline Challenge			•	•													
Unit 2: Revolution in the Colonies																	
Geography Challenge	•																
Chapter 5: Toward Independence					•		•				•			•	•	•	•
Chapter 6: The Declaration of Independence	•		•	•	•	•					•	•	•	•	•		
Chapter 7: The American Revolution	•	•			•		•	•		•	•		•	•	•		
Timeline Challenge		•	•	•													
Unit 3: Forming a New Nation																	
Geography Challenge	•																
Chapter 8: Creating the Constitution		•				•					•	•		•		•	
Chapter 9: The Constitution: A More Perfect Union								•	•	•	•		•				
Chapter 10: The Bill of Rights						•			•	•	•	•		•			
Timeline Challenge			•	•													

History Alive! The United States Through Industrialism Skills Correlation	Map Skills	Comparing and Contrasting	Sequencing Events	Creating a Timeline	Analyzing Cause and Effect	Making Predictions	Recognizing the Role of Chance, Error, and Oversight in History	Framing Questions to Research	Distinguishing Fact from Opinion	Selecting Useful Information	Selecting Credible Sources: Primary Sources	Selecting Credible Sources: Secondary Sources	Drawing Sound Conclusions	Identifying Frame of Reference and Point of View	Identifying Bias, Stereotyping, and Propaganda	Conducting a Cost-Benefit Analysis	Interpreting Political Cartoons
Unit 4: Launching the New Republic																	
Geography Challenge	•																
Chapter 11: Political Developments in the Early Republic		•									•	•		•	•		•
Chapter 12: Foreign Affairs in the Young Nation			•	•	•				•	•	•	•				•	•
Chapter 13: A Growing Sense of Nationhood	•	•				•		•		•	•			•	•		
Chapter 14: Andrew Jackson and the Growth of American Democracy			•	•	•	•		•	•	•	•	•	•	•	•	•	•
Timeline Challenge			•	•													
Unit 5: An Expanding Nation																	
Geography Challenge	•																
Chapter 15: Manifest Destiny and the Growing Nation	•		•		•	•	•			•	•	•	•	•			
Chapter 16: Life in the West	•				•	•			•		•	•				•	
Chapter 17: Mexicano Contributions to the Southwest			•		•	•			•	•	•	•	•		•	•	
Timeline Challenge			•	•													
Unit 6: Americans in the Mid-1800s																	
Geography Challenge	•																
Chapter 18: An Era of Reform			•	•	•	•				•	•			•		•	
Chapter 19: The Worlds of North and South	•	•			•	•	•		•	•	•			•		•	
Chapter 20: African Americans in the Mid-1800s		•	•		•	•			•	•	•				•	•	
Timeline Challenge			•	•													

History Alive! The United States Through Industrialism Skills Correlation	Map Skills	Comparing and Contrasting	Sequencing Events	Creating a Timeline	Analyzing Cause and Effect	Making Predictions	Recognizing the Role of Chance, Error, and Oversight in History	Framing Questions to Research	Distinguishing Fact from Opinion	Selecting Useful Information	Selecting Credible Sources: Primary Sources	Selecting Credible Sources: Secondary Sources	Drawing Sound Conclusions	Identifying Frame of Reference and Point of View	Identifying Bias, Stereotyping, and Propaganda	Conducting a Cost-Benefit Analysis	Interpreting Political Cartoons
Unit 7: The Union Challenged																	
Geography Challenge	•																
Chapter 21: A Dividing Nation	•	•			•	•					•			•	•		•
Chapter 22: The Civil War	•	•				•					•		•	•		•	
Chapter 23: The Reconstruction Era	•	•	•			•			•		•		•	•			•
Timeline Challenge			•	•													
Unit 8: Migration and Industry																	
Geography Challenge	•																
Chapter 24: Tensions in the West	•	•	•		•	•				•			•	•	•		
Chapter 25: The Rise of Industry				•		•							•	•	•		•
Chapter 26: The Great Wave of Immigration	•	•				•							•	•	•		•
Timeline Challenge			•	•													
Unit 9: A Modern Nation Emerges																	
Geography Challenge	•																
Chapter 27: The Progressive Era		•			•	•			•	•	•			•			•
Chapter 28: The United States Becomes a World Power					•			•	•	•	•				•		•
Chapter 29: Linking Past to Present		•		•							•					•	
Timeline Challenge			•	•													

Lesson Guide

Chapter 14
192: Anonymous, in Legends of America, "Native American Legends: The Cherokee Trail of Tears," at www.legendsofamerica.com.

Placards

Chapter 1
7: Chief Luther Standing Bear, in Valerius Geist, *Buffalo Nation: History and Legend of the North American Bison* (Stillwater, MN: Voyageur Press, 1998).

Chapter 4
10: William Penn, in William J. Buck, *William Penn in America* (Philadelphia: Historical Society of Pennsylvania, 1888), at www. books.google.com. **11:** English Bill of Rights, 1689, at www. constitution.org. **13:** Rev. Stephen Williams, in George C. Atwell, et al., *The Connecticut Quarterly: An Illustrated Magazine,* Vol. 2 (Hartford, CT: The Connecticut Quarterly, 1895), at www.books. google.com. **15:** Mary Cooper, in Nancy F. Cott, *Roots of Bitterness: Documents of the Social History of American Women* (Lebanon, NH: Northeastern University Press, 1996). **16:** Martha Ballard, in a diary entry on November 10, 1790, at www.dohistory.org

Lesson Guide

Art

132: QYA Design Studio

Placards

Photographs

9 R: Library of Congress **9 L:** Library of Congress **10:** Library of Congress **11:** The Granger Collection, New York **12:** Massachusetts Historical Society **13:** The Granger Collection, New York **14 L:** The Granger Collection, New York **14 R:** The Granger Collection, New York **15:** Library of Congress **16:** Library of Congress **17:** Gift of Mrs. Walter B. James Image © 2004 board of Trustees National Gallery of Art Washington DC **18:** The Metropolitan Museum of Art Gift of Mrs. Russell Sage: 1908. (08.228) Photograph @ The Metropoitan Museum of Art **19:** The Granger Collection, New York **20:** National Museum of American History Smithsonian Institution: Behring Center **21:** The Granger Collection, New York **22:** Getty Images **23:** Library of Congress **24:** Getty Images **25:** California State Library **26:** Library of Congress **27:** Cheryl Fenton Photography **28:** RF/Harris Shiffman/Shutterstock **29:** California History Section/California State Library **30:** Topical Press Agency/Getty Images **31:** Library of Congress **32:** Library of Congress **33:** Bettmann/Corbis **34:** Library of Congress **35:** Library of Congress **36:** Library of Congress **37:**The Historic New Orleans Collection 160.46 **38:** Hampton University Museum Hampton Virginia

Art

1–8: Richard Boles